Global Higher Education Practices in Times of Crisis

Global Higher Education Practices in Times of Crisis: Questions for Sustainability and Digitalization

EDITED BY

DIEU HACK-POLAY
Crandall University, Canada and University of Lincoln, UK

DEBORAH LOCK
Birmingham City University, UK

ANDREA CAPUTO
University of Lincoln, UK and University of Trento, Italy

MADHAVI LOKHANDE
WeSchool, India

AND

UDAY SALUNKHE
WeSchool, India

United Kingdom – North America – Japan – India – Malaysia – China

Emerald Publishing Limited
Emerald Publishing, Floor 5, Northspring, 21-23 Wellington Street, Leeds LS1 4DL.

First edition 2025

Editorial matter and selection © 2025 Dieu Hack-Polay, Deborah Lock,
Andrea Caputo, Madhavi Lokhande, and Uday Salunkhe.
Individual chapters © 2025 The authors.
Published under exclusive licence by Emerald Publishing Limited.

Reprints and permissions service
Contact: www.copyright.com

No part of this book may be reproduced, stored in a retrieval system, transmitted in any form or by any means electronic, mechanical, photocopying, recording or otherwise without either the prior written permission of the publisher or a licence permitting restricted copying issued in the UK by The Copyright Licensing Agency and in the USA by The Copyright Clearance Center. Any opinions expressed in the chapters are those of the authors. Whilst Emerald makes every effort to ensure the quality and accuracy of its content, Emerald makes no representation implied or otherwise, as to the chapters' suitability and application and disclaims any warranties, express or implied, to their use.

British Library Cataloguing in Publication Data
A catalogue record for this book is available from the British Library

ISBN: 978-1-83797-053-7 (Print)
ISBN: 978-1-83797-052-0 (Online)
ISBN: 978-1-83797-054-4 (Epub)

Printed and bound by CPI Group (UK) Ltd, Croydon, CR0 4YY

INVESTOR IN PEOPLE

Contents

About the Editors ... ix

List of Contributors ... xi

Preface ... xv

Introduction
Dieu Hack-Polay, Deborah Lock, Andrea Caputo and Madhavi Lohkande ... 1

Chapter 1 Next-Generation Innovative Teaching Ecosystems for Futuristic Management Education
Ragini N. Mohanty, Anu Thomas and Abhishek Kori ... 5

Chapter 2 Teaching in Times of Crisis or Pandemic Pedagogy
J.-F., Darren Pullen, Andy Bown, Zi Siang See, Naomi Nelson, Anita Heywood, Loan Dao, Yang Yang, Helena Winnberg and Stacie Reck ... 29

Chapter 3 Using Design Thinking to Redesign the Student Learning Experience: The Case of Higher Education
Farah Arkadan and Niloofar Kazemargi ... 49

Chapter 4 Educational Innovation and Digitalization During Crises
Jai Raj Nair ... 59

Chapter 5 Resilience and the Entrepreneurial University During Turbulent Times: A Model for the Higher Education Sector
Kiran Vazirani, Rameesha Kalra and Gnanendra M. ... 77

Chapter 6 Higher Education in Times of Crisis: Shifting Towards Better Inclusion of Students with Disabilities
Soad Louissi and Michelle Mielly   95

Chapter 7 Education and Resilience in the Entrepreneurial University: An Analysis of Past and Present Practice at Tangent, Trinity's Ideas Workspace
Maeve O'Dwyer and Daniel Rogers   111

Chapter 8 Resilience in Education: Unveiling the COVID-19-Induced Evolution of Architecture Pedagogy
Masoumeh Khanzadeh   127

Chapter 9 Challenges and Transformation of Pedagogy Towards Blended Learning: A Sequential Mixed-Method Study in Higher Education
Nagamani Nagaraja and Benny Godwin J. Davidson   151

Chapter 10 Deglobalizing Education: Perspectives, Challenges, and Sustainability
Pratika Mishra and Aurobindo Kiriyakere   169

Chapter 11 Technology-Enabled Education Innovation: The Hybrid Teaching-Learning Process
J. Meenakumari, Ramakrishnan N. and Sriharish Ramakrishnan   183

Chapter 12 Incorporation of Deep Learning-Based AI Tools in Education: A Statistical Evaluation of the Perceptions of Gen-Z and Millennials
Remya Nair   199

Chapter 13 Integrating AI Tools in Academic Curriculum: A Study on the Effectiveness of AI Tools in Higher Education
Santosh Rupa Jaladi, Hema Doreswamy and Radhika Uttam   229

Chapter 14 Post-COVID Scenario and E-Learning: Fate of Student Academia at Tertiary Level
Obaid Ullah, Shehnaz Tehseen, Khalid Sultan, Syed Arslan Haider and Azeem Gul   241

Chapter 15 Recent Trends in Deployment of Multi-Protocol Label Switching (MPLS) Networks in Universities
Siddhartha Goutam and Aradhana Goutam   *255*

Chapter 16 Educational Innovation and Digitalization During the Crisis
Sridhar Chakravarthi Mulakaluri   *271*

Chapter 17 Deconstructing Value Creation in Indian Management Education: A Learner Journey Perspective
Bharath Rajan and Sujatha Natarajan   *287*

Chapter 18 Business Education: COVID-19 and Beyond
Swapna Pradhan   *311*

Chapter 19 The Impact of Education 5.0's Personalized Learning Experience on Student Concentration
Vandana Panwar and Satarupa Nayak   *327*

Chapter 20 Assistive Technologies for Education: Fulfilling National Education Policy (NEP) Goals
Vijay T. Raisinghani   *353*

Conclusion
Dieu Hack-Polay, Deborah Lock, Andrea Caputo, Madhavi Lokhande and Uday Salunkhe   *371*

About the Editors

Dieu Hack-Polay is Professor of Management at Crandall University (Canada) and Associate Professor in Organizational Behaviour and Management in the Lincoln International Business School, University of Lincoln, UK. He worked for several years in various sectors of activity including the voluntary sector and local government as a human resources and training practitioner in the UK. He also has several years of experience as an academic. He worked for various institutions in the UK, Canada, and China. His main research interest is in the economic performance of migrants in host countries and international human resource management. He has authored two textbooks and several book chapters as well as published several research articles in international journals. His professional affiliations include chartered fellowship of the Chartered Institute of Personnel & Development, fellowship of the Higher Education Academy, and fellowship of the Society for Education and Training.

Deborah Lock is a Professor and Deputy Dean, Faculty of Business, Law and Social Science at Birmingham City University, UK. She is an experienced academic leader with more than 20 years strategic level experience in higher education. As a career-hopper, she has had numerous jobs (Bid Writer, Business Development Manager, Director of Enterprise, College Director of Education to name a few) through which she has developed a reputation for the successful delivery of education related change management projects. She is passionate about ensuring HE business education provides students and graduates with the opportunity to develop the skills required to enhance their employability prospects irrespective of whether they are at market entry or career progression level. She was awarded her professorship in 2019 based on her work around inclusive education practices.

Andrea Caputo is an Associate Professor in Management at the University of Trento, Italy, and at the University of Lincoln, UK, where in 2018, he co-founded with other academics the UNESCO Chair in Responsible Foresight for Sustainable Development. He received his PhD from the University of Rome Tor Vergata, Italy. His main research interests include entrepreneurial decision-making, negotiation, digitalization and sustainability, internationalization, and strategic management of small- and medium-sized enterprises. He is the Editor of the book series *Entrepreneurial Behaviour* (Emerald), and Associate Editor of the *Journal of Management & Organization*, *Management Decision*, and *BRQ*

Business Research Quarterly. His award-winning research was published in over 100 contributions, including articles in highly ranked journals, for example, *HRM Journal, Journal of Business Research, Journal of Small Business Management, Small Business Economics, International Small Business Journal, International Journal of Conflict Management, Studies in Higher Education, Business Strategy and the Environment*, and *IEEE TEM*, among the others. In 2021 and 2022, he was ranked among World's Top 2% Scientists List of outstanding researchers prepared by Elsevier BV, Stanford University, USA.

Madhavi Lokhande is the Dean at Welingkar Institute of Management Development and Research, WeSchool, Bengaluru. She is a Fellow of the Cost Accountants of India and the Institute of Management Accountants, USA. As a researcher, she has published several papers and case studies in leading journals and international and national case clearing houses. She was awarded by the Higher Education Forum for Excellence in Contribution to Management Education. She also holds the position of National Vice President – Homepreneurs Council, Women's India Chamber of Commerce and Industry and is the President of the Institute of Management Accountants, Bangalore Chapter. Her recent accolades include the prestigious fellowship from the Executive Leadership Academy from UC Berkeley. Her work with women micro entrepreneurs helped her get a PhD from SNDT Women's University and also led her to be a mentor for the ISB Goldman Sachs 10k programme. Her other interests are: She founded 'Padhaai', a charitable trust that promotes the cause for inclusive education. She is the cofounder of Imagilytica Leadership Consulting LLP that curates learning programmes using the philosophy of kinaesthetic learning.

Uday Salunkhe has headed WeSchool as its Group Director for over two decades. His passion for leadership, design thinking, and innovation, supported by 'Disruptive thinking' and encouraging 'Opposing minds', has helped WeSchool carve a niche in the space of design thinking and innovation-led management education. A strong believer in self and positivity, driven by a philosophy of 'Force Multiplier' effects, he has been singularly responsible for taking WeSchool Global, by building several partnerships worldwide, be it with his alumni, business, or the academia circle. A strong networker himself, he believes that one's net worth is determined by their network. An 'Edupreneur', with PhD in Turnaround Strategy and a recipient of the prestigious Eisenhower Fellowship, USA, he has also been a scholar at the Linnaeus–Palme programme at the Malardalen University, Sweden. He has to his credit various pioneering programmes and initiatives along with many research publications. Beyond his role at WeSchool, he is Chairman of the Education Committee of the Council of EU Chambers of Commerce in India, a former President of Association of Indian Management Schools (AIMS), among other regulatory and governing bodies in the strategic and advisory capacity.

List of Contributors

Farah Arkadan	*American University of Dubai, UAE*
Andy Bown	*University of Tasmania, Australia*
Loan Dao	*University of New South Wales, Australia*
Benny Godwin J. Davidson	*University of the Fraser Valley, Canada*
Hema Doreswamy	*Prin. L. N. Welingkar Institute of Management Development and Research, Karnataka, India*
Gnanendra M.	*Christ University, India (ORCID ID: 0000-0001-7972-9221)*
Aradhana Goutam	*Prin. L. N. Welingkar Institute of Management Development and Research (WeSchool), Maharashtra, India*
Siddhartha Goutam	*Prin. L. N. Welingkar Institute of Management Development and Research (WeSchool), Maharashtra, India*
Azeem Gul	*National University of Modern Languages, Pakistan*
Syed Arslan Haider	*Capital University of Science and Technology, Pakistan*
Anita Heywood	*University of New South Wales, Australia*
J.-F.	*Crandall University, Canada*
Santosh Rupa Jaladi	*Prin. L. N. Welingkar Institute of Management Development and Research, Karnataka, India*
Rameesha Kalra	*Christ University, India (ORCID ID: 0000-0001-6274-6324)*
Niloofar Kazemargi	*University of Pescara-Chieti, Italy*
Masoumeh Khanzadeh	*Nuh Naci Yazgan University, Turkey (ORCID ID: 0000-0003-4606-0490)*
Aurobindo Kiriyakere	*Presidency University, India*
Abhishek Kori	*Welingkar Institute of Management Development and Researchuaf, Maharashtra, India*
Soad Louissi	*Grenoble Ecole de Management, France*

List of Contributors

J. Meenakumari	Surana Educational Institutions, India
Michelle Mielly	Grenoble Ecole de Management, France
Pratika Mishra	Welingkar Institute of Management Development and Research (WeSchool), Maharashtra, India
Ragini N. Mohanty	Welingkar Institute of Management Development and Research (WeSchool), Maharashtra, India
Sridhar Chakravarthi Mulakaluri	XIM University, India
Nagamani Nagaraja	Centre for Learning, Leadership and Excellence, India
Jai Raj Nair	Welingkar Institute of Management Development and Research, Karnataka, India
Remya Nair	University of Mysore, India; Welingkar Institute of Management Development and Research, Karnataka, India
Sujatha Natarajan	Prin. L. N. Welingkar Institute of Management Development and Research (WeSchool), Maharashtra, India (ORCID ID: 0000-0002-5568-2059)
Satarupa Nayak	Prin. L. N. Welingkar Institute of Management Development and Research (WeSchool), Maharashtra, India
Naomi Nelson	Federation University Australia, Australia
Maeve O'Dwyer	Dublin City University, Ireland
Vandana Panwar	Prin. L. N. Welingkar Institute of Management Development and Research, Maharashtra, India
Swapna Pradhan	Welingkar Institute of Management Development and Research (WeSchool), Maharashtra, India
Darren Pullen	University of Tasmania, Australia
Vijay T. Raisinghani	Welingkar Institute of Management Development and Research (WeSchool), Maharashtra, India
Bharath Rajan	Prin. L. N. Welingkar Institute of Management Development and Research (WeSchool), Maharashtra, India (ORCID ID: 0000-0003-3015-5401)
Ramakrishnan N.	Christ University, India
Sriharish Ramakrishnan	Bosch Global Software Technologies, India
Stacie Reck	Maplehurst Middle School, Australia
Daniel Rogers	Tangent, Trinity's Ideas Workspace, Ireland

Khalid Sultan	*National University of Modern Languages, Pakistan*
Zi Siang See	*University of Tasmania, Australia*
Shehnaz Tehseen	*Sunway University Business School, Malaysia*
Anu Thomas	*Welingkar Institute of Management Development and Research (WeSchool), Maharashtra, India*
Obaid Ullah	*National University of Modern Languages, Pakistan*
Radhika Uttam	*Prin. L. N. Welingkar Institute of Management Development and Research, Karnataka, India*
Kiran Vazirani	*Christ University, Karnataka, India (ORCID ID: 0000-0001-5591-6874)*
Helena Winnberg	*Tasmanian Department for Education, Children and Young People, Australia*
Yang Yang	*University of Tasmania, Australia*

Preface

This book of collected works comments on some of the major changes and shifts in higher education teaching practices which emerged because of the COVID-19 pandemic socio-economic and political turbulence in the past four years. While the sector had been slowly moving towards hybrid delivery prior to this, the rapid acceleration of digital adoption due to lockdown restrictions provided academics and institutions alike with the opportunity to experiment with innovative ways of teaching and develop new pedagogies which reflect the nature of digital citizenship in an age of technological transformation. With the dramatic development of artificial intelligence, the past few years, new challenges have emerged that educators have to deal with to maintain standards and stimulate the learning environment. Many of the examples in this book highlight some of these key challenges for higher education which are constant themes irrespective of geographical boundaries and/or political systems: accessibility and inclusiveness, and how to use innovative learning technologies to the best effect to ensure students develop the skills and competences required to be successful.

As noted by George Couros (leader in innovative teaching, learning, and leading), 'Technology will never replace great teachers, but in the hands of great teachers, it's transformational', and this book aims to capture some of the transformations which have taken place over recent years. This book also raises fundamental questions about the future of teaching and learning and the necessity for the education sector to evolve alongside technological development. This book is an invitation to stakeholders in academia to continuously engage with debate and share experiences and good practice. Undoubtedly, the fast changes in the higher education environment command a greater flow of information sharing among practitioners to ensure comparability of the student's level of education, particularly as both student and professor mobility is increasingly normalized and on the increase. The significant number of chapters in this book and other similar books denote the fact that technological change is one of the greatest managerial and educational challenges of our time. The survival of the higher education sector and quality within it tightly hinges on the sector capacity to adapt.

This book provides a variety of chapters covering various socio-economic and cultural contexts. However, we were pleased to incorporate many chapters from the Global South whose good practices are often not heard of enough and integrated to global higher educational practices. Such practices have become important owing to the intertwining of global higher education systems, the increased mobility of teachers, graduates, and professionals. We hope that the readers will enjoy this additional text.

Introduction

Dieu Hack-Polay[a,b], Deborah Lock[c], Andrea Caputo[b,d] and Madhavi Lohkande[e]

[a]*Crandall University, Canada*
[b]*University of Lincoln, UK*
[c]*Birmingham City University, UK*
[d]*University of Trento, Italy*
[e]*WeSchool, India*

Our new book *Global Higher Education Practices in Times of Crisis: Questions for Sustainability and Digitalization* aims to shed some light on strategies that higher education practitioners and researchers have developed for the higher education sector to cope with crisis times (Tilak & Kumar, 2022). This new book is a good complement to our two earlier books (Caputo et al., 2022; Lock et al., 2022) addressing issues or borderlands higher education. The subject of the new book is topical given the successive crises that the world has gone through in the past three decades, e.g. economic crises, recessions, health pandemics, including the recent COVID-19 crisis which had significant economic and social ramifications (Hack-Polay, 2020; Lock et al., 2022). During these crises, the sector has undergone significant challenges but also innovations, including the deployment of technology and strategic partnerships in order to survive (Caputo et al., 2022). This book is therefore expected to provide a comprehensive contemporary portrayal of higher education practices from the perspective of sustainability and digitalization.

The principal premise of this book is to characterize the international environment of teaching in higher education institutions during crisis times and examine the challenges faced and how the sector has weathered those (Hack-Polay, 2022). Whether economic crises, political crises or health crises, these have often led higher education institutions across the globe to think outside the box and develop innovative practices suited for turbulent times (David, 2011; Hack-Polay, 2020). The global aspect of this book recognizes the intertwining of socio-political and economic realities which also encapsulate the higher education domain, with the increasing globalization of curricula and practices (Caputo et al., 2022). These are the good practices that this book aims to capture and disseminate widely.

Global Higher Education Practices in Times of Crisis:
Questions for Sustainability and Digitalization, 1–3
Copyright © 2025 by Dieu Hack-Polay, Deborah Lock, Andrea Caputo and Madhavi Lohkande
Published under exclusive licence by Emerald Publishing Limited
doi:10.1108/978-1-83797-052-020241001

The content of this book is purposefully kept broad to leave room for educators and practitioners around the globe to have their specific input and share what they deem engaging educational responses to crisis times. The various chapters of the book particularly reflect the global dimension that we sought to cover given that higher education realities are increasingly intertwined in our modern world. The themes covered are varied and include:

- Perspectives on higher education globalization
- Pedagogical issues in crisis time
- Crisis leadership and sustainability in higher education
- Economic issues in higher education
- Technological responses to structural transformations
- The post-crisis chrysalis effect and emergence of the digital citizen
- Educational innovation and digitalization during crises
- Resilience and the entrepreneurial university in turbulent times
- Crisis leadership
- Deglobalization of higher education during crisis time

Identifying good practices in these domains can enable higher education to rethink their development strategies and approaches to teaching and learning in crisis times which are becoming the new normal. The proposed contents allow me to say that it would be a timely and well-structured book.

We are seeking chapters on topics that are fluid, comprehensive, and cover coherent critical issues for research and discussion, and which could enable reflection in more than one socio-economic and political context of higher education. We encourage contributors to be creative and critical in telling their stories of resilience in crisis time. Relevant and attractive themes covering entrepreneurial higher education approaches in times of crisis are welcome.

The chapters submitted were initially presented at our Lincoln International Higher Education Practices conference in Bangalore. The conference was held at the Welingkar School of Management, Bangalore, India, in November 2023. This provided significant feedback to enhance the chapters. But in order to operate in the spirit of globality of this book, the editors have decided to draw on chapters from around the world. The chapters selected fulfil the aim and spirit of our book.

Taking forward the notion of the scholar without borders, this book provides a critical review of the teaching practices in higher education in international contexts in the post-COVID era. Sticky problems and debates about inclusivity, diversity, and cultural representation in the curriculum and classroom are explored through the eyes of the academics who negotiate complex teaching landscapes either on a temporary or permanent basis. The aspiration for universal nuanced teaching practices that reflect individual and national identities, along with newly emerging global ones that represent virtual academic citizenship that crosses geographical and political borders is presented as a foundation on which to instil borderless higher education. COVID-19 has challenged the international environment of higher education teaching. This has led colleagues and institutions across the globe to think outside the box and develop innovative practices suited for turbulent times. But often, these are confined to the local or regional levels. These are the good practices that this book aims to capture and disseminate widely.

This book will appeal to researchers in academia, higher education leaders and teachers, as well as postgraduate students. We hope that all who read this book will appreciate the significant topical issues that we raised and contribute to the ongoing debate on the globalization of higher education and its evolving context. We welcome comments and feedback that will help shape the next issue.

References

Caputo, A., Lock, D., & Hack-Polay, D. (2022). *International environments and practices of higher education*. Emerald Publishing Limited.

David, M. E. (2011). Overview of researching global higher education: Challenge, change or crisis? *Contemporary Social Science, 6*(2), 147–163. https://doi.org/10.1080/2158 2041.2011.580610

Hack-Polay, D. (2020). *Covid-19 and internationalization in higher education – Can an elusive virus redefine higher education international strategy?* Researchgate. https://www.researchgate.net/publication/341448317_Covid-19_and_HE_Covid-19_and_internationalization_in_higher_education_-Can_an_elusive_virus_redefine_higher_education_international_strategy?channel=doi&linkId=5ec1b823a6fdcc90d67dfcec&showFulltext=true

Hack-Polay, D. (2022). Conclusion: Borderlands – (Re)ordered lands. In D. Lock, A. Caputo, D. Hack-Polay, & P. Igwe (Eds.), *Borderlands* (pp. 247–250). Springer. https://doi.org/10.1007/978-3-031-05339-9_21

Lock, D. Caputo, A., Hack-Polay, D., & Igwe, P. (2022). *Borderlands: The internationalisation of higher education teaching practices*. Springer.

Tilak, J. B. G., & Kumar, A. G. (2022). Policy changes in global higher education: What lessons do we learn from the COVID-19 pandemic? *Higher Education Policy, 35*, 610–628. https://doi.org/10.1057/s41307-022-00266-0

Chapter 1

Next-Generation Innovative Teaching Ecosystems for Futuristic Management Education

Ragini N. Mohanty, Anu Thomas and Abhishek Kori

Welingkar Institute of Management Development and Research (WeSchool), Mumbai, Maharashtra, India

Abstract

The COVID-19 pandemic has profoundly impacted global education, with over 190 countries closing educational institutions, affecting 1.6 billion learners worldwide. This crisis led to a staggering 70% increase in Learning Poverty in low- and middle-income countries, with estimated lifetime earnings loss amounting to $17 trillion. In response, institutions swiftly implemented emergency remote learning (ERT), transitioning to online platforms and leveraging artificial intelligence and adaptive learning tools. This shift, embraced by all stakeholders, facilitated continuity in education amid unprecedented challenges. Moreover, social media platforms emerged as vital tools for promoting learning, fostering engagement, and facilitating global collaboration among students. However, sustainable education requires more than technological dissemination; it necessitates a holistic approach integrating technology, digital transformation, artificial intelligence, social media, and innovative pedagogies. This chapter explores the implications of these advancements in higher education, amid a deglobalized world, emphasizing the need for an integrated and futuristic approach to address contemporary challenges.

Keywords: Innovative learning ecosystem; social media; living labs; pedagogical innovations; educational technology

---

Global Higher Education Practices in Times of Crisis:
Questions for Sustainability and Digitalization, 5–28
Copyright © 2025 by Ragini N. Mohanty, Anu Thomas and Abhishek Kori
Published under exclusive licence by Emerald Publishing Limited
doi:10.1108/978-1-83797-052-020241002

Introduction

> Students must learn how to discard old ideas, how and when to replace them. Tomorrow's illiterate will not be the man who can't read; he will be the man who has not learned how to learn. (Toffler, 1971, p. 414)

During the COVID-19 pandemic, administrators, educators, and students struggled to sustain teaching and learning due to the inability to rapidly migrate and acclimatize to technology and pedagogical shifts. The global pandemic also triggered newer opportunities for the education industry. Insights in the form of a relook at curriculum design and structure, newer approaches of pedagogy and assessments, changes to the roles of educators and students, organization policies, culture and governance are found to be significant to help build more resilient educational systems that can adapt to the unforeseen future demands. Resilience is considered as the capacity of people, groups, and systems to deal with risks brought on by unforeseen external occurrences (Weick, 1993). Futuristic innovative and smart teaching ecosystems should offer enhanced learning experiences based on learning features, preferences, and progress and support mobile learning, flexible learning, personalized learning, adaptive learning, and mixed learning. Such systems should make it easier for people to have access to knowledge, engage and participate in activities, get feedback and assistance, utilize rich media, and get on-the-go mentoring (Singh & Hassan, 2017). Further, due to an increased emphasis on students' mental health and well-being and holistic development, the importance of soft skills such as emotional intelligence, resilience, adaptability, and empathy will be acknowledged.

Next-Generation Innovative Teaching Ecosystem: Dimensions and Implications

'Next-generation innovative teaching ecosystems and environments' refers to the integrated features, plans, and settings that encourage active, interactive, and immersive learning. Their goal is to aid transformation through knowledge with an emphasis on critical and analytical interdisciplinary thinking, collaboration, and practical skill development, and the curation of student mindset to prepare for success in their future career roles with sustainable impact. In doing so, technology is leveraged to enhance educational outcomes, boost student engagement, and personalize the learning experience. The emergent trends in education (Fig. 1.1) can be categorized as:

1. Global Citizenship and Global Citizenship Education
2. Technology Integration in Education
3. Innovative Learning Approaches and Pedagogy
4. Innovation in Content Creation
5. Social Media and Living Lab

Next-generation Innovative Teaching Ecosystems   7

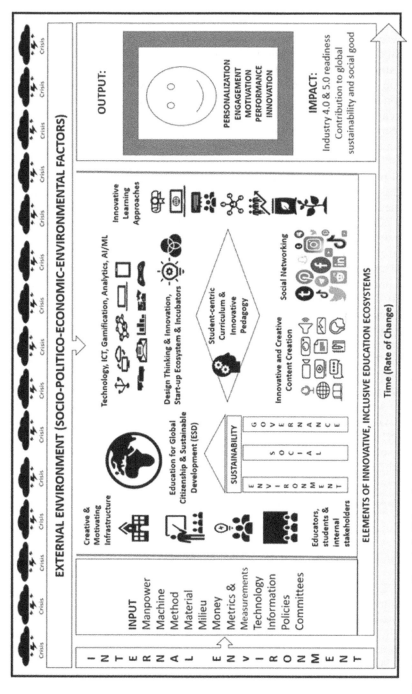

Fig. 1.1. Emergent Trends in Education. *Source*: Authors' representation.

Global Citizenship and Global Citizenship Education

Establishing more peaceful, tolerant, inclusive, and safe communities has become crucial, and hence the acknowledgement of the critical role of education for global citizenship has grown. Universities have a crucial role to sensitize and educate students on global citizenship and the impact of their behaviour and actions on the global society. According to the United Nations' (UN) Global Education First Initiative, 'It is not enough for education to produce individuals who can read, write and count'. Global Citizenship Education and Education for Sustainable Development place a high priority on relevant and efficient education with the objectives being to advance humanity, respect for all people, and assist students in becoming responsible and actively engaged global citizens. This will promote global citizenship, intercultural sensitivity, and the capacity for success in a multicultural society. Such complementary approaches using civic education enable individuals with the critical thinking abilities required to make educated decisions and actively participate in projects to solve challenges that address local, national, and worldwide social, political, economic, and environmental issues. Exposure of learners to a variety of cultures, opinions, and experiences through virtual exchanges, international partnerships, and cultural immersion programmes will promote global citizenship, intercultural sensitivity, and the capacity for success in a multicultural society. Real-world projects and activities will promote critical thinking, problem-solving, creativity, and cooperation abilities, during which learners can work in collaborative groups to tackle challenges and use their knowledge in real-world circumstances. *Example: The National Education Policy (NEP 2020) of India has introduced the Global Citizenship Education (GCED) that will support students in becoming informed about and active supporters of societies that are more peaceful, tolerant, inclusive, secure, and sustainable. The major themes included in NEP 2020 are* "Global Governance Systems, Structures, and Issues; Cultural Diversity and Tolerance; Inequality; Gender Equality; Human Rights Education; Peace and Non-Violence; Combating Climate Change and Its Impact; and Environmental Sustainability'.

Technology Integration in Education

The panorama of educational practices is rapidly changing to Education 4.0 as technology advances. Exposure and experience with the next-generation methodologies and technology tools has helped to improve industry-relevant learning. 'Virtually everywhere' may be the futuristic place of learning and enhanced learning experiences. Cloud computing, information and communication technology (ICT), Internet of Things, big data, artificial intelligence (AI), learning analytics, robots in education, and learning personalization are all gaining popularity. Online courses, foreign specialists, worldwide partnerships, searchable databases, and libraries are just a few of the many learning options offered virtually. Recently, machine learning using large language models and generative AI have opened up a new world of possibilities for the future of education. According to Holmes et al. (2019), AI and education (AI&ED) is significant under four dimensions:

- *Learning with AI* – where educators make use of AI-driven tools for teaching and learning.
- *Using AI to learn about learning* – where AI and analytics can be used to understand how students learn, how does learning progress, and which learning designs prove to be effective.
- *Learning about AI* – helping promote AI literacy and understanding about the technological aspects of AI, and
- *Preparing for AI* – helping promote AI literacy and understanding about the human aspect of AI.

AI and machine learning algorithms will help institutions gather and assess data on student performance, engagement, and conduct in order to pinpoint problem areas; personalize learning opportunities, learning pathways and experiences; provide customized material, adaptive assessments, and individualized feedback for development; and make data-driven administrative and instructional decisions. Inspired students are more committed to their own learning and form strong bonds with their classmates and teachers. Theoretically, using AI and personalized learning would be the perfect response to some of the most prevalent problems in education.

Examples about use of technology in education

1. AI-powered chatbot solutions: Bethel University, Indiana, increased student retention rate by 4% with the help of a messaging bot 'Wilhelm' that worked by conducting student surveys, connecting students to university services, and notifying university services of students seeking assistance. Nearly 85% of student users appreciated the app for privacy and comfort reasons. The University of Murcia in Spain used a chatbot to respond to students' inquiries on 'campus and careers', by assisting students beyond the regular office hours and enhanced their motivation, with an accuracy of 38,708 questions answered accurately more than 91% of the time. 'Woebot', the chatbot, aided students with mental well-being, stress reduction, and increased drive to study through 'intelligent mood tracking'. It provided comfort to the students immediately, amid an overburdened university health system with dangerously long waiting periods for on-campus mental health counselling.
2. Technology integrated pedagogy: During the COVID-19 epidemic, when it was difficult for face-to-face demonstration and adoption of technology applications and virtual tools for the practise of brainstorming, creative ideation, and prototype development while ensuring student participation, interactive engagement, and learning outcomes, the author used the technology integration matrix (TIM) to efficiently administer and improve the design

thinking course online. The Florida Centre for Instructional Technology has developed the TIM framework to analyse and target the use of technology to enhance learning. Traditionally, ethnography includes community-based interactions and observations, which is followed by problem definition, brainstorming, and insights generation. The student gains conversational, observational, and collaborative working skills through such problem-solving and project-based learning courses. Online technology tools and virtual collaborative design thinking was introduced during lockdown for course delivery and learning, which promoted cooperation, collaboration, creative and analytical thinking, simulations, skill development, and confidence-boosting motivation. TIM helped document and map student skill development and performance (see Tables 1.1 and 1.2). At the end of the course, students were highly motivated, satisfied with their ability to work in teams, and confident in their ability to use design tools and techniques for problem-solving for impact.

Innovative Learning Approaches and Pedagogy

Education Beyond Boundaries

A combination of blended, in-person and online learning experiences can help improve teaching and learning. Blended learning models include skill-driven, attitude-driven, and competency-driven learning. Interactions and cooperation can be enabled through ICT-based technologies, open educational resources, and Massive Open Online Courses (MOOCs), collaborative interactions with global experts and learning communities. Interaction and cooperation between students and instructors in attitude-driven learning helps students acquire new skills, attitudes, and behaviours. The competency-driven strategy seeks to convey learners' tacit knowledge via interaction and observation of professionals at work.

Examples

- *SWAYAM (Study Webs of Active Learning for Young Aspiring Minds), introduced in 2017, is a national programme offered by the Government of India to all students with the aim to overcome education gaps. It offers free online courses and learning resources across a variety of areas, from school to higher education level. These courses are curated by eminent academics from renowned Indian institutions. The focus on flexible learning alternatives is strongly emphasized in SWAYAM, which increases interactive learning via video lectures, learning resources, assessments in the form of quizzes and assignments, discussions, and debates.*
- *The Consortium for Educational Communication (CEC) and University Grants Commission (UGC, India) together created the CEC-UGC YouTube channel. which features a variety of educational material in the form of lecture sessions, interviews, webinars, and programmes spanning areas of business, humanities, arts, sciences, etc. This platform served as open access dissemination of video content created by higher education experts, to encourage knowledge sharing, research abilities, career guidance, and group learning via collaborative interactive involvement and live webinars.*

Table 1.1. Application of TIM Framework: Key Levels of Transformation Through Teaching and Learning (Framework).

Learning Environment	Capability Description	Entry	Adoption	Adaptation	Infusion	Transformation	Applications
Active	Students actively engage in the use of technology tools at an individual level.	The student is a passive recipient with the use of conventional tools.	→			Extensive, unconventional tool used (higher-order learning).	Engaging students in technology use for improved learning outcomes.
Collaborative	At all times, students use technology tools for collaborative work.	Use of conventional tools.	→			Use of technology tools with peers and experts.	Fostering collaborative working with peers, experts, and global connections.
Constructive	Students use technology tools to integrate new information into their prior knowledge.	Guided use of conventional tools.	→			Extensive use of technology tools for higher-order learning.	Deepening comprehension through unconventional technology use.
Authentic	Students link their learning meaningful activities in a context beyond the instructional setting and into the external world by use of technology tools.	Guided use of technology for meaningful activities.	→			Innovative use in higher-order learning connected to the external world.	Linking learning activities to the external world for real-world impact.

Note: This framework guides educators in tailoring technology integration strategies to enhance the learning experience.

Table 1.2. Technology Usage Levels in Teaching Learning Environments (Real-Time Application of TIM Framework).

Learning Environment	Capability (TIM) Description	Entry	Adoption	Adaptation	Infusion	Transformation
Active	Active learning at the individual level	Curriculum content and information passively received by students	Conventional and procedural use of tools	Individual use of conventional tools with some student choice and exploration	Student choice of tools and self-directed use regularly	Extensive, unconventional use of technology tools, with higher-order learning
	Students actively engage in the use of technology tools.	Course outline shared via a shared drive. Student participation. Online polls were conducted to assess student learning of concepts. Based on the response, doubts clarified before proceeding further.	Students used shared online Google documents for documentation of their contribution.	LMS was used for student interaction, assessments, and submissions. Classroom discussions and feedback through LMS.	Open-source free online design platforms and tools used for prototyping, working model, and process flow. Peer feedback was sought.	Students demonstrated individual contributions to create interactive and immersive prototypes with the use of virtual reality (VR) tools.
Collaborative	Collaborative	Use of technology tools	Use of conventional tools	Use of conventional tools with some student choice and exploration	Students choose tools and use them regularly	Use of technology tools with peers, outside experts, and others

	At all times, students use technology tools for collaborative work.	WhatsApp messaging apps were used for collaborative communications and interactions.	Students used shared online Google documents for collaborative working and sharing with teammates and faculty. The purpose was documentation of collaborative contribution, shared ideation, project discussions, and critical validation of content posted.	Students used design thinking collaboration and simulation tools like Miro and Mural	Students connected via Zoom. Google Meet, Webex, and MS Teams video conferencing platforms for group discussions, brainstorming and peer interaction sessions.	Students connected via Zoom. Google Meet, Weex, and MS Teams video conferencing platforms for idea validation, subject matter expert interactions, and prototype feedback.
Constructive	Constructive for knowledge building	*Information delivered to students*	*Guided use of conventional technology tools*	*Independent use with some student choice and exploration*	*Students choose tools and use them regularly*	*Extensive, unconventional use of technology tools, with higher-order learning*

(Continued)

Table 1.2. (Continued)

Learning Environment	Capability (TIM) Description	Entry	Adoption	Adaptation	Infusion	Transformation
	Students use technology tools for integrating new information to their prior knowledge.	Information of supplementary educational resources delivered as multimedia content, YouTube content and movies, TEDx, online courses, and other MOOC courses.	Students guided to use design thinking simulation tools like FIGMA for wireframe development.	- FIGMA for wireframes - Canva, Creatively for creative communications - VR software Unity for creating interactive project prototypes.	Use of design thinking collaboration and simulation tools like Miro, Canva, Creatively, Mural, FIGMA, and Strategyzer for collaborative working, creating product demos, prototypes and project briefs.	Use of VR software Unity and created interactive project prototypes.
Authentic (meaningful)	*Meaningful activities in context beyond the instructional setting*	*Technology use outside of the instructional setting*	*Guided use of technology tools for activities with some meaningful context*	*Independent use in activities with some student choice and exploration*	*Student choice of tools and use for meaningful activities regularly*	*Innovative use in higher-order learning activities that are connected to the external world*

Next-generation Innovative Teaching Ecosystems 15

| Students link their learning activities to the external world by use of technology tools. | Use of internet and online research databases of EBSCO, ProQuest, SCOPUS, and other research publications for research and project work. | Virtual conversations via Zoom and Google Meet video conferencing platforms for user interviews and interactions to gain authentic perspectives and external world insights. | Use of design thinking tools like Adobe Photoshop, Adobe InDesign for creating their infographics, digital portfolio, videos, etc. | Students post their project work and outcomes using appropriate technology tools on social media sites, blogs, webpages, etc. | Students made use of VR software like Unity for creating interactive project prototypes, and social media sites for maximum visibility and impact with external stakeholders. |

Framework Source: Adopted from the TIM of Florida Centre for Instructional Technology.

LMS, learning management system; FIGMA, FIGMA is a browser-based, collaborative UI (user interface) design tool that allows users to work together for creating vibrant and interactive prototypes (https://www.figma.com/about/).

CEC employs channels such as television and ICT in its endeavour to empower people with the power of knowledge. (https://www.youtube.com/channel/UCA7OQkX9AEIVQ6j9i0OSQhA)

Alternative Learning Approaches

When accessing the internet, students from diverse and difficult geographical terrains and places remote from cities face huge challenges, which impacts virtual education. In such circumstances, the community-enabled and -driven radio-based blended learning approach can function as a viable alternative learning option during any crisis that affects remote regions.

Example

- In India, SWAYAM PRABHA, a collection of 80 DTH channels that use the GSAT-15 satellite to continuously broadcast high-quality educational programming helps achieve this mission. The students may pick when they want to learn new material each day for at least four hours, which will then be repeated five more times during the day (https://www.swayamprabha.gov.in/).

Lifelong Learning and Micro-credentials

Continuous skill development and upskilling will be essential with the rapid pace of growth of technology and needs of the job markets. Micro-credentials, with shorter and more concentrated learning programmes, will become more popular since they provide learners with critical career-enhancing skills and information. Content, Technology-Digitization-AI, and Educators are the three main pillars of focus in the emerging lifelong learning ecosystems (UNESCO Institute for Lifelong Learning, UIL).

Gamification and Immersive Learning

Gamification approaches and immersive learning experiences can be used to increase engagement and motivation. Gamified components, such as badges, leader boards, and awards, will make learning more fun and encourage a feeling of success. Immersive and experiential learning environments will be created using VR, augmented reality (AR), and simulations.

Example

- *Associate Professor Sanghoon Park of the USF College of Education, along with a team of students and Reginald Lucien, Assistant Dean of the Judy Genshaft Honours College, have developed an educational tool. It includes an avatar, a maze, and a motivational chatbot named RAMI (Regulatory Advisor for Motivation Inhibition). RAMI serves as a learning companion, especially for online courses, engaging with students by inquiring about their emotions and challenges. This immersive programme combines gamification, personalized assistance, and an engaging narrative to guide* and motivate students throughout their educational journey. Park's well-designed courses and high-quality materials have resulted in over 90% of students consistently achieving top grades and supporting students in their career aspirations (https://youtu.be/OqxSUMcrLw0: *Innovation in Online Design & Teaching Award 2023*).

Next-Generation Pedagogy

The Organization for Economic Co-operation and Development (OECD) and the European University Association (EUA) 'University Missions 2030' guide universities in their mission to empower students as change-makers to address business and societal challenges within the framework of sustainability's three pillars: people, planet, and prosperity. They are consistent with the World Economic Forum's emphasis on diverse learning, active teaching and learning pedagogical techniques, relevant skills in research, innovation and culture, and continuous assessment. They see education as a catalyst for society growth, stimulating innovation and educating students to face global challenges while emphasizing practical skills and holistic learning methodologies. The IDEAS framework, as presented by Guàrdia et al. (2021), serves as a next-generation pedagogy guide, outlining key application areas for innovative pedagogical formats. This framework encompasses five crucial elements:

1. Intelligence (I): Utilizing learning analytics to identify challenges faced by students, popular courses, and encouraging participation in external digital networks. This element enhances decision-making, digital literacy, and the utilization of creative technologies beyond traditional classroom settings.
2. Distributed (D): Involving collaborations, open resources, acknowledgement of prior learning, shared ownership of learners' journeys by stakeholders, and engagement with a broader community. It promotes partnerships, separates services from instruction, and involves a wider range of stakeholders in both research and education.
3. Engaging (E): Prioritizing active student engagement through activities such as content production, portfolios, gamification, and peer feedback. This element focuses on problem-solving, knowledge expansion, and learner-centred content over traditional methods.
4. Agile (A): Encouraging learner adaptability through customization, modular curricula, self-assessment, and personalized resource access. It provides tailored learning experiences, recognizes prior knowledge, expands access, and fosters internationalization.
5. Situated (S): Emphasizing the relevance of learning to learners' goals and the real world. This element contextualizes activities, offers workplace-relevant learning, and addresses critical societal concerns.

The choice of pedagogical methods is contingent upon factors such as the level of education, effective learning theories, relevance, evidence of effectiveness, the development of industry-relevant skills, and the innovativeness of the chosen methods. Effective pedagogies, aimed at greater engagement and retention, employ active tactics like group work and problem-solving. Case-based learning enhances critical thinking, collaboration, and practical application. Data skills are honed through programmes like MS Excel and Tableau, while simulations and interactive technology improve technical, digital, critical thinking, and decision-making skills.

Examples

- The PICRAT approach was used by the Education University of Hong Kong to help incorporate modern technologies into a linguistics course. Even when face-to-face instruction was not possible due to the pandemic, Lixun Wang, the lecturer, made sure that every student received an equally high-quality education by involving them in a variety of technology-enhanced learning activities and implementing the PICRAT model for technology integration in the Year 1 undergraduate-level course 'Introduction to Linguistics'. In this teaching intervention, by augmenting, replacing, and changing traditional practices like in-person lectures and class discussions, the instructor made effective use of technology. Even if a pandemic recurs, the students will be able to overcome the obstacles since they gained important lifelong learning skills.
  - https://repository.eduhk.hk/en/publications/adoption-of-the-picrat-model-to-guide-the-integration-of-innovati

  Use cases: marketplaces for participatory, engaging, exciting, competitive learning:

- 'Shark Tank' pedagogy – where students pitch in their learning/business ideas and receive feedback and simulated/real expression of funding interest from the jury.
  - https://executiveeducation.wharton.upenn.edu/wp-content/uploads/2018/12/NanoTool-2019-01.pdf
  - https://executiveforum.com/leadership-lessons-from-the-shark-tank/
  - https://repository.escholarship.umassmed.edu/bitstream/handle/20.500.14038/34489/Shark_Tank_Submitted_Manuscript_Gravlin_et_al.pdf?sequence=3&isAllowed=y

- Real-life/virtual flea markets – students put up a bazaar to sell products and demonstrate outcomes (success). Student groups run an entire end-to-end business involving planning, budgeting, procurement, marketing, execution, financial management, and performance management.
  - https://www.deanza.edu/fleamarket/online-market?fbclid=IwAR31hyR2sJS5NoI2X-dLTaPfWJoQ0u08Z8xJmn1hCBf0Q0DBKFk6V6pEhnM
  - https://www.deanza.edu/fleamarket/?fbclid=IwAR3XgyMRTm3pQ7zqJWSQqEv-pjNBRIfCJlvPC6zK2XsdANMBKxrOf0U8DJ4

Innovation in Content Creation

The advent of instructional design and digital technologies has broadened learning material beyond conventional forms. Simulations, animations, and VR/AR-based materials boost engagement and motivation. Online VR classes improve attention, simplicity of use, and practical application. VR supplements current approaches by giving a novel solution for complicated learning scenarios, making it useful in conventional and case-based settings.

In INSEAD courses, each student may have a different experience within the boundaries of pre-established material (such as a boardroom scenario, factory tour, or market) thanks to a VR helmet that reacts to in-flight head movements. To the benefit of the group, these unique virtual experiences are often preceded and followed by in-depth shared discourse. VR could provide a brief but meaningful break from the typical classroom environment and can be considered as a useful tool in contemporary business education (https://www.insead.edu/vr-immersive-learning-initiative/experiences).

Social Media and Living Lab: Network, Collaboration, Engagement, and Growth

In the digitally connected world, educators can leverage the power of social media to teach digital and social media natives in more than one way (see Fig. 1.2 and Table 1.3). Social media usage in the classroom helps students become more effective communicators in the modern world. It supports the notion of lifelong learning and helps students keep their interest in the topic.

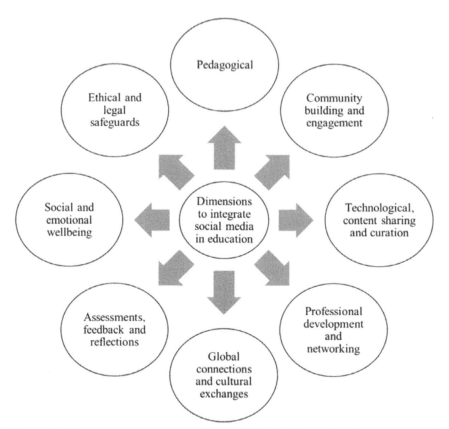

Fig. 1.2. Dimensions to Integrate Social Media in Education. *Source*: Authors' representation.

Table 1.3. Dimensions to Integrate Social Media Into Education.

Dimensions	Description	Benefits
Pedagogical	Real-time student interaction and participation on social media platforms enhance participatory and interactive learning. Peer-to-peer learning is facilitated through collaborative document sharing, discussion forums, and messaging apps.	Improved learning outcomes through enhanced communication, collaboration, and peer learning. Develops communication, problem-solving, and critical thinking skills.
Community building	Social media fosters community among students and professors, promoting dialogues and relationships. It can also teach principles of digital citizenship and safety.	Enhanced engagement, motivation, and learning retention. Equips students with online navigation skills, digital etiquette, and respectful online interactions.
Technology and content sharing	Appropriate selection of social media platforms aligns with learning goals, technology requirements, and privacy standards. Faculty and students can share content such as infographics, podcasts, and videos to complement the curriculum.	Enables deeper comprehension, independent study, critical thinking, and media literacy. Encourages resource exploration and diverse perspectives.
Professional development	Students can network with experts, professionals, and leaders, gaining insights and staying updated.	Exposes students to real-world applications and best practices. Facilitates sharing, advice-seeking, and keeping up with industry trends.
Global connections	Social media breaks geographical barriers, connecting students globally. Cross-cultural learning occurs through virtual interactions, group projects, and video conferences.	Enhances cultural understanding, global citizenship, and diversity appreciation. Encourages active participation in a global society.
Assessments and feedback	Social media enables quick feedback on discussions, assignments, and projects, promoting responsive learning.	Develops metacognitive skills through self-assessment and reflection. Cultivates constructive criticism, peer assessment, and continuous improvement.

Table 1.3. (*Continued*)

Dimensions	Description	Benefits
Social and emotional well-being	Faculty create inclusive and safe online environments, teaching students' online etiquette, safety, and balance.	Supports students' emotional and social needs, fostering overall well-being.
Ethical and legal awareness	Educates students on ethical and legal aspects of sharing and using content on social media, including terms of service, privacy policies, and safeguarding personal information.	Increases awareness of copyright, intellectual property, plagiarism, internet safety, and privacy concerns related to social media.

Living Lab

Living labs are defined as 'rigorous campus-based research with operational, academic partners, sustainable data collection/analysis, formal and informal learning activities, measurable outcomes and feedback loops'. A living lab is an experimental environment in which students, educators, researchers, community, and other stakeholders collaborate and interact to develop, implement (see Fig. 1.3), and evaluate innovative ideas, products, techniques, technologies, and solutions. Living labs are often placed in real-world settings, such as schools, universities, or community centres, allowing for realistic and practical experimentation. Living labs promote inclusive design and involve the communities in decision-making and innovation. The components of a living lab comprise 'innovation (central), technological resources (ICT and technology infrastructure), management and organizational structure, partners, stakeholders, users, research, funding and resources, and approach'. Living labs make the educational ecosystem and its users and stakeholders more resilient.

The future of education is dependent on the influences and interactions of a complex set of internal and external factors. Having understood the emergent trends in education, it is important to get an overview of the factors that can influence the implementation of an integrated futuristic new normal in the university education ecosystem.

Implementation and adoption of a new futuristic system invites the amalgamation and alignment of multifaceted themes that work together, in a synchronized fashion, to drive results and create an impact. The fundamental themes comprise:

    a. individual factors – faculty and students
    b. organizational factors
    c. environmental factors, and
    d. technological factors

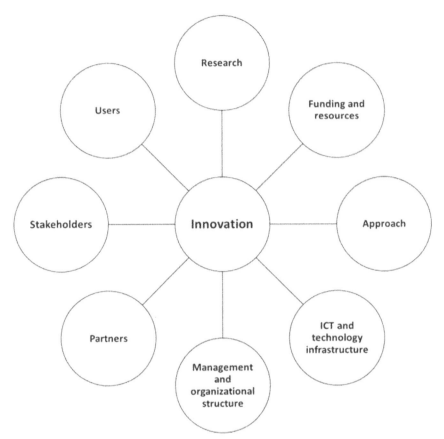

Fig. 1.3. Living Lab – Components. *Source*: Adopted from *The Living Labs Methodology Handbook* (Ståhlbröst & Holst, 2012).[a]

[a]https://www.slideshare.net/openlivinglabs/ws-8-living-lab-methodology-handbook

a. Individual factors – faculty and students

The journey towards a futuristic educational ecosystem commences with the diverse attributes of both faculty and students. Factors such as age, gender, and educational qualifications weave a rich tapestry of perspectives, each contributing to the holistic adoption of technology. The digital literacy of educators, coupled with their level of proficiency, forms the bedrock upon which digital transformation is built. Their ability, interest, and willingness to explore innovative avenues, combined with agility and behaviours that embrace change, are pivotal in steering the course towards an enriched educational experience. The symbiotic feedback loop between faculty and students fuels interactive learning, cultivates self-efficacy, and moulds attitudes that thrive in a technology-driven world.

b. Organizational factors

At the institutional level, a symphony of organizational factors orchestrates the harmonious integration of technology. Visionary leadership, equipped with a keen understanding of the evolving educational landscape, provides the compass guiding the institution's trajectory. Financial support and resource allocation act as pillars, empowering the creation of a robust technological infrastructure. Nurturing an organizational culture that reverberates with innovation, fuelled by continuous training and workshops, propels educators and learners towards a progressive horizon. The curriculum, underpinned by cutting-edge pedagogical approaches and assessments, reflects the institution's commitment to preparing students for a digital future. Rankings, accreditation, and stakeholder-centric policies cement the institution's dedication to excellence in education.

c. Environmental factors

The environmental underpinning is pivotal in shaping the receptiveness of technology integration. Capacity-building endeavours bolster the institution's ability to seamlessly adopt technological advancements, while ethical and legal considerations ensure the alignment with societal norms and standards. The preservation of privacy and the provision of comprehensive faculty support lay the foundation for a secure and nurturing digital ecosystem. The strategic selection of infrastructure locations and sizes, accompanied by reliable internet speed, serves as the backbone of accessibility and connectivity. The presence of familial support during virtual sessions fosters an inclusive learning environment, while tools and progress monitoring mechanisms facilitate the cultivation of a holistic educational journey.

d. Technology factors

The technical components of this paradigm for transformation start with awareness to promote change and inquiry. Simplified access enhances stakeholder involvement and engagement. Effective technology enhances the user experience for seamless, immersive learning. The digital world is strengthened by data and network security, maintaining trust. A plethora of resources and guidance assure continuous learning. Low-code technologies democratize content production and allow artists greater freedom. User-friendly design, multimedia integration, reliability, and constant support are used to create an atmosphere where technology drives innovation in education.

In essence, the use of this comprehensive framework can help institutions pave the way for a future where technology enhances education, fosters creativity, and equips learners and educators alike with the tools to thrive in an ever-evolving world.

Primary research was conducted via a focus group discussion with teaching faculty to gain insights on factors influencing implementation of an integrated futuristic new normal in the university education ecosystem.

A moderated focus group discussion was conducted with 10 faculty members who had taught during the pandemic, chosen across different areas, designations, and for their unique teaching styles and requirements. Content analysis using sentiment analysis technique and word cloud visualization was conducted. Insights, sentiments (see Table 1.4), and satisfaction level with online teaching during pandemic were assessed. Their views were matched with the dimensions of

Table 1.4. Sentiment Analysis (10 Faculty).

Statement Sentiment	Average Score (%)	Number of Statements
Positive	54	128
Negative	32	74
Neutral	14	33

the framework. This study confirmed that faculty views are closely aligned with the dimensions of the framework. From a success perspective, such insights will prove to be helpful when planning the implementation and integration of innovative teaching ecosystems and environments. An emphasis on pre-counselling, pre-sensitization as well as ongoing continued support should be designed to take care of the impacting factors.

Faculty Expressions – Sample Representation (see Figs. 4(a)–4(f))

- Feelings of 'embarrassed', 'digitally retarded', 'non/less tech savvy' compared to digital native students who are fast in adoption of technology changes.
- Digital environment creates a roadblock. It is a bottleneck to the learning experiences and outcomes.
- Missed the sense of 'immediate gratification' experienced during the physical classes. For successful online learning, assurance of continuous connectivity is required.
- Faculty with technical background and having prior exposure and experience of working with technology expressed moderate to high level of satisfaction with online education and had made significant personal financial investment to procure and install hardware and software for continuity of business and education learning process.
- Individual factors of attitude, agility, mindset, behaviours, willingness, flexibility, motivation, passion, and resilience are greater influencers. Digital literacy and level of digital competence is an important determinant.
- Leadership, vision, trust, organizational culture, and seniority should motivate, facilitate, and provide resources to encourage smooth transition and transformation. Training and workshops should be considered as investments and not an expense. Management should welcome feedback and improvement for effective learning. Over a period of time, a learning culture is developed in the organization.
- Rankings and accreditation can be considered as indirect factors driving technology implementation and adaptation.
- Product features, functionality, maturity, ease of use of technology, awareness of purpose for use of technology, cost, time, and project compatibility are important factors in implementation and adoption of technology.
- Conversations and communications are more important than just introducing technology as tools for working and getting the task done.

Next-generation Innovative Teaching Ecosystems 25

a. Faculty area

Faculty Area	Satisfaction level
HR	Moderate
Operations	High
Healthcare	Moderate
Retail	Moderate
Marketing	Low
Finance	Low
Media and Entertainment	Low
Rural	Low
Sustainability	Low
Design Thinking	Low

b. Satisfaction with online teaching

c. Technology factor

d. Personal factors (faculty and students)

e. Institutional/organizational factors

f. Environment support factors (faculty and students)

Fig. 1.4. Sentiment Analysis and Word Cloud Visualization. *Note*: Tool used: MS Excel Azure Machine Learning, www.wordclouds.com (https://www.zygomatic.nl/).

- Tech should be an enabler and not a replacer to physical interactions – should enhance productivity and make work better.
- Today, the relationship between faculty and students is interchangeable. Faculty, though teachers, can be considered learners for technology literacy and competence; sometimes, they also seek guidance and assistance from students. In such scenarios, the students can be considered teachers. Gradually,

a faculty's technology competence is transitioning from 'digitally challenged – digital migrant – digital citizen – digital native'.
- In a crisis situation, management and faculty should try to understand with the students and faculty fraternity about their environment, infrastructural issues and family issues and make efforts for a win-win arrangement.
- Management education is all about the in-betweens, the grey areas and understanding the grey areas, and offering solutions to address such grey areas.
- Cost–benefit analysis is very important for inclusive education, especially for those who were challenged in terms of access to and or ownership of devices suitable for online learning.

Conclusion

The implementation of next-generation innovative teaching ecosystems for futuristic management education has several important implications for its stakeholders.

For the students, it gets translated into greater accessibility to education, more flexibility of learning with the learn-from-anywhere model, and options for continuity of education. It provides for an enhanced learning experience resulting in effective learning outcomes and impact. It also creates improved employability potential and better career roles considering the skills and competencies developed, which are relevant to the global economy and market requirements.

For the faculty, there is an opportunity to explore and experiment with innovative teaching methods using traditional and advanced pedagogy techniques and better ways to foster good teacher–student relationships, resulting in greater student participation, engagement, and problem-solving. Exposure to such advanced teaching learning techniques and technologies helps with the professional development for the faculty, helping them become experts and stay current and relevant in their own domains. Eventually, it increases the intelligence quotient for an organization.

For the educational institution, such endeavours can create a differentiation and enhance the institutional reputation as a forward-thinking progressive innovation-driven institution, offering a competitive advantage. It can help form meaningful partnerships that would enable problem-solving opportunities for students through engagement in live projects, internship, and industry mentoring opportunities.

References

Al-Bashabsheh, W. T. F., & Pradhan, P. (2023). The importance of social media in education during COVID-19. *Journal of Advance Research in Science and Social Science (JARSSC)*, *5*(2), 1–13. https://doi.org/10.46523/jarssc.05.02.07

American Institutes for Research. (n.d.). Spotlight on personalized learning. https://www.air.org/resource/spotlight/spotlight-personalized-learning

Cheung, S. K. S., Kwok, L. F., Phusavat, K., & Yang, H. H. (2021). Shaping the future learning environments with smart elements: Challenges and opportunities. *International Journal of Educational Technology in Higher Education*, *18*(1), 16. https://doi.org/10.1186/s41239-021-00254-1

Consortium for Educational Communication (CEC). (n.d.). https://cec.nic.in/

Council of Europe. (n.d.). Artificial intelligence and education: A critical view through the lens. https://rm.coe.int/artificial-intelligence-and-education-a-critical-view-through-the-lens/1680a886bd

Evelyn Learning. (2019, December 6). Pedagogy as a tool of effective teaching and learning. https://www.evelynlearning.com/pedagogy-as-a-tool-of-effective-teaching-and-learning/

Florida Center for Instructional Technology. (n.d.-a). Frequently asked questions (FAQs). https://fcit.usf.edu/matrix/fetc-2021/

Florida Center for Instructional Technology. (n.d.-b). Frequently asked questions (FAQs). https://fcit.usf.edu/matrix/faqs/

Guàrdia, L., Clougher, D., Anderson, T., & Maina, M. (2021). IDEAS for transforming higher education: An overview of ongoing trends and challenges. *International Review of Research in Open and Distributed Learning*, *22*(2), 166–184. https://doi.org/10.19173/irrodl.v22i2.5206

Herodotou, C., Sharples, M., Gaved, M., Kukulska-Hulme, A., Rienties, B., Scanlon, E., & Whitelock, D. (2019). Innovative pedagogies of the future: An evidence-based selection. *Frontiers in Education*, *4*, 3. ISSN 2504-284X. https://doi.org/10.3389/feduc.2019.00113

Holmes, W., Persson, J., Chounta, I.-A., Wasson, B., & Dimitrova, V. (2022). *Artificial intelligence and education: A critical view through the lens of human rights, democracy and the rule of law*. Council of Europe.

How AI and data could personalize higher education. (2019, October). *Harvard Business Review*. https://hbr.org/2019/10/how-ai-and-data-could-personalize-higher-education

Liu, M., & Yu, D. (2023). Towards intelligent E-learning systems. *Education and Information Technologies*, *28*, 7845–7876. https://doi.org/10.1007/s10639-022-11479-6

Madni, S. H. H., Javed, A., Ali, H. H., Hasan, M. M., Saad, M., Junaid, S., Maray, M., & Hosseini, S. (2022). Factors influencing the adoption of IoT for E-learning in higher educational institutes in developing countries. *Frontiers in Psychology*, *13*, 915596. ISSN 1664–1078. https://doi.org/10.3389/fpsyg.2022.915596

McDiarmid, G. W., & Zhao (赵勇), Y. (2023). Time to rethink: Educating for a technology-transformed world. *ECNU Review of Education*, *6*(2), 189–214. https://doi.org/10.1177/20965311221076493

Mesquita, A., & Oliveira, A. (2022). The future of higher education and the use of newer technologies and pedagogical approaches – The perspective of students. *FAIMA Business & Management Journal, Suppl. Special Issue*, 141–162. https://www.proquest.com/scholarly-journals/future-higher-education-use-newer-technologies/docview/2765804242/se-2

Ministry of Education, Government of India. (n.d.). ICT initiatives. https://www.education.gov.in/ict-initiatives

MIT Office of Sustainability. (n.d.). *Defining living labs*. Massachusetts Institute of Technology. https://sustainability.mit.edu/defining-living-labs

Nietzel, M. T. (2020, March 12). *How colleges can chatbot their way to better student retention*. Forbes. https://www.forbes.com/sites/michaeltnietzel/2020/03/12/how-colleges-can-chatbot-their-way-to-better-student-retention/?sh=635744a96b34

Pantelimon, F.-V., Bologa, R., Toma, A., & Posedaru, B.-S. (2021). The evolution of AI-driven educational systems during the COVID-19 pandemic. *Sustainability*, *13*, 13501. https://doi.org/10.3390/su132313501

Prahmana, R. C. I., Hartanto, D., Kusumaningtyas, D. A., Ali, R. M., & Muchlas. (2021). Community radio-based blended learning model: A promising learning model in a remote area during the pandemic era. *Heliyon*, *7*(7), e07511. https://doi.org/10.1016/j.heliyon.2021.e07511

Quintana Borazon, E., & Chuang, H.-H. (2023). Resilience in educational system: A systematic review and directions for future research. *International Journal of Educational Development*, *99*, 102761. https://doi.org/10.1016/j.ijedudev.2023.102761

Rashid, S., & Yadav, S. (2020). Impact of Covid-19 pandemic on higher education and research. *Indian Journal of Human Development*, *14*, 340–343. https://doi.org/10.1177/09737 03020946700

Singh, A. D., & Hassan, M. (2017). *Pursuit of smart learning environments for the 21st century, current and critical issues in curriculum, learning and assessment.* IBE/2017/WP/CD/12.

Ståhlbröst, A., & Holst, M. (2012). *The living labs methodology handbook: A transnational Nordic smart city living lab pilot – SmartIES.* Social Informatics at Luleå University of Technology and CDT – Centre for Distance-spanning Technology. https://www.ltu.se/cms_fs/1.101555!/file/LivingLabsMethodologyBook_web.pdf

Stern, I., Epstein, A., & Landau, D. (2021, November 8). *Making VR a reality in business classrooms.* Harvard Business School Publishing. https://hbsp.harvard.edu/inspiring-minds/making-vr-a-reality-in-business-classrooms

SWAYAM. (n.d.). https://swayam.gov.in/

SWAYAM Prabha. (n.d.). About SWAYAM Prabha. https://swayamprabha.gov.in/index.php/about

Toffler, A. (1971). *Future shock* (p. 414). A Bantam Book/published by arrangement with Random House, Inc. https://ia801209.us.archive.org/6/items/FutureShock-Toffler/Future-Shock_-_Toffler.pdf

UNESCO Institute for Lifelong Learning. (n.d.). Learning ecosystems. https://www.uil.unesco.org/en/learning-ecosystems

United Nations. (n.d.). *Global citizenship education. United Nations academic impact.* https://www.un.org/en/academic-impact/page/global-citizenship-education

University Grants Commission. (2021). Educational framework for global citizenship in higher education. https://www.ugc.gov.in/e-book/GCED%20Book_WEB.pdf

University of South Florida. (2023, May 2). Associate Professor develops motivational chatbot and Candyland-like maze to ensure student success. https://www.usf.edu/news/2023/associate-professor-develops-motivational-chatbot-and-candyland-like-maze-to-ensure-student-success.aspx

Valiathan, P. (2002). *Blended learning models.* ASTD. Retrieved from https://www.academia.edu/17903067/Blended_Learning

Wang, L. (2023). Adoption of the PICRAT model to guide the integration of innovative technologies in the teaching of a linguistics course. *Sustainability*, *15*(5), 3886. https://doi.org/10.3390/su15053886

Weick, K. E. (1993). The collapse of sensemaking in organizations: The Mann Gulch disaster. *Administrative Science Quarterly*, *38*(4), 628–652.

World Bank. (2022, January 4). The global education crisis is even more severe than previously estimated. World Bank Blogs. https://blogs.worldbank.org/education/global-education-crisis-even-more-severe-previously-estimated

Chapter 2

Teaching in Times of Crisis or Pandemic Pedagogy

J.-F.[a], Darren Pullen[b], Andy Bown[b], Zi Siang See[b], Naomi Nelson[c], Anita Heywood[d], Loan Dao[d], Yang Yang[e], Helena Winnberg[f] and Stacie Reck[g]

[a]Faculty of Education, Crandall University, Canada
[b]School of Education, University of Tasmania, Australia
[c]Institute of Education, Federation University Australia, Australia
[d]Faculty of Medicine and Health, University of New South Wales, Australia
[e]College of Health and Medicine, Academic Division, University of Tasmania, Australia
[f]Tasmanian Department for Education, Children and Young People, Australia
[g]New Brunswick Education, Maplehurst Middle School, Australia

Abstract

Higher education institutions (HEIs), including universities, adult and vocational institutes, and technical and further education (TAFE) centres, faced the challenge of responding to the COVID-19 pandemic with limited data on how best to protect their communities and to continue educating their students. HEIs implemented various measures and adaptations by prioritizing the safety and well-being of students, staff, and the broader community while ensuring uninterrupted educational delivery. The pandemic presented a global educational challenge, requiring institutions to address complex organizational issues. These challenges encompassed topics such as information access, equity, diverse communication infrastructures, collaboration, logistics, the use of digital platforms, decentralization, redundancy, variation in virtual rituals and communication protocols, unstructured digital proxemics, Zoom fatigue, the absence of remote feedback loop models, and COVID-19 management protocols. Among the critical questions posed by the pandemic in the higher education sector in Australia and

---

Global Higher Education Practices in Times of Crisis:
Questions for Sustainability and Digitalization, 29–47
Copyright © 2025 by J.-F., Darren Pullen, Andy Bown, Zi Siang See, Naomi Nelson, Anita Heywood, Loan Dao, Yang Yang, Helena Winnberg and Stacie Reck
Published under exclusive licence by Emerald Publishing Limited
doi:10.1108/978-1-83797-052-020241003

Canada, whether at universities, technical institutes, or education centres, was how faculty enhanced the learning experience and fostered symbiosis among co-located/on-shore and remote/off-shore students. To gain a deeper understanding of the relationship between HEIs and COVID-19 educational mitigation, we analysed the actions taken by three HEIs in Australia and one in Canada during the crisis years of 2021–2022. This analysis was based on the personal reflections of the authors (academics from various HEIs), a synthesis of which is presented in this chapter.

Keywords: Technology; remote learning; pandemic; pedagogy

Introduction

On 30 January 2020, the World Health Organization (WHO) declared the COVID-19 outbreak as a public health emergency of international concern. The COVID-19 pandemic, also known as the coronavirus pandemic, has left an indelible mark on societies and economies globally, ranking it fifth among the deadliest epidemics and pandemics in history (Jarus, 2023; WHO, 2021). The pandemic was caused by a severe acute respiratory syndrome coronavirus 2 (SARS-CoV-2), which transmits primarily through respiratory droplets released when an infected individual coughs, sneezes, converses, or breathes. Physical isolation and reducing the proximity of individuals were, therefore, imperative in containing and minimizing the spread of the virus (Bennett, 2023). To counteract the transmissibility and for novel variants to potentially evade immunity, a range of measures were introduced, including lockdowns, social distancing regulations, mask mandates, travel restrictions, and vaccines (Australian Government Department of Health and Aged Care, 2023; Basseal et al., 2023; Littlecott et al., 2023). Consequently, the repercussions of the COVID-19 pandemic extended deeply into economic and social domains, many of which are still being discovered (Bennett, 2023). These repercussions or disruptions included interruptions to education, work, and social life, which caused mental health challenges (Brodeur et al., 2021).

Background

Educational institutions worldwide had to adapt to the challenges posed by the pandemic, leading to school closures, the adoption of remote learning methods, and disruptions to traditional educational practices such as examinations. This chapter will examine the pandemic responses of three Australian and one Canadian higher education institutions (HEIs) to determine whether the pandemic has expedited the ongoing trends and transformations in the higher education sector, specifically the transition from traditional on-site teaching to blended or hybrid and online programme delivery. Additionally, our examination will chronicle how each HEI had to reevaluate their educational strategies, focusing on design and delivery, adapting teaching methods for online environments, communicating with students, and redesigning student engagement/learning procedures and tasks to accommodate online assessment. We will also explore how educators collaborated across diverse settings and contexts, acknowledged expertise beyond institutional and disciplinary boundaries, and delved into the influence of technology on teaching and learning practices. Our institutional case studies, which are based on the individual reflections of the contributing authors (i.e., who were working at these institutions during the pandemic), will elucidate how the pandemic compelled educators and students to navigate new learning methods. The overall aim of this chapter is to analyse the changes made at these institutions as they were forced to adapt to new ways of teaching and delivering educational programmes during one of the deadliest pandemics in history.

Implications for HEIs

Due to the COVID-19 pandemic, every institution of higher education (HEI) implemented distinctive and comprehensive adjustments encompassing a variety of measures. Some of these measures were novel for faculty (professors, lecturers, and teachers) and students. These changes included the shift from conventional classroom-based instruction to remote learning, enforcing COVID-19 protocols and requirements for on-campus activities, and developing communication, engagement, and assessment strategies. These adaptations necessitated changes in teaching and learning methods, raised concerns about educational equity, and emphasized the importance of focusing on mental health and well-being.

Transition to Remote Learning and Use of Digital Technologies

In Australia and Canada, hybrid learning models were implemented in some schools, combining in-person and online instruction to reduce the number of students in classrooms at any given time (Kay et al., 2020). Students in hybrid models experienced a mix of in-person and online learning, necessitating adaptation to different learning environments and ways of learning, which was challenging for some. While this approach aimed to balance educational continuity with safety, it presented challenges for faculty who had to manage in-person and virtual classrooms simultaneously. One main challenge for students was learning to self-manage time and learning commitments. Additionally, some students found it challenging to stay engaged and motivated in remote learning environments away from their peers and teachers (Gustiani, 2020; Noor et al., 2022). Furthermore, the shift to remote learning highlighted the digital divide among students, with some facing difficulties due to limited access to technology and the internet, leading to disparities in learning experiences (Pullen, 2015).

The COVID-19 pandemic placed additional stress on faculty members, often leading to burnout as they adapted to new teaching methods and had to address the well-being of their students and their own well-being needs (Fray et al., 2023). This increased workload and the emotional toll of managing the pandemic's impact on students and their families were contributing factors to increased teacher burnout (Fray et al., 2023). While the long-term effects of these adjustments are still under study, they are anticipated to have a lasting impact on education and the teaching profession (Fray et al., 2023; Limniou et al., 2021; Sintema, 2020).

Many HEIs found it necessary to shift to remote learning as governments recognized the rapid spread of the virus (WHO, 2021). This transition mandated that faculty quickly depart from traditional in-person classroom environments and embrace innovative online teaching methods for off-campus or hybrid instruction. Moreover, in certain instances, this transition compelled reconsidering physical collaborative spaces to align with social distancing requirements while ensuring pedagogical effectiveness. The transition also imposed additional demands on faculty in terms of lesson planning, teaching formats, and assessment planning. For most HEIs, moving to remote learning involved adapting to new digital platforms, developing online teaching materials, and mastering the art of conducting virtual classes.

Educational institutions embraced video conferencing platforms like Zoom and Microsoft Teams to facilitate real-time virtual lectures and seminars, ensuring minimal disruption to the academic calendar and student learning. Learning management systems such as Moodle and Blackboard were also enhanced to attempt to seamlessly deliver course materials and assignments. Moreover, certain tertiary education institutions also invested in virtual labs, augmented reality (AR), and artificial intelligence (AI) tools to maintain the quality of practical education. This often meant utilizing technologies in unfamiliar ways while simultaneously grappling with technological infrastructure challenges, such as slow internet speeds that resulted in latency issues during video conferencing or when uploading large files (Greenhow et al., 2021).

Navigating COVID-19 Regulations and Mental Health Challenges

All HEIs put into practice mask mandates, social distancing requirements, and enhanced cleaning protocols to mitigate the risk of virus transmission. Faculty members were tasked with the responsibility of enforcing these protocols and setting an example by adhering to these measures in the classroom, thereby ensuring the safety of themselves and their students. This meant that many faculty members found themselves learning about universal health precautions concurrently with their students. Faculty also had another additional challenge of enforcing rules that might have been unsettling for students, particularly for younger students, those with learning disabilities, and students with developmental delays (Paulauskaite et al., 2021). The implementation of these measures required students to adapt to new routines, including wearing masks and maintaining physical distance from their peers. These adjustments had the potential to impact their social interactions, social learning, and overall school experience and performance (Limniou et al., 2021).

Faculty and students found it necessary to redefine their methods of socialization, interaction, and communication. It is crucial to address these issues since psychological stress negatively correlates with learning and active participation in university life (Dodd et al., 2021). COVID-19 adversely affected students' academic pursuits and interactions with peers and faculty. These challenges stemmed from the difficulties associated with online learning despite its reported time-saving benefits. Students also grappled with altered living conditions, financial pressures, anxiety, loneliness, motivation, and uncertainty about the future and employment, further compounding the existing stress induced by new modes of learning and engagement (Dodd et al., 2021).

The HEIs as a learning community underwent a significant transformation, prompting a newfound emphasis on supporting health, well-being, and engagement within higher education communities (Dodd et al., 2021). Many students experienced heightened levels of stress, anxiety, and social isolation during the pandemic, leading to an increased demand for mental health resources and support. This need was underscored by the surge in phone calls to mental health organizations, primarily from young women aged 19–25 (Gallo et al., 2020; Limniou et al., 2021; Paulauskaite et al., 2021). In recognition of the mental health challenges presented by the pandemic, HEIs expanded their mental health and well-being services, offering online counselling and support to both staff and students.

Communication, Engagement, and Assessment

Educational institutions arranged virtual gatherings, clubs, associations, and digital social environments to sustain student involvement and promote unity. These initiatives underscored HEIs' dedication to harmonizing their educational objectives with the need to preserve a sense of a learning community and well-being throughout the COVID-19 pandemic. Their capacity to adapt and resilience were indispensable in ensuring that students continued to enjoy a robust sense of community, even in the face of challenging circumstances. As a result of the transition to remote learning, numerous educational institutions found it necessary to adapt existing policies or craft new ones pertaining to assessment and grading. Some schools postponed or revised high-stakes exams, such as Grades 11 and 12, prompting faculty and education assessment agencies to adapt their assessment methods to account for the challenges posed by the pandemic (Sintema, 2020). Substitute evaluation techniques and professional methods for overseeing high-stakes examinations from a remote context needed to be rapidly activated to validate students' learning achievements through technology (Fluck et al., 2009; Pullen, 2013). While these alterations in assessment may have reduced stress for certain students, they also prompted inquiries into how their academic advancement could be adequately appraised.

To better understand specific responses during the pandemic and the implications for post-pandemic study, four case studies will be provided, three Australian universities and one Canadian university, from the perspective and insights of faculty who worked and taught during the pandemic.

Experiences From the University of Tasmania (UTAS), Australia

The UTAS is a prominent state university in Australia, boasting a rich history as one of the country's oldest educational institutions. It holds the 20th position among Australian universities and serves as a research-focused university, catering to approximately 33,000 students.

Transition to Remote Learning and Use of Digital Technologies

UTAS has a well-established tradition of providing a hybrid approach (combining face-to-face and online, initially through postal methods and later transitioning fully online) for course and programme delivery. Consequently, when UTAS shifted to exclusive online course delivery during the COVID-19 pandemic, the transition was exceptionally smooth and built upon pre-existing policies and procedures (UTAS, 2020). In the School of Education, the majority of undergraduate students had already experienced some level of online learning. Typically, courses and lectures were delivered asynchronously online, giving students the flexibility to attend on-campus tutorials or engage in online sessions at their convenience. Consequently, the transition to 100% online delivery was relatively smooth, reducing anxiety for administrators, students, and faculty members. Notably, during the pandemic, live (synchronous) online session attendance appeared higher, possibly because students had limited social interactions.

One of the initial actions taken during the pandemic crisis was to find innovative ways to maintain teaching and learning activities in the field of education. This necessitated the adoption of digital tools and creative methods for real-time communication and collaboration (Matthews et al., 2020). As a result, Microsoft Teams and Zoom were integrated as meeting options within online learning platforms, facilitating various teaching and learning activities. The extent to which this integration led to potential fatigue remains uncertain.

This solution allowed faculty and students to engage in project-based discussions, enabling all participants to provide real-time feedback and input within a shared workspace. It was utilized in conjunction with teleconference teaching and learning sessions, permitting the integration of multimedia elements such as screenshots, notes, and diagrams. This made it suitable for digital presentations accessible via commonly available web browsers, offering accessibility anytime and anywhere, provided an internet connection was available. It is crucial to consider how digital technologies contribute to developing digital literacy across the curriculum (Australian Curriculum, Assessment and Reporting Authority (ACARA), 2022).

Apart from commonly utilized collaborative tools such as Outlook for email and Zoom for virtual meetings, there has been notable progress and a growing demand for Extended Reality (XR) and simulation applications in teaching and learning. This trend has been particularly pronounced during the pandemic, where digital technologies and tools have been employed in unconventional and inventive ways, enhancing spatial capabilities and fostering immersive and effective learning outcomes (Bower et al., 2020; Horst & Dorner, 2019; MacDowell & Lock, 2022). These technologies, such as AR and virtual reality (VR), offer educators and students innovative avenues for creating and engaging with educational content. XR opens opportunities for novel learning methods and data visualization, particularly in STEM (Science, Technology, Engineering, and Mathematics) and HASS (Humanities and Social Sciences) contexts.

For instance, in Science, students could visualize scientific data through virtual simulations, while Math students could manipulate shapes and engage in simulations within digital environments. Media Arts students found avenues to digitize

Teaching in Times of Crisis or Pandemic Pedagogy   35

their work and experiment with fresh creative techniques and tools. HASS students were empowered to explore local places and pose new questions about digital citizenship. Fig. 2.1 shows a three-dimensional (3D) scanned terrain based on geological data from Table Cape, an extinct volcano located northwest of Tasmania with rich cultural and tourism significance for educational applications. Users could interact with elements in the simulation, including using a magnifying glass to examine objects and points of interest in the 3D scanned model.

Fig. 2.2 illustrates how educators and students acted as 'creators,' designing digital worlds for simulation-based learning and promoting interactive

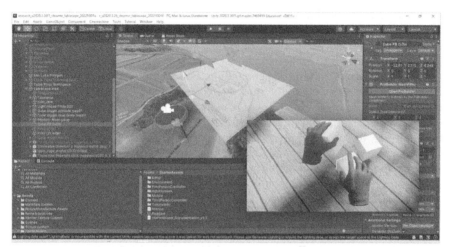

Fig. 2.1.   Interactive VR Prototype and 3D Scanned Terrain Based on the Geology Data of Table Cape, Which Is an Extinct Volcano in Tasmania.

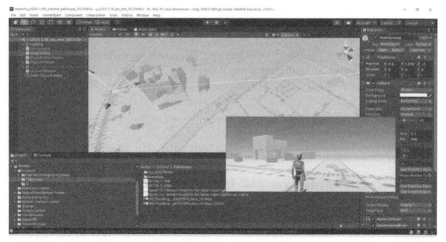

Fig. 2.2.   Digital Tools and Workflow for Creating Playable Educational Experiences in Simulated Digital Spaces.

experiences in technology-enhanced inquiry-based learning. These examples were developed using Unity Technologies, allowing content to be deployed in various scenarios, as readily available educational XR content on virtual platforms, such as Oculus and Steam.

Incorporating different AI tools into the curriculum has reshaped the teaching and learning paradigm to stimulate students' experience and success. One of the projects in the College of Health and Medicine was endorsed to use H5P – an interactive digital learning platform, to develop adaptive AI-driven teaching and assessment resources for a short lesson to address diverse learning needs and students' barriers during the onset of the COVID-19 pandemic. The target students were those who were interested in developing a better understanding of dementia care for patients from different cultural backgrounds. The course explored the varying perspectives of people with dementia, carers, and people living with dementia to facilitate a better understanding of what dementia is in the absence of cross-cultural understanding. For example, one adaptivity was to develop an interactive guide for students to explore the dementia care story by choosing the role of the interviewee. Customized learning resources, including our previous personalized interview videos from current family caregivers, have been tailored to student's special learning needs. The advent of the COVID-19 pandemic precipitated a rapid acceleration in the development of various technologies and the adoption of AI technologies within education. This trajectory signifies an enduring commitment to unlocking AI's potential to transform pedagogical practices, challenge conventional paradigms, and offer new horizons for learning and teaching.

Navigating COVID-19 Regulations and Mental Health Challenges

UTAS followed all the COVID-19 protocols and mandates set by State and Commonwealth Governments. Student well-being was paramount to UTAS, and several macro- and micro-level support mechanisms were implemented, from online tailored support to open and flexible options of support and care in relation to how a student could seek support, submit their work and assessments. UTAS created several support strategies to safeguard faculty, and a short-term response to COVID-19 included scaling back the use of casual and fixed-term staff and executive salary cuts. 'Tasmania's package of COVID-19 employment measures include cancellation of a 2% pay increase and deferral salary increases associated with promotions, for time fractions for some staff, and early retirements and voluntary redundancies' (Tjia et al., 2020). These measures allowed those concerned faculty to accept voluntary or early retirements.

Communication, Engagement, and Assessment

A large part of the UTAS student cohort was used to interact with faculty and their colleagues entirely online (discussion boards, emails, and webinars). Considering the pandemic, rather than overuse an impersonal online announcement via a post in the discussion board, faculty sent out personalized emails to minimize the feeling of isolation and anxiety. A unique observation was in the use of language on online learning discussion posts and on the online synchronous tutorials; there were notable expressions of care and concern from students for others' welfare appearing to the extent that perhaps had not previously been witnessed; students among themselves were communicating a genuine concern and empathy.

Faculty deliberately tried to actively involve students by introducing a more personalized approach to the learning experience, incorporating relatively informal video clips as means of communicating. The instructional material was complemented by brief introductory videos delivered in an informal 'selfie mode', wherein faculty greeted the students and provided an overview of the forthcoming topics and tasks. This straightforward addition, utilizing a smartphone, received positive feedback from students. This was evident in unsolicited comments in discussion forums and emails and more formal teaching evaluations. Students appreciated the humanized communication that deviated from conventional methods.

In an endeavour to compensate for the absence of on-campus learning opportunities, videos and synchronous video tutorials were integrated at various points throughout the semester. This aimed to fill the void created by the removal of in-person learning. Furthermore, additional support and guidance for assessment tasks were offered, enabling students to seek clarification on any course-related matters.

Several alternative assessment strategies were employed, and one example was an AI-driven adaptive assessment that was also developed and embedded to measure student success. For example, one question asked students to reflect on the strategy that has been used when meeting with a person from Germany with dementia. A series of multiple-choice questions was used to test students' understanding, which allowed for rich experience and increased the knowledge base. If the correct answer for a given question is provided, the student moves on to the next question. However, if an incorrect answer is provided, it is evident that the student needs more support to understand the question and reach the correct answer. Instead of offering straightforward feedback or revealing the correct answer outright, the AI-driven approach involved intelligently guiding students along an entirely different learning pathway, accompanied by new educational resources. This AI-enhanced pathway was designed to address and rectify misconceptions through automated feedback when the student triggered an incorrect answer. The benefits of such an approach lie in the provision of specific support and feedback to enable learners to make full use of learning opportunities (Kiesewetter et al., 2022).

Experiences From Federation University (FU), Australia

FU is the fourth oldest tertiary institution in Australia and is ranked 36th out of 37 universities in Australia (*Times Higher Education*, 2023). FU is a regional multi-campus institution with around 8,000 students, of whom a significant proportion of students are the first in their families to attend university. Within the university, the Institute of Education, Arts, and Community is dedicated to preparing future educators, specifically those likely to work in regional and remote educational settings. One notable feature of this institution is the relatively small class sizes and tutorials designed for pre-service teachers (PSTs), typically consisting of fewer than 25 students. This enables faculty and teaching assistants to establish a deeper understanding of their students, allowing for tailored instruction and fostering an environment conducive to building vital connections. The quality of the teacher–student relationship is widely recognized as a pivotal factor influencing students' learning engagement, overall well-being, and academic success (Darling-Hammond et al., 2020). This sense of connection and support contributes significantly to students' overall satisfaction with their educational experience and enhances their motivation to excel academically.

The COVID-19 pandemic presented unprecedented challenges for FU. The university's dedication to nurturing robust teacher–student relationships remained steadfast; nonetheless, the pandemic did affect the university's capacity to engage with students in various respects.

Transition to Remote Learning and Use of Digital Technologies

The shift to online teaching and learning, while imperative for public health, posed risks to the academic, emotional, and social well-being of students (Wang, 2023). With the necessity for social distancing and safety protocols, teaching and learning transitioned to online platforms. Although classes were scheduled and conducted as live, synchronous online sessions, some students encountered substantial disadvantages in terms of accessibility. For instance, a weak internet connection often compelled students to disable their webcams to prevent lag and others faced health challenges related to COVID-19 infections that prevented them from attending. While online learning and teaching are often regarded as more challenging and isolating, the crisis stimulated innovation and fostered the development of creative solutions to enhance the quality of virtual education (Gillett-Swan, 2017).

In FU, a Centre for Academic Development (CAD) team was created to provide ad hoc or just-in-time support for staff. This also included facilitating a centralized space for staff to share materials, resources, and activities to engage students. The provision of ongoing professional development, enhanced course and curriculum design, and the creation and sustainability of high-quality digital resources helped advance online teaching and learning practices.

FU also bought a licence to use Adobe Creative Cloud, a comprehensive suite of applications to bring creativity to teaching and learning online. The ITS Training and Development team created a site for access to all Creative Cloud resources, which included short video guides, courses, and examples of how staff implemented this innovative technology. This supported the development of digital fluency and 21st-century skills to enhance the learning experience.

Lastly, FU joined IComm to create technology-rich teaching spaces – Connected Classrooms – to enable synchronous learning for students, regardless of their geographic location. The Connected Classroom Initiative transformed hybrid learning, providing students with a seamless and immersive learning experience, with opportunities to participate in tutorials, interact with their peers, and develop essential skills critical to success.

Navigating COVID-19 Regulations and Mental Health Challenges

Like UTAS, FU also followed all government COVID-19 protocols and mandates. Like other Australian universities, FU had safety and support information accessible on their websites, including COVID-19 updates throughout the pandemic. FU took student well-being seriously, and given its focus on connectedness and community building, supporting students and their well-being was paramount.

Communication, Engagement, and Assessment

FU adapted and implemented strategies to mitigate the effects of the pandemic on student–teacher relationships and academic outcomes. To ensure continuity and connectedness, FU increased written, asynchronous communication methods such as emails, forums, and audio and video recordings for interactions between students and lecturers. Students came to rely more heavily on their lecturers for assistance in understanding assignments and receiving feedback. FU created spaces and opportunities and provided various digital and web-based additional supports for students' well-being, enhancing online engagement strategies and maintaining open lines of communication to ensure that students felt connected and supported throughout this challenging period.

Experiences From the University of New South Wales (UNSW Sydney), Australia

The UNSW Sydney is one of the founding universities in the group of eight universities in Australia and is ranked fourth in Australia. UNSW Sydney is a research university with around 66,000 students.

Transition to Remote Learning and Use of Digital Technologies

UNSW, like many universities globally, recognized the need to adhere to social distancing and public health guidelines. As a result, traditional in-person lectures, seminars, tutorials, and laboratory classes were swiftly moved to digital platforms. This shift allowed students to continue their studies remotely, reducing the risk of virus transmission on-campus. Digital technologies played a crucial role in enabling this transition, as educators and students turned to online platforms for communication and collaboration.

Throughout the health crisis, UNSW relied heavily on digital assets for its teaching and learning initiatives. Microsoft Teams and Zoom seamlessly became part of the university's online education infrastructure, enabling immediate communication and cooperation. These solutions not only facilitated virtual classroom environments but also empowered educators to engage with students through diverse channels, including virtual office hours and group discourse sessions. However, while these digital tools played a vital role in maintaining educational consistency, they also presented fresh challenges. Educators needed to acclimate to these platforms, generate online teaching materials, and acquire proficiency in conducting virtual class sessions. UNSW, both centrally and through faculties and schools, supported students and educators with virtual training and resources, facilitating the rapid uptake of these platforms.

In addition to Microsoft Teams and Zoom, educators at UNSW embraced various digital tools in their teaching. For example, educators adopted a range of polling and online quiz software to support learning, including Poll Everywhere, Mentimeter, Slido, and Kahoot! In contrast to the adoption of Microsoft Teams and Zoom, the adoption of polling software was organic and user-led, with no preferred platform provided and supported by the UNSW central information technology support unit. Therefore, support was generally peer-led within teaching teams and schools. Several courses within the School of Population Health utilized Mentimeter at the beginning of virtual lectures, quizzing students on the prior week's key learning outcomes. In addition to synchronous polling, this platform allowed asynchronous learning in which students could answer questions, view the overall class results, and check their learning, thus providing engaging learning opportunities for students to learn in different modalities.

Navigating COVID-19 Regulations and Mental Health Challenges

Like UTAS and FU, the UNSW Sydney followed all government COVID-19 protocols and mandates. Several provisions and support mechanisms were implemented to support the well-being of faculty and students. One was the option of working from home for faculty. The other was the flexibility around working conditions and allowing faculty and students to exercise their own judgements in utilizing the best feasible way to engage and interact with others.

Communication, Engagement, and Assessment

In response to the transformed learning landscape, UNSW adjusted the assessment and examination procedures. The university restructured its assessment methods and exam formats to suit remote learning conditions and align with social distancing guidelines. These adaptations encompassed the implementation of alternative assessment approaches. Because UNSW did not utilize online remotely proctored exams, primarily due to privacy concerns, the chosen alterations were crafted with the intent of alleviating the pressure on students while preserving the fairness of their academic evaluations. In the absence of remote proctoring of exams, educators were tasked with designing new approaches to assessment that either used alternative online options, such as Moodle (learning management system) quizzes or Inspera (online assessment platform), or educators moved to more authentic assessment tasks.

The procedures related to assessments also required adaptation throughout the COVID-19-induced lockdowns, with a particular need to support student well-being. For example, postgraduate students in the Master of Public Health programme are primarily working in the health sector, and many were intimately involved in the COVID-19 response while juggling part-time postgraduate study and domestic issues such as home-schooling. Leniency with special consideration for written assessment due dates was implemented to support student progression and successful completion of courses, even while this had a substantial administrative burden on educators.

Experiences From Crandall University (CU), Canada

CU is a modest-sized Christian institution situated in Atlantic Canada, boasting an enrolment of approximately 1,200 students. Nestled within a maritime setting, CU primarily conducts its teaching through traditional in-person classroom settings, maintaining a small class size. While most courses and learning activities at CU take place in physical, on-campus settings, a limited number of courses are delivered through online platforms, utilizing Microsoft Teams in conjunction with Moodle as the primary learning and teaching platform. CU's education programme began about 25 years before the pandemic and was designed to offer a highly hands-on, interactive, and relationship-based approach to teacher training. The Bachelor of Education (BEd) programme was not offered online because the founding faculty members believed in face-to-face interaction with experienced teachers, including practical components and many opportunities for faculty and students to practise and demonstrate effective pedagogical approaches. The BEd programme was developed in the context of powerful teacher–mentor relationships. The same model was maintained when CU began to offer its Master of Education programme in subsequent years.

Transition to Remote Learning and Use of Digital Technologies

When the global COVID-19 pandemic began to impact all aspects of life in the Canadian context in early 2020, due to location and size, it was not immediately clear that online learning would be necessary since the student population was relatively small. However, when the Canadian government required educational institutions to shut down, CU had no choice but to pivot and begin offering online and face-to-face classes throughout the pandemic with social distancing in place. Most professors utilized Moodle and Microsoft Teams, with some using Zoom to teach courses in real time to allow students to maintain their pre-pandemic schedules. Faculty members were able to establish and continue to develop strong relationships with students through small class sizes and additional one-on-one support using Teams meetings. Faculty demonstrated flexibility as most learned to utilize the platform along with the students. Despite the extremely challenging global context, this 'we are all in it together' mentality contributed to a positive experience for most students.

Navigating COVID-19 Regulations and Mental Health Challenges

Like UTAS, FU, and UNSW, CU followed all government COVID-19 protocols and mandates. CU considered the stress and anxiety of faculty and students and provided information on where to seek support, be it on-campus, off-campus, or online.

Communication, Engagement, and Assessment

The primary mode of communication was through emails. A COVID-19 Advisory Group was formed to support faculty and students in navigating the official mandatory orders and operations. The Advisory Group also developed a set of guidelines to align with the provincial orders and would regularly pass on relevant information about operations and management, and the Advisory Group was available to support faculty and students. All faculty and students were highly engaged and positively maintained a sense of care in the community. While COVID-19 did bring academic and learning challenges, assessments were done in the traditional setting (i.e., paper-based task) with social distancing where exams were necessary, and assessments were submitted in paper or email.

Overall Impact of the COVID-19 Pandemic on the Higher Education Landscape From the Lens of Faculty

The COVID-19 pandemic has had a profound impact on the higher education landscape in both Australia and Canada. It compelled an abrupt and unprecedented shift from traditional on-campus learning to remote and online education, necessitating rapid adaptation from educators and institutions. During this transformative period, several key findings and crucial recommendations for post-pandemic teaching practices have surfaced.

Throughout the pandemic, educators contended with many challenges, chief among them being the need to swiftly attain proficiency in digital tools and online teaching and assessment methods. This experience prompted many educators to explore innovative approaches to engage students within virtual learning environments. Since digital tools were unfamiliar to teaching staff and students, the shift in approach underscored the enduring importance of digital literacy for educators.

Furthermore, the pandemic accelerated the widespread adoption of several technologies, including novel ones such as Extended Reality (XR) and simulation technologies. AR and VR emerged as potent tools for enhancing spatial comprehension and immersive learning experiences relevant to STEM and HASS disciplines. These technologies opened novel avenues for engaging students and merit further integration into curriculum design post-pandemic for both online and on-campus classrooms.

As educators and HEIs navigated these transformative changes, they also developed a heightened sensitivity to the mental health needs of students and staff. The pandemic brought into sharp focus the critical importance of mental well-being. Educators found themselves in the role of providing support to students grappling with heightened stress, anxiety, and social isolation. This necessitated an expansion of mental health resources and the provision of online counselling services. Simultaneously, educators themselves contended with burnout resulting from the demands of adapting to new teaching modalities and the responsibility of managing the emotional well-being of their students.

The impacts on students and their learning experiences during the pandemic were many and profound. The abrupt transition to remote and online learning, sometimes with only a few days' notice, created disparities in access to technology and digital resources, exacerbating the digital divide. Some students found it challenging to stay engaged and motivated in a remote learning environment without key support from peers and direction from staff, while other students faced difficulties due to limited access to technology and the internet, in addition to having additional care needs for learning from home.

Furthermore, the shift to remote learning disrupted traditional classroom dynamics and social interactions, affecting students' social learning and overall school experience. The changes in assessment and grading methods, including the postponement or revision of high-stakes invigilated exams, raised questions about how academic progress could be evaluated fairly and with a high degree of authenticity or assignment trust.

Amid these challenges, what we have learnt about pandemic teaching and learning experiences has yielded valuable lessons that can be applied in our current teaching practices. From these learnings, we have identified five key experiences.

First, the pandemic accelerated the adoption of digital tools and online teaching methods among educators and students. Educators and students became proficient in using platforms such as Zoom, Microsoft Teams, and various learning management systems for content creation, file sharing, and engagement tools. This digital integration should persist post-pandemic to improve teaching practices, as these new practices offer increased flexibility in content delivery, fostering engagement, and catering to diverse learning and teaching styles. This approach can create a more dynamic and accessible learning experience for students and teaching staff if done with care and understanding of the learning needs.

Second, the pandemic introduced many hybrid learning models that combined in-person and totally online elements. These hybrid models offered flexibility and inclusivity, accommodating students with varying needs and preferences. In a post-pandemic era, educators should continue to embrace hybrid approaches to ensure that education remains accessible to all, regardless of location or circumstances.

Third, additionally, AR and VR emerged as powerful tools for immersive and experiential learning, particularly in STEM and HASS fields. These technologies can potentially deepen students' comprehension of complex concepts and enhance engagement. Integrating XR and simulations into teaching practices can elevate student learning outcomes by providing interactive and memorable learning experiences.

Fourth, the pandemic highlighted the critical importance of mental health support for students and educators. Institutions should maintain their focus on mental well-being by offering counselling services, providing self-care resources, and promoting a supportive learning environment. They should also provide educational opportunities for staff and students to learn about well-being needs and support services. Addressing the mental health needs of the education community can positively impact student retention, engagement, and overall learning outcomes and study success.

Lastly, the pandemic emphasized the significance of adaptability and flexibility in teaching practices. Educators learned to adjust to changing circumstances and evolving student needs swiftly. These skills should be retained and incorporated into future teaching approaches to respond to disruptions or changing educational requirements effectively. Prioritizing adaptability can lead to more responsive teaching practices and improved student learning outcomes.

Incorporating these pandemic learnings into teaching practices and institutional policies can create a more dynamic, inclusive, and supportive educational environment for staff and students. This, in turn, can enhance student learning outcomes, success, and overall educational quality.

Conclusion

As we reflect on our individual institutions' teaching and learning approaches during the pandemic and prepare for future educational challenges, we propose five key areas where we still need to gain a deeper understanding and develop better preparations.

1. *Assessment and Evaluation*: The pandemic prompted a significant shift in assessment and evaluation methods, with educators adapting to online and remote learning environments. There is a need to continue exploring and refining effective assessment strategies suitable for various learning contexts, ensuring fairness, reliability, and accuracy in measuring students' understanding and skills. Additionally, research should focus on leveraging technology to enhance assessment practices and maintain academic integrity in online evaluations.
2. *Digital Inclusivity*: The digital divide became more evident during the pandemic, highlighting the need to bridge this gap and ensure digital inclusivity for all students. The pandemic also highlighted a digital divide among teaching faculty, with some embracing the new and others struggling to transition from on-campus modes to fully digital online methods. Further research is necessary to understand the specific challenges teaching staff and students face in accessing online resources and technology. Institutions should invest in infrastructure and support systems to provide equitable access to technology, and educators should design courses that accommodate different technology levels and ensure accessibility both online and offline while also catering to a diverse digital literacy level among educators and students.
3. *Mental Health and Well-being*: The pandemic underscored the importance of addressing mental health and well-being in the education community. We need ongoing research to understand the long-term impacts of the pandemic on students' mental health and to develop comprehensive support systems. Institutions should continue prioritizing mental health services and resources, offering accessible counselling and support. Educators need to receive training in recognizing signs of mental health issues in students and colleagues and in providing appropriate assistance and referral to support services, which aims to foster a supportive and empathetic learning environment for all.

4. *Pedagogical Adaptation*: The pandemic moved quickly both in terms of virus spread and in terms of how quickly we all had to adapt to new challenges. The rapid transition to remote and online teaching required educators to adjust their pedagogical approaches and assessment strategies. Further exploration is needed to understand the effectiveness of these adaptations and how they can be integrated into future teaching practices. Educators should continue to refine their online teaching skills and embrace hybrid learning models that combine in-person and online elements to enhance flexibility and inclusivity. This is particularly important as we become more aware of staff and students' needs, such as family, self-care needs, learning/work, and well-being.
5. *Technological Integration*: The pandemic accelerated the integration of technology innovations in education. Future research should focus on best practices for leveraging digital tools to enhance the learning experience and promote engagement. Institutions should invest in technology infrastructure and support systems, and educators should stay updated on emerging technologies that can benefit student learning outcomes.

These five areas – assessment and evaluation, digital inclusivity, mental health and well-being, pedagogical adaptation, and technological integration – are critical for preparing for future educational challenges based on the lessons learned during the pandemic. Collaborative efforts among educators, institutions, and policymakers will be essential to address these concerns effectively and ensure the resilience of the education system in the face of uncertainty.

In conclusion, the COVID-19 pandemic has reshaped the landscape of higher education in Australia and Canada, as well as globally. While it brought unprecedented challenges, it also spurred innovation and heightened awareness of the mental health needs of faculty and students. As educators and institutions navigate the current and future educational landscape, the lessons learned from this transformative pandemic period should serve as valuable guides to enhance teaching practices, ensuring a more adaptable, inclusive, and supportive educational experience for all stakeholders.

References

Australian Curriculum, Assessment and Reporting Authority (ACARA). (2022). Australian curriculum technologies F-10 version 9.0 about the learning area. https://v9.australiancurriculum.edu.au/content/dam/en/curriculum/ac-version-9/downloads/technologies/digital-technologies/technologies-about-the-learning-area-f-10-v9.docx

Australian Government Department of Health and Aged Care. (2023). What we're doing about COVID-19. https://www.health.gov.au/topics/covid-19/about/what-were-doing

Basseal, J. M., Bennett, C. M., Collignon, P., Currie, B. J., Durrheim, D. N., Leask, J., & Marais, B. J. (2023). Key lessons from the COVID-19 public health response in Australia. *The Lancet Regional Health–Western Pacific*, *30*, 1–8.

Bennett, C. M. (2023). Covid-19 in Australia: How did a country that fought so hard for extra time end up so ill prepared? *BMJ*, *380*, 469. https://doi.org/10.1136/bmj.p469

Bower, M., DeWitt, D., & Lai, J. W. M. (2020). Reasons associated with preservice teachers' intention to use immersive virtual reality in education. *British Journal of Educational Technology*, *51*, 2215–2233. https://doi.org/10.1111/bjet.13009

Brodeur, A., Gray, D., Islam, A., & Bhuiyan, S. (2021). A literature review of the economics of COVID-19. *Journal of Economic Surveys*, *35*(4), 1007–1044.

Darling-Hammond, L., Schachner, A., & Edgerton, A. (2020). Restarting and reinventing school: Learning in the time of COVID and beyond. Learning Policy Institute. http://learningpolicyinstitute.org/product/restarting-reinventing-school-covid.

Dodd, R. H., Dadaczynski, K., Okan, O., McCaffery, K. J., & Pickles, K. (2021). Psychological wellbeing and academic experience of university students in Australia during COVID-19. *International Journal of Environmental Research and Public Health*, *18*(3), 866. https://doi.org/10.3390/ijerph18030866

Fluck, A., Pullen, D., & Harper, C. (2009). Case study of a computer based examination system. *Australasian Journal of Educational Technology*, *25*(4), 509–523.

Fray, L., Jaremus, F., Gore, J., Miller, A., & Harris, J. (2023). Under pressure and overlooked: The impact of COVID-19 on teachers in NSW public schools. *The Australian Educational Researcher*, *50*(3), 701–727.

Gallo, L. A., Gallo, T. F., Young, S. L., Moritz, K. M., & Akison, L. K. (2020). The impact of isolation measures due to COVID-19 on energy intake and physical activity levels in Australian university students. *Nutrients*, *12*(6), 1865. https://doi.org/10.3390/nu12061865

Gillett-Swan, J. (2017). The challenges of online learning: Supporting and engaging the isolated learner. *Journal of Learning Design*, *10*(1), 20–30.

Greenhow, C., Lewin, C., & Staudt Willet, K. B. (2021). The educational response to Covid-19 across two countries: A critical examination of initial digital pedagogy adoption. *Technology, Pedagogy and Education*, *30*(1), 7–25.

Gustiani, S. (2020). Students' motivation in online learning during Covid-19 pandemic era: A case study. *Holistics (Hospitality and Linguistics): Journal Ilmiah Bahasa Inggris*, *12*(2), 23–40. https://jurnal.polsri.ac.id/index.php/holistic/article/view/3029

Horst, R., & Dorner, R. (2019). Opportunities for virtual and mixed reality knowledge demonstration. 2018 IEEE international symposium on mixed and augmented reality adjunct (ISMAR-adjunct).

Jarus, O. (2023). The worst epidemics and pandemics in history. https://www.livescience.com/worst-epidemics-and-pandemics-in-history.html

Kay, J., McRae, N., & Russell, L. (2020). Two institutional responses to work-integrated learning in a time of COVID-19: Canada and Australia. *International Journal of Work-Integrated Learning*, *21*(5), 491–503.

Kiesewetter, J., Hege, I., Sailer, M., Bauer, E., Schulz, C., Platz, M., & Adler, M. (2022). Implementing remote collaboration in a virtual patient platform: Usability study. *JMIR Medical Education*, *8*(3), e24306 https://mededu.jmir.org/2022/3/e24306

Limniou, M., Varga-Atkins, T., Hands, C., & Elshamaa, M. (2021). Learning, student digital capabilities and academic performance over the COVID-19 pandemic. *Education Sciences*, *11*(7), 361.

Littlecott, H., Herd, C., O'Rourke, J., Chaparro, L. T., Keeling, M., James Rubin, G., & Fearon, E. (2023). Effectiveness of testing, contact tracing and isolation interventions among the general population on reducing transmission of SARS-CoV-2: A systematic review. *Philosophical Transactions of the Royal Society A*, *381*(2257), 20230131.

MacDowell, P., & Lock, J. (2022). *Immersive education, designing for learning*. Springer. https://link.springer.com/book/10.1007/978-3-031-18138-2

Matthews, B., See, Z. S., & Day, J. (2020). Crisis and extended realities: Remote presence in the time of COVID-19. *Media International Australia*, *178*(1), 198–209. https://doi.org/10.1177/1329878X20967165

Noor, U., Younas, M., Saleh Aldayel, H., Menhas, R., & Qingyu, X. (2022). Learning behavior, digital platforms for learning and its impact on university student's motivations and knowledge development. *Frontiers in Psychology, 13*, 7246.

Paulauskaite, L., Farris, O., Spencer, H. M., EPICC-ID Group, & Hassiotis, A. (2021). My son can't socially distance or wear a mask: How families of preschool children with severe developmental delays and challenging behavior experienced the covid-19 pandemic. *Journal of Mental Health Research in Intellectual Disabilities, 14*(2), 225–236.

Pullen, D. (2013). Doctors online: Learning using an internet based content management system. *International Journal of Education and Development Using ICT, 9*(1), 50–63.

Pullen, D. (2015). An investigation of pre-service teachers' attitude and learning through a learning management system. *Australian Educational Computing, 30*(1), 1–20.

Sintema, E. J. (2020). Effect of COVID-19 on the performance of grade 12 students: Implications for STEM education. *EURASIA Journal of Mathematics, Science and Technology Education, 16*(7), em1851.

Times Higher Education. (2023). *Best universities in Australia 2024.* https://www.timeshighereducation.com/student/best-universities/best-universities-australia

Tjia, T., Marshman, I., Beard, J., & Baré, E. (2020). *Australian university workforce responses to COVID-19 pandemic: Reacting to a short-term crisis or planning for longer term challenges?* https://melbourne-cshe.unimelb.edu.au/__data/assets/pdf_file/0006/3501987/HE-Response-to-COVID-19-2020-09-25-Final-rev.pdf

University of Tasmania (UTAS). (2020). *Position statement: Next steps in the university's response to COVID-19.* https://www.utas.edu.au/__data/assets/pdf_file/0017/1312253/COVID-update-16-March.pdf

Wang, Y. (2023). The research on the impact of distance learning on students' mental health. *Education and Information Technologies (Dordr), 28*, 1–13. https://doi.org/10.1007/s10639-023-11693-w

World Health Organization (WHO). (2021). *Listings of WHO's response to COVID-19.* https://who.int/news/item/29-06-2020-covidtimeline

Chapter 3

Using Design Thinking to Redesign the Student Learning Experience: The Case of Higher Education

Farah Arkadan[a] and Niloofar Kazemargi[b]

[a]*American University of Dubai, UAE*
[b]*University of Pescara-Chieti, Italy*

Abstract

The health crisis in 2020 resulted in accelerated digitalization and technological innovation in higher education. However, digital technologies and innovation pose challenges and issues in pedagogy (Caputo et al., 2022). This chapter explains how to (re)design student learning experiences addressing pedagogical issues and challenges experienced by students using digital innovation. In response, we adopted design thinking allowing for a deeper understanding not just of students' needs but also their thoughts, feelings, and overall experience. Design thinking is a user-centred problem-solving method. It starts with empathizing with users, followed by identifying the real problems, generating ideas, prototyping, and testing solutions. The design thinking method allowed engagement with students in the innovation process as the main users. Primary data were collected using interviews with students over two main waves of data collection during the health crisis in 2020 and 2021 and the post-pandemic period in 2022–2023. In total, more than 300 students from seven different programmes were engaged. For data analysis, we used thematic analysis and reflection. In analysing, we adopted a sociotechnical perspective and the nature of experience. Our findings illustrate design principles that instructors need to keep in mind while (re)designing distance (online) education to enhance the student learning experience. We discuss the practical implications of the study and how the findings can help instructors and higher education managers in innovating higher education. As digital technologies and innovation are becoming critical for teaching and learning in higher education, the findings of this study can be generalized to the post-pandemic period.

Keywords: Design; user experience; higher education; design thinking; online learning

Introduction

The outbreak of the health crisis in 2020 has disrupted education and forced universities around the world to leverage digital innovation and technologies for a shift from a face-to-face environment to a virtual environment. 'Institutions and instructors previously resistant or indifferent to tools such as videoconferencing, team-based platforms, and virtual classrooms have come to rely on those tools as essential ingredients in their work' (EDUCAUSE Association, 2021, p. 8). As digital technologies and innovation brought a diverse set of new opportunities for pedagogical strategies, recent studies anticipated a shift to hybrid teaching and learning in higher education (Whiting, 2020). Many universities have revisited their strategies to offer hybrid/fully digital programmes (Healy et al., 2020) by becoming more student centric in addressing the post-COVID-19 pandemic social changes.

However, the adoption of digital technologies and innovation has introduced new pedagogical issues and challenges in customer experience. Customer experience entails multifaceted customer responses to various interactions with an organization, including sensorial, emotional, cognitive, physical, and social responses (Berry et al., 2002; Brakus et al., 2009; Gentile et al., 2007; Meyer & Schwager, 2007; Verhoef et al., 2009). Customer experience management means managing the customer's experience with a product or service, including the various interactions and touchpoints between the customer and a product/service (Lusch et al., 2008; Prahalad & Ramaswamy, 2000).

In this study, we focus on the student learning experience. This is because education is no longer limited to the boundaries of the classroom (Domae, 2017) as the advancement of digital technologies has created new opportunities and touchpoints for learning such as self-learning and peer-to-peer interactions (Cunningham & Walton, 2016).

Organizations increasingly focus on their customer experiences to build and sustain their competitive advantage (Berry et al., 2002; Brakus et al., 2009; Homburg et al., 2017; Lemon & Verhoef, 2016; Meyer & Schwager, 2007; Pine & Gilmore, 1998; Rawson et al., 2013; Verhoef et al., 2009); however, we know little about how design thinking can be used to enhance and innovate student learning experiences.

This study addresses the question of how to (re)design student learning experiences addressing pedagogical issues and challenges experienced by students using digital innovation. To answer this question, we adopted design thinking allowing for a deeper understanding not just of students' needs but also their thoughts, feelings, and overall experience.

Design thinking has been defined as a 'human-centred approach to innovation that puts the observation and discovery of often highly nuanced, even tacit, human needs right at the forefront of the innovation process' (Gruber et al., 2015). It has been proposed as a methodology that infuses innovation in all its forms – such as products, services, processes, or even strategy – with a focus on the human element (Brown, 2008). This approach enables a deeper understanding of not only customer requirements but also their emotions, insights, and overall journey. There is a growing adoption of design thinking in organizations across diverse fields as a means of creating compelling offerings (Elsbach & Stigliani, 2018) including higher education (Severino et al., 2021; Vaugh et al., 2020; Victorino et al., 2022). Various methods are employed such as interviews, ethnography, visual anthropology, workshops (Kummitha, 2018), customer journey mapping, empathic design, and personas (Andreassen et al., 2016) to gain an in-depth understanding of customer/user requirements. Design thinking adopts an agile and iterative approach to problem-solving (Prasad et al., 2018), guaranteeing the fulfilment of user expectations.

Our findings illustrate design principles that instructors need to keep in mind while (re)designing distance (online) education to enhance the student learning experience. We discuss the practical implications of the study and how the findings can help instructors and higher education managers in innovating higher education. As digital technologies and digital innovation are becoming critical for teaching and learning in higher education, the findings of this study can be generalized to the post-pandemic period.

Method

The outbreak of the health crisis in 2020 led to a shift to the virtual learning environment. However, the adoption of new digital technologies and innovation posed some challenges and issues especially related to student learning experiences. To tackle pedagogical issues and challenges experienced by students using digital innovation, we adopted an exploratory qualitative method to shed light on students' learning experiences and reflect on design principles. We defined a design thinking project named 'Redesign a digital program'. The project was incorporated as class activities in several courses (including Innovation Management, Digital Innovation and Organizational Design). The project was introduced to the students during the course. The goal of the project was to redesign a digital experience for students by collecting and analysing qualitative data during and after the health crisis. Primary data were collected using interviews with students over two main waves of data collection during the health crisis in 2020 and 2021 and the post-pandemic period in 2022 and 2023. In total, more than 300 first- and second-year graduate students were engaged. For the project, each project team was composed of 5–7 students. Project teams were provided with instructions and a timeframe indicating deliverables for each phase. Digital tools were used to collect and record all students' activities and deliverables.

Design thinking allowed for gaining a deeper understanding of user experience and engaging students as the main users in the innovation process. Design thinking is a user-centred problem-solving process, which entails five phases: (1) empathy, (2) define, (3) ideate, (4) prototype, and (5) test. Each phase of the design thinking process is outlined below.

In the *empathy phase*, the aim is to gain a deeper understanding of the real needs of users and obtain new insights. Interviews and observation are the most common methods to collect data. In this stage, two rounds of interviews were conducted. In the first round, two/three team members took the role of designers. They interviewed their peers to gain insights into real experiences and challenges of distance learning. In the second round, group members changed their respective roles. Interview instructions were provided to all students in order to enhance the quality of the collected data.

In the *define phase*, the aim is to define a problem that needs to be addressed in the design thinking process. The overarching problem statement to be addressed in this process was, 'How might we (re)design distance (online) education to enhance the learning experience?' Based on data analysis, different issues and challenges emerged. Each team (re)formulated the most important problem raised by users during the interviews. Some examples included 'How might we help students focus more during online classes?'; 'How might we boost interaction of students with the institution?'; 'How might we enhance students' involvement in online sessions?'; 'How might we support students to acquire useful skills for the job market?' They also identified for whom the core issues need to be addressed (persona). For instance, the persona varied from fresh students to final-year and exchange students. The teams were provided with transcribing and coding techniques to analyse the interviews.

In the *ideate phase*, the aim is to explore potential solutions. To ensure students' creativity and out-of-the-box thinking, the students were engaged in several creativity exercises. Then, the team members were engaged in brainstorming sessions to come up with a diverse set of ideas to address the identified problem. No judgement was allowed in the early phase. The students were encouraged to generate a large quantity of ideas. Then, the team members were provided an opportunity to exchange and discuss their thoughts and ideas with the aim of refining, combining, or developing ideas to form innovative solutions. Some examples of solutions included introducing community apps, new features and interfaces for online sessions, and collaboration tools and developing rules of games for online sessions (i.e., switching on webcam) and digital spaces for learning (i.e., metaverse based).

In the *prototype phase*, tangible representations of ideas are created. Prototypes are simple representations of the working models of the final product or service. They serve to communicate the idea and evaluate the solutions. Prototypes can significantly economize time and resources while ensuring that the solution is designed in a way that addresses the user's need. For this phase, the teams were provided with different types and techniques of prototyping (from sketches to Click-Through, video, and interactive models) and different digital tools (such as wireframing and prototyping tools). For the project, each team had one day to develop a prototype of their ideas.

In the *test phase*, the aim is to test and validate ideas at a very early stage with users. At this phase, users provide feedback about whether and how the proposed solution functions and meets their needs. Such feedback allows designers to make further refinements and adjustments to ensure that the final solution effectively meets user needs. The students were encouraged to present their prototypes to the whole class to collect feedback. All feedback was recorded and used to refine the solution in an iterative approach to ensure that the solution truly meets user needs.

Design Principles for Digital Higher Education

From 2020 to 2023, the design thinking approach was used to identify students' challenges and issues in digital education and introduce innovative solutions for tackling such challenges.

Design thinking was an effective tool for gaining in-depth insights into real students' experiences in the digital environment. The design thinking project was based on collaborative efforts of educators and students in higher education, aimed at enhancing the student learning experience. In the subsequent sections, we elaborate on design principles for enhancing student learning experiences that were identified.

Principle 1 – Co-create Learning Experience

The ultimate users of digital higher education are students. Students' viewpoints and experiences are valuable sources for higher education innovation. Their ideas and feedback can be incorporated into designing digital higher education (Abusidualghoul, 2022; Bovill et al., 2011). Conducting interviews and direct observation provides an in-depth understanding of the preferences and needs of a diverse set of students (e.g., different backgrounds, origins, and family status). In this way, we can ensure the alignment between the designed programme and the needs and expectations of students. Students must be engaged in the early phase of design.

Principle 2 – Keep It Flexible

Our findings show the importance of flexibility in the designed digital spaces and systems. Flexibility is needed to ensure that different and emerging needs can be accommodated without a huge investment. This requires an adaptable technology infrastructure and using modular digital solutions to mix and match different solutions and facilitate 'plug and play' to create a wide range of solutions.

Principle 3 – Focus on Team Activities

What has emerged from our findings was that often 'team activities and contacts between team members are taken for granted' (student). The dynamics of interactions in a digital environment are different from in-person experience. Students often expressed a lack of trust and accountability among team members. As team interactions occur online, not all team members contribute equally to teamwork leading to a higher workload for some members, which consequently influences the quality of teamwork. Some students also mentioned different time zones and cultures influence synchronous collaboration and communication. The digital programmes need to not only provide space and structure for teams to interact but also develop team-building skills. This includes supporting team members to get to know each other, feel comfortable, coordinate tasks, and solve conflicts.

Principle 4 – Activate Feedback Loops

Feedback loops involve iterative feedback collection and information exchange between students and instructors with the aim of enhancing the learning experience. This enables instructors to continuously monitor and assess the effectiveness of teaching and learning. Establishing a fast feedback loop allows students to communicate issues and problems in a timely manner, thus allowing improvement and adjustment of lessons and activities to students' emerging needs. Designing an effective feedback loop in digital courses is crucial as perceptions and observations of instructors are limited. To ensure the effectiveness of teaching and learning several feedback points are needed. They can be designed in both synchronous and asynchronous parts. Our findings show that anonymous feedback, one-to-one checkpoints, and surveys are perceived by students to be effective. Instructors need to ensure they design feedback loops to collect both quantitative (e.g., rating) and qualitative (e.g., suggestions) feedback as they are complementary.

Principle 5 – Motivate Participation

In interviews with students, it became clear that there was great concern about the decreased span of attention in online classes. In general, monolog online lectures were boring for students, and they mentioned that after a while it became difficult to remain focused and concentrated. Some students underlined different sources of distraction (e.g., smartphones, TV, and family members). To address the loss of focus, instructors need to design interactive sessions by adopting gamification, competitions, and collaboration activities. Such activities by nature create incentives for students to participate and interact.

Principle 6 – Consider Students' Well-being

In interviews, students stressed that they experienced physical and mental fatigue in online courses. Following long hours of lessons mediated by computers augments physical and mental issues such as eye strain, bad posturing, and anxiety. Students also stressed that online courses demand more self-organizing and time management skills. The designed spaces and systems need to foster well-being and mental health. Embedding practices and enhancing self-awareness can develop skills and the ability to manage time better, balance study and life, and address physical and mental fatigue. Solutions proposed by the participants for enhancing well-being include sending notifications to students in a certain interval of time, integrating short sessions of yoga or meditation, time management skills, and so on.

Principle 7 – Consider the Whole Students' Experience

Touchpoints refer to the interactions between an individual and a firm which serve in gaining information, selection, and usage of products/services (Homburg et al., 2017; Lemon & Verhoef, 2016). Although digital touchpoints' distinctive nature offers many opportunities to interact and engage with students, students of online courses felt they had fewer touchpoints compared to in-presence courses with the university. Especially during the fully digital courses, students stated that 'experiencing university with some limitations and feeling of having missed opportunities' (student). Thus, both higher education institutions and instructors need to consider the overall interaction that students have with a university and its services throughout their entire journey. In digital courses, instructors and higher education institutions need to add new touchpoints to ensure that students effectively and efficiently interact with a diverse set of offers and services. This includes new touchpoints for career services and mentorship programmes and offered seminars and events. Considering the whole experience is crucial as it leads to the higher satisfaction of students.

In higher education, besides academic knowledge, students need to develop job-related skills and knowledge. Such skills include but are not limited to problem-solving, critical thinking, cultural competence, diversity skills, emotional intelligence, negotiation, and public speaking. In particular, during the health emergency, many students stressed difficulties in developing employability skills while completing internships online as they were not able to interact with employees and managers to develop their skills and knowledge. To foster the development of complementary skills, new services and features need to be integrated into traditional university offers and services. The solutions put forth by students vary from co-projects with companies to a platform to facilitate interactions between students and potential future employers and a platform offering training courses for complementary skills.

Principle 8 – Focus on Complementary Skills

In higher education, besides academic knowledge, students need to develop job-related skills and knowledge. Such skills include but are not limited to problem-solving, critical thinking, cultural competence and diversity skills, emotional intelligence, negotiation, and public speaking. In particular, during the health emergency, many students stressed difficulties in developing employability skills: completing internships online, students were not able to interact with employees and managers to develop their skills and knowledge. To foster the development of complementary skills, new services and features need to be integrated into traditional university offers and services. The solutions put forth by students vary from co-projects with companies to a platform to facilitate interactions between students and potential future employers and a platform offering training courses for complementary skills.

Principle 9 – Keep Students' Community Alive

Lack of social bonding and feelings of isolation became evident from the interviews. Similarly, students expressed that all their interactions with peers were limited during synchronous sessions. Thus, the design of digital courses needs to extend interactions from synchronous classes to peer-to-peer interactions. Creating new platforms for students to interact with each other and providing guidelines related to the norms and 'netiquette' of online interactions, as what is appropriate behaviour in face-to-face interactions might change in online interactions. Higher education institutions and instructors need to incorporate different technological features to foster peer-to-peer interactions and a sense of belonging to the community. One solution proposed by students was peer-to-peer platforms where students can know and interact with each other and blogs to share experiences and stories. Other examples of solutions include group discussion, language exchange, and virtual coffee breaks.

Conclusion

Like all sectors, the COVID-19 pandemic has caused radical changes in the pedagogy approach. However, shifting to digital environments was not without problems. Designing effective student learning students requires a deep understanding of pedagogical issues and challenges experienced by students in digital environments.

Design thinking as a user-centred problem-solving method can be an appropriate tool to develop and evaluate solutions in a timely manner. It can help educators and instructors transform challenges into an opportunity for enhancing student learning experience. By using design thinking as an exploratory qualitative method and participatory process, we shed light on design principles that instructors need to keep in mind while (re)designing digital education to enhance the student learning experience.

Design thinking allowed us to gain a better understanding of students' challenges and issues in digital environments and test and reflect on design principles for digital learning environments. Our findings show that the adoption of new technologies and adding new functionalities are not enough. Rather, higher education needs to carefully adapt and adjust digital technologies that meet students' needs such as human interactions.

It is worth pointing out that enhancing and innovating the student learning experience requires an iterative approach and continuous improvement which pushes for higher flexibility and innovation in the pedagogy system. Moreover, we believe that the fast pace of digital transformation accelerated during the COVID-19 pandemic will continue; thus, the findings of this study can be generalized to designing digital environments in the post-pandemic period.

References

Abusidualghoul, V. (2022). Students' perspectives on teaching practices: A focus on feedback for a highly diverse cohort. In A. Caputo, D. Lock, & D. Hack-Polay (Eds.), *International environments and practices of higher education* (pp. 21–29). Emerald Publishing Limited.

Andreassen, T. W., Kristensson, P., Lervik-Olsen, L., Parasuraman, A., McColl-Kennedy, J. R., Edvardsson, B., & Colurcio, M. (2016). Linking service design to value creation and service research. *Journal of Service Management, 27*(1), 21–29.

Berry, L. L., Carbone, L. P., & Haeckel, S. H. (2002). Managing the total customer experience. *MIT Sloan Management Review, 43*(3), 85–89.

Bovill, C., Cook-Sather, A., & Felten, P. (2011). Students as co-creators of teaching approaches, course design, and curricula: Implications for academic developers. *International Journal for Academic Development, 16*(2), 133–145.

Brakus, J. J., Schmitt, B. H., & Zarantonello, L. (2009). Brand experience: What is it? How is it measured? Does it affect loyalty? *Journal of Marketing, 73*(3), 52–68.

Brown, T. (2008). Design thinking. *Harvard Business Review, 86*(6), 84.

Caputo, A., Lock, D., & Hack-Polay, D. (Eds.). (2022). *International environments and practices of higher education*. Emerald Publishing Limited.

Cunningham, M., & Walton, G. (2016). Informal learning spaces (ILS) in university libraries and their campuses: A Loughborough University case study. *New Library World, 117*(1/2), 49–62.

Domae, L. (2017). *Planning the campus with place in mind: A phenomenological exploration of the lifeworlds of community college campuses in British Columbia*. Doctoral dissertation.

EDUCAUSE Association. (2021). *2021 EDUCAUSE horizon report*. https://library.educause.edu/-/media/files/library/2021/4/2021hrteachinglearning.pdf?la=en&hash=C9DEC12398593F297CC634409DFF4B8C5A60B36E

Elsbach, K. D., & Stigliani, I. (2018). Design thinking and organizational culture: A review and framework for future research. *Journal of Management, 44*(6), 2274–2306.

Gentile, C., Spiller, N., & Noci, G. (2007). How to sustain the customer experience: An overview of experience components that co-create value with the customer. *European Management Journal, 25*(5), 395–410.

Gruber, M., De Leon, N., George, G., & Thompson, P. (2015). Managing by design. *Academy of Management Journal, 58*(1), 1–7.

Healy, E., Kinsella, D., & Cremin, M. R. (2020, September 30). *Understanding the impact of covid-19 on higher education institutions*. Deloitte.

Homburg, C., Jozić, D., & Kuehnl, C. (2017). Customer experience management: Toward implementing an evolving marketing concept. *Journal of the Academy of Marketing Science, 45*, 377–401.

Kummitha, R. K. R. (2018). Institutionalising design thinking in social entrepreneurship: A contextual analysis into social and organizational processes. *Social Enterprise Journal, 14*(1), 92–107.

Lemon, K. N., & Verhoef, P. C. (2016). Understanding customer experience throughout the customer journey. *Journal of Marketing, 80*(6), 69–96.

Lusch, R. F., Vargo, S. L., & Wessels, G. (2008). Toward a conceptual foundation for service science: Contributions from service-dominant logic. *IBM Systems Journal, 47*(1), 5–14.

Meyer, C., & Schwager, A. (2007). Understanding customer experience. *Harvard Business Review, 85*(2), 116.

Pine, B. J., & Gilmore, J. H. (1998). *Welcome to the experience economy* (Vol. 76, No. 4, pp. 97–105). Harvard Business Review Press.

Prahalad, C. K., & Ramaswamy, V. (2000). Co-opting customer competence. *Harvard business review, 78*(1), 79–90.

Prasad, W. R., Perera, G. I. U. S., Padmini, K. J., & Bandara, H. D. (2018, May). Adopting design thinking practices to satisfy customer expectations in agile practices: A case from Sri Lankan software development industry. *2018 Moratuwa engineering research conference (MERCon)* (pp. 471–476). IEEE.

Rawson, A., Duncan, E., & Jones, C. (2013). The truth about customer experience. *Harvard Business Review, 91*(9), 90–98.

Severino, L., Petrovich, M., Mercanti-Anthony, S., & Fischer, S. (2021). Using a design thinking approach for an asynchronous learning platform during COVID-19. *IAFOR Journal of Education*, *9*(2), 145–162.

Vaugh, T., Finnegan-Kessie, T., Donnellan, P., & Oswald, T. (2020). The potential of design thinking to enable change in higher education. *All Ireland Journal of Higher Education*, *12*(3), 1–21.

Verhoef, P. C., Lemon, K. N., Parasuraman, A., Roggeveen, A., Tsiros, M., & Schlesinger, L. A. (2009). Customer experience creation: Determinants, dynamics, and management strategies. *Journal of Retailing*, *85*(1), 31–41.

Victorino, G., Bandeira, R., Painho, M., Henriques, R., & Coelho, P. S. (2022). Rethinking the campus experience in a post-COVID world: A multi-stakeholder design thinking experiment. *Sustainability*, *14*(13), 7655.

Whiting, K. (2020). *Is this what higher education will look like in 5 years*. World Economic Forum.

Chapter 4

Educational Innovation and Digitalization During Crises

Jai Raj Nair

Welingkar Institute of Management Development and Research, Bangalore, Karnataka, India

Abstract

The recent COVID-19 pandemic underscores the need for educational innovation and digitalization during crises where many educational institutions were forced to shift to online and remote learning. This chapter is a discursive review of problems and solutions and key trends that have emerged because of crises. One of the key benefits of educational innovation and digitalization during crises is the ability to continue providing education and learning opportunities to students even when traditional face-to-face learning is not possible. Educational institutions need to invest in building resilient online learning ecosystems to ensure that education can continue uninterrupted even in the face of unforeseen disruptions. This ecosystem should include robust technological infrastructure, a diverse range of digital resources and tools, and training and support for educators. Ultimately, a resilient online learning ecosystem is not just a response to crises but a proactive investment in the future of education.

Keywords: Educational innovation, digitalization, online learning ecosystem, distance learning; educational crises

Introduction to Educational Crises and Digitalization

Defining Educational Crises

An educational crisis is one where an education system is unable to meet the needs of all students due to lack of resources, inequity, and conflict. Educational crises have a devastating impact on students' lives, leading to low learning outcomes, high dropout rates, and limited opportunities.

Recent examples of educational crises include:

- COVID-19 pandemic
- Syrian refugee crisis
- Hurricane Katrina
- Earthquake in Haiti
- War in Afghanistan
- Rohingya refugee crisis in Myanmar

Understanding the Need for Digitalization During Crises

Crises can disrupt education on a massive scale. In such situations, digitalization can play a vital role in ensuring the continuity of educational systems.

a. *Continuity*: Digital platforms help maintain educational activities.
b. *Flexibility and adaptability*: Digital tools and platforms provide the flexibility to adjust and adapt instructional methods.
c. *Reach and accessibility*: Digitalization removes geographical boundaries and promotes accessibility.
d. *Innovation and pedagogical advancement*: Crises necessitate creative solutions, and educators adopt new and effective ways to engage students through technology.

In a nutshell, digitalization in education during crises is important because it:

a. Keeps education going when schools are closed.
b. Allows educators to adjust teaching methods to meet the changing needs of students.
c. Makes education more accessible to students in underserved areas.
d. Promotes innovation in teaching and learning.
e. Helps educators identify and support struggling students.

Technology's Transformative Role in Education

Technology has revolutionized the field of education. It goes beyond integrating gadgets into classrooms; it fundamentally changes the dynamics of education. Some of the far-reaching implications of technology's pivotal role in education include:

a. *Enhancing access and equity*: Technology democratizes access to learning.
b. *Personalized learning*: Technology empowers educators to tailor instruction to individual student needs.

c. *Enriching content*: Digital technology enriches educational content by offering multimedia resources, interactive simulations, and virtual labs.
d. *Collaboration and communication*: Technology facilitates seamless collaboration.
e. *Digital literacy*: Students learn how to navigate information, critically evaluate online sources, and responsibly use digital tools.
f. *Innovation in teaching*: Educators can experiment with innovative teaching methods to create engaging and immersive learning experiences.
g. *Global perspective*: Technology exposes students to global perspectives, connecting them with learners and resources from around the world.

Technology's role in education is transformative and multifaceted. It breaks down barriers, enhances learning experiences, fosters innovation, and equips students with skills necessary for success in the digital age.

Impact of Educational Crises on Learning

Natural Disasters and Their Impact on Education

Natural disasters have a significant impact on education systems. A summary of the various ways in which these disasters affect learning are given below:
Impacts on learning:

a. *Disruption of schools*: Natural disasters often result in the physical destruction of school infrastructure leading to gaps in students' education.
b. *Emotional trauma*: Experiencing a natural disaster can traumatize students. The fear, stress, and loss can lead to psychological distress, making it challenging for students to focus on their studies.
c. *Interrupted academic calendar*: Schools may need to close temporarily or operate on reduced schedules during and after natural disasters.
d. *Health concerns*: Natural disasters can lead to health hazards which can affect students' learning.
e. *Resource allocation*: In the wake of a natural disaster, resources may need to be redirected towards immediate relief and recovery efforts.
f. *Long-term impact*: The effects of natural disasters can extend beyond the immediate aftermath. Students who experience significant disruptions in their education may struggle to catch up.

Economic Crises and Educational Challenges

Economic crises have a profound impact on education systems. A summary of the intricate relationship between economic downturns and the educational challenges is given below:

a. *Budget cuts*: Governments cut education budgets during economic crises to save money.
b. *Exacerbated educational inequality*: Economic crises tend to worsen educational inequality.
c. *Reduction in education quality*: Strained budgets can lead to a reduction in the quality of educational programmes, such as cuts to extracurricular activities.

Economic crises can significantly impact education, affecting funding, accessibility, and the overall quality of learning experiences. Proactive measures to safeguard education during economic downturns are crucial for ensuring that students have equitable access to quality learning opportunities and that their long-term prospects are not unduly hampered by economic challenges.

Digital Tools and Technologies for Education

Digitalization and Its Significance on the Education Space

Digitalization is the integration of digital technologies into various aspects of life. The significance of digitalization in reshaping education is explained in the following points:

a. *Access to education*: Digitalization has democratized access by removing geographical barriers.
b. *Personalized learning*: Digital tools enable personalized learning experiences by tailoring content.
c. *Flexibility and convenience*: Education has become more flexible and convenient with digitalization.
d. *Diverse learning resources*: Digitalization offers an abundance of learning resources, including interactive simulations, virtual laboratories, and open educational resources (OERs).
e. *Global collaboration*: Digital tools facilitate global collaboration and cultural exchange.
f. *Enhanced engagement*: Gamification and interactive elements in digital education enhances student engagement.
g. *Innovation and future readiness*: Adopting digitalization prepares students for the future by equipping them with digital literacy skills.
h. *Lockdown resilience*: The COVID-19 pandemic highlighted the importance of digitalization in education, underscoring the value of digital tools in crisis response.

Virtual Classrooms and Online Learning Platforms

Virtual classrooms and online learning platforms have emerged as transformative tools in education, revolutionizing the way students access knowledge and interact with educators, in terms of:

a. *Flexibility in learning*: Online platforms offer unprecedented flexibility, allowing students to customize their learning experiences.
b. *Global reach*: Virtual classrooms transcend geographical boundaries.
c. *Cost efficiency*: Online education is cheaper than traditional ones.
d. *Professional development*: Online platforms offer opportunities for educators to upskill themselves.

Virtual classrooms and online learning platforms have redefined the landscape of education, offering accessibility, flexibility, and engagement that were once unimaginable. While they bring immense benefits, challenges such as the digital divide and maintaining student motivation must be addressed.

Learning Management Systems (LMS)

LMSs have emerged as invaluable tools for educators, institutions, and learners alike. LMS platforms, such as Moodle, Canvas, and Blackboard, have significantly reshaped the landscape of education, providing a comprehensive solution to navigate the complexities posed by educational crises and the digital revolution.

LMS platforms have played a pivotal role in facilitating the seamless transition from traditional classroom settings to remote and hybrid learning models during crises. These systems offer a centralized hub for course materials, communication, assignments, and assessments.

Digitalization, on the other hand, has transformed the way we access, consume, and share information. LMS platforms align with this trend by providing a user-friendly, online interface that caters to the needs of both educators and learners. LMSs have become indispensable in the face of educational crises and the ongoing digitalization of education. They offer a robust and adaptable framework to ensure continuity, accessibility, and engagement in learning.

Open Educational Resources (OER)

OERs have emerged as a transformative force in education. These freely accessible and openly licensed learning materials have played a pivotal role in reshaping the educational landscape, making quality education more accessible and adaptable to the changing needs of learners.

OERs serve as a powerful tool for ensuring continuity, equity, and innovation in learning. OERs also promote equity in education by providing all students with access to high-quality learning materials. As the world continues to grapple with evolving educational challenges, OERs remain a vital force for positive change, poised to shape the future of learning and ensure educational opportunities for all.

EdTech Tools and Innovations

The integration of EdTech tools has become paramount in addressing the evolving landscape of education. These tools encompass a wide range of applications ranging from virtual classrooms to artificial intelligence (AI)-driven personalized learning, and they also facilitate synchronous and asynchronous learning.

a. *Personalized learning*: AI-powered EdTech solutions support personalized learning.
b. *Interactive content and gamification*: EdTech tools provide interactive and gamified learning experiences. Gamification elements, such as badges, leader boards, and simulations, make learning enjoyable while promoting active participation.
c. *Augmented reality (AR) and virtual reality (VR)*: AR and VR technologies bring immersive experiences to education.

d. *Global collaboration and remote learning*: Digital tools facilitate global collaboration.
e. *Teacher professional development*: EdTech tools support educators' professional development.

EdTech tools and innovations have revolutionized education by providing solutions to navigate educational crises. As technology continues to advance, these tools will remain at the forefront of educational transformation. The integration of EdTech is a catalyst for the ongoing evolution of education, promoting accessibility, equity, and innovation in learning.

Models of Educational Innovation

❖ *Blended Learning and Hybrid Education*

Blended learning and hybrid education have emerged as flexible instructional models that hold significant promise in addressing educational crises. By combining the strengths of in-person and online learning, these models provide a dynamic approach to education.

Flipped Classrooms and Asynchronous Learning

Amidst educational crises and the rapid digitalization of education, flipped classrooms and asynchronous learning have emerged as innovative pedagogical approaches.

Flipped classrooms: In traditional classroom settings, content delivery occurs during in-person lectures. Flipped classrooms invert this model by providing students with advance materials to study independently before class. In-class time is then devoted to interactive discussions, problem-solving, and collaborative activities.

Asynchronous learning: Asynchronous learning removes the constraints of real-time learning by allowing students to engage with course materials and assignments on their own schedules.

Successful implementation of flipped classrooms and asynchronous learning requires robust digital infrastructure, access to technology, and effective communication between educators and students.

Gamification and Game-based Learning

Gamification and game-based learning are innovative approaches in the education sector. These methods leverage the principles of game design and interactive gameplay to enhance engagement, motivation, and learning outcomes, making them valuable tools for addressing the evolving needs of education.

Gamification involves incorporating game elements and mechanics into non-game context to motivate and engage learners. This can include point systems, badges, leaderboards, and challenges designed to make learning more enjoyable and interactive. The benefits include:

a. *Engagement and motivation*: Gamification techniques tap into intrinsic human motivations, such as competition and achievement, to keep students engaged.
b. *Progress tracking*: Gamification elements allow students to track their progress and compete with themselves or peers.
c. *Problem-solving skills*: Games often require critical thinking, problem-solving, and decision-making skills that help in developing valuable cognitive skills.
d. *Game-based learning*: This involves using actual games as part of the curriculum.
e. *Immersive learning*: Digital game-based learning immerses students in virtual worlds, historical settings, or interactive simulations.
f. *Collaboration and social learning*: Many educational games encourage collaboration and social interaction.

Successful integration of gamification and game-based learning requires careful planning, alignment with learning objectives, and appropriate use of technology. As technology continues to evolve, these innovative approaches will continue to play a pivotal role in shaping the future of education, providing effective alternatives to traditional instructional methods.

Personalized Learning and Adaptive Technologies

The rapid advancement of technology has significantly transformed the integration of personalized learning and adaptive technologies. This leverages technology to tailor educational content and experiences to each learner. Adaptive technologies employ algorithms and artificial intelligence to analyse student performance and adapt learning materials in real time.

Personalized learning and adaptive technologies are pivotal elements of educational innovation and digitalization during crises. By tailoring education to individual needs, maintaining engagement, and addressing disparities in access, these approaches ensure that learning continues perpetually.

Teacher Professional Development in Digital Pedagogy

In the face of global crises, teacher professional development in digital pedagogy has emerged as a critical component of ensuring quality education continuity. The effective integration of digital tools and methodologies into teaching practices has become essential for educators to meet the challenges presented by these crises.

Digital pedagogy refers to teaching and learning in digital environments. It encompasses the use of various technologies, online resources, and innovative teaching methods to engage students effectively in the absence of traditional classrooms.

Teacher professional development in digital pedagogy is a linchpin in educational innovation and digitalization during crises. It empowers educators to adopt technology for effective teaching, ensuring that students continue to receive quality education perpetually.

Pedagogical Strategies for Crisis-Resilient Education

Adapting Curriculum and Content Delivery

Crisis-resilient education demands flexible and adaptable pedagogical strategies. Adapting curriculum and content delivery is a key pillar of such strategies, ensuring that education remains accessible and effective even in the most challenging circumstances.

Content delivery focuses on how the curriculum is delivered to students. Crisis-resilient pedagogical strategies emphasize the use of digital technologies and online resources to ensure learning can continue outside of traditional classrooms.

Content delivery should incorporate strategies that promote active engagement and interaction among students, even in virtual settings. This can involve virtual group projects, discussion forums, and real-time Q&A sessions to mimic the collaborative and participatory aspects of traditional classroom learning.

Building a Resilient Online Learning Ecosystem

In the digital age, a resilient online learning ecosystem is essential for pedagogical strategies that promote crisis-resilient education. This ecosystem encompasses the infrastructure, resources, and practices necessary to ensure that learning can continue seamlessly at all times. At the core of a resilient online learning ecosystem is robust technological infrastructure. This includes a reliable LMS, high-speed internet access, and adequate hardware for both educators and students. In times of crisis, this infrastructure provides the foundation for educational continuity, enabling seamless communication, content delivery, and assessment.

Building a resilient online learning ecosystem is a critical component of pedagogical strategies for crisis-resilient education. It fosters adaptability, connectivity, and accessibility, ensuring that education remains uninterrupted in the face of unforeseen challenges. By investing in technology, resources, and educator training, educational institutions can build a solid foundation for resilient and sustainable learning ecosystems.

Illustrations of Educational Innovation

Success Stories of Educational Innovations during Crises

Amidst the challenges and disruptions brought about by crises such as the COVID-19 pandemic, several educational institutions have showcased remarkable resilience and adaptability through innovative approaches to digital education. These success stories highlight the transformative potential of technology and pedagogical innovation during times of adversity:

a. *Harvard University's online transition*: When the pandemic forced the closure of campuses worldwide, Harvard University swiftly transitioned to online learning. They not only leveraged established online platforms but also collaborated with EdTech companies to enhance the virtual classroom experience.

b. *Khan Academy's free resources*: Khan Academy, a non-profit organization, provided free access to their extensive library of educational resources during the pandemic. Their commitment to equity and accessibility made high-quality education available to students worldwide, particularly those facing financial barriers.
c. *Singapore's Smart Nation initiative*: Singapore's government accelerated its Smart Nation initiative during the pandemic, investing heavily in digital infrastructure and resources for education. This comprehensive approach enabled seamless online learning and teacher training, ensuring minimal disruptions to the education system.
d. *California Community Colleges' online transition*: The California Community Colleges system, one of the largest in the world, rapidly transitioned to online instruction during the pandemic. They focused on faculty development and support, fostering a community of educators sharing best practices in digital teaching.
e. *Virtual science labs at Arizona State University*: Arizona State University pioneered virtual science labs, allowing students to conduct experiments remotely. This innovation ensured that science education remained hands-on and engaging, even in a virtual environment.
f. *Rwanda's One Laptop per Child programme*: In Rwanda, the One Laptop per Child programme distributed laptops and tablets to primary school students. This initiative aimed to bridge the digital divide, ensuring that all students had access to online resources for remote learning.
g. *UNICEF's Learning Passport*: UNICEF launched the Learning Passport, a digital platform offering free access to quality education resources. This initiative aimed to reach vulnerable and displaced children during crises, providing them with the opportunity to continue learning.

These success stories illustrate that educational institutions can not only weather crises but also thrive by embracing educational innovation and digitalization. They demonstrate the power of adaptability, collaboration, and a commitment to ensuring that learning remains accessible and effective, even in the most challenging circumstances. These institutions serve as inspirations and models for others looking to build crisis-resilient education systems in an increasingly digital world.

Indian Success Stories of Educational Innovations during Crises

India, like many countries, faced significant disruptions to its education system during the COVID-19 pandemic. However, several educational institutions in India showcased impressive resilience and adaptability by embracing educational innovation and digitalization. These success stories are emblematic of the nation's commitment to ensuring continued learning, even in the face of unprecedented challenges:

a. *Amrita Vishwa Vidyapeetham's virtual labs*: Amrita Vishwa Vidyapeetham, a prominent Indian university, pioneered the development of virtual labs in

various scientific disciplines. These labs allowed students to conduct experiments remotely, ensuring that hands-on learning remained a cornerstone of science education.
b. *National Digital Library (NDL) of India*: The NDL of India, initiated by the Ministry of Human Resource Development, offers a vast repository of digital educational resources. During the pandemic, it proved invaluable in providing students and educators with access to a wide range of digital content, including textbooks, videos, and research materials.
c. *Indian Institutes of Technology (IITs) and online classes*: India's prestigious IITs quickly adapted to online learning. They offered online courses and lectures, making high-quality education accessible to a broader audience, including students from underserved regions.
d. *Schools embracing EdTech*: Numerous schools across India embraced EdTech during the pandemic. Many adopted online LMSs and video conferencing tools to facilitate remote classes and ensure that students' academic progress continued.
e. *Government initiatives*: The Indian government launched several digital education initiatives, such as the 'SWAYAM' platform, which offers online courses across a variety of subjects. These initiatives aimed to bridge the digital divide and provide education to all, regardless of geographical location.
f. *Teacher training programmes*: Recognizing the need to equip educators with digital teaching skills, various organizations and institutions in India initiated teacher training programmes. These programmes empowered teachers to adapt their pedagogical approaches to online instruction effectively.
g. *Private EdTech companies*: Indian EdTech startups and companies played a crucial role in offering e-learning solutions. Platforms like Byju's and Vedantu saw a surge in users during the pandemic, providing students with interactive and engaging online learning experiences.

These Indian success stories highlight the nation's resilience in the face of crises through educational innovation and digitalization. They underscore the importance of leveraging technology to ensure the continuity of education, reach underserved populations, and equip educators with the tools needed for effective digital instruction. These efforts not only helped India navigate the challenges posed by the pandemic but also hold the potential to transform the future of education in the country.

Lessons From Real-World Experiences

Real-world experiences in educational innovation during crises have yielded valuable lessons that can inform future strategies for educational continuity. Some of the key lessons include:

a. *Flexibility is key*: The ability to adapt quickly to changing circumstances is paramount. Educational institutions that had flexible curricula, adaptable teaching methods, and contingency plans in place were better equipped to respond to crises.

b. *Digital literacy is non-negotiable*: Both educators and students require digital literacy skills to navigate online learning effectively. Training programmes for teachers and initiatives to enhance students' digital literacy proved essential in making digital education successful.
c. *Engagement requires creativity*: Engaging students in virtual environments requires innovative approaches. Lessons learned include the importance of interactive content, gamification, peer collaboration, and teacher–student interaction to maintain student engagement.
d. *Assessment redefined*: Rethinking assessment methods is essential.
e. *Hybrid learning is the future*: Many institutions discovered that hybrid learning offers flexibility and resilience. This approach allows for a seamless transition between physical and virtual classrooms in times of crises.
f. *Adaptability is a skill*: Crises underscored the importance of adaptability in both educators and students. The ability to embrace new technologies and teaching methods, as well as navigate uncertain circumstances, is a crucial skill as we go forward.
g. *Collaboration is key*: Collaborative efforts among educational institutions, EdTech companies, governments, and communities have been pivotal. Sharing best practices, resources, and expertise fosters collective resilience in the face of crises.

These lessons from real-world experiences in educational innovation during crises provide a roadmap for building resilient and adaptable education systems. By prioritizing equity, digital literacy, engagement, security, and adaptability, educational institutions can prepare for unforeseen challenges and provide quality education regardless of the circumstances.

Evaluating the Impact of Digitalization

Assessment and Measurement of Student Learning Outcomes

In the era of digitalization in education, assessing and measuring student learning outcomes has undergone a transformative shift. Traditional assessment methods have been supplemented and, in some cases, replaced by innovative digital tools and techniques. This evolution not only allows for more accurate and comprehensive evaluation but also offers insights into the impact of digitalization on educational outcomes. Some of the key features are:

a. *Formative vs summative assessment*: Digitalization has enabled a more balanced approach to assessment. Formative assessments, which occur throughout the learning process, provide real-time feedback to both students and educators, facilitating adjustments to teaching strategies. Summative assessments, which evaluate overall learning outcomes, have also benefited from digital tools that enhance their reliability and validity.
b. *Adaptive assessments*: Adaptive assessments use algorithms to adjust the difficulty of questions based on a student's previous responses. This approach provides a personalized assessment experience, ensuring that students are appropriately challenged and accurately evaluated.

c. *Online portfolios and projects*: Digitalization has facilitated the creation of digital portfolios and project-based assessments.
d. *Game-based assessment*: Gamification elements, such as quizzes with game-like features, offer an engaging way to assess student understanding.
e. *Global benchmarking*: Digital assessments can be used for global benchmarking, allowing educators and policymakers to compare student performance across regions and nations.
f. *Feedback and continuous improvement*: Digital assessment tools enable more timely and detailed feedback for students.

The assessment and measurement of student learning outcomes have been significantly enhanced by digitalization in education. These advancements offer educators a deeper understanding of student progress, provide personalized learning experiences, and enable continuous improvement in teaching and curriculum design.

Monitoring and Improving the Quality of Digital Education

As digitalization continues to reshape education, it becomes essential to prioritize the monitoring and improvement of the quality of digital education. Ensuring that the integration of technology enhances learning outcomes and educational experiences requires ongoing evaluation and strategic adjustments. Some key considerations for evaluating the impact of digitalization and improving its quality include:

a. *Define clear learning objectives*: Start by establishing clear learning objectives and outcomes that align with the institution's educational mission. These objectives should guide the selection of digital tools and content:
b. *Regular assessment and evaluation*: Implement a system for regular assessment and evaluation of digital education practices. Collect data on student performance, engagement, and satisfaction and use it to identify areas for improvement.
c. *Learning analytics*: Leverage learning analytics to gain insights into student behaviour and performance.
d. *Feedback loops*: Establish feedback loops with students, educators, and other stakeholders and use this feedback to make data-driven improvements.
e. *Content quality assurance*: Evaluate the quality and relevance of digital content regularly. Ensure that materials align with curriculum objectives, are up to date and meet accessibility standards.
f. *Pedagogical innovation*: Encourage pedagogical innovation by fostering a culture of experimentation and exploration.
g. *Global benchmarking*: Participate in global benchmarking efforts to assess how digital education practices compare to those in other regions or countries.
h. *Research and evaluation*: Invest in research and evaluation studies to assess the long-term impact of digitalization on education.

By actively monitoring and improving the quality of digital education, institutions can harness the transformative potential of technology while ensuring that students receive a high-quality learning experience.

Long-term Effects and Sustainability

The impact of digitalization in education extends beyond immediate changes; it holds long-term effects and sustainability implications that shape the future of learning. Evaluating the following aspects is essential to ensure that digitalization delivers enduring benefits and remains a sustainable force in education:

Long-term effects:

a. *Skill development*: Digitalization equips learners with essential digital skills that enhance employability and adaptability.
b. *Lifelong learning*: Digitalization fosters a culture of lifelong learning, in line with changing career demands and personal interests.
c. *Pedagogical transformation*: Digitalization encourages pedagogical innovation. Educators adapt their teaching methods, incorporating technology and new approaches to enhance learning outcomes.
d. *Global collaboration*: As digital education fosters global collaboration, the long-term effects include an increased awareness of global issues, cultural understanding, and the potential for collaborative problem-solving on a global scale.

Sustainability:

a. *Infrastructure*: Ensuring the sustainability of digitalization requires consistent investment in technology infrastructure. Regular updates and maintenance are necessary to tackle obsolescence.
b. *Content quality*: The sustainability of digitalization relies on the continuous development of high-quality, up-to-date digital content that aligns with evolving educational standards.
c. *Policy and regulation*: Sustainable digitalization requires adaptive policies and regulations that keep pace with technological advancements and evolving educational needs.
d. *Pedagogical adaptation*: Ongoing pedagogical adaptation is necessary to ensure that digitalization remains effective and aligned with evolving educational goals.

In evaluating the impact of digitalization in education, it is imperative to consider both the long-term effects and sustainability factors. While digitalization offers transformative potential, sustaining its benefits requires a commitment to the above, thereby ensuring that digitalization remains a powerful and sustainable force for positive change in education.

Educational Policies and Governance

Government Policies and Support for Digital Education

Government policies and support play a pivotal role in shaping the impact and effectiveness of digitalization in education. Evaluating these policies and their outcomes is essential to understand how they contribute to the broader goals of enhancing learning outcomes, accessibility, and equity.

Policy frameworks:

a. *Digital inclusion initiatives*: Governments have launched various digital inclusion programmes to bridge the digital divide.
b. *Curriculum integration*: Many governments have integrated digital literacy and technology skills into the standard curriculum.
c. *Data privacy regulations*: Governments have enacted data privacy regulations, such as the General Data Protection Regulation (GDPR) in Europe, to safeguard student data and privacy.

Financial support:

a. *Funding for technology infrastructure*: Governments allocate funds for the development and maintenance of technology infrastructure in educational institutions.
b. *Digital content creation*: Financial support may also be provided for the creation of high-quality digital educational content, including e-books, videos, and interactive materials, to enhance the learning experience.
c. *Teacher training*: Governments invest in teacher training programmes to enhance educators' digital pedagogy skills.

Quality assurance:

a. *Standards and assessment*: Governments establish standards for digital education content and assessments to maintain quality and ensure that digital resources align with educational goals.
b. *Research and evaluation*: Policymakers support research and evaluation studies to assess the impact of digitalization on learning outcomes.

Public–private partnerships:

a. *Collaboration with EdTech companies*: Governments collaborate with EdTech companies to provide digital resources and platforms for educational institutions. These partnerships expand the range of available educational tools and content.

Evaluating the impact of government policies and support for digital education involves assessing their effectiveness in achieving educational goals, promoting equity, ensuring data security, and fostering digital literacy. A well-designed and implemented policy framework, combined with adequate financial support and a commitment to equitable access, can harness the full potential of digitalization in education and benefit students, educators, and society at large.

Regulatory Frameworks and Standards

In the context of evaluating the impact of digitalization in education, regulatory frameworks and standards play a crucial role in ensuring quality, equity, and accountability.

Quality assurance:

a. *Content standards*: Regulatory bodies often establish content standards to ensure that digital educational materials align with curriculum objectives and educational goals.
b. *Assessment standards*: Standards for digital assessments and evaluations are essential to ensure the fairness and reliability of testing methods.

Ethical and legal considerations:

a. *Ethical guidelines*: Regulatory frameworks incorporate ethical guidelines related to digital education. These guidelines address issues such as online safety, and responsible technology use.
b. *Intellectual property rights*: Regulatory standards also encompass intellectual property rights in digital education. They define how copyrighted materials can be used, shared, and distributed in educational settings.

In evaluating the impact of digitalization in education, regulatory frameworks and standards serve as essential benchmarks. They are crucial in maintaining accountability, safeguarding student interests, and ensuring that digitalization enhances the educational experience.

The Future of Education in a Digital Age

Emerging Trends in Educational Technology

EdTech is continually evolving, and several emerging trends are shaping the landscape of education for enhancing learning and digitalization:

a. *AI and machine learning (ML)*: AI-driven tools and ML algorithms are being employed to personalize learning experiences.
b. *Hybrid and blended learning*: Hybrid and blended learning models have gained prominence. These approaches offer flexibility and resilience, allowing for seamless transitions during crises.
c. *Immersive technologies*: VR and AR are being used to create immersive learning experiences through which students can explore historical sites, conduct virtual science experiments, and engage in interactive simulations.

d. *Gamification and game-based learning*: Gamification elements, such as rewards, badges, and leaderboards, are integrated into educational platforms to motivate students.
e. *EdTech ecosystems*: Comprehensive EdTech ecosystems are emerging, offering a suite of integrated tools and resources.
f. *Blockchain for credentials*: Blockchain technology is being explored for securely storing and verifying educational credentials.
g. *Collaborative learning platforms*: Collaboration tools and platforms enable students to work together on projects, fostering teamwork and communication skills even in remote settings.
h. *Global learning networks*: Online platforms connect students and educators worldwide, promoting cross-cultural understanding and collaborative projects.

These emerging trends in EdTech are not only transforming how education is delivered but also enhancing its resilience during crises.

Conclusion and Action Points

The Role of Educators, Policymakers, and Researchers

Educational digitalization during crises necessitates the concerted efforts of educators, policymakers, and researchers to ensure the effective delivery of education and address the unique challenges posed by unforeseen circumstances. The stakeholders' roles in this context are as follows:

Educators:

a. *Adaptation and innovation*: Educators are at the forefront of implementing digital education during crises. They must adopt innovative tools and approaches to engage students effectively.
b. *Professional development*: Educators should engage in ongoing professional development to enhance their digital pedagogy skills, stay updated on emerging technologies.
c. *Data utilization*: Educators should use data analytics to monitor student progress and adapt instruction accordingly.

Policymakers:

a. *Policy formulation*: Policymakers play a crucial role in crafting policies and regulations that support the digitalization of education during crises.
b. *Resource allocation*: Policymakers allocate resources for digital infrastructure, teacher training, and student support services.
c. *Collaboration*: Policymakers collaborate with educational institutions, technology providers, and other stakeholders to develop comprehensive strategies for digital education during crises.

Researchers:

a. *Innovation and best practices*: Researchers contribute by conducting studies and experiments to identify innovative technologies and best practices in digital education.
b. *Data analysis*: Researchers analyse data from digital education initiatives to assess their impact on student learning outcomes and identify areas for improvement.
c. *Evaluation*: Researchers conduct rigorous evaluations of digital education programmes to determine their effectiveness and efficiency.
d. *Evidence-based recommendations*: Researchers provide evidence-based recommendations to educators and policymakers, helping them make informed choices about digital tools, curriculum design, and teaching methods.
e. *Anticipating future needs*: Researchers anticipate future educational needs and challenges, helping educators and policymakers prepare for the future.

The collaborative efforts of educators, policymakers, and researchers are essential for the successful implementation of educational digitalization during crises. By working together, these stakeholders can ensure that digital education remains inclusive, effective, and responsive to the evolving needs of students and the challenges posed by unforeseen circumstances.

A Vision for a Resilient, Digitally-enabled Education System

A vision for a resilient, digitally enabled education system in the context of educational and digitalization during crises is one that is:

a. Accessible to all learners, regardless of their location, circumstances, or background.
b. Flexible and adaptable to meet the needs of all learners.
c. Equitable and inclusive.
d. High-quality and effective.

To achieve this vision, the following areas need investments:

a. *Infrastructure*: Reliable internet connectivity and devices.
b. *Professional development*: Training and supporting educators.
c. *Curriculum and content:* Digital curricula and content aligned with the latest learning standards.
d. *Assessment*: Digital assessment tools.
e. *Digital skill development:* Skills such as digital literacy and information and communication technology (ICT) skills.

By investing in these areas, a resilient, digitally enabled education system that can withstand crises can be created.

Bibliography

Bates, T. (2019). *Teaching in a digital age: Guidelines for designing teaching and learning.* Tony Bates Associates Ltd.
Dede, C. J., Mishra, A., & Kizilcec, M. (2021). *Learning in the time of COVID-19: A global perspective.* Routledge.
Dhawan, S. (2020). Digital innovation in times of crisis: How mashups improve quality of education. *Journal of Educational Technology Systems, 49*(1), 3–16.
Ewell, P. D. (2021). *Teaching online: A guide to learning design, delivery, and assessment.* Routledge.
Garrison, D. R., & Vaughan, N. D. (2013). *Blended learning in higher education: Framework, principles, and guidelines.* John Wiley & Sons.
Hodges, C., Moore, S., Lockee, B., Trust, T., & Bond, A. (2020). *The difference between emergency remote teaching and online learning.* EDUCAUSE Review.
Means, B., Neisler, J., & Hill, H. C. (2020). *How much have teacher-student interactions in hybrid and remote settings changed? Evidence from COVID-19 spring-season.* NBER Working Paper.
OECD. (2020a). *Education responses to COVID-19: Education policy outlook.* OECD
OECD. (2020b). *How learning continued during the COVID-19 pandemic: Global lessons from initiatives to support learners and teachers.* OECD Education Working Paper No. 242.
OECD. (2021). *Educational innovation and digitalisation during the COVID-19 crisis: Lessons for the future.* OECD Paper No. 178.
Schleicher, A. (2020). The future of education in a post-COVID-19 world. *Educational Researcher, 49*(7), 455–462.
Smith, D. A., O'Brien, M. A., & Keane, M. T. (2021). Mashing up technologies for innovation in online teaching: Lessons from a virtual hackathon during the COVID-19 pandemic. *Teaching in Higher Education, 26*(5), 508–521.
Spector, J. M. (2020). *Remote teaching and learning: A practical guide.* Routledge.
The OECD's Education. (2022). https://www.oecd.org/education/
The World Bank's Education. (2023). https://www.worldbank.org/en/topic/education
UNESCO. (2020a). *Digital education in the time of COVID-19 and beyond.* UNESCO.
UNESCO. (2020b). *Education in a post-COVID world: Nine ideas for public action.* UNESCO's publication discusses strategies for reshaping education in the wake of the COVID-19 pandemic, with a focus on digitalization and innovation.
UNESCO's COVID-19 Education Response. (2020). https://en.unesco.org/covid19/educationresponse
Vlachopoulos, D., & Makri, A. (2017). Online learning in higher education: A review of research on interactions and transactions. *The International Review of Research in Open and Distributed Learning, 18*(3), 1–33.
Wang, Q. (2017). A generic model for guiding the integration of ICT into teaching and learning. *Innovations in Education and Teaching International, 54*(5), 411–419.
Watson, J., & Gemin, B. (2008). *Promising practices in online learning: Using online learning for at-risk students and credit recovery.* North American Council for Online Learning.
World Bank. (2020). *Education in the time of COVID-19: Disruptions, responses, and lessons for the future.* World Bank.
Zhao, Y. (2020). COVID-19 as a catalyst for educational change. *Prospects,* 1–6. https://link.springer.com/content/pdf/10.1007/s11125-020-09477-y.pdf
Zhao, Y., Lei, J., Yan, B., Lai, C., & Tan, H. S. (2005). What makes the difference? A practical analysis of research on the effectiveness of distance education. *Teachers College Record, 107*(8), 1836–1884.

Chapter 5

Resilience and the Entrepreneurial University During Turbulent Times: A Model for the Higher Education Sector

Kiran Vazirani, Rameesha Kalra and Gnanendra M.

Christ University, Bangalore, Karnataka, India

Abstract

Turbulent times include economic crises, recessions, health pandemics, war situations, including the recent COVID-19 crisis which had significant economic and social ramifications. Turbulence impacts the economy, businesses, and societies as whole. Crises impact the education industry not only in terms of teaching and learning but also the next level of learning outcome as job opportunities and career growth of the stakeholders. University systems play a major role in handling turbulence and generating resilience methods to ensure the least possible impact on the sector. The entrepreneurial mindset of the universities encourages them towards risk-taking, becoming initial movers, and being innovators in their approaches (Etzkowitz et al., 1998). This chapter provides a broader understanding of different types of turbulence, as well as the intensity of impact on the higher education sector. It also discusses how these turbulent times come with opportunities which can be leveraged by institutions. With an extensive literature review and understanding, it proposes a conceptual multilayered model to support entrepreneurial development. This study employs desk research methods to understand, review, and propose methods and methodology to encourage and adapt universities handling turbulence and crises. Lack of research in handling crises and turbulence in the case of higher education makes this study imperative. The outcome extends the conceptual understanding of turbulent situations and will help the universities to self-introspect and understand the ways for reacting to these changes, crises, and turbulences.

Global Higher Education Practices in Times of Crisis:
Questions for Sustainability and Digitalization, 77–94
Copyright © 2025 by Kiran Vazirani, Rameesha Kalra and Gnanendra M.
Published under exclusive licence by Emerald Publishing Limited
doi:10.1108/978-1-83797-052-020241006

Discussion on National Education Policy enhances the understanding for educators and universities to utilize added opportunities.

Keywords: Turbulent times; resilience; entrepreneurial university; impact on stakeholders; National Education Policy 2020

Introduction

The recent hit pandemic had a major impact on all sectors of life. The education sector was also the hardest hit due to the pandemic (Bortoló et al., 2023). With the lack of knowledge and direction of how educational institutions could handle the pandemic without much loss to its stakeholders, it became challenging for them to plan for the future. The regulatory bodies had to implement a lot of quick decisions like implementing lockdowns, switching to e-learning classrooms, social distancing, travel restrictions, to name a few (Cai et al., 2023). While the challenges faced by higher educational institutions (HEIs) were substantial in terms of training the existing faculty members and provide them sufficient infrastructure and digital tools to deliver sessions online, the pandemic was catalyst in introducing new and innovative ways of teaching-learning, cost-effectiveness, research collaborations, and improved resilience (Cunningham, 2022; Nayak et al., 2023).

Crises are situations that are highly disruptive and complex and therefore demand strategic responses (Brennan & Stern, 2017). It is understood that crises are unexpected and cannot be forecasted, but there has to be a contingency crisis management plan that can guide the universities in moving forward. Prywes and Sobel (2015) in their article suggested the importance of crisis management plan to be in place during current times and proposed a seven-step approach to crisis management, comprising the following:

a) Developing relationships with police officials/journalists who will ensure effective communication among the public and management.
b) Formation of a crisis management team that will ensure proper planning and legal advice whenever required.
c) Train the core crisis management team.
d) Identify strong people from the crisis management team and train them well in their communication skills so that they can act as spokespersons during times of crisis.
e) Updated crisis management team training on sensitive information that must not be disclosed to the public.
f) Regularly train the crisis management team on the key information that must be shared with the public.
g) Plan the social media strategy effectively, ensuring that the crisis management team can rapidly respond via social media whenever any crisis situation occurs.

In an article by Lott (2012), suggestions have been offered to the management of HEIs to ensure any communication during periods of crisis is made timely and is disseminated among all stakeholders. Yet another research (Hussain, 2014) suggested that management of HEIs would be better able to handle crises if they have a proper crisis management plan in place and well-established communication channels are proper and well-coordinated.Frigotto et al. (2022), stated that universities and HEIs that plan for crisis and resilience will be able to effectively serve their stakeholders in a better manner. This will ensure minimum disruptions that may occur due to a crisis. The first step for crisis management, as discussed above, would be laying down a well-coordinated plan for crisis management which should not only focus on the long-term but also be viable in the long run. These plans would lay down the guidelines and steps required to communicate with the stakeholders. In the absence of an effective crisis communication plan, crisis management would be entirely ineffective (Mykhailova et al., 2023).

There exists a close relationship among crisis planning, crisis management, and resilience; if employees are resilient and have planned well for the crisis, the organizations would be in a better position to manage the crisis effectively (Bross et al., 2020). The crisis management plan should specify the course of action, resources/tools required, channels of communication, feedback mechanism system that the management should follow when the crisis is around (Hedner et al., 2011). Regular follow-ups, meetings, and review of the plans must also be ensured in order to identify the gaps and the areas of improvement in the existing plans. Thus, an effective planning and control system in place will ensure an effective execution of the plans (Oleksiyenko et al., 2023).

As defined by Sutcliffe and Vogus (2003), resilience is the capability of an organization to absorb stress/shocks received from the external/internal environment and still have the ability to recover well from an adverse situation. Thus, resilience acts as a safety cushion to absorb chaos/shocks/unfavourable situations efficiently. Koronis and Ponis (2018) listed the drivers for ensuring organizational resilience – preparedness, responsiveness, adaptability, and development of learning processes that support problem identification and probable solutions.

Crisis management by HEIs during tough times involves a multifaceted and holistic approach that will not only ensure continuity of learning but will also ensure the safety and well-being of its stakeholders. Krishnamurthy (2020) suggested the use of artificial intelligence to help maintain the continuity of learning during periods of crisis; however, since the fundamental components of teaching-learning are deeply related to human interaction, personalized touch, and understanding. To meet the challenges posed by the current environment and prepare the learners and facilitators for the growth of an entrepreneurial ecosystem that will encourage a culture of innovation, risk-taking, response to challenges, and an entrepreneurial mindset (Karlsson & Offord, 2023).

Entrepreneurial university refers to a university that can adapt to turbulent and uncertain situations. Entrepreneurial universities are focused on ensuring a balance between teaching, research, and innovative activities. For this, the universities should ensure fostering a culture of risk-taking and a conducive environment for promoting innovation, research, and quality teaching. Clark (1998) suggested that entrepreneurial universities focus on the following aspects: (a) presence of a strong management team that helps the universities adjust flexibly and be more adaptive to the external environment, (b) self-reliant in case of funding (no reliance upon government funds), (c) flexible enough to adapt to the changing environment, and (d) presence of a strong entrepreneurial culture to embrace change.

Guenther and Wagner (2008), Philpott et al. (2011), and Miller et al. (2018) have provided the essential traits of an entrepreneurial university to include the following which have been combined as follows:

a) Training the undergraduate and postgraduate students with the requisite skills in order to be employable.
b) Ensuring that entrepreneurship concepts are taught and practised in the class.
c) Offering the courses outside the curriculum of the university to ensure lifelong learning.
d) Quality research which in turn would contribute to effective class teaching
e) Providing consultancy services to organizations to help them improve their functioning.
f) Industry–academia collaborative research output.
g) Incubation facilities with the objective of doing research and developing new ventures.
h) Prepare students of today for a world full of complexity and uncertainty tomorrow.
i) Pursuit of interdisciplinary research and development by teachers and students.

Different School's Thoughts for Entrepreneurial University

Etzkowitz identifies two significant academic transformations in the roles of universities. Initially, the first generation of universities primarily focused on teaching, and their primary mission was imparting established knowledge. The first revolution occurred in Germany in the late 19th century when universities began integrating research activities into their mission. Subsequently, during the latter half of the 20th century, following the emergence of science-driven innovations during World War II, the second revolution materialized. Universities expanded their missions to encompass economic and social development in addition to their traditional roles in teaching and research (Etzkowitz, 2004). This type of university is called 'entrepreneurial university'.

The 'entrepreneurial university', in the literature, has so many implications. Clark (1998) and Van Vught (1999) mention 'Innovative Universities', while Slaughter and Leslie (1997) noted 'Market Universities' and 'Academic Capitalism', Dill (1995) refers to 'University Technology Transfer', and Röpke (2000) considers the entrepreneurial university as an 'Entrepreneur Organization'. Aronowitz (2000) presents a concept known as the 'Corporate University', where activities and practices that generate profits hold significance, and teaching and research endeavours without commercial outcomes are not as highly regarded. According to Schulte (2004), an entrepreneurial university is primarily tasked with two key responsibilities: educating aspiring entrepreneurs and adopting an entrepreneurial mindset and approach (Kirby, 2002). These universities are characterized by their innovation, ability to identify and generate opportunities, and proficiency in teamwork.

They exhibit a willingness to take risks and proactively address challenges. Table 5.1 summarises the perspectives of different authors about the concept of Entrepreneurial University and its characteristics. Gurrero et al. (2006) conducted research into the environmental factors influencing the establishment and growth of entrepreneurial universities. Guerrero and Urbano (2012) acknowledge the relatively early stage of research in this domain and attempt to outline a framework. Their proposed model incorporates both environmental factors (comprising formal and informal elements) and internal factors (encompassing resources and capabilities). An entrepreneurial society denotes regions where knowledge-driven entrepreneurship has emerged as a key catalyst for economic expansion, job generation, and competitiveness in the global marketplace (Audretsch, 2007).

Table 5.1. Entrepreneurial University as Defined by Different Authors.

Author and Year	Definition	Key Points/Features
Salarnzadehl et al. (2011)	This is a dynamic system characterized by distinct inputs (such as resources, culture, rules and regulations, etc.), processes (including teaching, research, managerial operations, logistical activities, etc.), and outcomes (like entrepreneurial human resources, relevant research aligned with market demands, innovations and discoveries, entrepreneurial networks, and entrepreneurial hubs). The system's objective is to effectively harness all its resources, skills, and capacities to accomplish its 'Third Mission'.	The input–output model, where input as resources and the output as the innovation, effective research and entrepreneurial centres.
Clark (1998)	The entrepreneurial university is proactively engaged in redefining its operational methods, thereby instigating a change in its cultural dynamics, with the goal of adopting a more promising stance for the future. In this context, university entrepreneurship is not only a result but also an ongoing process.	The entrepreneurial mindset is both a process and an outcome.
Deem (2001)	The idea of the entrepreneurial university is intricately linked with the notion of new managerialism, which involves the pursuit of innovative, efficient, and effective approaches to tasks and the establishment of novel organizational structures.	Inclination towards innovation and culture of innovation.

(Continued)

Table 5.1. (*Continued*)

Author and Year	Definition	Key Points/Features
Slaughter and Leslie (1997)	In a more specific context, entrepreneurial universities primarily participate in what can be termed 'academic capitalism'. In this scenario, researchers essentially function as entrepreneurs and capitalists supported by state funding within a neoliberal framework.	Emphasis more on academic research.
Peterka and Salihovic (2012)	An entrepreneurial mindset provides a blueprint for the institutional advancement of a university. In this model, the university proactively establishes its autonomy, diversifies its funding sources (thus reducing reliance on government funding), creates new academic departments and initiatives aligned with societal needs, and undertakes structural transformations. These changes collectively enhance the university's ability to effectively adapt to evolving circumstances.	Emphasis is on differentiated characteristics of entrepreneurial university, like autonomy, looking forward for society as whole, structural changes to adapt to the new environment.
Röpke (2000)	The concept of an entrepreneurial university can be understood in three ways: First, the university as an institution transforms itself to adopt an entrepreneurial character. Second, individuals within the university community, including faculty, students, and staff, cultivate entrepreneurial attributes. Third, the university's interaction with its external environment, particularly its engagement with the region or locality, aligns with entrepreneurial principles, characterized by a dynamic and innovative approach.	The three major interaction – university itself, its internal stakeholders, and the interaction with society as a whole.
Guerrero and Urbano (2012)	An entrepreneurial university serves as a tool that not only contributes to the workforce and adds value through knowledge creation or transformation but also enhances individuals' values and attitudes regarding various cultural, educational, institutional,	Emphasis is on the change in the basic culture of academic university to entrepreneurial university.

Table 5.1. (*Continued*)

Author and Year	Definition	Key Points/Features
	and legislative challenges. This adaptation is essential for thriving in a highly competitive global landscape.	
Khoshhall et al. (2023)	The academic community has become entrepreneurial both in its internal dynamics and in its external relations with businesses for research contracts and the transfer of knowledge and technology.	Transfer of knowledge and technology with business researches.
Awad and Salaimeh (2023)	Entrepreneurship is considered an integrated process consisting of a group of elements and relationships among universities, industry, government, citizens, and environment	Multilayered relationship among different stakeholders of a university.

Source: From multiple authors.

Characteristics of Entrepreneurial University

Universities are navigating a transformative landscape marked by significant political and economic shifts. This includes heightened public demands for increased accessibility to higher education, governments' expectations for universities to actively contribute to a nation's socio-economic progress, and the growing need for universities to adopt market-oriented principles and effective organizational management within their institutions. These factors collectively shape a new framework for the advancement of higher education (Hannon, 2013). In today's fiercely competitive global landscape, universities cannot be seen solely as integral components of the national education system, sheltered and funded by the government, responsible only for academic programmes and research. Instead, universities must actively compete for students, research opportunities, and financial resources. This necessitates a significant shift in their traditional approaches to management, funding, internal organization, external partnerships, and the execution of their core functions (Van Ginkel, 2002).

The shift towards becoming an entrepreneurial university is a result of a dual influence: internal changes within the university itself and external factors affecting it. This evolution is closely tied to the growing importance of knowledge in society and the increasing emphasis on knowledge-driven innovation. Universities are adopting an entrepreneurial approach not only to meet the requirements of their local context but also to actively play a role in fostering regional and national economic development (Gibb, 2013).

An entrepreneurial university serves as a tool that not only contributes to the workforce and adds value through knowledge creation or transformation but also enhances individuals' values and attitudes regarding various cultural, educational, institutional, and legislative challenges. This adaptation is essential for thriving in a highly competitive global landscape (Etzkowitz, 2004).

At present, experts widely acknowledge that the concept of an 'Entrepreneurial University' plays a significant role in fostering self-improvement, promoting innovation, and serving as an effective strategy for thriving in highly dynamic and unpredictable markets (Hannon, 2013).

The original primary role of universities was centred around teaching. The secondary mission, which is research, gained equal significance alongside teaching primarily in the 19th century (Etzkowitz, 1998). Etzkowitz contends that the third mission of universities involves their active contribution to innovation and societal transformation. In this context, university professors assume a pivotal entrepreneurial role to ensure that ideas are effectively translated into practical applications (Gulbrandsen & Slipersæter, 2007).

In developed economies, universities tend to be more focused on specific academic disciplines compared to their counterparts in post-Soviet countries (Seniuk, 2018). Additionally, they often have stronger connections with local communities and government authorities. In this context, there is a growing need for the triple integration model (TIM) rather than the triple helix model. TIM can be effectively implemented through contemporary digital multi-tier, globally integrated platforms. These platforms serve as potent institutional tools to facilitate the gradual transformation of traditional universities into research-driven and entrepreneurial institutions in the future.

Challenges of Turbulence Time

There are various challenges faced by HEIs during periods of turbulence which not only leads to disruptions in their functioning but also impact the institutions financially and operationally. Turbulent times would require the universities to revive their long-term strategic plans in view of the crisis management needs. The changing and dynamic external environment has motivated universities to become more entrepreneurial in order to better meet the challenges posed and contribute towards long-term sustainable development. Baporikar (2022) highlighted a few challenges of the entrepreneurial university as follows:

a) Establishment/partnering with strong incubators who can assist in commercializing entrepreneurial ideas and provide a conducive/supportive environment for new business ventures.
b) Ensuring greater collaboration with industry, through alumni or industry professionals. Universities can offer degree courses that are offered in collaboration with industry and that in turn will support the students in internships and final placement.
c) Innovation is considered as a key when it comes to entrepreneurship. For universities to have an entrepreneurial mindset, their focus must be on the development of new programmes, collaborative research with industry, and ensuring ways of strengthening relationships with all the stakeholders.
d) Being self-reliant and avoiding too much dependence on government support and funding.

e) Promotion of research and development, collaborative research opportunities, participation in conferences, workshops, seminars, and consultancy services in collaboration with industry professionals.
f) Innovative strategies to ensure partnership with industry so that the university curriculum can be framed keeping in mind the corporate requirements.
g) Ensuring quality of teaching, staff, and systems in place so that entrepreneurial universities can contribute towards growth and innovation in the long run.
h) Developing a strong conducive culture that reflects positivity throughout the university.

Some of the challenges faced by entrepreneurial universities include resource constraints, encouraging faculty to get involved, industry–academia collaboration, compliance with regulatory and legal requirements, interdisciplinary research initiatives, continuous adaptation as per the needs of the stakeholders, and ensuring incubation cells within the universities to promote a culture of entrepreneurship among staff and students (Kawamorita et al., 2020). Rubens et al. (2017) argued some major challenges faced by entrepreneurial universities: faculty attitude towards third mission and entrepreneurship, changing attitudes towards traditional teaching institutions, faculty assessment process, funding to universities and growth of administration, and limited support and commitment to third mission (Anderson et al., 2018). Fostering connections between business and management schools, often termed 'real-world engagement' or 'knowledge exchange' activities, is becoming increasingly essential. External stakeholders are no longer viewed solely as recipients of higher education offerings but are increasingly acknowledged as active collaborators in shaping valuable management knowledge, theory, and practical applications.

Stages of Development of the Entrepreneurial University

A university works with external and internal environmental situations which create the base for the future. The university model has been developing for decades, starting from an academic university, whose main goal and objective of presence in the society was to provide as much as education to all the stakeholders and society as a whole. This was during the early stage of the concept of higher education. Then came the research era, which forced universities to incorporate the research mindset especially among the internal stakeholders. This led to the establishment of research centres in the university premises. The economic growth of various economies across world have shown a significant impact and change in educational universities as well. The evolution of entrepreneurial mindset and the scope of the acceptance of new entrepreneurs by the society and the industry made universities to go beyond the academic teaching and academic research. The incubation of entrepreneurial culture and mindset became the base reason for the entrepreneurial universities. But if the whole process of developing an entrepreneurial university has to be looked into, it starts with the basic three levels: preparation stage, development stage, and the outcome stage.

Stage 1: Stage of Preparation

Being the first stage of establishment, universities should look forward to some basic add-ons to the existing model. Major universities follow the academic research mindset, so the major change which needs to be adopted is the regular research on the external environmental opportunities including the local, regional, and international markets. This is one of the major sources of understanding the existing gap which can be taken as a business or entrepreneurial opportunity in the future. With the same, a regular analysis of the resources and capability of the university plays an important role to understand how the external environmental opportunities can be aligned and being grabbed for the benefit of students and the society as a whole. The nature of autonomy brings a backbone to university to work in the alignment of the requirements of the industry and the society. Autonomy gives a liberty and responsibility to universities to build an ecosystem to ensure enhanced learning and experience for the learners as well as the teaching fraternity. This gives a scope of empowering the teaching fraternity to understand, anticipate, and plan the right path for the young entrepreneur. Even the governing body, especially in India, supports the autonomous nature of universities which resulted in around 871 universities conferred with autonomous status by University Grants Commission (UGC) as of February 2022. Proactiveness and risk-taking attitude of leaders in the universities plays a key role to move ahead in the preparation stage. As the leaders govern the universities or institutions or organizations, they create a culture, value, and path of the system.

Another key factor which can be treated as the base for the entrepreneurial university is the level of acceptance for innovativeness – by each of the internal stakeholders. Innovative mindset is the key for any entrepreneur and looking from the university perspective the acceptance for innovation at every level – by course facilitator, mentor, management, administrative staff, and students. The collective innovative mindset of each of the above parties will lead an ecosystem which accepts and promotes the creative innovation. Also, the inclination of today's industry towards the multidisciplinary knowledge forces the universities to provide an interdisciplinary exposure to their students and course facilitators. This leads these parties to look forward to every situation from a 360 degree, with a solution which provides a better solution to any current situation.

Experiential learning – learning with experience – gives a practical approach towards the given situation. And for anyone with such an experience leads to see the problems of society or the country in a more practical way and in a solution-oriented way. Providing such an exposure to all the internal stakeholders of a university, enhances the real-time experience. More amount of internship and industry-related projects, involvement of entrepreneurial projects, social projects, political and industrial projects, etc. for all the parties directly associated with universities will enhance the in-depth knowledge of problem identification. The right identification of any problem gives a base for the entrepreneurial opportunity. On the same, it enhances the entrepreneurial mindset which is the base for the upcoming entrepreneurial university (see Fig. 5.1).

Model for the Higher Education Sector 87

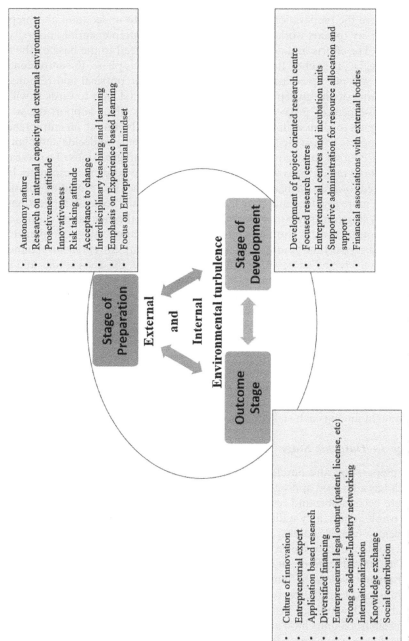

Fig. 5.1. Stages of Development of the Entrepreneurial University. *Source*: Authors.

Stage 2 – Development Stage

The development stage acts as a second phase of reflection of the preparation stage, where the preparation stage has given a scope to understand and prepare the university to start working on the road map of entrepreneurial university or a system. The efforts and acceptance of Stage 1 will lead to the base of the second phase, i.e., the act of the development stage. In this phase, the entrepreneurial group will put up collective efforts to build up the physical and resourceful requirements of the entrepreneurial university. The first step towards it will be the establishment of project-oriented research centres which support the young entrepreneurs to align with their passionate dream of becoming an entrepreneur. It also supports course facilitators and teaching fraternity to decide and plan for their own courses to ensure the high impactful learning sessions. The research centres whose major focus was only to look forward to academic researches have been moved towards the real-time research-related issues and providing solutions which are more practical and have higher managerial and societal implications.

At this stage, the support of management towards the incubation centres and entrepreneurial centres should be more. An active and effective entrepreneurial centre will support the young mind to execute the young entrepreneurial mindset more effectively and successfully. On the same ground, the associations and collaboration with diversified financial assistance leads to a more established network and strong base for each type of centres in the universities. The diversified financial assistance leads to more reward system and recognition for every internal stakeholder of the universities.

All the above-mentioned centres, networks, mindset, and changes could only be possible only if the supportive administrative staff carries the same mindset. Without the support of the administrative staff – which include the leader and management at top level with the support provider from admin staff or non-teaching members of the community, the execution of the extended entrepreneurial thought among each stakeholder would become challenging.

Stage 3 – Outcome Stage

The preparation and development stage results in the outcome as a university which has a focused approach towards entrepreneurship. Such types of universities are accountable and responsible towards the industry as well as the society as a whole. They carry a differentiation and unique approach towards real-time problem-solving situations. The acceptance towards innovation is very high. Such an ecosystem encourages a risk-taking mindset and supports entrepreneurship. The major outcome of such efforts includes the culture and entrepreneurship environment within the university. This culture gets embedded as a part of the teaching and learning process as well. Katholieke Universiteit Leuven and The Standfort's Technology Venture Programme are some examples where teachers and established units have autonomy to act and plan. Also, the absence of a hierarchical structure gives a freedom for a course instructor to design, plan, and execute his course and research agenda. Also, the university model of incorporating entrepreneurial activities at every level supports and enhances the entrepreneurial mindset within the university. Universities having a programme like The

Standfort's Technology Venture Programme support networking and knowledge sharing, in terms of organizing and participating multiple conferences, with an objective of sharing knowledge with other institutes as well as society for a better understanding of real-time situations. Such networking strategies will help to build long-term academia–industry relationships and support to be more engaged and related to industry and societal-related issues. All such activities result in more of application-based research outcome than restricting to only academia-based research. Another example of supporting more of an entrepreneurial mindset is by the UnLtd Higher Education Support System, UK. This helps with funding and its procedure to different entrepreneurs including internal and external stakeholders. One of the major results of entrepreneurial university is the increase in the number of legally owned models, procedures, and products. Universities encourage such initiatives by providing them support in legal and financial requirements to its internal and external stakeholders. Also, the increase in terms of diversified financing leads to motivating its stakeholders, with a better reward system and financial independency.

Impact on the Stakeholders of Universities

University stakeholders are those set of people or groups of people or organizations, who have direct or indirect impact from the presence, acts, and efforts of the university (see Fig. 5.2). It includes individuals or groups of people having direct impact both in the short and long run. Also, the indirect impact could be seen on different bodies like other institutions, accreditation agencies, etc. which could be evident in the long-run scenario.

According to Kotler and Fox (1995), the following are the stakeholders who are related to any university. Adaptation of entrepreneurial mindset will have a strong and long-term impact on every stakeholder in the given list. These stakeholders get impacted by the entrepreneurial mindset of university at different intensity. The details are as follows:

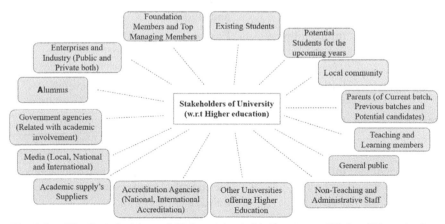

Fig. 5.2. The Stakeholders of Universities (with Respect to Higher Education). *Source*: Authors.

Figure 5.2 identifies the various stakeholders associated with an entrepreneurial university. However, the influence of the university's entrepreneurial mindset on each stakeholder varies in strength and nature. Table 5.2 provides a detailed explanation of the nature and intensity of the impact that an entrepreneurial mindset has on the stakeholders of a university.

Table 5.2 – The Nature and Strength of Impact of Entrepreneurial Mindset on Stakeholders of a University.

Stakeholder	Nature/Strength of Impact	Description of Impact
Current students	Direct, high	Enhances the scope of entrepreneurial mindset and internationalization
Potential students	Direct, high	Acting as guiding path, higher aspirations
Local community	Direct, high	More number of entrepreneurs, supporting with real-time solutions
Parents	Indirect, medium	Indirect impact but more responsible towards their act and support to their ward
Faculty members	Direct, high	More empowered, risk takers, change acceptors, open-minded contributors
General public	Indirect, medium	More educated and accountable towards society
Administrative staff	Indirect, medium	Exposure to multi-industry experience with more practically oriented work culture
Competitors	Direct, medium	Enhances competition and drives industry for the betterment of society and students
Accreditation agencies	Indirect, low	Ensures the accreditation bodies to aspire high and support with more autonomous guidelines and policies
Suppliers	Indirect, low	Suppliers will see a higher level of differentiation among the universities
Media	Indirect, low	Media will have indirect long-term impact with better skilled and ethically responsible contributors
Government agencies	Indirect, medium	Higher scope to support and delegation of societal-related issues with entrepreneurial universities
Alumnus	Indirect, high	Leads to high networking and internationalization, higher knowledge exchange

Table 5.2. (*Continued*)

Stakeholder	Nature/Strength of Impact	Description of Impact
Enterprises and industry	Direct, high	More number of entrepreneurs, more ethically responsible citizens
Foundation parties	Direct, high	Responsible leadership, participative management style

Source: Authors.

Role of National Education Policy (NEP) 2020 – As a Supporting Policy for Entrepreneurial University

The role of higher education in promoting societal well-being cannot be undermined. Ensuring quality of education is one of the sustainable development goals reflected in Sustainable Development Goal (SDG) 4 provided by the United Nations. With the changing knowledge landscape, world of data analytics, and machine learning, it is becoming increasingly evident that the education system should provide holistic and all-round development for learners. The National Education Policy, 2020 led by The Ministry of Human Resource Development, India, in year 2020 focused on holistic and entrepreneurial mindset of individuals. The thrust areas of NEP are aligned with the thrust areas and characteristics of an entrepreneurial university focusing on promoting quality research, providing opportunities for faculty development and lifelong learning, conducive environment and support for students and staff, focus towards holistic education, and emphasis on innovation and entrepreneurship.

The NEP has paved the way for an entrepreneurial university by supporting in the following ways:

a) To promote quality research, the government has proposed setting up a National Research Foundation (NRF) to strengthen the quality of research in India, comprising the board of members who are passionate and best researchers in their respective domains. The members would help foster a culture of research and innovation in the country.
b) The focus area of NEP is also towards promoting a culture of entrepreneurship and innovation through quality research initiatives. Opportunities for multidisciplinary learning, internship opportunities, and skilling to advance learners with the practical skill set are required to survive in the future. The policy provides a platform for vocational education through industry–academia linkage, that will help build entrepreneurial competencies and development of cognitive abilities.
c) Ensuring curriculum design and development in accordance with the skill set required by leaders of tomorrow. Introduction of Entrepreneurship Development course, covering aspects relating to all facets of business, right from the idea to its implementation.
d) Formation of incubation centres to assist learners in implementing their business ideas, obtaining project approvals, obtaining seed money, and preparing the final report.

e) Quality teaching which is reflected in pedagogy, classroom delivery, hands-on training, innovative ways of teaching, and experiential learning experience for learners.
f) Greater autonomy to the universities on matters of curriculum, pedagogy, evaluation, and assessment.
g) Offering financial assistance to underprivileged sections of the society so as to offer equitable learning opportunities to all and encouraging students to avail the benefits of online/Swayam Massive Open Online Course (MOOC) courses.
h) Integration of technology in education to enhance learning experience and access to all levels of learners.

The NEP focuses on skilling the country by ensuring a comprehensive, holistic approach towards ensuring entrepreneurial revolution. Quality education (SDG 4) adopted by the United Nations can be easily achieved if the entire education system is transformed and that requires the active participation and support from all stakeholders.

Conclusion

It has been seen over decades that universities and the education sector get evidently impacted by changes in the external factor in an economy. It could be at the micro level – related to the same industry or geographical location or at the macro level – situations like COVID-19 pandemic. The resilience and the entrepreneurial mindset act as a defensive strategy to respond to the change in the external environmental turbulence. Such universities are characterized by autonomy, risk taker, change acceptor, differentiator, proactive, inclined towards entrepreneurship, real-time research oriented, interdisciplinary or multidisciplinary exposure to learners and course facilitators, socially oriented and strong leadership as a culture. All these characteristics act as a source of defence for the external environmental turbulence and crisis. The support of new education policy towards the multidisciplinary approach and the entrepreneurial mindset opens the scope of private universities to look ahead for entrepreneurial mindset.

References

Anderson, L., Hibbert, P., Mason, K., & Rivers, C. (2018). Management education in turbulent times. *Journal of Management Education, 42*(4), 423–440.
Aronowitz, S., & Giroux, H. A. (2000, December). The corporate university and the politics of education. In *The educational forum* (Vol. 64, No. 4, pp. 332–339). Taylor & Francis Group.
Audretsch, D. B. (2007). *The entrepreneurial society*. Oxford University Press.
Awad, I. M., & Salaimeh, M. K. (2023). Towards an entrepreneurial university model: Evidence from the Palestine Polytechnic University. *Journal of Innovation and Entrepreneurship, 12*(1), 9.
Baporikar, N. (2022). Entrepreneurial university challenges and critical success factors to thrive. *International Journal of Applied Management Theory and Research (IJAMTR), 4*(1), 1–15.

Bortoló, G. M., Valdés, J. Á., & Nicolas-Sans, R. (2023). Sustainable, technological, and innovative challenges post Covid-19 in health, economy, and education sectors. *Technological Forecasting and Social Change, 190*, 122424.

Brennan, J. A., & Stern, E. K. (2017). Leading a campus through crisis: The role of college and university presidents. *Journal of Education Advancement & Marketing, 2*(2), 120–134.

Bross, L., Wienand, I., & Krause, S. (2020). Batten down the hatches – Assessing the status of emergency preparedness planning in the German water supply sector with statistical and expert-based weighting. *Sustainability, 12*(17), 7177.

Cai, P., Ye, P. Z., Dai, R. F., Hambly, B. D., & Tao, K. (2023). The outcomes of lockdown in the higher education sector during the COVID-19 pandemic. *PloS One, 18*(4), e0282907.

Clark, B. (1998). *Creating entrepreneurial universities: Organizational pathways of transformation*. Emerald Group Publishing Limited.

Cunningham, J. A. (2022). COVID-19: Entrepreneurial universities and academic entrepreneurship. In D. B. Audretsch & I. A. M. Kunadt (Eds.), *The COVID-19 crisis and entrepreneurship. International studies in entrepreneurship* (Vol. 54). Springer.

Deem, R. (2001). Globalisation, new managerialism, academic capitalism and entrepreneurialism in universities: Is the local dimension still important? *Comparative Education, 7*–20.

Dill, D. D. (1995). University-industry entrepreneurship: The organization and management of American university technology transfer units. *Higher Education, 29*(4), 369–384.

Etzkowitz, H. (2004). The evolution of the entrepreneurial university. *International Journal of Technology and Globalisation, 1*(1), 64–77.

Etzkowitz, H., & Leydesdorff, L. (1998). A triple helix of university – Industry – Government relations: Introduction. *Industry and Higher Education, 12*(4), 197–201.

Frigotto, M. L., Young, M., & Pinheiro, R. (2022). Resilience in organizations and societies: The state of the art and three organizing principles for moving forward. *Towards resilient organizations and societies: A cross-sectoral and multi-disciplinary perspective, 3*–40.

Gibbs, G. (2013). Reflections on the changing nature of educational development. *International Journal for Academic Development, 18*(1), 4–14.

Guerrero, M., Urbano, D., & Kirby, D. (2006). A literature review on entrepreneurial universities: An institutional approach. *Working Paper Series*, 06/8. Business Economics Department. Autonomous University of Barcelona.

Guenther, J., & Wagner, K. (2008). Getting out of the ivory tower – New perspectives on the entrepreneurial university. *European Journal of International Management, 2*(4), 400–417.

Guerrero, M., & Urbano, D. (2012). The development of an entrepreneurial university. *The Journal of Technology Transfer, 37*, 43–74.

Gulbrandsen, M., & Slipersæter, S. (2007). The third mission and the entrepreneurial university model. In A. Bonacorssi & C. Daraio (Eds.), *Universities and strategic knowledge creation – Specialization and performance in Europe* (p. 112). MPG Book Limited.

Hannon, P. D. (2013). Why is the entrepreneurial university important? *Journal of Innovation Management, 1*(2), 10–17.

Hussain, S. B. (2014). Crisis communication at higher education institutions in South Africa: A public relations perspective. *Journal of Economics and Behavioral Studies, 6*(2), 144–151.

Karlsson, P. S., & Offord, M. (2023). Higher education during crisis: A case study on organic resilience. *Continuity & Resilience Review, 5*(2), 185–197.

Kawamorita, H., Salamzadeh, A., Demiryurek, K., & Ghajarzadeh, M. (2020). Entrepreneurial universities in times of crisis: Case of Covid-19 pandemic. *Journal of Entrepreneurship, Business and Economics, 8*(1), 77–88.

Khoshhall, A., Yaghoubi, N. M., & Salarzehi, H. (2024). Designing an entrepreneurial university model in higher education in South Khorasan province. *International Journal of Nonlinear Analysis and Applications, 15*(6), 187–200.

Kirby, D. A., Guerrero, M., & Urbano, D. (2011). Making universities more entrepreneurial: Development of a model. *Canadian Journal of Administrative Sciences/Revue Canadienne des Sciences de l'Administration, 28*(3), 302–316.

Koronis, E., & Ponis, S. (2018). A strategic approach to crisis management and organizational resilience. *Journal of Business Strategy, 39*(1), 32–42.

Kotler, P., & Fox, K. (1995). Strategic marketing for educational institutions. Prentice-Hall.

Krishnamurthy, S. (2020). The future of business education: A commentary in the shadow of the Covid-19 pandemic. *Journal of Business Research, 117*, 1–5.

Lott, M. K. (2012). *Crisis management plans in higher education: Commonalities, attributes, and perceived effectiveness.* Gallaudet University.

Miller, K., McAdam, R., & McAdam, M. (2018). A systematic literature review of university technology transfer from a quadruple helix perspective: Toward a research agenda. *R&D Management, 48*(1), 7–24.

Mykhailova, Y., Savina, N., & & Tymoschuk, I. (2023). The management strategy in the educational institution during the crisis caused by COVID-19 pandemic. In *CTE workshop proceedings* (pp. 139–152).

Nayak, A., Dubey, A., & Pandey, M. (2023). Work from home issues due to COVID-19 lockdown in Indian higher education sector and its impact on employee productivity. *Information Technology & People, 36*(5), 1939–1959.

Oleksiyenko, A., Mendoza, P., Riaño, F. E., Dwivedi, O. P., Kabir, A. H., & Shchepetylnykova, I. (2023). Global crisis management and higher education: Agency and coupling in the context of wicked COVID-19 problems. *Higher Education Quarterly, 77*(2), 356–374.

Peterka, S. O., & Salihovic, V. (2012). What is entrepreneurial university and why we need it. *Economy of Eastern Croatia: Yesterday, Today, Tomorrow, 1*(1), 98–107.

Philpott, K., Dooley, L., O'Reilly, C., & Lupton, G. (2011). The entrepreneurial university: Examining the underlying academic tensions. *Technovation, 31*(4), 161–170.

Pinheiro, R., Frigotto, M., & Young, M. (Eds.) (2022). *Towards resilient organizations and societies.* Public Sector Organizations.

Prywes, D. I., & Sobel, S. (2015). Planning for university crisis management: The seven-step approach. *Planning for Higher Education, 44*(1), 20.

Röpke, R. (2000). The entrepreneurial university: Innovation, academic knowledge creation and regional development in a globalized economy. In *Proceedings of the 2014 IEEE ICMIT,* Germany.

Rubens, A., Spigarelli, F., Cavicchi, A., & Rinaldi, C. (2017). Universities' third mission and the entrepreneurial university and the challenges they bring to higher education institutions. *Journal of Enterprising Communities: People and Places in the Global Economy, 11*(03), 354–372.

Salarnzadehl, A., Salarnzadeh, Y., & Daraei, M. R. (2011). Toward a Systematic Framework for an entrepreneurial university: A study in Iranian context with an IPOO model. *Global Business and Management Research: An International Journal, 3*(1), 30–37.

Schulte, P. (2004). The entrepreneurial university: A strategy for institutional development. *Higher Education in Europe, 29*(2), 187–191.

Seniuk, Y. V. (2018). Entrepreneurial university as innovation hub in transitional economy: New digital platform for SME globalization. In *16th IEEE international conference on emerging eLearning technologies and application* (pp. 489–498), Slovakia.

Slaughter, S., & Leslie, L. (1997). *Academic capitalism: Politics, policies, and the entrepreneurial university.* Johns Hopkins University Press.

Sutcliffe, K. M., & Vogus, T. J. (2003). Organizing for resilience. In K. S. Cameron, J. E. Dutton, & R. E. Quinn (Eds.), *Positive organizational scholarship: Foundations of a new discipline.* Berrett-Koehler Publishers.

Thomas, H., Abouzeedan, A., & Klofsten, M. (2011). Entrepreneurial resilience. *Annals of Innovation & Entrepreneurship, 2*(1), 7986.

Van Ginkel, H. (2002). Academic freedom and social responsibility – The role of university organisations. *Higher Education Policy, 15*(4), 347–351.

Van Vught, F. (1999). Innovative universities. *Tertiary Education and Management, 5*, 347–355.

Chapter 6

Higher Education in Times of Crisis: Shifting Towards Better Inclusion of Students with Disabilities

Soad Louissi and Michelle Mielly

Grenoble Ecole de Management, France

Abstract

The COVID-19 pandemic led to a tumultuous, emergent and dynamic *new normal* across all facets of society as strikingly illustrated in the field of education, with school closures affecting 94% of the global student population. Higher education institutions (HEIs), confronted with growing fears of long-term effects on academic outcomes and enrolment statistics, were compelled to reckon directly with the vast inequalities revealed through remote instruction. With the classroom's intrusion into the private domain, the most vulnerable learners, specifically students with disabilities (SWDs) often avoided disclosing their disability due to fear of stigma, leading to fewer receiving the accommodations necessary for optimal outcomes. In response, many HEIs were obliged to swiftly move towards greater transparency, engagement, and proximity with their disabled student constituencies. The case of a French Business school presented in this chapter reveals that such a shift eventually resulted in increased levels of disclosure of the SWD population. We review the institutional response to student inequalities in the post-COVID return to campus and relate it to theories of organizational diversity and disability inclusion to better understand how, despite contradictory tensions, institutional shifts during crises can ultimately lead to better disclosure and inclusion outcomes for SWDs.

Keywords: Organizational shifts; students with disabilities; HEIs in crisis; inclusion; disability disclosure

Introduction

The global COVID-19 pandemic outbreak called for urgent and immediate action to survive the crisis and eventually bounce back. Government lockdowns and public health authorities forced all working communities to identify and implement stay-at-home solutions overnight, and higher education institutions (HEIs) were no exception.

HEIs traditionally rely on in-person interaction, key to the overall student learning journey (Camilleri, 2021; Clemes et al., 2008; Quinn et al., 2009; Solomon et al., 1985). The pandemic propelled educators into online teaching scenarios with little space or time to reflect on optimal adaptation strategies. Social distancing and lockdown '... heightened the need for online learning' and presented a unique opportunity to 'create a flexible, equitable and inclusive system of learning' (UNESCO, 2022, p. 8). As we collectively witnessed, the forced study-from-home lockdown exposed the vulnerabilities of the most precarious, including students with disabilities (SWDs). Yet interestingly, this situation simultaneously compelled greater transparency and a crucial moment of institutional, social, and cultural reckoning.

HEIs are traditionally on the committed end of the inclusion spectrum and make significant efforts to connect with their diverse constituents to provide the conditions necessary for all to succeed (EU, 2017). This, however, requires identifying students with specific learning needs and relying on voluntary self-disclosure. In 2016, only 37% of SWDs in HEIs disclosed their disabilities (NCES, 2016). Fast-forward to the 2020–2021 academic period, where institutions saw a 14% spike in the number of disability disclosures (AdvanceHE Report, 2022; AHEAD Report, 2022). This can be attributed to a variety of factors, including heightened awareness and decreased stigmatization of disability.

The pandemic forced HEIs globally to examine the integration and inclusion of their vulnerable populations and incited a fresh examination of their practices and policies. Some emergent inclusion strategies allowed for better student proximity, which in turn encouraged the trust levels required for disability disclosure, and this ultimately served to improve post-crisis well-being. The physical classroom emerged for many educators as the 'great equalizer' in reflecting upon the many ways that the virtual classroom had unwittingly exposed myriad hidden inequalities. All of this enabled a comeback for HEIs in the form of novel opportunities to better accommodate students with specific needs (Tilak & Kumar, 2022).

This chapter therefore examines disability inclusion in the pandemic's aftermath at a HEI, exploring policy responses and how these encouraged higher rates of disability disclosure. It is organized into the following thematic sections:

- Diversity, Inclusion, and Disability
- Higher Education and Disability Inclusion
- National Policy and Disability Inclusion in France: An Illustrative Case
    - Disability and Higher Education in France
    - The Case of *Grande Ecole*
    - The Shift
    - Lessons Learned

Diversity, Inclusion, and Disability

Intensified internationalization and globalization have generated tremendous growth in organizational diversity, obliging organizations to reflect on management practices to accompany such trends in the global labour market. Diversity management policies have had to keep up with shifting workforce demographics, leading to new regulatory and HRM realities, in particular, a sharpened focus on inclusion policy. In what they refer to as *the tragedy of the uncommons,* Jonsen et al. (2013) suggest that more organizational resources should be channelled towards diversity management which would sharpen the focus on the collective good instead of individual goals and achievements.

Organizations are increasingly encouraged to create an attractive and inclusive workplace setting for a diversifying workforce and the value it brings. Inclusive leadership and practices have been shown to bear positively on employee well-being, job satisfaction, and job performance to name a few (Shore et al., 2011). Whereas disability inclusion has been broadly treated in the fields of psychology, behavioural science, law, occupational health, and social work, the diversity, equity and inclusion (DEI) scholarship in management and organization studies (MOS) has traditionally examined issues of gender, class, or racial justice with less focus on disability. While much of the research on diversity is relatively recent, gender and racio-ethnic approaches have historically provided the privileged lens of analysis for studying inequalities in organizations (Amis, 2018; Zanoni et al., 2010). Kudlick (2003) suggests that research on gender, race, and sexuality can provide valuable tools for exploring disabilities, often excluded from what she refers to as an *anti-oppression analysis.* This points to the relevance of an intersectional approach (Crenshaw, 1991) to better interrogate how various forms of identity intersect to oppress *or* privilege individuals and may explain how it has increasingly become a preferred means for MOS scholars to avoid excessive focus on a single strand of diversity (Özbilgin et al., 2011).

Deconstructing Disability Categories and Ableism. The predominant view on disability has shifted from a *medical pathology* orientation to a *social* one, implying that better inclusion can emerge when disability is considered as a *social category* rather than a medical condition; i.e., as an illness (Sloan et al., 2018). Nevertheless, disability cannot be understood through the sole lens of *social category* because it requires considering the *nature* of the person's impairment and often necessitates accommodations that enable better occupational adaptation. Unlike impairment, which constitutes a material medical condition, disability can be perceived as a *social construct* emanating from environments created for able-bodied people (i.e., *ableist* worldviews). From this perspective, it becomes the responsibility of society and organizations to make inclusion occur by removing exclusionary barriers.

Due to its disassociation from other social categories such as race, gender, age, or religion, continued discrimination against people with disabilities is perpetuated and, in some cases, expected, since 'people are sorted by ability' and,

> [...] Indeed, in job applications and promotions, where discrimination by age, sex, race or religion is prohibited, it is the task of the interview panel to discriminate between individuals exclusively by ability – just as long as they don't make inferences from gender or skin color, etc. (Wilkinson & Pickett, 2010, p. 43)

Given that an estimated 16% of the world's population – or one in every six of us – experience significant disability (World Health Organization (WHO), 2023), educators preparing students for the job market cannot remain ignorant of their own *ableist blindspots*. Understanding the exclusionary mechanisms arising from the unfair conditions faced by individuals with disabilities, whether stigma, discrimination, or lower economic prospects (WHO, 2023) can push all HEI stakeholders to shift their discourse, practices, and SWD outcomes.

The diversity literature clearly indicates that ableist discourses in organizations do not stem from a macro-level perspective but are produced from within the organization by singling out specific socio-demographic profiles and associating them with certain skills. The able-bodied/disabled binary is '… deployed in distinct ways to regulate disabled workers' identity, and by so doing sustain specific understandings of the ideal worker' (Jammaers & Zanoni, 2021, p. 443). Taking it a step further, recent calls have shifted towards *able-bodied allyship* which can serve to 'co-produce disability knowledge in the field of MOS', which is currently 'dominated by (assumptions of) able-bodiedness' (Jammaers & Ybema, 2023, p. 787).

Higher Education and Disability Inclusion

Higher education in the Global North had already experienced a general decline in enrolment numbers due to the global financial crisis, with the pandemic further threatening HEIs' viability (HESA, 2022). The necessity to increase student enrolment has propelled institutional shifts in policies and practices to ensure their survival. Schools must integrate inclusive educational practices into their management systems, which should lead to greater social cohesion and the ability to provide creative and original research and pedagogy for a broader range of students and academics (League of European Research Universities, 2019).

The general move to social responsibility and greater inclusion has been broadly observed across HEIs. This could be partly thanks to the adoption of Sustainable Development Goals (SDGs) promoting *inclusive education,* defined by UNICEF as '… an education system that includes all students, and welcomes and supports them to learn, whoever they are and whatever their abilities or requirements' (UNICEF, 2023).

With the growing number of SWDs entering universities (Pumfrey, 2008), inclusion has become a red-hot priority. In some schools, professors receive lists including personalized details for each student's accommodation needs. Staff and faculty workshops on inclusive practices and disability awareness have proliferated. Yet a variety of disability inclusion-related challenges have simultaneously surfaced. The first is that educators are often reluctant to overtly guide or accommodate SWDs in the classroom, citing a lack of knowledge, training, or time for individualized student support. The second issue faced is student concealment of disability, often due to fear of stigma, compounding problems of academic performance and general well-being.

The COVID-19 crisis yielded complex effects on SWDs and their willingness to disclose special learning needs. The overnight shift to remote teaching afforded more privacy and opportunity to self-accommodate for SWDs while paradoxically isolating them even further (Lederman, 2020). Campus support services for learning and crisis management were made more widely available during and after the pandemic through student accessibility services (Mullins & Mitchell, 2021). While the impact has varied widely based on individual circumstances and the measures taken by the institutions, a number of factors influence how the pandemic might have encouraged or discouraged SWDs from disclosing their special learning needs.

Among them, we have identified the following encouraging factors:

1. *Transition to Online Learning*: As many educational institutions shifted to remote or hybrid learning models, SWDs faced new challenges. This shift prompted some students to disclose their needs in order to receive appropriate accommodations for online learning environments, and today, more SWDs are enrolled in higher education than ever before (Grimes, 2020).
2. *Increased Flexibility*: The pandemic forced educators and institutions to become more flexible in their teaching approaches. This might have created a more inclusive environment that encouraged SWDs to come forward and request necessary support (UNESCO, 2021).
3. *Changes in Support Systems*: SWDs often rely on various support systems, such as in-person aides, therapists, or specialized equipment. The disruption caused by the pandemic might have made these support systems less accessible, prompting some students to disclose their needs to ensure they could continue learning effectively (Mullins & Mitchell, 2021).
4. *Health-Related Concerns*: Students with certain disabilities might have been at a higher risk of severe illness from COVID-19. This concern could have motivated them to disclose their condition in order to access necessary accommodations or safety measures (OECD, 2020).
5. *Advocacy and Awareness*: The pandemic shed light on the importance of inclusion and equal access to education. This increased awareness might have encouraged students to speak up about their disabilities, hoping to contribute to a more accessible education system (French Ministry of Education, 2018).

Among the disclosure-discouraging factors, we have identified, for example:

1. *Barriers to Disclosure*: The pandemic also brought about economic challenges and emotional stress for many families. Some students most likely chose not to disclose their disabilities due to concerns of being a family burden or adding extra pressures during an already trying time. In addition, decision-making was greatly impaired during the pandemic due to stress, which disproportionately impacted communities of colour and other vulnerable groups (APA Monitor on Psychology, 2022).
2. *Lack of Connection*: Remote learning could lead to a sense of isolation, making it more difficult for students to connect with teachers or peers who might have otherwise encouraged them to disclose their needs (Hollister et al., 2022).
3. *Privacy Concerns*: The online learning environment also raised concerns about privacy and the security of personal information. Some students might have been hesitant to disclose their disabilities due to worries about how their private information would be handled in an online context (Jiang et al., 2022).

In essence, the impact of the COVID-19 pandemic on SWD willingness to disclose special learning needs is nuanced and multifaceted. It has become increasingly crucial to recognize that while some students might have felt more encouraged to disclose their needs due to the changing educational landscape, others might have faced new barriers that made disclosure more challenging. As we move forward, it will be increasingly essential for HEIs to remain flexible, supportive, and inclusive.

National Policy and Disability Inclusion in France: An Illustrative Case

In February 2005, French law 2005-102 was introduced to guarantee the rights of citizens with disabilities. Disabled individuals were henceforth expected to participate in society as any other citizen, and inclusion was deemed not contingent on the nature of their disability (French Ministry of Labour, 2023). In September 2018, the French government included Article L5213-6-1 in national labour law, stipulating that every organization with more than 250 employees must appoint a disability officer in charge of supporting disabled staff members in their occupational lives (French Ministry of Labour, 2020). As outlined in the new French quality control label *Qualiopi*, all educational institutions are required to complete compulsory training certification, to appoint a disability officer, and to comply with accessibility (French Ministry of Labour, 2020).

In September 2018, the French government included Article *L5213-6-1* in national labour law, stipulating that every organization with more than 250 employees must appoint a disability officer in charge of supporting disabled staff members in their occupational lives (French Ministry of Labour). As outlined in the new French quality control label *Qualiopi,* all educational institutions are required to complete compulsory training certification, to appoint a disability officer, and to comply with accessibility and accommodations criteria for their students (French Ministry of Labour).

Disability and Higher Education in France

In 2020, 87.7% of students with recognized disabilities were granted the right to a *personalized support plan* summarizing the accommodations available during their studies, including among others, human or technical assistance and pedagogical adjustments; 95.3% of students with recognized disabilities benefit from special accommodation for exams (Conférence des Grandes Ecoles, 2019).

The Case of Grande Ecole

A series of semi-directive interviews and empirical observations conducted in 2022 and 2023 at *Grande Ecole* revealed a long-standing history of organizational interest in disability inclusion for students among faculty and staff. From 2005 onwards, following the passage of the aforementioned national legislation, a variety of developments were implemented in the school, including a dedicated disability team and disability funding from organizations seeking to recruit qualified disabled students in compliance with the new labour laws. Despite this, during the pre-COVID period, the school experienced below-national-average enrolment rates for SWDs and yet surprisingly a rapid increase in the SWD disclosures occurred in the post-COVID period. Interestingly, in its efforts to increase student engagement and attendance, both negatively impacted by the successive lockdowns and remote learning environment, the institution enacted a much more stringent in-person attendance policy beginning in the Fall of 2022. Simultaneously, the newly appointed disability officer updated and modified the announcement sent out to students each Fall to identify those with special needs. Both of these efforts, intentionally or not, led to almost doubling the number of students disclosing their disability compared to previous years.

Grande Ecole has campuses in two cities with disability accessibility integrated in the buildings' architecture, excepting a few older classrooms. The disability team ensures that SWDs are aware of their accommodation options and resources available. The pedagogical development team at *Grande Ecole* began in this same period to offer a range of workshops to train professors and staff on disability concerns (e.g., how to create inclusive pedagogical material). Although 250 faculty members are employed at the institution, training session organizers cite frustratingly low attendance numbers and are often forced to cancel events.

In addition, a Sustainability Committee at the institution has been developed to cover four specific axes of institutional development including

1. Climate Strategy
2. Sustainable Purchasing and Responsible Consuming
3. Diversity and Zero Inequalities
4. Sustainable and Inclusive Internationalization

The disability officer is an active member of the committee and contributes to the work and research with the collective. They officially meet three times a year to discuss progress made as well as to define objectives for future initiatives. The institution's diversity and inclusion team advocates for various forms of diversity, including disability, and has developed a set of documents detailing how to manage official instances of student disability disclosure, with specifics on the requirements for programme coordinators, managers, and teachers. In addition, *Grande Ecole* has negotiated official partnerships and exchanges with 51 other HEIs across 22 countries for study abroad opportunities. In order to better advise SWDs in their choices of foreign programmes of study, the disability officer has published an extensive 68-page document outlining partner schools and how each specifically organizes accommodations by disability type. The excerpt in Fig. 6.1 provides two examples from this document.

In addition to the above initiatives, *Grande Ecole* currently partners with 21 local and national companies and associations who participate in a special programme enabling student access to a special fund covering disability-related costs incurred during their educational lifecycle. The disability officer also participates in and hosts a wide range of events and activities to raise awareness on disability inclusion and to assist students in finding internship and job opportunities.

Country: Canada
Host Institution: ▮▮▮▮▮
Existing Disability and Wellbeing service: Yes
Contacts: Student Services Support for disabled students ▮▮▮▮▮

Fields of intervention: One-to-one Disability Need Assessments, Implementation of the services/accommodations needed, Access to psychological support, Pedagogical counselling units offered by teachers and students, Career counselling

Services and accommodation available at the Host Institution:

Wheelchair	
Visibly Impaired	
Hearing Impaired	
Dyslexia/Dyscalculia	Depending on the student's 25%, 33% or exceptionally 50% extra time. A student may be in a smaller group depending on their assessed needs.
Psychological disabilities (for example: Autism, AD(H)D etc.)	Depending on the student's needs, 25%, 33% or exceptionally 50% extra time. A student may be in a smaller group depending on the assessment of his or her needs. They may also be on their own. Permission to go out unaccompanied without recovery lost time. Food or medication may be authorized.
Other services/ accommodations provided	– help to succeed – psychological support – follow-up on the implementation of accommodations – special accommodations can be made to meet specific needs, – referral of students to different services depending on their needs (help center in math, French, financial aid, orientation…)

Partner's website link: https://www.▮▮▮▮▮

Country: Argentina
Host Institution: ▮▮▮▮▮
Existing Disability and Wellbeing service: No

Services and accommodation available at the Host Institution:

Wheelchair	Only classrooms in the new building are wheelchair accessible. Public buses are wheelchair friendly; not all subway stations provide access for wheelchairs.

Visibly Impaired	There are no policies in place for visually impaired students.
Hearing Impaired	There are no policies in place for hearing impaired students.
Dyslexia/Dyscalculia	There are no policies in place for dyslexia or dyscalculia.
Psychological disabilities (for example: Autism, AD(H)D etc.)	There are no policies in place for students with psychological disabilities.
Other services/ accommodations provided	

Fig. 6.1. Internal Document. 'Inclusion and Diversity: Host Institutions Services and Accommodations' (Translated from French for this Publication).

As a key 'externally-focused' aspect of the school's inclusion policy, this work is financially significant, as it enables partner companies and organizations to earmark funds to cover both accommodation costs for the students while in a course of study and to ensure their possibility of recruiting them postgraduation. This enables the organizations to simultaneously comply with the legal requirements for disabled employee recruitment while suggesting their commitment to corporate social responsibility (CSR) initiatives, with special attention to the 'S' for social responsibility covering disability inclusion.

The disability officer recently led a group of students to collaborate on an internal communication and advocacy project where they designed and produced posters to be displayed across the school. In all, nine different thematic posters were created, ranging from cancer to autism to invisible impairments and physical disability. Fig. 6.2 depicts excerpts of three such posters, abridged for purposes of anonymity.

Prior to the 2018 changes in French legal requirements for disability inclusion, *Grande Ecole* had already initiated a special track for both SWDs and financially disadvantaged students to facilitate their admission and integration. An optional certificate course on disability inclusion was created in 2014 and was made available to all. Since its debut, 351 students (and counting) have successfully completed the course. In recent years, many new initiatives were implemented including a programme focused on Data Science tailored to neurodiverse students. See Fig. 6.3 for a timeline reconstructed with the assistance of key informants.

The Shift

The disability inclusion officer is a key informant-participant in our empirical study. In the tradition of researcher reflexivity in interactions with human subjects, our work with her has led to concrete outcomes: after one of our discussions

Fig. 6.2. Example Posters Created by Students to Spread Awareness on Disability.

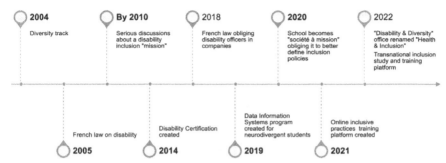

Fig. 6.3. Timeline of Institution's Diversity and Inclusion Developments.

on how language leads to the social construction of disability, she decided to change the wording of her annual introductory communication with students in the Fall. Specifically, her original emails sent out in the 2021–2022 school year advised SWDs to contact the 'Disability and Diversity Office' if a student presented a 'disability'. The 2022–2023 campaign shifted the language euphemistically, inciting students with 'specific needs' to contact the office with *no mention of disability*, and changed its name from the 'Disability and Diversity Office' to the new 'Health and Inclusion Office'.

This information was prominently displayed on digital screens in the halls all throughout the month of September 2022, highlighting examples of specific learning needs, which could be signalled to the office (dyslexia, attention-deficit hyperactivity disorder (ADHD), depression, and more). This new communicative enactment appears to have shifted towards 'solution-centricity' to remove the stigma associated with the term 'disability'. Ultimately, this helped students better identify with the communication – and the subsequent actions associated with it.

In September 2021, a total of 82 SWDs disclosed their needs to the disability officer to set up the necessary learning accommodations. In September 2022 that number swelled to 140 SWD disclosures. The dramatic increase has a number of potential explanations, but our analysis identified three triggering factors that led to this trend.

1. First, the increase can be partially attributed to the aforementioned *modified communication strategy* adopted by the disability team, heightening student identification with 'specific needs' instead of 'disability'.
2. Second, the implementation of *more stringent attendance rules* obliging students to justify any unexcused absences (or risk failing the course) held serendipitous yet unintended consequences. Those with undisclosed disabilities found themselves much more compelled than before to officially disclose their disability in order to justify any disability-related absences or late arrivals.
3. Lastly, the corporate partnerships developed with 21 different organizations provided essential funding to cover disability-related accommodation costs and held out the attractive offer of potential future employment.

Lessons Learned

Like many HEIs in France and elsewhere, legal compliance has provided a key driving factor for disability inclusion policy and awareness. Despite the presence in most HEIs of highly dedicated teams centred on improving disability inclusion, it seems that the stick prevails over the carrot when it comes to implementing real institutional change towards disabled student constituencies. The COVID crisis revealed not only the vast inequities and precariousness among students but also the extent to which many had been concealing their disability. The various incentives ushered in through new policy in the post-COVID period – whether serendipitous or causal – increased the disclosure rates and now begs the question of what lessons can be gleaned.

The disability officer at this institution recognized the need to develop a completely new discourse on disability, inclusion, and accommodation. Whether in terms of attendance policy, a shift in disability-relevant terminology, or the potential of job prospects with firms seeking to recruit qualified SWDs, disclosure moved in the desired direction and legitimized the institutional commitment to disability inclusion. Yet greater rates of SWD disclosure bring new costs, intensifying faculty and staff workloads and requiring individualized learning approaches. Faculty will require more formal and deliberate disability inclusion onboarding, for example, pedagogical training, potential ethics training, and a personal commitment to making their classroom as welcoming and inclusive as possible.

HEIs worldwide have had to contend with radical changes in pedagogy and technology adoption while being thrust into uncharted ethical considerations of student well-being. In the aftermath, they found themselves faced with the new challenges or lower enrolment, lackadaisical student engagement and low attendance alongside a widespread crisis in mental health and overall decreases in student well-being. The drop in enrolment pushed them to attract and include a broader array of students, many requiring customized tailoring for their specific needs.

These multifaceted challenges generated new forms of institutional vigilance which should be maintained post-crisis to not give way to complacency when it comes to disability inclusion policy. Most faculty and staff could benefit from relevant training, first of all. HEI disability officers should experiment in a greater variety of creative approaches to continue to innovate their approaches to incentivizing SWDs disclosure and institutional inclusion. Finally, an institutional policy grounded in an *ethics of care*, based on moral education and ethical ideals (Bergman, 2004) with attention to student connection formation and character education (Noddings, 2017) can go a long way in better addressing the myriad causes of student absenteeism, disengagement, mental health struggles, and disability concealment.

Conclusion

COVID-19 impacted the quality of service in HEIs (Camilleri, 2021) and while some believe that it widened the gap of social inequalities (Delès, 2022; Picard et al., 2023), others suggest that it can also serve as a catalyst for organizational change (Alkan et al., 2022). As we have seen, the crisis imposed a new reckoning with disability disclosure in HEIs with residual challenges remaining for improving the overall educational experience of SWDs. Such improvements hold long-term significance for SWD outcomes when it comes to level of educational attainment and professional trajectories. As our case illustrates, the organizational shift required to respond to the health crisis inadvertently and unintentionally created an environment where students felt more at ease to disclose their disabilities and to request the accommodations needed. The French legal and institutional context reveals just how important small policy tweaks can be in setting the stage for better educational and economic prospects among SWDs. The COVID-19 pandemic was the single greatest disruption known to contemporary HEIs, and yet more crises appear on the horizon – whether environmental degradation, shifts towards authoritarian, anti-democratic regimes, or increased social unrest due to police violence, racial injustice, war, or gender-based grievances. HEIs will increasingly find themselves at the crux of new social movements and can fall back on the lasting lessons learned from the pandemic on how a combination of policy tweaks and serendipitous, often unintended consequences helped some navigate their way through the eye of the storm.

References

AdvanceHE Report. (2022). Equality in higher education: Statistical reports. https://www.advance-he.ac.uk/news-and-views/equality-higher-education-statistical-reports-2022

AHEAD Report. (2022). Students with disabilities engaged with support services in higher education in Ireland 2020/21. https://www.ahead.ie/userfiles/files/Students%20with%20Disabilities%20Engaged%20with%20Support%20Services%20in%20Higher%20Education%20in%20Ireland%202020%2021.pdf.

Alkan, D. P., Ozbilgin, M., & Kamasak, R. (2022). Social innovation in managing diversity: COVID 19 as a catalyst for change. *Equality, Diversity and Inclusion: An International Journal*, *41*(5), 709–725.

Amis, J. M., Munir, K. A., Lawrence, T. B., Hirsch, P., & McGahan, A. (2018). Inequality, institutions and organizations, special issue. *Organization Studies*, *39*(9), 1131–1152.

APA Monitor on Psychology. (2022). High stress levels during the pandemic are making even everyday choices difficult to navigate. https://www.apa.org/monitor/2022/06/news-pandemic-stress-decision-making.

Bergman, R. (2004). Caring for the ethical ideal: Nel Noddings on moral education. *Journal of Moral Education*, *33*(2), 149–162.

Camilleri, M. A. (2021). Evaluating service quality and performance of higher education institutions: A systemic review and a post-COVID-19 outlook. *International Journal of Quality and Service Sciences*, *13*(2), 268–281.

Clemes, M. D., Gan, C. E., & Kao. T. H. (2008). University student satisfaction: An empirical analysis. *Journal of Marketing for Higher Education*, *17*(2), 292–325.

Conférence des Grandes Ecoles. (2019). Baromètre handicap 2019. https://www.cge.asso.fr/publications/2020-01-16-barometre-handicap-2019-2/.

Crenshaw, K. (1991). Mapping the margins: Intersectionality, identity politics, and violence against women of color. *Stanford Law Review*, *43*(6), 1241–1299.

Delès, R. (2022). Educational inequalities in France: A survey on parenting practices during the first COVID-19 lockdown. *International Review of Education*, *68*, 539–549.

European Union. (2017). *Communication from the Commission to the European Parliament, the Council, the European Economic and Social Committee and the Committee of the Regions: A renewed EU agenda for higher education.* (COM 52017) 247 Final. European Commission. https://eur-lex.europa.eu/legal-content/EN/TXT/HTML/?uri=CELEX:52017SC0164&from=EN

French Ministry of Education. (2018). International perspectives on inclusive education. https://www.education.gouv.fr/international-perspectives-inclusive-education-9734

French Ministry of Labour. (n.d.). https://travail-emploi.gouv.fr/

Grimes, S. (2020). Student suggestions for improving learning at university for those with learning challenges/disability. In G. Crimmins (Ed.), *Strategies for supporting inclusion and diversity in the academy: Higher education, aspiration and inequality* (pp. 329–352). Springer International Publishing.

HESA. (2022). Falling student enrolment is a key trend in Global North. https://www.universityworldnews.com/post.php?story=20220318140456226

Hollister, B., Nair, P., Hill-Lindsay, S., & Chukoskie, L. (2022). Engagement in online learning: Student attitudes and behavior during COVID-19. *Frontiers in Education*, *7*, 1–16.

Jammaers, E., & Ybema, S. (2023). Oddity as commodity? The body as symbolic resource for other-defying identity work. *Organization Studies*, *44*(5), 785–805.

Jammaers, E., & Zanoni, P. (2021). The identity regulation of disabled employees: Unveiling the 'varieties of ableism' in employers' socio-ideological control. *Organization Studies*, *42*(3), 429–452.

Jiang, X., Goh, T. T., & Liu, M. (2022). On students' willingness to use online learning: A privacy calculus theory approach. *Frontiers in Psychology*, *13*, 1–11.

Jonsen, K., Tatli, A., Ozbilgin, M., & Bell, M. P. (2013). The tragedy of the uncommons: Reframing workforce diversity. *Human Relations*, *66*(2), 271–294.

Kudlick, C. (2003). Disability history: Why we need another 'Other'. *American Historical Review*, *108*(3), 763–793.

League of European Research Universities. (2019). Equality, diversity and inclusion at universities: The power of a systemic approach. https://www.leru.org/files/LERU-EDI-paper_final.pdf

Lederman, D. (2020). How teaching changed in the (forced) shift to remote learning. How professors changed their teaching in this spring's shift to remote learning. https://www.insidehighered.com/digital-learning/article/2020/04/22/how-professors-changed-their-teaching-springs-shift-remote

Mullins, L., & Mitchell, J. (2021). The transition online: A mixed-methods study of the impact of COVID-19 on students with disabilities in higher education. *International Journal of Higher Education*, *11*(2), 13.

Noddings, N. (2017). The search for meaning and connection. *Educational Studies*, *53*(1), 183–190.

NCES. (2016). A *majority of college students with disabilities do not inform school.* New NCES Data Show. https://nces.ed.gov/whatsnew/press_releases/4_26_2022.asp

OECD. (2020). The impact of COVID-19 on Student equity and inclusion: Supporting vulnerable students during school closures and school re-openings. https://www.oecd.org/coronavirus/policy-responses/the-impact-of-covid-19-on-student-equity-and-inclusion-supporting-vulnerable-students-during-school-closures-and-school-re-openings-d593b5c8/

Özbilgin, M. F., Beauregard, T. A., Tatli, A., & Bell, M. P. (2011). Work–Life, diversity and intersectionality: A critical review and research agenda. *International Journal of Management Reviews*, *13*(2), 177–198.

Picard, H., Mielly, M., & Rose, J. (2023). Exploring the intersectional facets of unbounded flexible work: Remote work, home life and tangible inequalities during COVID-19 lockdown. *EGOS 23rd colloquium*, Cagliari, Italy.

Pumfrey, P. K. (2008). Moving towards inclusion? The first-degree results of students with and without disabilities in higher education in the UK: 1998-2005. *European Journal of Special Needs Education, 23*(1), 31–46.

Quinn, A., Lemay, G., Larsen, P., & Johnson, D. M. (2009). Service quality in higher education. *Total Quality Management and Business Excellence, 20*(2), 139–152.

Shore, L. M., Randel, A. E., Chung, B. G., & Dean, M. A. (2011). Inclusion and diversity in work groups: A review and model for future research. *Journal of Management, 37*(4), 1262–1289.

Sloan, L. M., Joyner, M. C., Stakeman, C. J., & Schmitz, C. L. (2018). *Critical multiculturalism and intersectionality in a complex world* (2nd ed.). Oxford University Press.

Solomon, M. R., Surprenant, C., Czepiel, J. A., & Gutman, E. G. (1985). A role theory perspective on dyadic interactions: The service encounter. *Journal of Marketing, 49*(1), 99–111.

Tilak, J. B. G., & Kumar, A. G. (2022). Policy changes in global higher education: What lessons do we learn from the COVID-19 pandemic? *Higher Education Policy, 35*, 610–628.

UNESCO. (2021). *Reimagining our futures together: A new social contract for education*. International Commission on the Futures of Education. https://unesdoc.unesco.org/ark:/48223/pf0000379707.locale=en

UNESCO. (2022). *Understanding the impact of COVID-19 on the education of persons with disabilities: Challenges and opportunities of distance education: Policy brief*. UNESCO Institute for Information Technologies in Education [286]. https://unesdoc.unesco.org/ark:/48223/pf0000379117

UNICEF. (2023). *15 Pacific Island countries join hands to improve inclusive education*. https://www.unicef.org/pacificislands/press-releases/15-pacific-island-countries-join-hands-improve-inclusive-education

World Health Organization (WHO). (2023). Global report on health equity for persons with disabilities https://www.who.int/teams/noncommunicable-diseases/sensory-functions-disability-and-rehabilitation/global-report-on-health-equity-for-persons-with-disabilities

Wilkinson, R. G., & Pickett, K. (2010). *The spirit level. Why equality is better for everyone*. Penguin Books.

Zanoni, P., Janssens, M., Benschop, Y., & Nkomo, S. (2010). Guest editorial: Unpacking diversity, grasping inequality: Rethinking difference through critical perspectives. *Organization, 17*(1), 9–29.

Chapter 7

Education and Resilience in the Entrepreneurial University: An Analysis of Past and Present Practice at Tangent, Trinity's Ideas Workspace

Maeve O'Dwyer[a] and Daniel Rogers[b]

[a]Dublin City University, Ireland
[b]Tangent, Trinity's Ideas Workspace, Ireland

Abstract

As universities globally strive to balance the priorities of teaching and research with the needs of economy and enterprise, it is increasingly important that university-based entrepreneurship programmes foster a culture that is ethically informed and globally aware. Entrepreneurship has become a popular career path for university students, with many universities offering programmes to aid students in realizing their entrepreneurial ambitions. In a truly entrepreneurial university, all staff and students can benefit from developing an entrepreneurial mindset, a way of thinking that emphasizes innovation, creativity, and problem-solving, leading to better flexibility and resilience. This mindset is valuable in times of crisis because it allows us to adapt quickly to changing circumstances, identify new opportunities, and develop innovative solutions to complex problems. This chapter will offer a critical reflection on practice undertaken at Tangent, Trinity's Ideas Workspace, an interdisciplinary unit offering entrepreneurship education at Trinity College Dublin, the University of Dublin, and offer recommendations for practice around the ethics of entrepreneurial education. This chapter will be of interest to educators who want to foster a more globally aware and ethically responsible approach to entrepreneurship education.

Global Higher Education Practices in Times of Crisis:
Questions for Sustainability and Digitalization, 111–125
Copyright © 2025 by Maeve O'Dwyer and Daniel Rogers
Published under exclusive licence by Emerald Publishing Limited
doi:10.1108/978-1-83797-052-020241008

Keywords: Entrepreneurship education; ethics; design thinking; GBL (game-based learning); EntreComp

Introduction

An entrepreneurial mindset is fast becoming an essential attribute for many graduates entering employment. The existing model for financing higher education institutions, which relies mainly on public funding, is increasingly regarded by policymakers and institutional leaders as unsustainable (Gallo, 2014). At Trinity College Dublin, the University of Dublin (Trinity), this governmental support has declined in recent years, putting increasing pressure on alternative sources of revenue.

With increased reliance on philanthropic funding, higher education institutions throughout the world are coming under pressure to align their activities with the needs of the marketplace through internationalization and engagement with private industry. Consequently, the number of graduate entrepreneurship programmes has increased dramatically, and university students are increasingly likely to consider entrepreneurship as a career path, according to the 2019 GUESSS (Global University Entrepreneurial Spirit Students' Survey) National Report Ireland (Enterprise Ireland, 2019). The appeal of entrepreneurship among Irish graduates has shifted away from inheriting family-owned businesses in traditional industries, to an expectation that entrepreneurship will involve the creation of a new or innovative product or service: 'The least popular career option for graduates was business succession (taking over a family or other business). When asked to consider their career five years after university, the most popular career was entrepreneur (33%, $n = 478$)' (Enterprise Ireland, 2019, p. 2).

Although such programmes have been shown to impact the entrepreneurial intention in students (Fayolle et al., 2006), many are largely outcomes focused with an emphasis on starting a venture and raising finance. This approach inevitably excludes certain demographics of students and can underestimate the potential impact on students of early-stage venture failure as part of a lifelong career. There are therefore discrepancies between aims and practices with respect to the development of entrepreneurship programmes in third-level education (Seikkula-Leino et al., 2010). Students who are not in a position to develop a start-up, or to engage in extra-curricular activities such as clubs or societies, have little opportunity to informally develop so-called softer transferable skills such as creative thinking, resilience, global citizenship, working with others, and leadership. Yet these skills are crucial for their adaptation to a constantly changing economic and social environment (World Economic Forum, 2023, p. 42).

This chapter argues that the potential of higher education institutions to adapt and thrive in the face of adversity depends largely on the development of an entrepreneurial mindset within faculty, staff, and students. Challenges such as climate change, economic uncertainties, technological disruptions including artificial intelligence, and unforeseen crises such as the global COVID-19 pandemic, have created additional pressures within the sector. This chapter will explore what it means to have an entrepreneurial mindset and how nurturing this mindset in both staff and students can greatly enhance a university's ability to respond to crises and challenge conventional notions of success in higher education.

The authors will critique current practice at Tangent, Trinity's Ideas Workspace (Tangent), a leader in European university-based entrepreneurship education, to explain how we work to support student learning which builds resilience during global crises, past and present, and take a self-reflective approach to examine how we might better promote ethical entrepreneurship. We will reflect on our approach to embedding the United Nations (UN) Sustainable Development Goals (SDGs) in curricula, and consider whether this is sufficiently impactful for students attending one of Europe's most successful universities for student start-ups (Pitchbook, 2020).

Tangent is an interdisciplinary centre open to all Trinity staff and students as well as the Irish workforce. The centre educates over 1,000 learners annually in creativity, innovation, and entrepreneurship across a variety of domains including healthcare, well-being, climate, and creative and cultural entrepreneurship. Tangent aims to provide a coherent journey for the aspiring student entrepreneur from idea generation through to venture development and works to increase student adaptability and resilience more widely through an entrepreneurial mindset. This chapter will analyse whether the opportunities Tangent provides students to enhance their transferable skills, including during turbulent times, are sufficiently linked to ethical and sustainable innovation. This includes briefly explaining our focus on the SDGs and innovation for good in our educational programmes and the existence of start-ups that have achieved success in our accelerator programmes.

This chapter will also examine the concept of the entrepreneurial university through the lens of entrepreneurial education, exploring its prevalence, importance, current delivery, impact and, finally, interrogating how educators can improve educational initiatives towards ethical and sustainable innovation and entrepreneurship.

University Entrepreneurship Programmes: European Context

Exploring the concept of the entrepreneurial university through the lens of entrepreneurship education allows us to consider the importance of mindset, taking the scope of investigation beyond those students who have confirmed entrepreneurship as their desired career path. Similarly, the full scope of activity at Tangent is focused not solely on specific qualifications or start-ups, but on nurturing the entrepreneurial mindset across the Trinity student body and the Irish workforce. To contextualize this activity, this section will briefly explore the approach to entrepreneurship in higher education across the European Union (EU).

The production of goods and services by socially conscious entrepreneurs has the potential to positively impact the world. The COVID-19 pandemic has heightened global inequalities, particularly in disadvantaged regions. Now more than ever, entrepreneurial universities globally have a responsibility to consider additional measures for preparing future-ready and resilient graduates to face future crises. In its Strategic Plan, Trinity declared, 'we challenge our students to think independently, communicate effectively, act responsibly, and develop continuously, equipping them for lives of active citizenship (Trinity College Dublin, the University of Dublin, 2020, p. 8). In times of crisis, these attributes are even more important, and the entrepreneurial mindset, or transferable skills outlined above, is now under increased focus by the EU and by the world's most highly rated universities.

The EU responded to the needs of a post-COVID-19 pandemic workforce by designating 2023 as the European Year of Skills, to help implement the 2020 EU Skills Agenda and the 2018 Key Competencies for Lifelong Learning. This includes entrepreneurial ability as a symbol of a subset of characteristics and competencies required to survive and thrive in a volatile, uncertain, complex, and ambiguous (VUCA) world. On 18 January 2022, an EU Press Report introducing two new strategies related to higher education stated,

> Today, European society needs the contribution of universities and other higher education institutions more than ever … Universities, and the entire higher education sector, have a unique position at the crossroads of education, research and innovation, in shaping sustainable and resilient economies, and in making the European Union greener, more inclusive and more digital. (European Commission, 2022)

With limited ability to train incoming students in the specific skills they need to succeed in unknown roles and facing unknown crises, the importance of supporting the development of ethically aware, adaptable, and resilient graduates is evident. Entrepreneurial education holds a significant role in the upskilling of all students in the competencies required to succeed. The development of the European Framework in Entrepreneurial Competencies (EntreComp) reveals the importance placed by the EU on developing these skills (Bacigalupo et al., 2016). Entrepreneurial programmes, including at Tangent, now map learning to EntreComp to allow students to realize their learning both in terms of learning outcomes and in relation to their specific progress in key competencies. EntreComp comprises three areas of activity (ideas and opportunities, resources, and into action), subdivided into 15 competencies, each with a description of the level of proficiency from foundational to expert (Bacigalupo et al., 2016, pp. 23–35). With many companies now holding competency-based interviews, EntreComp allows students to understand their personal development in language accessible to them and useful for the world of work.

The inclusion of entrepreneurial ability in Irish policy, including Ireland's National Skills Strategy 2025 (Department of Education and Skills, 2016, pp. 23–24), reveals its increasing prioritization across the Irish higher education sector. Globally, the importance of entrepreneurship education is reflected in best practice. As a quick test, in the Quacquarelli Symonds (QS) World University Rankings 2024, the highest scoring institutions all celebrate and support entrepreneurial ability across staff and students. In the top five universities for 2024, the Martin Trust Center for MIT Entrepreneurship, the Cambridge Entrepreneurship Centre, Oxford University Innovation, the Technology and Entrepreneurship

Centre at Harvard, and the Stanford Entrepreneurship Network all either provide entrepreneurship programmes directly or pull together activity from multiple centres, teams, and faculties across their institution to provide a portfolio of support for entrepreneurs. It is worth noting that sustainability now forms part of the QS ranking criteria (QS, 2024).

Each university likely has their own numerical targets related to entrepreneurial activity, such as commercialization of research, number of spin-outs and student start-ups, or amount of investment achieved. Tangent offers its own student start-up programme, called LaunchBox, which has had notable successes, both in terms of supporting student entrepreneurship, and nurturing the creation of ethical and sustainable enterprises. Established in 2013, LaunchBox is an annual accelerator programme that aims to empower Trinity students to forge their own career paths. Each year, potential businesses pitch to secure a place on the programme, during which teams receive training and mentoring to develop their ideas. Ten student enterprises receive €10,000 in equity-free funding each, an approach which helps break down financial barriers to engaging in the programme during the summer period, when many students might otherwise partake in part-time work. The final pitch involves answering questions from industry-based judges to designate the winning team.

A truly entrepreneurial education does not mean creating financially literate graduates but is about creating critical and creative global citizens. Existing enterprises are slowly being held to account with regard to their sustainability and ethical business practices, with sites like Ethical Consumer (www.ethicalconsumer.org), and start-ups related to the circular economy becoming more popular with consumers. The homepage for the International Sustainability Standards Board (ISSB), part of the Sustainability activity of the International Financial Reporting Standards Foundation (IFRS), launched in 2021 at COP26 in Glasgow, notes, 'Sustainability factors are becoming a mainstream part of investment decision-making. There are increasing calls for companies to provide high-quality, globally comparable information on sustainability-related risks and opportunities, as indicated by feedback from many consultations with market participants' (IFRS, 2023).

It is therefore important for graduates joining the workforce to understand the key concept of sustainability for industry. Some notable successes arising from LaunchBox which contribute to global citizenship include Food Cloud in 2013, which aims to solve supermarket food waste, ReFunk in 2021 which specialises in the circular economy, particularly upcycling of furniture, and Field of Vision in 2021, which offers the visually impaired new ways to follow live sporting events. Regardless of the subsequent success of start-ups, the process of developing from idea to venture offers a transformative learning experience, towards which the approach of awarding equity-free funding is crucial.

This global focus on entrepreneurial ability is not just what the EU needs from its workforce but also what the workforce needs to survive. According to the 2023 World Economic Forum Future Jobs Report, the transferable skills most in demand by employers include creative and analytical thinking (World Economic Forum, 2023, p. 42). Graduates face a competitive job market – according to the

Higher Education Authority Graduate Outcomes Report 2020, 8.1% of graduates in the Republic of Ireland were unemployed nine months after graduation, up from 4.3% in 2018, with arts and humanities and information and communication technologies students most affected (Higher Education Authority, 2020, Section 1). By supporting student learning towards developing an entrepreneurial mindset, regardless of their discipline, students can graduate with an improved ability to articulate their learning and transferable skills.

Practice at Tangent, Trinity's Ideas Workspace: A Reflection

Post-COVID-19 pandemic learning in more sustainable ways of working can be seen across the higher education sector. At Trinity, initiatives to reduce waste in labs, reduce the environmental impact of catering, and support greater biodiversity in green areas have been trialled in the past few years. These initiatives, just some of many, can be considered part of a wider movement required towards a more sustainable approach to academia and higher education in general. Researchers are calling for a post-pandemic window of opportunity to revolutionize practice, 'We are now at a critical point of creative destruction where we can dismantle existing practices and radically reimagine academia to align with our sustainability values'(Wassénius et al., 2023). But is this increased awareness visible in the curriculum? What part might entrepreneurial education, specifically design thinking, play in creating global citizens resilient to change?

Design thinking is a common process in corporate innovation culture as a user-centred approach to problem-solving (Martin, 2009). According to Brown (2009), design principles are no longer applied to just physical products but also to user experience, interactivity, aesthetics, and functionality. As an innovation process, design thinking incorporates the needs of people with what is technologically feasible and what can be translated into value and market opportunity (Brown, 2008). Its origins can be traced as far back as 1987 where it was first introduced by Peter Rowe (1987) to describe methods and approaches used by architects and urban planners. The methodology engages human-centred design for the purposes of innovation. It is sometimes described as an analytic and creative process that engages a person in the opportunity to experiment, create, and prototype models, gather feedback, and design and re-design (Razzouk & Shute, 2012). Traditionally, designers focused solely on product development, considering concepts in isolation and from a particular disciplinary perspective, usually engineering. Design thinking has now become a common process used by educators and industry alike for idea generation and problem-solving within a multidisciplinary context.

Since 2018, Tangent has integrated design thinking, usually towards engaging with the UN SDGs, in its curricula. It then provides a pathway to realize innovations through incubation and accelerator programmes such as LaunchBox. The purpose is to align curricula with global priorities, encourage critical thinking and problem-solving, and promote awareness of the SDGs. This chapter will now interrogate the curriculum design, past and present, of our main offerings, to assess whether they offer students the opportunity to develop the key entrepreneurial skills they need to succeed. It is simplistic to measure in terms of student numbers, but an estimated 600 or more undergraduate (UG) and postgraduate (PG) students annually are encouraged to innovate using the SDGs as inspiration, as part of deliberate curriculum design aiming to introduce students to real-world problems and engage in socially aware ideation.

Tangent offers a five-European Credit Transfer and Accumulation System (ECTS) elective module in design thinking to 100 second- or third-year UG students annually, undertaken as part of their degree, and delivered over one semester. From the early design of this module, ethical entrepreneurship has been built into the content and assessment design, with a key focus on supporting students to innovate against the SDGs. Students form interdisciplinary teams to employ the design thinking framework to solve a real-world problem and apply new learning in entrepreneurship. At the end of the module, students pitch their solutions in a live presentation to judges, including industry-based assessors who can offer real advice on how they might take their business ideas forward. The design of this assessment was previously considered innovative and is still fit for purpose but has the potential for greater impact by introducing an increased requirement for sustainability into the analysis of the feasibility and practicality of the identified solution. This would ensure the assignment better matches current developments in the world of work and might help reduce the number of students prioritizing purely financial measures of success. For example, a checklist for ethical and sustainable entrepreneurship, or a mandatory projection for costings to achieve carbon-neutral activity, could pivot the focus away from the 'billion-dollar market' frequently mentioned by students in their pitches and help them understand the hidden impact of enterprise. By introducing higher scrutiny on the ethics of the idea, the assessment would more closely mirror real-world implementation of enterprise, in a world where industry is being held to sustainability targets and consumers are becoming increasingly aware of the hidden environmental and social costs of product generation.

Tangent also offers a variety of PG qualifications, but of particular note in terms of entrepreneurship education towards developing an entrepreneurial mindset is the Postgraduate Certificate in Innovation and Entrepreneurship. This programme is designed for PhD students, post-doctoral researchers, and early career research staff from all disciplines. The course is at Level 9 on the Irish National Framework of Qualifications and comprises two 10 ECTS modules (Creative Thinking and Innovation Pathways for Researchers) and two 5 ECTS modules (Opportunity Generation and Recognition and Leadership). It is part-funded by the Irish Government via the Human Capital Initiative. The programme begins with students fostering innovation and entrepreneurship skills in multidisciplinary research teams, ideating against the SDGs, and pitching new solutions to global issues. Over the duration of the programme, students begin to apply their learning to their own context and experience the benefits of learning as part of a cohort of researchers from multiple disciplines and career stages. A key element of this programme is assignments designed to ensure that students can tailor their coursework to be practically useful to their own career development, whether that be within academia through commercialization of research or consultancy, in a new role outside of academia or as an entrepreneur. Regardless of their career ambitions, training in key innovation processes such as design thinking can both support their research activity and be used to address societal challenges and develop creativity, enhancing ideation and problem-solving capacities.

There is clear value in the application of the design thinking process in higher education, particularly entrepreneurship education. Giving students a set of skills that might enable them to transfer their knowledge into other domains is of immense importance. Exploring a problem within a multidisciplinary context using design thinking methodology helps in the acquisition of transferable skills such as problem-solving, communication, and teamwork and ultimately the adoption of the entrepreneurial mindset. To help students articulate this development of entrepreneurial ability, both programmes are mapped to EntreComp. A special content area on the virtual learning environment (Blackboard) explains the EntreComp framework, maps their learning to specific competencies, and invites them to partake in an online self-assessment of their ability against key competencies at the start and end of their learning journey at Tangent.

However, the approach of student self-assessment has weaknesses, and it is in applied learning that the students fully realize the potential of their skills. Therefore, we recently sought to design learning activities whereby students not only embrace their learning in design thinking but personally experience the application of a truly entrepreneurial mindset. This required first articulating what is meant by 'mindset'. Colombelli et al. (2022) give tangible meaning to the term 'entrepreneurial mindset'. They propose that at its core it refers to a set of attitudes, behaviours, and qualities that enable individuals and institutions to approach challenges and opportunities in an innovative, proactive, and adaptable way. For the individual, it encompasses a set of skills and traits that are relevant in a variety of situations, including education, career, and personal development. It equips individuals to think creatively, generate novel ideas, and find innovative solutions to problems. Mindset describes the sense of initiative and attitude towards challenges, while entrepreneurship skills could be summarized in creativity, planning, and managing ambiguity. Finally, connectedness to the labour market is how knowledge and skills are integrated in order to acquire funding and realize entrepreneurial ambition. This is evidenced by the appearance in many successful entrepreneurs of traits such as problem-solving, resilience, and the ability to recognize opportunity.

With this in mind, we sought to innovate in the curriculum to enhance student learning and also push the boundaries of entrepreneurship education. Introducing gamified elements to the learning experience can result in increased learner motivation levels and improved knowledge retention (Buckley et al., 2017). Gamification and game-based learning (GBL) has been shown in multiple studies to facilitate development of skills such as problem-solving, critical thinking, social awareness, collaboration, and dealing with failure (James, 2020). GBL allows the educator and student to be fully immersed in a participatory educational experience which has the potential to create a meaningful connection between the curriculum and learner. It allows both educator and student the opportunity to assess the overall impact of their learning, or in this context, the development of the somewhat difficult to measure and ephemeral entrepreneurial mindset as it is applied in practice. GBL is a growing phenomenon and more evidence is required to understand the long-term benefits (de Freitas, 2018). Promising examples of GBL applied to entrepreneurship education include the University of Szeged Implementing Serious Games in Entrepreneurship Education (ISGEE) project, which resulted in an online game called Entrepoly (available at www.isgee.eu) and University College London's SPERO programme which employs roleplay in entrepreneurial education for doctoral students.

Thus, Tangent sought to design entrepreneurship activities for delivery in a game-based, experiential learning environment, to assess the development of entrepreneurship competencies and mindset through an in-person-guided role-play game. For illustration purposes, Table 7.1 is an example of the gameplay overview for a game testing entrepreneurial ability and teamwork, usually applied in the context of an entrepreneurship module, but which can be easily simplified for participants new to entrepreneurial education or for public engagement events. It was developed in 2022 by Dr Maeve O'Dwyer, Programme Manager at Tangent, and Dr Colin Keogh, Senior Innovation Consultant, as a roleplay activity intended to facilitate demonstration of skills acquired through participation on the PGCert Innovation and Entrepreneurship (creativity, communication, leadership, opportunity generation, teamwork, and dealing with ambiguity or failure). Open access resources for the game are available at osf.io/yrkga.

Students were pre-assigned roles such as Chief Executive Officer (CEO), Chief Financial Officer (CFO), intern, etc. which had both straightforward characteristics and hidden attributes. Hidden attributes could be positive, such as financial literacy, or negative, such as the ability to defect to another team with core intellectual property. In addition to the students as the main players, additional roles were created for staff and alumni, to mimic the real-world process of networking and raising capital for a business idea. Investor roles could include CEO, retiree, venture capitalist, altruist, environmentalist, or academic. The addition of elements of luck, such as chance cards designed to create unexpected surprises, added a level of difficulty and fun to the game. The game promotes narrative development, immediate feedback through interaction and pitching, and progress indicators through the accumulation of points or funding. Students react positively to the game and, when participating at the end of a programme, are surprised to find the impact of their learning when applied in practice in a hypothetical test of their entrepreneurial ability.

Gamified and GBL can offer an interactive and experiential learning experience that helps students achieve the proposed learning objectives, apply their skills, and build confidence in communicating with others. For entrepreneurial educators, GBL could incorporate industry leaders, entrepreneurs, academics, and students to play roles and participate and offers the opportunity to re-engage graduates who previously participated as students but who can now play an alternate role. Games can ultimately provide a showcase opportunity where students both apply and articulate the knowledge, skills, and confidence gained during their learning.

Table 7.1. Introduction to Gameplay.

Stage	How to Play
Team formation	Each student arrives playing a pre-assigned role. CEOs put together a team with one of each role. Teams pick a team name and ideate briefly using a challenge based on the UN SDGs
Networking	Newly formed teams make connections – looking for insights, mentors, or prospective investors – at a networking session with alumni and educators. Investors have points or resources to award, and team members may also have secrets to hide
Funding	Students roll the dice for initial funds and are encouraged to return to investors to give their value proposition and story to win further resources. Students are reminded that people invest in people!
Ideation and problem-solving	Students take their investor feedback and resources to polish their ideas. They will need a solid problem statement and business idea/solution to convince
Prepping for the pitch	Each team uses whiteboards or creates props to polish their pitch. Last-minute gambles are possible via chance cards and could take the form of pivots, penalties, or even mergers
Pitches	Each team delivers a three-minute pitch to all game participants, in any format they like, and responds to questions. Following all pitches, the audience votes, and the winning team receives a point bonus
Counting points	All the points awarded during the game are counted. Each team has been accompanied by a staff member during the game who keeps track of player and team points. Alternatively, investors are given physical cards used to represent points or investment
Results	A winning pitch receives a reward. However, chance cards or awkward questions can arise, and hidden attributes can cause last-minute surprises. The final winners may surprise everyone!
Reflection and open discussion	Once the game has finished, take some time to think about the experience and how students will apply the learning going forward. Many students only realize their ability and development of their skills after they finish the game and reflect with their peers

Future-Ready Graduates: Recommendations for Ethical and Globally Aware Entrepreneurship Education

Entrepreneurship education is not only achieved by programmes or workshops focusing solely on entrepreneurship but can be built into any curriculum by considering the most important aspects of the entrepreneurial mindset or, in other words, the most important transferable skills related to agility, problem-solving, and effective communication. This chapter offers a selection of best practice to draw on, from mapping activity to EntreComp to the use of the SDGs to challenge student thinking. It is essential that educators not only look to increase the resilience and creativity of their students, but that they do so with a lens towards ethically and globally aware citizenship to create truly future-ready graduates. Based on the analysis of past and present practice at Tangent, we have devised some recommendations:

- Entrepreneurship education can take many forms and does not need to be labelled 'entrepreneurship', which can be off-putting to students
- Design thinking is a useful framework for students at any level of education or in any discipline
- Designing learning against the key values or competencies you identify for development in your students, or which they self-identify, is useful
- Students benefit from understanding their learning in accessible language or as competencies (e.g., via EntreComp)
- Building in a sustainability lens when choosing your problem or challenge prompts focuses student attention on global issues and supports citizenship
- Building in experiential, gamified, or GBL and roleplay can help develop entrepreneurial abilities beyond traditional 'business topics'
- Solutions to problems or challenges are often assessed for feasibility and innovation, but we suggest adding some additional requirements around ethics and sustainability
- Blended programme design offers the benefits of both in-person experiential learning and the flexibility of online learning.

Since its inception in 2018, all courses at Tangent were designed to be blended, comprising both in-person and online learning. This expertise in online delivery proved critical during the recent COVID-19 pandemic as all programmes had to be moved entirely online in a matter of days. Adapting curricula intended to be delivered in the classroom to an online environment required rapid upskills of delivery personnel and regular communication to students to ensure that technology did not pose a barrier to student learning. The teamwork and adaptability of staff and students alike made this transition relatively seamless.

However, it was not without impact on the student experience-our records show that student attrition across Tangent programmes increased from 5% to 15% in 2020. When surveyed, students cited childcare, family commitments, and illness as key reasons, therefore changes in individual circumstances appeared to be the key cause of attrition. This suggests that, personal circumstances notwithstanding, students were not discouraged by the different and challenging learning experience.

Responses to GBL, even a simplified version trialled with visiting students new to entrepreneurship education, have been overwhelmingly positive, which suggests that game literacy, whether digital or in person, will be of significant use to educators in future. Universities which foster an entrepreneurial mindset among students are more likely to create an environment where students are encouraged to take initiative and pursue innovative projects. This has the potential to lead to greater engagement, motivation, and meaningful learning experiences, as students are empowered to take ownership of their education and drive their own learning paths. This is increasingly evident through the current focus on transferable skills development and microcredentials.

Most pedagogical studies on an entrepreneurial mindset have been conducted in Europe and focus on UG university students (Daspit et al., 2023), but development for PG students is also crucial. The incorporation of experiential learning, interdisciplinary collaborations, and innovation-focused curricula is essential to the development of entrepreneurial characteristics. While celebrating innovation and growth, the necessity for responsible business practices that address income inequalities should be acknowledged.

Teaching staff at Tangent are encouraged to use case studies and examples that are diverse, inclusive, and demonstrate social and commercial value. Facilitating critical discussions that encompass not only financial success but also social impact will lead to greater analysis of the role of entrepreneurship in society and ultimately a more sustainable approach to entrepreneurship. Tangent curricula and assessments encourage students to consider the SDGs and how their innovative solutions or proposed ventures could help solve global challenges or local subsets of global issues like water scarcity. To build on this, we hope to develop more content around the circular economy, understanding the impact of treatment of the workforce, and the environmental impact of the supply chain for products, etc. This also includes positive results such as job creation, value creation, etc. Often students can misunderstand the financial models of non-traditional enterprises such as charities, and it is an area for development in our curricula to help students better understand the financial makeup of how charities and non-profit organizations function.

In order to ensure graduates leave the university with an understanding and appreciation of ethics, it needs to be integrated in the curriculum. All entrepreneurship programmes should promote ethical discussion and highlight successful entrepreneurs who can act as ethical role models. Ideally, all those studying entrepreneurship will develop critical thinking skills that encourage them to analyse ethical implications of different business decisions as well as clarifying alignment with individual and/or organizational values. As a university-based innovation hub, Tangent has a clear mission and value set, among which is a commitment to creating a more sustainable planet and an equitable and inclusive society. Students and staff are made aware of these values when participating or contributing to programmes, but there is further work to do to build them into the curriculum in an engaging and meaningful way.

Ideally, entrepreneurial education would take place not just within centres for innovation and entrepreneurship like Tangent but as a core activity embedded in all programs for students and as part of work-loaded time for staff. Entrepreneurship education is not just about students. Academic faculty who engage in entrepreneurship are likely to be more proactive in seeking out research and funding opportunities with industry and business. This in turn benefits students, who may gain practical experience through placements and access to real-world projects. Industry-academia partnerships can also help universities better prepare graduates for the job market and adapt their curriculum to changing industry trends. However, academic entrepreneurship can be difficult – academic research and publishing in peer-reviewed journals are traditionally prioritized by universities, which can leave limited time for engagement in entrepreneurship, and motivations and incentives for academics as opposed to industry-based researchers can differ (Lacetera, 2009, p. 455).

According to Connell (2019), the current university system is facing various challenges, including rising tuition costs, outdated teaching methods, and a mismatch between academic offerings and real-world needs. One way to address this would be to highlight the societal relevance and impact of many entrepreneurial ventures that began as university-based research projects, to create a culture for more ventures to thrive. Institutional support, resources, and mentorship for academics interested in entrepreneurship is essential to build interest and capability.

Conclusion

Universities and higher education institutions serve several key functions in addition to education. Perhaps most notable is knowledge creation through research and the translation of research into impact. However, universities with a culture of entrepreneurship may be more inclined to embrace innovative approaches to teaching and research. Therefore, they can quickly adapt to changing circumstances, such as shifts in learning technology, modalities, and unexpected crises. University leadership plays a pivotal role in promoting an entrepreneurial mindset within a given institution. Leadership can promote a culture that encourages experimentation and collaboration and fosters an environment conducive to adaptation. When students and staff with this mindset begin to view life challenges as opportunities to learn and evolve, rather than as insurmountable obstacles, the cumulative effect over time can build institutional resilience and agility needed to overcome financial and economic obstacles and disruptions. Such resilience is crucial in times of crisis, as it enables universities to adapt and continue educating students. This was never more evident than during the COVID-19 pandemic when universities globally were forced to move their activity online until it was safe to attend in person.

It is clear that graduates who possess an entrepreneurial mindset and entrepreneurship skills can better contribute to their countries becoming global innovation leaders. Fostering an entrepreneurial mindset in higher education, whereby graduates can be job shapers and job seekers, is crucial to ensuring successful graduate outcomes in an increasingly competitive market. By embracing the entrepreneurial mindset, universities can not only effectively navigate crises but also position themselves as centres of innovation, adaptability, and long-term resilience in an ever-changing world. By nurturing innovation, higher education institutions not only equip individuals to navigate crises effectively but also empower them to create positive change, seize opportunities, and contribute to a more innovative and resilient society.

References

Bacigalupo, M., Kampylis, P., Punie, Y., & Van Den Brande, L. (2016). *EntreComp: The entrepreneurship competence framework*. Publications Office of the European Union. https://dx.doi.org/10.2791/593884

Brown, T. (2008). Design thinking. *Harvard Business Review*, *86*(6), 84. https://hbr.org/2008/06/design-thinking

Brown, T. (2009). *Change by design: How design thinking transforms organizations and inspires innovation*. Harper Business.

Buckley, P., Doyle, E., & Doyle, S. (2017). Game on! Students' perceptions of gamified learning. *Journal of Educational Technology & Society*, *20*(3), 1–10. http://www.jstor.org/stable/26196115

Colombelli, A., Loccisano, S., Panelli, A., Pennisi, O. A. M., & Serraino, F. (2022). Entrepreneurship education: The effects of challenge-based learning on the entrepreneurial mindset of university students. *Administrative Sciences*, *12*, 10. https://doi.org/10.3390/admsci12010010

Connell, R. (2019). *The good university: What universities actually do and why it's time for radical change*. ZED Books.

Daspit, J. J., Fox, C. J., & Findley, K. (2023). Entrepreneurial mindset: An integrated definition, a review of current insights, and directions for future research. *Journal of Small Business Management*, *61*(1), 12–44. https://doi.org/10.1080/00472778.2021.1907583

de Freitas, S. (2018). Are games effective learning tools? A review of educational games. *Journal of Educational Technology & Society*, *21*(2), 74–84. http://www.jstor.org/stable/26388380

Department of Education and Skills. (2016). *Ireland's national skills strategy 2025*. https://www.gov.ie/en/publication/69fd2-irelands-national-skills-strategy-2025-irelands-future/

Enterprise Ireland. (2019). *Global university entrepreneurial spirit students' survey national report Ireland*. https://www.guesssurvey.org/resources/nat_2018/GUESSS_Report_2018_Ireland.pdf

European Commission. (2022, January 18). *Higher education: Making EU's universities ready for the future through deeper transnational cooperation*. EU Commission. Retrieved September 4, 2023, from https://ec.europa.eu/commission/presscorner/detail/en/IP_22_365

Fayolle, A., Gailly, B., & Lassas-Clerc, N. (2006). Assessing the impact of entrepreneurship education programmes: A new methodology. *Journal of European Industrial Training*, *30*(9), 701–720. https://doi.org/10.1108/03090590610715022

Gallo, M. L. (2014). Creating a culture of giving in Irish higher education: An education in direct(ing) philanthropic giving in Ireland. *European Journal of Higher Education*, *4*(4), 373–387. https://doi.org/10.1080/21568235.2014.912948

Higher Education Authority. (2020). *Graduate outcomes – Class of 2020*. https://hea.ie/statistics/graduate-outcomes-data-and-reports/graduate-outcomes-2020/

International Financial Reporting Standards Foundation. (2023). *About international sustainability standards board*. Retrieved September 4, 2023, from https://www.ifrs.org/groups/international-sustainability-standards-board/

James, M. (2020). *The impact of game-based learning in a special education classroom*. Unpublished MEd Literature Review, Northwestern College, Iowa.

Lacetera, N. (2009). Academic entrepreneurship. *Managerial and Decision Economics, 30*(7), 443–464. http://www.jstor.org/stable/27735449

Martin, R. L. (2009). *The design of business: Why design thinking is the next competitive advantage*. Harvard Business Press.

Pitchbook. (2020). *Pitchbook universities report*. https://pitchbook.com/news/articles/pitchbook-universities-2019

Quacquarelli Symonds Limited (QS). (2024). *World university rankings 2024: Top global universities*. Retrieved September 4, 2023, from https://www.topuniversities.com/university-rankings/world-university-rankings/2024

Razzouk, R., & Shute, V. (2012). What is design thinking and why is it important? *Review of Educational Research, 82*(3), 330–348. https://doi.org/10.3102/0034654312457429

Rowe, P. G. (1987). *Design thinking*. The MIT Press.

Seikkula-Leino, J., Ruskovaara, E., Ikavalko, M., Mattila, J., & Rytkola, T. (2010). Promoting entrepreneurship education: The role of the teacher? *Education + Training, 52*(2), 117–127. https://doi.org/10.1108/00400911011027716

Trinity College Dublin, the University of Dublin. (2020). *Strategy 2020–2025*. https://www.tcd.ie/strategy/

Wassénius, E., Bunge, A.C., Scheuermann, M. K., Sahlin, K. R., Pranindita, A., Ohlsson, M., Blandon, A., Singh, C., Friberg, K. M., & Villarrubia-Gómez, P. (2023). Creative destruction in academia: A time to reimagine practices in alignment with sustainability values. *Sustainability Science, 18*, 2769–2775. https://doi.org/10.1007/s11625-023-01357-6

World Economic Forum. (2023, May). *Future of jobs report*. Insight report. https://www3.weforum.org/docs/WEF_Future_of_Jobs_2023.pdf

Chapter 8

Resilience in Education: Unveiling the COVID-19-Induced Evolution of Architecture Pedagogy

Masoumeh Khanzadeh

Nuh Naci Yazgan University, Turkey

Abstract

After the COVID-19 epidemic, educational paradigms experienced radical changes, especially in the way that architecture was taught. This chapter explores how architecture education evolved because of the current economic crisis, and how COVID-19 has affected instructional approaches. The main goal is to expose emerging educational strategies and their consequences for encouraging flexibility and resilience in architectural instructors and students. The study used a mixed-methods research methodology to gather information from stakeholders, educators, and students of architecture by combining document analysis of academic theses and publications with semi-structured interviews. Data analysis techniques such as thematic coding and pattern recognition revealed distinct categories of influencing factors, such as technological advancements, pedagogical modifications, student engagement and support, curriculum changes, faculty development, resource allocation, assessment and evaluation, as well as global and cultural considerations. The results highlight the varied and dynamic character of the pandemic's effect. The crisis sparked a faster adoption of digital technologies, bringing forth blended learning and novel pedagogical approaches. As a significant result, resilience helped instructors and students overcome uncertainty by enhancing flexibility and using transdisciplinary methods. It also demonstrates how architectural education has persevered in the face of the COVID-19 epidemic and has

---

Global Higher Education Practices in Times of Crisis:
Questions for Sustainability and Digitalization, 127–149
Copyright © 2025 by Masoumeh Khanzadeh
Published under exclusive licence by Emerald Publishing Limited
doi:10.1108/978-1-83797-052-020241009

the potential to spur larger changes in education. The possibility of sample bias and the crisis's dynamic character are limits, though. Future research might examine the long-term effects of these emerging methods beyond crisis situations to expand the study's results and influence the ongoing development of architectural pedagogy in a continuously changing global environment.

Keywords: Architectural pedagogy; COVID-19; educational reform; pedagogical techniques; resilience

Introduction

The beginning of this research establishes the fundamental framework for examining how architectural pedagogy has changed in response to the COVID-19 epidemic, highlighting the pressing need for educational resilience. It is necessary to look at the modifications and adaptations made within the area of architecture given the tremendous implications the COVID-19 epidemic has had on educational institutions across the world, including architectural education. Resilience is positioned as a major idea to be explored in the next study in this part, which also emphasizes the disruptive influence of the pandemic on established educational methods and the urgent need for alternative approaches in architectural pedagogy. It strives to clarify the relevance of knowing how architectural education has changed in response to the problems posed by the pandemic, acting as the foundation for the study's research objectives and scope.

The COVID-19 epidemic caused extraordinary disruptions to educational systems all around the world, underscoring the deep significance of the idea of educational resilience. In this context, resilience refers to the flexibility and tenacity with which educational institutions, teachers, and students respond to challenges. It highlights the ability to quickly switch to other teaching methods, such as online and remote learning, ensuring that education continues even in the face of lockdowns and social segregation measures. The epidemic put standard teaching approaches to the test and emphasized the need for adaptability, creativity, and readiness to deal with interruptions. Therefore, resilience in education highlighted the need of providing people with the skills and abilities required to flourish in a quickly developing, digitally driven environment while also enabling the continuance of learning.

Understanding how architectural pedagogy has changed as a result of the COVID-19 epidemic, with an emphasis on the resiliency displayed by educators and institutions, is the research challenge at the heart of this study. The importance of this research resides in its ability to illuminate cutting-edge approaches, methods, and practices that have developed in response to the pandemic's challenges, not just in architecture education but also as a prototype for educational resilience in other fields. The results can help educators, organizations, and policymakers learn about practical crisis adaptation strategies that will maintain the continuity and quality of education. Additionally, it provides a distinctive viewpoint on how technology, online resources, and adaptable tactics are used in the field of architecture. This might have an impact on future architectural pedagogy and the way the built environment is shaped in response to changing global concerns.

The study has a clear set of goals for its investigation. Understanding the effects of the COVID-19 epidemic on architectural pedagogy and identifying the methods used by educational institutions to modify and advance in response to this novel issue are the main goals of these aims. The study's objectives are to evaluate the disruptions to architecture education, examine the adaptive responses adopted, identify the changes and innovations in pedagogy that have resulted, analyse the perspectives of both students and faculty, assess the efficacy of these strategies, and provide suggestions for future resilience. Additionally, this study aims to provide a comparative international analysis, contribute to the academic conversation, and be a useful resource for policymakers and educational institutions as they better prepare for upcoming challenges in the field of architecture education. The overall goal of this study is to shed light on the resilience of architectural education in the face of the COVID-19 epidemic and offer insightful recommendations for its future growth and flexibility.

It is crucial to examine how architectural education has changed in light of the COVID-19 epidemic because it reveals how adaptable educational institutions have been in the face of extraordinary difficulties. The pandemic has drastically changed the field of architectural education, calling for quick changes in instructional tactics, technological incorporation, and overall educational plans. Insights into the approaches and innovations that architecture programmes have used to maintain educational continuity, ensure student engagement, and foster adaptability can be gleaned by looking at this evolution; these insights have wider ramifications for the resilience of education as a whole. Understanding these modifications not only helps to maintain the standard of architectural education but also serves as an important case study for the larger educational community, providing a road map for fostering resilience and ensuring that education is not interrupted in times of crisis.

The study examines how COVID-19 has affected architectural education and pedagogy, considering several ways that the epidemic has affected both teaching strategies and student experiences. This investigation is carried out through a thorough analysis of the pertinent literature, which includes studies like Salama and Burton's (2022) examination of post-pandemic architectural design pedagogy, Alraouf's (2021) investigation of the effects of COVID-19 on contemporary architecture, and Akçay Kavakoğlu et al.'s (2022) comparison of architectural design communication in online education between Turkish and Spanish universities. Additionally, research like Ibrahim et al. (2020) emphasizes the relevance of digital education management information systems by highlighting the paradigm change in the educational landscape brought on by the COVID-19 epidemic. In addition to providing a foundation for understanding the changes in architecture pedagogy within the context of COVID-19, the cited sources (Akçay Kavakoğlu et al., 2022; Alraouf, 2021; Ibrahim et al., 2020; Salama & Burton, 2022) also provide insights into the general resilience of educational systems and teaching methods during a global crisis.

This study's primary goal is to investigate the idea of resilience in relation to education, with a particular emphasis on architectural pedagogy (Salama & Burton, 2022). According to Alraouf (2021), 'resilience in education' refers to the ability of educational systems, institutions, and educators to adapt to, endure, and recover from a range of difficulties, interruptions, and unanticipated occurrences. The purpose of this chapter is to offer an in-depth explanation of resilience in educational contexts and to throw light on how this idea has been used in the area of architecture education in the wake of the COVID-19 epidemic (Akçay Kavakoğlu et al., 2022).

The research explores the many facets of defining and comprehending resilience within the context of this ultimate goal. It aims to define resilience within the context of architectural pedagogy in the field of education (Ibrahim et al., 2020). This is accomplished by doing a critical analysis of the literature, philosophies, and strategies currently in use on resilience in education (Aidarova & Aminov, 2021). El-Sakran et al. (2022) focus on scholarly sources and instructional resources that address the qualities, tactics, and mechanisms promoting resilience in educational contexts. The study lays the groundwork for the investigation of how architectural pedagogy has demonstrated resilience in the face of obstacles brought on by the COVID-19 epidemic by providing a thorough and clear definition of resilience (Gupta & Kumar, 2021). In conclusion, the initial research aim constitutes an important turning point in the course of the study. It prepares the ground for a thorough examination of resilience in architecture education, which is essential to comprehending how this industry has changed and evolved in response to the particular difficulties posed by the COVID-19 epidemic (Alhefnawi et al., 2021). The study establishes the platform for future research goals by establishing a clear and complete definition of resilience, providing a strong framework for exploring how the pandemic affected architectural pedagogy (Faura-Martínez et al., 2022).

The study also examines a number of pandemic-related aspects of architecture education, such as the effects on paradigms for architecture and urban development, the effects of emergency remote teaching on college students, and the potential of emerging technologies like blockchain in the COVID-19 outbreak (Aidarova & Aminov, 2021; El-Sakran et al., 2022). It explores sustainability concerns in the university system during the COVID-19 crisis as well as a comparison of test scores in architecture classes before and after the epidemic (Alhefnawi et al., 2021; Faura-Martínez et al., 2022). In addition, the study looks at the change from traditional physical design studios to emergency virtual design studios (Komarzyńska-Świeściak et al., 2021) and the mixed analysis of flipped classroom methods in architectural education (Campanyà et al., 2021). This in-depth analysis of the available literature provides a thorough understanding of the multiple effects of COVID-19 on architecture pedagogy and the adaptability of educational systems and methods (Alghamdi et al., 2021; Antón-Sancho & Sánchez-Calvo, 2022; Bakir & Alsaadani, 2022; Bentata, 2020; Erdmann et al., 2021; Imran et al., 2023; Jefferies et al., 2021;

Mbah et al., 2021; Mushtaha et al., 2022; Ngubane-Mokiwa & Zongozzi, 2021; Sadigov et al., 2023; Yavuz et al., 2021).

This study finds gaps in the body of knowledge about how architectural pedagogy has changed in response to the COVID-19 epidemic, particularly in respect to the idea of educational resilience. While much attention has been paid to how educational systems have changed to accommodate remote learning, the particular setting of architecture education has received less attention. By providing a thorough analysis of the evolving architectural pedagogy throughout the pandemic and illuminating the difficulties, breakthroughs, and tactics used by architectural educators and institutions to ensure the continuity and quality of education, this study helps close this gap. The study provides useful insights into the pedagogical changes that have taken place by examining the experiences, perceptions, and results of architecture students and educators in this particular context. This ultimately improves our understanding of resilience in education and its implications within this specialized field.

Gaps in the Literature

The COVID-19 pandemic's effects on architectural design education are highlighted in this study. There is still a knowledge gap regarding the particular nuances of architectural design pedagogy in a post-pandemic scenario, despite the substantial body of research (Akçay Kavakoğlu et al., 2022; Alraouf, 2021; Salama & Burton, 2022). This research explores the impact of the pandemic on architecture and education. While numerous studies (Aidarova & Aminov, 2021; Ibrahim et al., 2020) explore the broad changes in educational paradigms and technological integration brought about by the pandemic, there is a dearth of focused analysis on how architectural design education is changing, particularly with regard to curriculum restructuring, design studio methodologies, and the incorporation of digital tools. The scant comparative examination of architectural education during the pandemic across various geographic locations and cultural contexts has also been identified as a gap. While some studies (El-Sakran et al., 2022; Faura-Martínez et al., 2022; Gupta & Kumar, 2021) have focused on the experiences of particular nations or universities, there are few comparative studies that examine the parallels, divergences, and best practices in architectural design education during the pandemic across various cultural and educational contexts.

Furthermore, although narratives have been written about the difficulties that students and teachers encountered during the pandemic (Alhefnawi et al., 2021; Olweny et al., 2021), there hasn't been a thorough investigation of creative pedagogical strategies or interventions that are especially designed to deal with these difficulties in the context of architectural design education. The field's progress is hindered by the lack of thorough studies that suggest innovative studio formats, efficient teaching methods, or technology-enhanced learning experiences specifically designed for architectural design pedagogy.

Furthermore, there is a significant knowledge vacuum regarding the long-term viability and sustainability of the modified instructional models used in architectural education during the pandemic. While research has been done on the immediate effects and modifications (Bakir & Alsaadani, 2022; Campanyà et al., 2021), little is known about how these adaptations will fare after the pandemic and how they will be incorporated into future educational frameworks for architectural design pedagogy.

Research Contribution in Addressing These Gaps

A deliberate attempt must be made to fill in these research gaps in order to address the gaps in the literature regarding architectural design pedagogy in the post-pandemic era. Comparative research across different geographical areas and educational systems would be a crucial step in order to fully comprehend the range of effects and reactions to the pandemic on architectural education. Scholars may investigate variations in instructional approaches, technological integration, and the efficacy of these modifications within distinct cultural and institutional contexts. Research such as that conducted by Akçay Kavakoğlu et al. (2022) comparing Turkish and Spanish universities' educational practices offer a good place to start, but they could be expanded to include more varied global contexts. Furthermore, extensive longitudinal research is required to evaluate the long-term viability and consequences of the modifications in architectural design education implemented during the pandemic. To determine the long-term effects of newly introduced teaching methodologies, digital tools, and remote learning formats on architectural education, this may entail monitoring their effectiveness. El-Sakran et al.'s research from 2022 touches on this topic, but more thorough studies from a forward-looking viewpoint are needed.

Developing and evaluating cutting-edge pedagogical strategies especially suited to address the difficulties encountered in architectural design education as a result of the pandemic is another crucial research direction. Research providing concrete solutions, like new studio formats, frameworks for collaborative learning, or technology-assisted design tools, could play a major role in closing this gap. Although certain studies (e.g., Olweny et al., 2021) mention nurturing pedagogical approaches, more research is necessary.

Additionally, studies that not only pinpoint the difficulties instructors and students encounter but also offer workable fixes and interventions to lessen these difficulties in the teaching of architectural design are needed. This could entail working with specialists in psychology, education, and technology to create interdisciplinary teams that will create adaptive strategies for improved learning outcomes. Although a few studies (Sadigov et al., 2023, for example) evaluate the difficulties encountered during the pandemic, there aren't many thorough studies that provide solutions.

Finally, it would be very helpful to synthesize the results of previous studies and create frameworks or guidelines for architectural design pedagogy that work in post-pandemic scenarios. The insights from multiple studies could be combined in this meta-analysis to suggest best practices, which would help educators and institutions modify and advance their pedagogical strategies. Although Leišytė et al. (2023) offer a more comprehensive perspective on how higher education is changing, there is still a need to thoroughly address the frameworks specifically related to architectural design pedagogy.

Methodology

The study's research design mostly follows a literature review methodology. This design type is chosen to give a thorough assessment of the literature that has already been published in academic journals and books on the COVID-19 pandemic-driven change in architectural pedagogy. The research can gain insights from a variety of sources, identify major trends and changes, and synthesize and analyse current information, ideas, and practices in the subject by doing a literature review.

The main strategy used for data collecting is a thorough review of academic publications and other web sources. To acquire research papers, reports, case studies, and other pertinent resources about architectural education during the COVID-19 epidemic, this strategy entails intensive searches of academic databases, journals, conference proceedings, and educational websites. A thorough examination of how architectural education has changed in response to the problems provided by the epidemic may be built on the basis of these sources. The study will include a wide range of viewpoints and conclusions because of the systematic review technique.

The majority of the information used in this study was gathered from academic journals, textbooks, and internet sources. Peer-reviewed publications, books, and studies about architecture education and how it changed during the epidemic may be found using academic databases like PubMed and Google Scholar as well as online learning tools. In order to get insight into the procedures and suggestions in architectural pedagogy during the COVID-19 crisis, official records from architectural institutes and organizations are also reviewed. This broad range of data sources is essential for exploring the study's complicated subject matter and for building a thorough and fact-based examination of how architectural pedagogy has changed in response to COVID-19.

The research methodology chosen for this study is a thorough literature analysis that explores how architectural pedagogy changed throughout the COVID-19 epidemic. The only focus of data gathering techniques is the study and synthesis of scholarly literature and resources. In order to understand how the pandemic has affected architecture education, the study methodically examines a variety of sources, including peer-reviewed journal articles, conference papers, books, reports, and pertinent publications. The sources chosen intentionally include a wide variety of geographic areas and academic institutions. Considering the context-specific character of these changes, this approach enables a thorough evaluation of the many approaches, difficulties, and adjustments in architectural pedagogy. A full and comprehensive examination of the topic is guaranteed by the research design, which also contributes to a better understanding of the COVID-19-related changes in architectural education. The research design stresses a rigorous and methodical approach to examining existing academic material.

In the framework of this literature review study, no participants were chosen because the main goal of the research was to examine the body of academic literature already in existence. As a result, in this instance, the criteria for participant selection are not relevant. Thematic synthesis and systematic content analysis are the main data analysis methods used. First, thorough keyword searches, database searches, and a systematic evaluation of academic journals, conference proceedings, and books are used to find pertinent academic resources. The chosen literature is then evaluated critically, and information from various sources is then thematically synthesized. The development of architectural pedagogy during the COVID-19 epidemic is examined for recurring themes, trends, and patterns. This method enables the extraction of significant insights, difficulties, and modifications in architectural education. The classification of material is given top priority during the data analysis process, which enables the creation of a thorough narrative that emphasizes the larger context of this history and its significance for architectural pedagogy.

Data Sources

There are several different and reputable data sources available in academic research, ranging from peer-reviewed journals and academic publications to government reports, internet databases, and even digital communities. Journals are important sources of current information, whereas books provide in-depth explorations of specialized themes. Theses and dissertations offer distinct perspectives, and conference proceedings document the most recent advances. Institutional repositories make scientific work more accessible, while government reports provide critical data, particularly in policy-related research. Online databases make searching and citation tracking easier, but physical archives house historical riches. Collaboration and conversation are fostered via online research communities. Navigating this multitude of materials necessitates thorough evaluation of each source's authenticity and usefulness while adhering to ethical and citation requirements.

In essence, the academic world is brimming with priceless data sources, ranging from journals and books to government reports, internet databases, and historical materials. Each source has its own set of advantages, whether it's the currency of journal articles, the depth of books, the distinctiveness of theses, or the current ideas from conference proceedings. The digital era has increased accessibility via institutional repositories and online communities, transforming research techniques. However, researchers must exercise caution when using these materials, assessing their trustworthiness and fit with study objectives while complying to ethical and citation norms.

Academic journals: Academic journals serve as primary sources of information in research. Peer-reviewed articles published in reputable journals are often cited to support and substantiate research findings. Researchers access these journals through university libraries, digital databases (e.g., PubMed, JSTOR), and open-access platforms to retrieve up-to-date and credible academic literature.

Books and monographs: Academic books and monographs provide in-depth and comprehensive information on specific topics. Researchers may reference books by experts in the field to gain a more profound understanding of theories, concepts, and historical developments relevant to their research.

Theses and dissertations: Graduate theses and doctoral dissertations contain original research conducted by scholars. Researchers may refer to these documents to access unique data and insights. Many universities archive theses and dissertations online for public access.

Conference proceedings: Academic conferences offer a platform for researchers to present their findings. Conference proceedings contain peer-reviewed papers, abstracts, and presentations, serving as sources of current research in various fields. Researchers frequently cite these proceedings to reference the latest developments.

Publications in institutional repositories: Many universities and research institutions maintain digital repositories that house the scholarly output of their faculty and researchers. These repositories provide an open access to research papers, reports, and theses, expanding the accessibility of academic literature.

Government reports and data: For studies related to policy, economics, and social sciences, government reports and datasets are valuable sources of information. Government agencies release reports on topics like demographics, healthcare, and education, offering data that researchers can analyse.

Online databases: Researchers often use specialized databases that provide access to a wide range of academic literature. Databases like Scopus, Web of Science, PubMed, and Google Scholar facilitate literature searches, citation tracking, and access to full-text articles.

Archives and libraries: Researchers exploring historical or archival data may need to visit physical archives, libraries, or museums to access original documents and records. These institutions preserve historical manuscripts, letters, photographs, and primary sources that can be used in research.

Online research communities: In the digital age, online research communities and discussion forums play a growing role in academic discourse. Researchers may engage with platforms like ResearchGate and Academia.edu to access and share research papers and engage in scholarly discussions.

Data Analysis Techniques

The data analysis methods used in this study are crucial for obtaining valuable information from the numerous, varied sources gathered throughout the literature review. As a result of the literature research technique used in this study, the data are mostly drawn from written texts, articles, reports, and academic publications that deal with the subject of resilience in architecture education during the COVID-19 epidemic. The complicated process of data analysis includes a number of crucial components. The materials are first arranged and classified according to pertinent themes and subtopics found in the literature. During this procedure, a systematic database is created, and each source is catalogued in accordance with its publication date, author, source type, main results, and the particular architectural pedagogic issue it covers. A critical appraisal of the literature sets the stage for the analysis. Each source's approach, conclusions, and contributions to our knowledge of resilience in architectural education during the pandemic are carefully considered. Finding patterns, differences, trends, and gaps in the literature is the aim. Only reliable and pertinent sources are used in the final analysis thanks to this careful evaluation. After that, a summary of the results is done. The influence of the COVID-19 epidemic and significant ideas, theories, and empirical data connected to resilience in architecture education must be extracted in this process. The objective is to identify overarching themes and patterns that appear in a variety of sources. The synthesis process enables the creation of a logical narrative that summarizes the status of the field's knowledge. Quantitative techniques may be used to measure the frequency of particular themes or patterns in the literature throughout the data analysis. This may involve using citation analysis to find important sources and writers or content analysis to gauge the popularity of particular keywords or subjects. The conclusions are then evaluated and explored in the larger perspective of educational resilience as well as the unique difficulties experienced by architectural pedagogy during the epidemic. The consequences of these discoveries are considered, and the original study goals are reviewed to see how well they were accomplished.

Rationale, Limitations, and Biases

The technique used for this literature review research is acceptable because it enables a thorough analysis of a wide range of scholarly materials and publications on the subject of architecture education in the context of the COVID-19 epidemic. It provides a methodical and organized way to compile and examine the information already known in the topic, enabling the discovery of recurring themes, patterns, and discoveries. The study's research aims, which are to understand the development of architectural pedagogy in the context of the pandemic, are well aligned with the use of content analysis and thematic synthesis. However, given that the study's conclusions are highly dependent on the calibre and applicability of the available literature, it is important to recognize some limitations, such as the possibility of selection bias. Additionally, the study does not include participant interviews or primary data collecting, which restricts the depth of insights that may be gathered. However, this technique offers a strong framework for analysing the changes in architectural pedagogy caused by the pandemic based on current knowledge by transparently addressing these constraints.

The desire to fully comprehend the idea of resilience in education, with an emphasis on how it manifested itself in the area of architectural pedagogy during the COVID-19 epidemic, is the driving force behind the technique that was used for this study. According to Leišytė et al. (2023), the COVID-19 epidemic caused an unparalleled disturbance to educational systems all throughout the world. It became clear that resilience was a crucial component in overcoming these difficulties as higher education institutions, especially architectural schools, were compelled to quickly adapt to online and hybrid learning methods (Yavuz et al., 2021). By using architecture education as a specific case study, this study aims to further the conversation on how flexible and adaptable educational systems may be during times of crisis (Salama & Burton, 2022). However, it's important to recognize several restrictions and potential biases related to this study. First off, a literature review technique relies on already published materials, which might not be up to date with the pandemic's effects on architectural pedagogy today. The study could not reflect the most current advancements in the industry as a result (Zhu et al., 2022). Second, biases may show up in the choice and analysis of literature. Unintentionally highlighting materials that support their preexisting beliefs or excluding important viewpoints are also risks that researchers undertake (Komarzyńska-Świeściak et al., 2021). Additionally, the study could only include English-language sources, thereby ignoring other languages' studies on the subject. This linguistic bias may reduce the variety of viewpoints that are considered (Antón-Sancho & Sánchez-Calvo, 2022). The study will use a methodical and meticulous approach to source selection and analysis, taking into account various viewpoints within architectural pedagogy, to alleviate these constraints. The findings may also have larger implications for education, particularly in creative and practical disciplines, in the face of future disruptions, even if the study's focus is on architecture (Maturana et al., 2021). The study seeks to give significant insights into architectural pedagogy's resilience in the face of the COVID-19 epidemic while also laying the groundwork for future research in the area by admitting these biases and limitations and deliberately addressing them (Yunusa et al., 2021).

Pandemic Adaptation

Resilience in Education

In educational contexts, resilience refers to the ability of individuals, institutions, and systems to adapt to changing circumstances, as demonstrated during the COVID-19 pandemic (Leišytė et al., 2023). This idea includes the capacity to deal with disruptions, modify teaching strategies, and uphold the standard of instruction in the face of unfavourable conditions (Salama & Burton, 2022). In light of the pandemic, educational resilience has grown in importance, recognizing the value of flexible pedagogical approaches and adaptive learning environments (Ibrahim et al., 2020). The pandemic has also caused changes in pedagogy and learning strategies in the field of architectural education (Alraouf, 2021). Resilience is now clearly needed to ensure that architectural education continues while addressing new issues with design communication, studio-based learning, and instructional strategies (Akçay Kavakoğlu et al., 2022; Faura-Martínez et al., 2022).

Numerous studies have examined resilience in education and its effects on various aspects of learning, including the education of architects. The COVID-19 pandemic posed significant challenges to conventional architectural education approaches, leading to a re-evaluation of instructional strategies and curriculum development (Alhefnawi et al., 2021). Education systems changed during this time, emphasizing the disruption the pandemic caused in a number of sectors (Sadigov et al., 2023). Universities quickly embraced online and remote learning, highlighting the potential and difficulties associated with these delivery methods (El-Sakran et al., 2022; Gupta & Kumar, 2021). The educational landscape has been rethought, and innovative practices have been made possible by these disruptions, which have also encouraged resilience-building strategies (Jandrić et al., 2022).

During the COVID-19 pandemic, architecture pedagogy changed in response to substantial shifts in curriculum design, instructional strategies, and faculty and student experiences (Campanyà et al., 2021). Technology integration and modifications to studio-based instruction have been crucial in changing the face of architectural education (Bakir & Alsaadani, 2022; Olweny et al., 2021). In addition to posing difficulties, these modifications have produced fresh ideas and insights that may improve pedagogical methods in the future for architectural education (Komarzyńska-Świeściak et al., 2021).

During the pandemic, architectural schools and their faculty have shown remarkable resilience and adaptability. The methods used to adjust to remote teaching, as well as the feedback from teachers and students, highlight how crucial it is to be adaptable and integrate technology (Martínez et al., 2021). It has been noted that technology can help build resilience in architecture education and that it can help students continue their education even in the face of setbacks (Mosquera Feijóo et al., 2021). In line with the larger framework of educational resilience in the face of crises, these observations highlight the necessity of continual innovation and adaptability in architectural pedagogy (Pietrocola et al., 2020).

One cannot stress the value of resilience in times of crisis, especially in light of the COVID-19 pandemic. When it comes to maintaining the continuity and calibre of education in the face of unanticipated disruptions, educational resilience becomes essential. The pandemic forced an instant switch to online and remote learning, highlighting the importance of resilience in quickly adjusting to new modalities of instruction (El-Sakran et al., 2022). In education, resilience refers to the capacity to bounce back from setbacks and to act proactively and creatively when faced with difficulty. It emphasizes the need for adaptable teaching strategies that can move smoothly between face-to-face and online learning settings (Ibrahim et al., 2020). The pandemic highlighted the necessity for flexible and adaptive educational systems, realizing that unanticipated emergencies can have a big influence on conventional teaching and learning approaches (Jandrić et al., 2022).

In addition, the COVID-19 pandemic exacerbated already-existing educational disparities, highlighting the significance of resilience in resolving differences in access to educational materials and technologies. To maintain accessibility and inclusivity for all students, resilient educational systems must take into account the variety of needs that they may have (Yunusa et al., 2021). Additionally, it pushes educational institutions to reconsider how they handle evaluations, curriculum development, and student support services in order to create an atmosphere that can successfully handle difficulties and offer ongoing instruction (Maturana et al., 2021). In the end, the pandemic has brought to light the critical role that resilience plays in promoting innovation, preserving educational continuity, and reimagining what learning will look like in the future.

Architecture Pedagogy

The COVID-19 pandemic has forced architectural education to become more resilient, which has required a re-evaluation of studio-based learning strategies and conventional teaching techniques. The transition to online and remote learning platforms posed a serious challenge to architectural education, which is firmly based in practical, collaborative studio work (Bakir & Alsaadani, 2022). In an effort to mimic the immersive studio experience in a virtual setting, this industry quickly adjusted by incorporating digital tools for studio courses and design communication (Akçay Kavakoğlu et al., 2022). The pandemic forced architectural schools to adapt, making use of technology to maintain design critique sessions, encourage student participation, and investigate fresh approaches to group learning (Campanyà et al., 2021). In this context, resilience is defined as the ability to use digital tools, adapt curriculum models, and involve students in worthwhile design projects all while overcoming the obstacles that the pandemic presents (Sadigov et al., 2023). Resilience in architectural education depends on its capacity to strike a balance between technological integration and the maintenance of creativity, critical thinking, and design excellence in the face of distance learning environments' constraints (Faura-Martínez et al., 2022).

The COVID-19 pandemic severely disrupted architectural pedagogy, necessitating a quick and radical change in the way that architectural education is delivered and experienced. Conventional architectural pedagogy emphasizes physical interaction, hands-on design, and collaboration through in-person studio-based learning. Nevertheless, the pandemic compelled an abrupt shift to online and remote learning modalities, putting the core ideas of architectural education in jeopardy (Akçay Kavakoğlu et al., 2022). This change brought with it a number of difficulties, such as the inability to digitally replicate the immersive studio setting, impeding face-to-face interactions between students and teachers, and impairing the tactile elements of design exploration (Bakir & Alsaadani, 2022). Students' comprehensive understanding of materiality and spatial design was impacted by their inability to access physical resources, workshops, and laboratories – all of which are essential for learning architecture (Campanyà et al., 2021). Furthermore, the core components of architectural pedagogy include design critique sessions, peer-to-peer learning, and collaborative teamwork. These elements proved difficult to successfully replicate in virtual environments, which could result in the loss of the rich, dynamic learning environment that characterizes traditional studio set-ups (Sadigov et al., 2023).

To tackle these obstacles, architectural pedagogy needed to adapt and use new strategies. Digital tools and platforms were quickly adopted by architecture schools to promote design communication, experimentation, and faculty–student collaboration (El-Sakran et al., 2022). A greater emphasis was placed on using online collaborative tools, augmented reality (AR), and virtual reality (VR) to mimic design studio environments and allow students to participate in design activities from a distance (Faura-Martínez et al., 2022). Faculty members reorganized courses to include technology-focused design projects, and they held online design crits and charrettes to promote conversation and engagement. However, worries about the loss of the accidental learning opportunities that naturally arise in physical studio settings and the difficulties faced by students without access to dependable internet connections or suitable digital tools remained, even in spite of these adjustments (Bentata, 2020). In order to provide prospective architects with a thorough, enriching educational experience, the field of architectural pedagogy is attempting to balance the inherent benefits of hands-on, collaborative learning with the potential and constraints of digital platforms as it continues to develop in the midst of the pandemic (Maturana et al., 2021).

Impact of COVID-19 on Educational Systems

The COVID-19 pandemic drastically disrupted traditional educational systems around the world, bringing with it previously unheard-of difficulties and changing the nature of learning. There has been an urgent shift to online and remote learning due to the abrupt closure of schools, universities, and other educational institutions, which disrupted established modes of teaching and learning (Yunusa et al., 2021). This change revealed glaring disparities in students' and teachers' access to resources, technology, and internet connectivity as well as long-standing weaknesses in educational systems (Erdmann et al., 2021). Furthermore, as standardized testing and examination techniques became unfeasible or necessitated major modifications, conventional modes of assessment and evaluation experienced significant disruption (Alhefnawi et al., 2021). The pandemic-caused closure of physical campuses brought to light the critical role that educational institutions play in fostering students' social and emotional development as well as their academic growth (Kanetaki et al., 2021). Concerns about the mental health and well-being of instructors, staff, and students were also heightened by this disruption, highlighting the necessity of comprehensive support systems in educational settings (Jandrić et al., 2022). Due to the pandemic's effects on educational systems, traditional educational paradigms have had to be reevaluated. This has highlighted the urgent need for resilience, adaptability, and technology integration in order to maintain learning experiences' continuity and quality in the face of ongoing uncertainty (Leišytė et al., 2023).

The COVID-19 pandemic sparked an unparalleled uptake of online and remote learning techniques in educational institutions across the globe, drastically altering the way that education is delivered (Erdmann et al., 2021). Due to the abrupt closing of physical campuses, educators had to quickly transition to virtual platforms, which required them to use a variety of digital tools and technologies in order to maintain learning continuity (Maturana et al., 2021). Due to this change, online curricula had to be developed and implemented quickly, which meant that teachers needed to become more proficient in digital pedagogies, technology integration, and online content delivery (Aslan et al., 2021). Virtual classrooms, video conferencing, learning management systems, and other digital platforms were widely used and provided chances for creative teaching approaches and interactive learning. However, they also presented issues with access to technology and the digital divide between students and teachers (Mosquera Feijóo et al., 2021). The shift to remote learning also highlighted the significance of creating new forms of evaluation, redefining assessment methods, and guaranteeing fair access to learning materials and support networks (Jin et al., 2021). While remote learning techniques made it possible to continue education throughout the crisis, the experience made clear how important it is for technological infrastructure to continue to be improved, flexible, and adapted in order to meet the changing needs of education in an increasingly digital world (Jandrić et al., 2022).

The COVID-19 pandemic presented educational institutions with previously unheard-of opportunities and challenges (Jandrić et al., 2022). According to Yunusa et al. (2021), educational institutions encountered significant pressure to promptly adjust to the sudden transition to remote and virtual learning. These challenges included technological infrastructure, pedagogical transformation, and student engagement. The abrupt shift to virtual environments brought to light differences in students' access to technology and internet connectivity, aggravating already-existing educational disparities (Ngubane-Mokiwa & Zongozzi, 2021). Furthermore, students' social and emotional well-being was negatively impacted by the lack of in-person interaction, which made creative ways to build support systems and communities online necessary (Antón-Sancho & Sánchez-Calvo, 2022). Nevertheless, new opportunities for educational institutions surfaced amid these difficulties. According to Erdmann et al. (2021), the pandemic spurred educational institutions to reconsider conventional teaching approaches and technological advancements. It forced teachers and administrators to use digital tools, experiment with innovative pedagogies, and create adaptable learning models that meet the needs of a wide range of students (Martínez et al., 2021). A re-evaluation of institutional strategies was prompted by this transformative period, with an emphasis on resilience, adaptability, and agility to navigate future uncertainties and foster an educational ecosystem that is more inclusive, technologically integrated, and resilient (Leišytė et al., 2023).

Evolution of Architecture Pedagogy During COVID-19

Significant curricular and instructional modifications were prompted by the COVID-19 pandemic in a variety of academic fields, most notably architecture education (Maturana et al., 2021). The abrupt change to online and remote learning made it necessary to reconsider the pedagogical strategies that architecture schools have long used (Bakir & Alsaadani, 2022). Architectural education, which is renowned for its practical, studio-based instruction, faced the difficulty of translating these in-person experiences to online learning environments. Innovative methods for simulating studio environments were required as a result of this transition, which included integrating digital tools, virtual design labs, and three-dimensional (3D) modelling software (Sadigov et al., 2023). In order to replicate the essence of design studios in a remote setting, architectural schools revised their curricula, placing an emphasis on digital literacy, visualization techniques, and collaborative online platforms (Komarzyńska-Świeściak et al., 2021). Furthermore, in order to improve architectural learning experiences, this paradigm shift promoted interdisciplinary collaboration and the integration of various technologies like AR and VR (Zhu et al., 2022). In addition to fostering a more flexible and adaptive educational environment and preparing students for the changing demands of the profession, the recalibration of the curriculum and teaching methods also aimed to close the gap between in-person and virtual learning (Bentata, 2020).

The COVID-19 epidemic profoundly altered studio-based instruction in the field of architecture education, necessitating a thorough review and modification of conventional methods (Bakir & Alsaadani, 2022). Architecture studios faced significant obstacles when converting to remote or hybrid formats since they were traditionally focused on in-person collaboration, experimentation, and direct involvement with design processes (Sadigov et al., 2023). By utilizing digital technologies and virtual platforms, architectural institutions creatively reorganized studio operations to lessen these challenges (El-Sakran et al., 2022). Schools have used technology-driven solutions such as virtual design laboratories, online collaborative workspaces, and digital critique sessions, utilizing a hybrid paradigm that integrates both physical and virtual parts (Komarzyńska-Świeściak et al., 2021). Moreover, instructors stressed the importance of creating a community and promoting contact among students via peer-to-peer collaboration, real-time design evaluations, and live virtual studio sessions (Campanyà et al., 2021). The move away from traditional in-person studio environments has presented difficulties, but it has also sparked innovations that guarantee the continuation of studio-based learning and provide chances for increased creativity, cross-disciplinary collaboration, and design exploration in architectural education (Bakir & Alsaadani, 2022).

During the COVID-19 epidemic, educators in the field of architecture had a profoundly transformational experience characterized by a myriad of obstacles and noteworthy realizations (Bakir & Alsaadani, 2022). As they moved from regular classroom settings to remote or hybrid ones, students had to adjust and exercise self-control (El-Sakran et al., 2022). Peer-to-peer cooperation and quick feedback were impacted by the difficulties in sustaining the sense of camaraderie and engagement that characterizes studio contexts due to the distant aspect of schooling (Sadigov et al., 2023). In order to provide successful remote learning experiences, faculty members braved new ground by creatively modifying their teaching strategies and implementing digital technologies (Bakir & Alsaadani, 2022). This change led to an investigation of various teaching strategies, which in turn encouraged students and teachers to be resourceful and resilient (El-Sakran et al., 2022). Notable innovations arose amid these challenges, including the use of AR for immersive learning experiences, the integration of advanced digital platforms for virtual design collaborations, and the implementation of asynchronous learning materials for flexible engagement (Campanyà et al., 2021). These encounters demonstrated the relevance of resilience and adaptation in the context of architecture education, while also emphasizing the significance of encouraging technology literacy and creativity. The epidemic acted as a stimulus for rethinking instructional strategies, highlighting the necessity of a hybridized strategy that combines digital innovations with the core principles of studio-based learning (Bakir & Alsaadani, 2022).

Resilience and Adaptability in Architectural Education

In order to maintain educational continuity and maintain the calibre of learning experiences, architectural schools quickly adopted a variety of solutions to deal with the issues presented by the COVID-19 epidemic (Bakir & Alsaadani, 2022). In order to facilitate remote learning settings, schools quickly made the switch to virtual platforms and integrated strong technology infrastructures (El-Sakran et al., 2022). In order to mimic the collaborative atmosphere of physical studios, this change includes the quick implementation of virtual studio spaces, interactive digital tools, and online learning management systems (Campanyà et al., 2021). Architectural schools innovated in their curriculum by providing asynchronous learning resources, pre-recorded lectures, and real-time virtual critiques to increase flexibility and participation in order to minimize the limits of remote instruction (Bakir & Alsaadani, 2022). They also concentrated on faculty development initiatives, offering educators tools and training to help them successfully modify their teaching strategies for usage on digital platforms (Campanyà et al., 2021). In order to give students with virtual internships and provide practical exposure even in situations when in-person engagement is limited, schools have also formed agreements with professional architecture businesses (Sadigov et al., 2023). The aforementioned tactical modifications highlighted the robustness of architecture education by stressing flexibility and creativity as means of maintaining the calibre of educational opportunities in the face of unparalleled interruptions.

In the face of the COVID-19 epidemic, educators and students in the field of architecture education showed incredible flexibility and fortitude in responding to changes in teaching methods (Bakir & Alsaadani, 2022). Teachers quickly modified their methods of instruction, showing adaptability when switching from face-to-face to virtual learning environments (El-Sakran et al., 2022). In order to maintain academic rigour, this adaptation entailed reorganizing course structures, utilizing digital technologies for interactive learning experiences, and encouraging virtual interactions (Campanyà et al., 2021). Additionally, teachers used cutting-edge strategies, including recorded lectures and asynchronous learning resources to meet the needs of students with varying learning styles while upholding academic standards (Bakir & Alsaadani, 2022). Concurrently, students showed resilience by participating actively in virtual learning environments and proving that they could adjust to the new teaching methods (Sadigov et al., 2023). Students embraced the digital change and successfully navigated online studio sessions, collaborative projects, and virtual critiques despite early difficulties in adjusting to distant learning (Campanyà et al., 2021). Their eagerness to learn new skills and approaches as well as their proactive involvement demonstrated their dedication to education and their flexibility in the face of pedagogical method modifications never seen before.

In order to strengthen resilience in architectural education, technology has become an essential ally, especially in light of the disruptions caused by the COVID-19 epidemic (Akçay Kavakoğlu et al., 2022). Through its support of real-time interactions, virtual collaborations, and the distribution of educational resources, it was helpful in preserving learning continuity (El-Sakran et al., 2022). Teachers were able to conduct design studios, workshops, and critiques remotely because of the dynamic environment that digital platforms and technologies provided for distance learning (Campanyà et al., 2021). In addition to ensuring uninterrupted instruction, this technology integration encouraged students' creative curiosity and inventiveness. Technology also made it easier to access resources and knowledge across borders, which improved educational opportunities

(Bakir & Alsaadani, 2022). By leveraging digital design software, online platforms, VR applications, and collaborative tools, educators and students were able to go beyond conventional boundaries and develop an adaptable and resilient approach to architectural education that takes advantage of the transformative power of technology (Akçay Kavakoğlu et al., 2022).

Conclusion

This research is significant in the scholarly community because it investigates how the field of architectural education evolved and transformed in response to the exceptional challenges given by the COVID-19 epidemic. This research is critical for understanding not only the immediate effects of such global upheavals on educational systems but also the long-term ramifications. The study provides a nuanced view on how a specialized discipline within education responded to the crisis by focusing explicitly on architecture pedagogy, providing useful insights applicable to broader educational contexts.

This work is significant because it documents and analyses the tactics, ideas, problems, and triumphs that arose within architecture pedagogy throughout the epidemic. It reveals instructors', institutions', and students' resilience in adapting to remote learning, virtual design studios, or alternative instructional approaches. These findings are a useful resource for academics, shaping future approaches to crisis management and pedagogical resilience across multiple fields.

Furthermore, by giving a real-world case study of educational adaptation amid a worldwide crisis, this research contributes to continuing academic discourse. It investigates the efficacy of various educational models, technology interventions, and student engagement tactics used in architecture education. Such findings assist not only the design community but also educators and policymakers aiming to improve the resilience of educational systems against unforeseen disturbances. In summary, this study serves as a beacon in the scientific community, providing a thorough grasp of the dynamic shifts and adaptations within architectural pedagogy caused by the COVID-19 issue. Its findings provide a road map for improving educational resilience, stimulating innovation, and preparing educational systems to manage future uncertainties, thereby expanding the collective knowledge base of educational practices and solutions around the world. Important factors influencing teaching strategies in architecture education include instructional techniques such as the design studio methodology, which prioritizes experiential, project-based learning. The integration of technology in design education is crucial, with an emphasis on combining digital tools with creative processes. Through site visits and experiential learning, curriculum design promotes practical understanding in architectural education. These components emphasize student-centred approaches, especially through the critique and review processes, and shape teacher roles through interdisciplinary learning. Furthermore, historical and theoretical research enhances the learning environment, and feedback and assessment frequently highlight sustainable design principles. The role of faculty is influenced by culture and society, with a focus on mentoring and advising students in the field of architecture (Table 8.1).

Table 8.1. Key Elements Shaping Architectural Pedagogy.

Key Elements Impacting Educational Approaches	Key Elements in Architecture Pedagogy
Pedagogical methods	Design studio methodology
Technology integration	Technology integration in design
Curriculum design	Experiential learning and site visits
Teacher role and pedagogical practices	Interdisciplinary learning
Student-centred approaches	Critique and review process
Learning environment	Historical and theoretical studies
Assessment and feedback	Sustainable and environmental design
Cultural and societal influences	Faculty role and mentorship

Experiential learning and site visits are important components of architecture education because they expose students to real-world architectural places and provide hands-on experience. These exercises help them learn spatial linkages and practical design issues. Furthermore, interdisciplinary research and collaboration with sectors such as engineering and environmental science broaden viewpoints, creating a thorough understanding of architecture's larger influence. Cultural and socioeconomic elements reinforce inclusiveness and diversity in education, while historical and theoretical studies increase students' understanding of architectural growth and societal influences on design. Emphasizing sustainable and environmental design principles teaches students about environmental issues, energy efficiency, and ethical duties in design work.

Teachers have a tremendous impact on student involvement and achievement in architecture education. Faculty advise and help students through the critique and review process, which is critical in this industry. This procedure, which includes peer assessments, instructor criticisms, and presentations, lets students express their design ideas and accept constructive feedback. Technological integration, mentoring, and varied viewpoints are critical in educating students for the multifarious needs of the architectural profession. These characteristics influence educational techniques, notably in architectural pedagogy, emphasizing the significance of practical, experiential, and interdisciplinary learning methods.

The main conclusions have important ramifications for how architecture education will develop in the future. Above all, the research (Salama & Burton, 2022) indicates that using resilience principles in educational contexts calls for a fundamental change in teaching techniques. The design of the curriculum for architectural education must be flexible and adaptable, emphasizing the development of students' various skill sets and readiness for unforeseen circumstances.

The way that conventional educational systems are changing (Erdmann et al., 2021) emphasizes how important it is for architecture schools to smoothly incorporate technology into their teaching methods. Since virtual platforms are already essential, there may be a continuing need to develop and improve these resources for successful remote learning. But the importance of studio-based learning shouldn't be diminished (Bakir & Alsaadani, 2022). Rather, there's a chance for hybrid methods that combine digital resources with practical training to produce a comprehensive architectural education.

Furthermore, a proactive approach to change management is required given the possibilities and constraints found in educational institutions (Jandrić et al., 2022). This should serve as a spur for architectural schools to reassess their instructional approaches, highlighting their strengths and weaknesses, encouraging creativity, and promoting student–faculty collaboration. Finally, the recognition of the varied experiences and lessons that teachers and students have learnt (Sadigov et al., 2023) points to the necessity of inclusion in educational practices, guaranteeing that different learning styles and views are accommodated within the context of architecture education.

Future studies in architectural education have a solid basis thanks to the body of current research. First and foremost, it is imperative to investigate the durability and long-term impacts of the modifications made to architectural education in response to the epidemic. To learn more about these adaptations' long-term effects and efficacy, research may explore how they might develop or last after the current crisis.

It would also be beneficial to look at how cutting-edge technology might promote cooperative learning opportunities in the field of architecture education. It would be interesting to investigate how new technologies such as artificial intelligence (AI)-driven design platforms, AR, and VR may improve faculty–student cooperation and creativity in architectural schools. A comparative analysis of how different nations or areas have responded differently to the problems provided by the pandemic might also offer valuable cross-cultural insights, given the global character of architecture education. This might involve analysing various educational responses, integrating technology, and analysing the results of these techniques.

Finally, studies that concentrate on the mental health and general well-being of architectural teachers and students in the face of these shifts may prove to be very helpful. Researching the psychological effects of social isolation, the transition to remote learning, and the general stresses in architecture education during emergencies such as the COVID-19 pandemic can direct the creation of treatments and support mechanisms to improve the learning environment as a whole.

References

Aidarova, G., & Aminov, A. (2021). COVID-19 – Global transition to a new architecture and urban development paradigm of the environment? *E3S Web of Conference, 274*, 01008. https://doi.org/10.1051/e3sconf/202127401008

Akçay Kavakoğlu, A., Güleç Özer, D., Domingo-Callabuig, D., & Bilen, Ö. (2022). Architectural design communication (ADC) in online education during COVID-19 pandemic: A comparison of Turkish and Spanish universities. *Open House International, 47*(2), 29–42. https://doi.org/10.5843/ohi.v47i2.1761

Alghamdi, A. K. H., El-Hassan, W. S., Al-Ahdal, A. A. M. H., & Hassan, A. A. (2021). Distance education in higher education in Saudi Arabia in the post-COVID-19 era. *World Journal on Educational Technology: Current Issues*, *13*(3), 485–501. E-ISSN: 1309-0348.

Alhefnawi, M. A. M., Dano, U. L., Istanbouli, M. J., Al-Gehlani, W. A. G., Afify, H. M. N., Elghany, G. A., & Rahal, M. S. (2021). Exam grades in architecture classes: A comparative assessment of before and during COVID-19 pandemic modes of teaching and learning. *International Journal of Innovation, Creativity, and Change*, *15*(2), 54. www.ijicc.net

Alraouf, A. A. (2021). The new normal or the forgotten normal: Contesting COVID-19 impact on contemporary architecture and urbanism. *Archnet-IJAR*, *15*(1). https://doi.org/10.26687/archnet-ijar.v15i1.1645

Antón-Sancho, Á., & Sánchez-Calvo, M. (2022). Influence of knowledge area on the use of digital tools during the COVID-19 pandemic among Latin American professors. *Education Sciences*, *12*(9), 635. https://doi.org/10.3390/educsci12090635

Aslan, S. A., Turgut, Y. E. & Aslan, A. (2021). Teachers' views related the middle school curriculum for distance education during the COVID-19 pandemic. *Education and Information Technologies*, *26*, 7381–7405. https://doi.org/10.1007/s10639-021-10587-z

Bakir, R., & Alsaadani, S. (2022). A mixed methods study of architectural education during the initial COVID-19 lockdown: Student experiences in design studio and technology courses. *Open House International*, *47*(2), 338–360.

Bentata, Y. (2020). COVID-2019 pandemic: A true digital revolution and birth of a new educational era, or an ephemeral phenomenon? *Medical Education Online*, *25*(1), Article 1781378. https://doi.org/10.1080/10872981.2020.1781378

Campanyà, C., Fonseca, D., Amo, D., Martí, N., & Peña, E. (2021). Mixed analysis of the flipped classroom in the concrete and steel structures subject in the context of COVID-19 crisis outbreak: A pilot study. *Sustainability*, *13*(11), 5826. https://doi.org/10.3390/su13115826

El-Sakran, A., Salman, R., & Alzaatreh, A. (2022). Impacts of emergency remote teaching on college students amid COVID-19 in the UAE. *International Journal of Environmental Research and Public Health*, *19*(5), 2979. https://doi.org/10.3390/ijerph19052979

Erdmann, A., Estrada Presedo, A., & De Miguel Valdés, M. (2021). Digital transformation of universities: The influence of COVID-19 and students' perception. *Multidisciplinary Journal for Education, Social and Technological Sciences*, *8*(2), 19–41. https://doi.org/10.4995/muse.2021.16007

Faura-Martínez, U., Lafuente-Lechuga, M., & Cifuentes-Faura, J. (2022). Sustainability of the Spanish university system during the pandemic caused by COVID-19. *Educational Review*, *74*(3), 645–663. https://doi.org/10.1080/00131911.2021.1978399

Gupta, M., & Kumar, V. (2021). Revealing the demonstration of blockchain and implementing scope in COVID-19 outbreak. *EAI Endorsed Transactions on Scalable Information Systems*, *8*(29), 1–10. https://doi.org/10.4108/eai.13-7-2018.165520

Ibrahim, F., Susanto, H., Khodaparast Haghi, P., & Setiana, D. (2020). Shifting paradigm of education landscape in time of the COVID-19 Pandemic: Revealing of a digital education management information system. *Applied System Innovation*, *3*(4), 49. https://doi.org/10.3390/asi3040049

Imran, R., Fatima, A., Salem, I. E., & Allil, K. (2023). Teaching and learning delivery modes in higher education: Looking back to move forward post-COVID-19 era. *The International Journal of Management Education*, *21*(2), 100805.

Jandrić, P., Fuentes Martinez, A., Reitz, C., Jackson, L., Grauslund, D., Hayes, D., Lukoko, H. O., Hogan, M., Mozelius, P., Arantes, J. A., Levinson, P., Ozoliņš, J. J., Kirylo, J. D., Carr, P. R., Hood, N., Tesar, M., Sturm, S., … Hayes, S. (2022). Teaching in the age of Covid-19 – The new normal. *Postdigital Science and Education*, *4*, 877–1015. https://doi.org/10.1007/s42438-022-00427-w

Jefferies, T., Cheng, J., & Coucill, L. (2021). Lockdown urbanism: COVID-19 lifestyles and liveable futures opportunities in Wuhan and Manchester. *Cities & Health*, *5*(sup1), S155–S158. https://doi.org/10.1080/23748834.2020.1788771

Jin, R., Adamu, Z., Chohan, N., & Kangwa, J. (2021). *A critical analysis of collaborative and disruptive digital-driven built environment education*. Association of Researchers in Construction Management (ARCOM).

Kanetaki, Z., Stergiou, C., Bekas, G., Troussas, C., & Sgouropoulou, C. (2021). Analysis of engineering student data in online higher education during the COVID-19 pandemic. *iJEP*, *11*(6), 27–49. https://doi.org/10.3991/ijep.v11i6.23259

Komarzyńska-Świeściak, E., Adams, B., & Thomas, L. (2021). Transition from physical design studio to emergency virtual design studio. available teaching and learning methods and tools – A case study. *Buildings*, *11*(7), 312. https://doi.org/10.3390/buildings11070312

Leišytė, L., Dee, J. R., & van der Meulen, B. J. R. (Eds.). (2023). *Research handbook on the transformation of higher education*. Edward Elgar Publishing.

Martínez, F., Jacinto, E., & Montiel, H. (2021). The use of online learning environments in higher education as a response to the confinement caused by COVID-19. *Journal of e-Learning and Knowledge Society*, *17*(1), 1–7. https://doi.org/10.20368/1971-8829/1135309.

Maturana, B., Salama, A. M., & McInneny, A. (2021). Architecture, urbanism and health in a post-pandemic virtual world. *Archnet-IJAR*, *15*(1), 1–9. https://doi.org/DOI

Mbah, M., Bang, H., & Ndzo, J. A. (2021). Community health education for health crisis management: The case of COVID-19 in Cameroon. *Community Health Equity Research & Policy*, *43*(4), 443–452. https://doi.org/10.1177/0272684X211031

Mosquera Feijóo, J. C., Suárez, F., Chiyón, I., & García Alberti, M. (2021). Some web-based experiences from flipped classroom techniques in AEC modules during the COVID-19 lockdown. *Education Sciences*, *11*(5), 211. https://doi.org/10.3390/educsci11050211

Mushtaha, E., Abu Dabous, S., Alsyouf, I., Ahmed, A., & Abdraboh, N. R. (2022). The challenges and opportunities of online learning and teaching at engineering and theoretical colleges during the pandemic. *Ain Shams Engineering Journal*, *13*(6), Article 101770.

Ngubane-Mokiwa, S. A., & Zongozzi, J. N. (2021). Exclusion reloaded: The chronicles of COVID-19 on students with disabilities in a South African open distance learning context. *Journal of Intellectual Disability – Diagnosis and Treatment*, *9*, 137–147. E-ISSN: 2292-2598.

Olweny, M., Morkel, J., Delport, H., Whelan, D., & Ndibwami, A. (2021). Zombies in the studio: Towards nurturing pedagogical approaches for architectural education in sub-Saharan Africa. *Charrette*, *7*(2), 57–83.

Pietrocola, M., Rodrigues, E., Bercot, F., & Schnorr, S. (2020). Risk society and science education: Lessons from the Covid-19 pandemic. *Science & Education*, *30*(2), 209–233.

Sadigov, R., Yıldırım, E., Kocaçınar, B., Akbulut, F. P., & Catal, C. (2023). Deep learning-based user experience evaluation in distance learning. *Cluster Computing*, *27*, 443–455. https://doi.org/10.1007/s10586-022-03918-3

Salama, A. M., & Burton, L. O. (2022). Defying a legacy or an evolving process? A post-pandemic architectural design pedagogy. *Proceedings of the Institution of Civil Engineers – Urban Design and Planning*, *175*(1), 5–21. https://doi.org/10.1680/jurdp.21.00023

Yavuz, M., Kayali, B., & Tutal, Ö. (2021). Trend of distance education research in the COVID-19 period: A bibliometric and content analysis. *Journal of Educational Technology and Online Learning*, *4*(2), 256–279. https://doi.org/10.31681/jetol.922682

Yunusa, A. A., Sanusi, I. T., Dada, O. A., & Oyelere, S. S. (2021). The impact of the COVID-19 pandemic on higher education in Nigeria: University lecturers' perspectives. *ijEDict – International Journal of Education and Development using Information and Communication Technology*, *17*(4), 43–66.

Zhu, J., Weng, F., Zhuang, M., Lu, X., Tan, X., Lin, S., & Zhang, R. (2022). Revealing public opinion towards the COVID-19 vaccine with Weibo data in China: BertFDA-based model. *International Journal of Environmental Research and Public Health*, *19*(20), 13248. https://doi.org/10.3390/ijerph192013248

Chapter 9

Challenges and Transformation of Pedagogy Towards Blended Learning: A Sequential Mixed-Method Study in Higher Education

Nagamani Nagaraja[a] and Benny Godwin J. Davidson[b]

[a]Centre for Learning, Leadership and Excellence, India
[b]University of the Fraser Valley, British Columbia, Canada

Abstract

Two essential components, a robust information technology (IT) infrastructure and faculty training in student-centred pedagogies and technology usage, are necessary for effective blended learning designs. Many universities invest in IT infrastructure such as bandwidth, high-end subscriptions, servers, SMART boards, projectors, Wi-Fi enhancement, learning management systems, IT support, and other tools. Faculty training is crucial and includes instruction on using the new infrastructure and adopting pedagogical methods associated with blended learning. This study's primary objective is to explore the challenges and pedagogical transformation towards blended learning designs in India. The research also investigates the impact of social context and emotional support on blended learning. It examines the mediating role of technostress among teachers between hybrid mode transformation and blended learning. The study's results will provide critical insights for academic institutions' higher management to encourage the adoption of learning designs and blended techniques by their employees during unforeseen events in the future, utilizing effective leadership and management skills. The study aims to assist academic institutions in meeting the demand for experiential learning in the classroom by incorporating blended learning. It acts as a bridge between industry expectations and academic outcomes. The study uniquely addresses the need for increased student engagement in the classroom.

Keywords: Blended learning pedagogy; challenges and transformation; techniques; technostress; leadership

Introduction

In the wake of the COVID-19 pandemic, with metaphors the world witnessed a rapid acceleration of technological innovations across various sectors, including education. Post-pandemic experiences were disruptive, deep, and transformative in nature. The world witnessed 'the New Normal' as tertiary institutions adapted to remote and hybrid learning models while educators were faced with the challenge of navigating digital platforms, online pedagogy, and new teaching methodologies. The pandemic forced educators to quickly adapt to new teaching environments, pushing them to acquire digital skills and utilize various educational technologies. These experiences have transformed the traditional role of educators, expanding their responsibilities to include proficiency in digital tools, online instructional design, and the ability to engage students in virtual learning environments.

Consequently, the post-pandemic period presents an opportunity to capitalize on this momentum and leverage technological innovations such as blended learning, which integrates the face-to-face teaching-learning process with web-based learning (Anthony et al., 2022). Poon (2014) clinched that blended learning would be developed as the principal teaching method as one of the top 10 educational trends to transpire in the 21st century. This worldwide pandemic had an unfathomable impact on educators, and the forced adoption led to a transformed focus on the need to raise the bar for teacher training. Moreover, the existing system for teacher training is inadequate owing to a lack of knowledge, skills, technological know-how, academic and institutional support which hampers their preparedness to teach in blended learning environments, leading to technostress among educators.

Recent research evidences the need to raise the bar. A study by the National Council for Accreditation of Teacher Education (NCATE) stated that only 37% of educators are equipped with skills to prepare students or graduates to practice the use of technology. Consequently, this is an attempt to explore the impact of technological innovations that have transformed higher education, the challenges and the transformation of pedagogy, teaching-learning processes, continuous professional development, learning design, and blended techniques and most significantly will investigate and examine the mediating role of technostress among educators between hybrid mode transformation and blended learning.

Contextually, providing critical insights and a comprehensive framework to investigate the complex relationship between blended learning, technostress, and pedagogical transformation and how institutions of excellence should utilize effective academic leadership to bridge the gap between industry expectations and academic outcomes and, last but not least, address the need for increased student engagement in the classroom.

In this chapter, we contextually discuss the impact, challenges, and transformation of pedagogy towards blended learning among academicians in higher education institutions (HEIs) and the phenomenon of technostress with its social and emotional impact. We aim to bring a deeper understanding of the learning designs, coping strategies, challenges, implications, and the multifaceted interplay between pedagogical evolution, well-being, and technological adaptation among educators. This chapter seeks to acquaint universities, stakeholders, and policymakers with a framework to effectively develop institutional policies, effective leadership, training programmes, learning designs, and mechanisms in the post-pandemic landscape to successfully integrate blended learning and confront unpredicted events in the future.

The post-pandemic technological shifts in the teaching-learning practices in HEIs have caused technostress among educators more so because of the technological transformations in pedagogy especially towards blending learning. Studies conducted by institutions like the University of California, National Institute of Educational Planning and Administration (India), and University of Pennsylvania state that 40–60% of educators experienced technostress leading to diminished productivity, creativity, and job satisfaction.

This chapter will encompass diverse dimensions. A few such dimensions are (1) the assessment and identification of the sources of technostress and comprehending its impact on teaching practices; (2) the exploration of pedagogical transformations observed in institutions of higher education; (3) academicians' perspectives and their coping strategies; (4) how the pedagogical transformation is influencing professional development, student engagement, and learning outcomes; (5) the impact of institutional policies and support systems while examining long-term implications; and (6) a holistic approach and frameworks with evidence-based recommendations to HEIs. This chapter will also attempt to answer the below questions to bring more clarity to the framework:

1. What are the significant challenges encountered in HEIs while acclimatizing to the transformation of pedagogy towards blended learning subsequent to the pandemic? How will educators navigate the technological and pedagogical shift?
2. How has technostress evolved? What are the long-term implications of technostress on their job satisfaction, burnout, and well-being?
3. What kind of strategies will impact educators' ability to manage and successfully implement blended learning methods? How do institutional policy, leadership, and administrative support relate to change and unanticipated future?

Blended Learning – What is it?

Blending learning is the most practised form of e-learning in HEIs today. Though there is an ambiguity and multiple interpretations of the term, blended learning characteristically refers to the incorporation of conventional in-person instruction with online instruction (Garrison & Vaughan, 2008; Ward & La Branche, 2003). It is an integration of different web-based technologies such as collaborative learning platforms, interactive virtual classes, multimedia, self-paced modules, and text to achieve educational objectives; it is where diverse teaching approaches like constructivism, behaviourism, and cognitivism are blended to achieve the best possible learning outcomes; it merges different instructional technology like web-based courses, video recordings, films, CD-ROMs, with in-person instructor-led training sessions, and it seamlessly combines instructional technology with real tasks, creating synergy between learning and working experiences (Friesen, 2012). Since 2006 to the present day, it has been tacit as an amalgamation of 'face-to-face and technology-mediated instructional forms and practices' (Friesen, 2012). It uses multiple distinct approaches to training plus a mixture of blending 'classroom instruction with online instruction', with access to a faculty member, structured courses, blending job training, and managerial training with e-learning activities (Clark, 2003).

Blended learning is a varied approach combining online and in-person instruction, with manifold interpretations accentuating its hybrid nature (Lawless, 2019). Few other research definitions view it as a 'blend of offline and online practices' (Cheung & Wang, 2019), a blend of technologies to augment teaching-learning experiences (Cronje, 2020), or reconstruction of conventional teaching with digital technology. Blended learning combines online and traditional classroom techniques (Joksimović et al., 2015). Moreover, it incorporates a mix of didactic methods for optimum outcomes (Caner, 2012). Last but not least, it is a teaching-learning process, an instructional methodology and a pedagogical approach that combines computer-mediated activities and face-to-face classroom methods to deliver instructions. Contextually, it is an integrated pedagogical approach that transforms student learning and engagement, but it also comes with its challenges. The most significant challenges are (1) sound pedagogical and instructional design, (2) digital literacy, (3) academic and administrative support, (4) technical skills, (5) efficient use of time, (6) professional training, and (7) leadership and institutional support.

This learning thus integrates synchronous and asynchronous learning tools to optimize the effective learning processes (UGC, 2021). Post-pandemic teaching-learning practices orbit around digital technologies where an instructor uses a variety of media to engage while creating diverse learning environments through different teaching strategies (Garrison & Kanuka, 2004). The role of technology is undeniable. Its integration into classroom instructions is essential (Singh, 2021), of course with its challenges and pedagogical transformations. Olitsky and Cosgrove (2014) stated how blended learning should be a pedagogical method that assimilates the 'effectiveness and socialization opportunities' of the technologically vigorous learning potentials of the online setting with the classroom.

Challenges and Pedagogical Transformation Towards Blended Learning

For decades, blended learning has been prefigured as a transformative teaching-learning method, and its practice has become progressively more prevalent in global higher education as technological systems advance and universities seek better means to engage with learners (Alammary et al., 2014). Aguti et al. (2014) specified that in developed nations, 80% of institutions dynamically engage in blended learning methods to aid teaching and learning and 97% of HEIs deployed more forms of technology-mediated learning. Norberg et al. (2011) proposed 'blended learning' effectually as 'the new normal', influenced by technology and evolving subsequently to the discovery of the printing press. Though these results were noteworthy, blended learning is not fully integrated in the majority of HEIs (Graham et al., 2013; Smith & Hill, 2019).

At the university level, challenges exist while aligning blended learning methods with universities' core priorities. Habitually, the focus is on technological tools, infrastructure, and related training but less prominence to the development of instructional approaches to blended teaching-learning practices (Norberg et al., 2011). Bansal (2014) states that inherently blended learning is about 'rethinking and redesigning the teaching and learning relationship'. However certain studies have pointed out that blended learning keys fail to live up to the potential approach and are not capable of showing predictable results due to a lack of methodological, technical, or organizational experience and knowledge. HEIs are also challenged due to a lack of skilled educators to engage with blended learning; resistance to change and innovation, scarcity of informed research models to support adoption, and more importantly blended learning research and practices are predominantly individual endeavours rather than institutional (Smith & Hill, 2019).

Boelens et al. (2017) highlighted four challenges in the design of blended learning in the context of students: (a) the question of flexibility, how to incorporate, and its feasibility into the course design; (b) facilitating interaction with tutors and peers: face-to-face, synchronous, or asynchronous digital communication; (c) the question of learning processes: the transition from traditional learning environments to a blended learning model that is self-regulated; and (d) fostering 'affective learning climate', communities of learning, motivation, acceptance, safety, values, and positive attitude towards learning.

Further, blended learning engages in a blend of face-to-face and online-mediated instruction to help educators reach pedagogical goals in educating students, enhance teaching-learning potentials, and attain social order (Subramaniam & Muniandy, 2019). It also offers personalization, enhanced student outcomes, and development of autonomy while learning can become self-directed enhancing the prospects of professional learning and increasing interaction between students and educators (So & Brush, 2008; Spring et al., 2016). Blended learning reforms pedagogic policies with a perspective to recapture the ideals of HEIs (Heinze & Procter, 2004). Consequently, blended learning remains an important pedagogical concept as its key focus is associated with dynamic teaching and learning experience (Wang et al., 2004).

Research studies have stated that blended learning focuses on collective collaboration, pedagogical efficiency, self-development, access to knowledge, cost efficacy, streamlines corrections, and solves problems such as attendance (Mustapa et al., 2015). It offers benefits and is more productive than conventional e-learning (Nguyen, 2017; Wai & Seng, 2015). Implementation of blended learning involves computer-mediated tools with face-to-face delivery methods creating an environment to promote learning engagements and learner outcomes (Moskal et al., 2013). Graham et al. (2013) and Moskal et al. (2013), in their research, have identified key aspects of blended learning such as technology-mediated online activities and human-mediated face-to-face activities. Further Anthony et al. (2022) have identified clusters of issues to be addressed while implementing blended learning. Cluster 1 discusses the administrative impact of diffusing blended learning, the evaluation of students' learning and learning efficacy, educators' teaching practices, the effectiveness of e-learning, the adoption of massive open online courses (MOOC) application, and the assessment of students' perception and readiness. Cluster 2 talks about effectiveness and efficiency; attitude and intention; students' acceptance, experience, and satisfaction; analysis of students' interactions; learning tools and the teacher, students' self-regulatory behaviour; and gender influence and satisfaction. Cluster 3 deliberates on institutions and higher education decision-makers and blended learning adoption, structure and development, acceptability and potential use, elements of success, learning behaviour, and best practices.

Further to their research Anthony et al. (2022) comprehensively deliberate the constructs and factors in three parts in the adoption of blended learning in higher education: first at the level of educators, second at the level of students, and lastly at the level of administration. Each of these levels is further classified into educators' level of satisfaction, course management, ease of use, and teaching experience; students' attitude, perspective, supporting factors, and learning effectiveness; and institutional management and administration, resources support, ethics, and administrative effectiveness. These are further categorized to bring clarity to the constructs while adapting to blended learning mode.

Consequently, HEIs, post looking beyond traditional classrooms, should strategically develop learning management systems (LMS) to incorporate diligent utilization of learning materials, assessments, discussion forums, best practices, and submission of assignments. This can be done by augmenting their existing best practices and replacing them with advances in learning and collaborative technologies to provide meaningful chances for learning development and social interactions. The teaching fraternity should prudently design courses with multiple engagements, instructions, representations, and expressions to scaffold and aid students in using their creativity to create individual blends where they can develop skills as self-regulating, self-directed, and reflective to eventually become self-determined learners (De George-Walker & Keeffe, 2010).

Five key factors that the pandemic has impacted are diagrammatically represented in Fig. 9.1 addressing factors like students' competency, learning outcomes, teaching-learning process, learning designs, technology, and blended learning techniques, thus emphasizing the need for transformation.

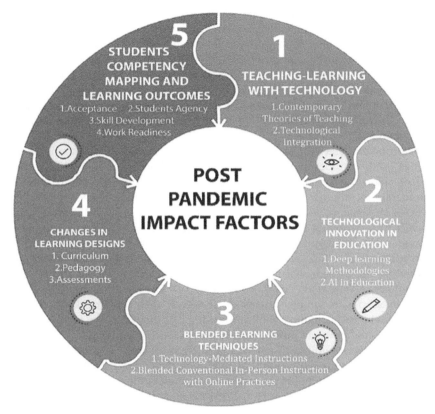

Fig. 9.1. Key Post-Pandemic Impact Factors. *Source*: Authors' own work.

Conceptual Frameworks

The conceptual framework of blended learning is often associated and grounded in constructivist philosophy. It employs research methods akin to grounded theory and often an ethnographic approach. By closely observing and scrutinising the collected data of student behaviour over a given period of time, researchers can develop hypotheses about the learning process within this educational model. (Creswell & Creswell, 2018). This conceptual framework defines an institutional approach to blended learning by developing conceptual clarity, a comprehension of blended frameworks and mechanisms to implement blended learning at the institutional level (McCarthy & Palmer, 2023). What is more significant is the need for accountability factors like (1) effective curriculum development and delivery, (2) learners' requirement, (3) support mechanisms, (4) appropriate technology, (5) organizational preparedness, (6) process of continuous improvement, (7) factors of risks, and (8) stakeholders roles (Adekola et al., 2017; Garrison & Vaughan, 2008).

Contextually, any proposed frameworks should be associated with the implementation policy and examine the degree to which a HEI adopts and implements this policy to support the blended learning approach (Graham et al., 2013). Research also states that there are conflicting views concerning the requirements of the blended learning frameworks in four blending levels – activities, courses, programmes, and at the institution level (Bonk & Graham, 2012). McCarthy and Palmer's (2023) research discusses the factors responsible for the blended learning framework like designing the curriculum, strategy and pedagogy for teaching, tech integration, the role of students, teaching-learning support, the role of the teacher, the role of the institution, infrastructure, partnerships, ethics, evaluation, and research.

Additionally, few studies discussed the 'organizational preparedness for change' while considering stakeholders' responsibilities associated with the process of change. A proposed transitional framework composed of institutional considerations, change agents, organizational preparedness, and stakeholder roles for implementation was also discussed (Adekola et al., 2017). Research and practice were evaluated at the institutional level along with the demonstration of the use of the framework. They also found the relationship between the institution and the teacher was significant in redefining the role of promoter of learning, facilitator, and advisor while supporting this through continuous professional development (Wang et al., 2015). Lim et al. (2019) furnished comprehensive strategic dimensions to complement all the themes in their framework to reinforce institutional implementation. Collectively, Fig. 9.2 showcases the factors reflecting institutional practices and policies that need crucial attention.

A few research findings also state that there is no single approach and every institution has to search for a pathway to reshape their course design, programme, teaching methods, and tailor the broader teaching-learning process accessible by learners (Galvis, 2018; Smith & Hill, 2019). Graham et al. (2013) stated that there is very little data to show how blended learning is integrated into higher education, due to its definition and measurement. Vaughan et al. (2017) pointed out in their evidence-based case study that 'without a universal definition of blended learning there is no shared language by which the education field can describe the phenomena or address its opportunities and challenges'. A significant area is lack of support and leadership and the way these factors impact institutional transformation is diagrammatically represented in Fig. 9.3.

Social Context and Emotional Support on Blended Learning

The social and the emotional contexts are associated with concepts like technological difficulties, poor integration, teacher scepticism, increased workload, and diminishing academic productivity according to Carbonell et al. (2013). Few other research also talk about how interest, independent learning, external expectations, self-efficacy, skills, and social perception are also integrated with the above contexts (Lu et al., 2012). Brown (2016) categorizes extrinsic and intrinsic practices based on experiences. It is a fact that educators' motivation is significantly affected by technology readiness (Nicolle & Lou, 2008). One such factor influencing the social and emotional context of educators is technostress.

Pedagogy Towards Blended Learning 159

Fig. 9.2. Key Impact Factors Reflecting Institutional Practices and Policy. *Source*: Authors' own work.

Fig. 9.3. Key Factors of Leadership Impact. *Source*: Authors' own work.

Technostress

Leaders at HEIs face multifaced burdens in managing change and management of institutional decisions (Strielkowski, 2020). Educators' working conditions changed (Sokal et al., 2020) as they abruptly adapted to the online learning system (VanNuland et al., 2020) which impacted professional and personal lives resulting in physical and emotional exhaustion as they realized their critical role in integrating technology into teaching and learning processes. Not only educators' perspectives but their workload, attitude, time, and pedagogy were also affected (Panisoara et al., 2020).

Educators commonly considered technology to lessen their preparation, but they lacked the skills and competencies to design and implement successful integration in their teaching-learning processes (Munyengabe et al., 2017). They are exposed to chronic technostress due to their lack of technology adoption (Li & Wang, 2020). This is due to a lack of training, inadequate infrastructure, and support from technology specialists, causing mental and physical stress because of technology use (Joo et al., 2016). This is true for institutional leaders as well who are under immense psychological strain to cater to the day-to-day requirements like reassurance and support (Mousa, 2021). Additionally, it complicates decision-making due to time constraints, lack of knowledge, uncertainty, and stress. Technology is here to stay, a survey conducted by the economist on the 'Future of Higher Education and How Technology Will Shape the Learning' highlighted how 63% of the survey respondents from both public and private sectors stated that 'technological innovation will have a major impact on teaching methodologies over years'. Contextually, the 2019 pandemic swiftly adopted into 'non-face-to-face' instructional design in education using information and communication technology (ICT) complemented by gadgets like iPads, smartphones, kiosks, and tablets (Ali, 2020; Rahiem, 2020). The survey further mentions how many HEIs are struggling with the challenges of raising ICT, costs, inadequate instructional design, insufficient staff, resources, and other technological support issues while it's enabling changing curricula, multi-model teaching, collaboration, and rich online resources.

Though technology is beneficial, the phenomenon, identified as 'technostress' (Weil & Rosen, 1997), refers 'to a sense of inferiority due to a perceived inability to use ICT well and a sense of being overwhelmed by too much information provided by ICT' (Nimrod, 2018) prevails. If one fails to respond well to technostress, the end-user experience and productivity are greatly impacted (Rachmawati et al., 2021; Sharma & Gupta, 2022). Technostress is defined as stress that is created by the use of ICT where individuals struggle to transact with the evolving ICTs, the shifts in changing cognitive, and the social necessities associated with its use (Ragu-Nathan et al., 2008).

Technostress denotes the problem of 'adaptation'; individuals experience when they cannot handle or acclimatize to ICT (Weil & Rosen, 1997). It is also an emotional reaction ICT users experience (Ayyagari et al., 2011). Technostress is a direct or indirect stressful experience that individuals go through while using ICT in daily life (Lee et al., 2016). Nimrod (2022) states how COVID-19 stressed people through inclusion – an inferiority complex perceived by their inability to use ICT and overload – where they are overwhelmed by the overload of ICT information. He also lists five factors which induce technostress:

1. Overload – information overload provided by ICT
2. Invasion – the use of ICT in personal contexts
3. Complexity – the complications and difficulties of learning, using, and mastering ICT in the ever-changing environment
4. Privacy – issues of exploitation, tracing, and overstepping personal boundaries in the use of ICT
5. Inclusion – complexes like inferiority and pressure in optimum utilization of ICT (Nimrod, 2018)

Fig. 9.4 showcases the factors influencing and impacting technostress in educators. It highlights a few noteworthy technological, social, and emotional challenges that have impacted educators across institutions.

Today, technology is a significant concern in education, and the pandemic has critically affected well-being due to the mandatory remote working requirements (Molino et al., 2020). The educators' willingness to continue with digitalization is needed to interpret their behaviour as an educational cognitive decision. There is research evaluating whether educators in multiple settings want to continue technology-mediated teaching (Yurkofsky et al., 2019), behaviour, emotions, skills, gender, attitude, and age but nothing on educators' willingness. The

Fig. 9.4. Key Impact Factors – Technostress. *Source*: Authors' own work.

intention of applying technology is to focus on 'perceived satisfaction, motivation, e-learning effectiveness, engagement and learning outcomes, disregarding negative feelings such as technostress' (Panisoara et al., 2020).

Recognizing the problems that evade educators' desire to use technology is critical for educational institutions to prosper in extremely competitive academic settings. The three kinds of technostress inhibitors are literacy facilitation, technical support provision, and involvement facilitation (Hwang & Cha, 2018). To conclude, technostress is reported because of difficulties such as social media, mobile applications, collaborative tools, digital data processing equipment, and learning management systems. A few other factors linked to technostress are instructional experience and teachers' psychological capital. Consequently, research also reveals how it can lead to mental and physical harm affecting performance and productivity (Salo et al., 2018). Further, this research has identified five critical frameworks that HEIs should critically engage and foresee as solutions to the challenges and transformation towards blended learning pedagogy. Various frameworks and their critical insights and solutions are presented in Table 9.1, such as:

1. Pedagogical Transformations
2. Social and Emotional Contexts
3. Technostress
4. Institutional Practices and Policy
5. Future of Learning and Work

Implications and Conclusion

Investments in the development and implementation of structured learning methods must be prioritized in the pedagogical realm. Student understanding and retention of course materials should be enhanced by these methods. At the same time, educators should explore innovative, adaptable, and flexible teaching methods that can accommodate diverse learning styles and abilities. Educators should become facilitators and classrooms should adopt the student-centric approach to learning. In order to maintain relevance and alignment with the evolving educational landscape, curricula and learning materials need to be reviewed and updated regularly.

It is also possible to provide students with a more holistic and engaging learning experience by incorporating a five-component strategy that incorporates active learning, collaboration, and formative assessment into course design. Student agency is imperative. It is imperative that educators remain current with emerging technologies and pedagogical trends so that their teaching approaches can be adapted. To stay on top of educational trends, educators should cultivate a culture of continuous professional development. Education is a demanding profession, so comprehensively training teachers is essential to their success. Education policies must be evidence based and reflect best practices through collaboration between educators, policymakers, and researchers. Furthermore, educators should be taught how to incorporate resilient and brain-based teaching methods into their training programmes to support students' emotional wellness.

Table 9.1. Frameworks – Critical Insights and Solutions.

Pedagogical Transformations	Social and Emotional Contexts	Technostress	Institutional Practices and Policy	Future of Learning and Work
• Structured learning methods • Creative, flexible and inclusive teaching and learning pedagogies • Rethinking and Redesigning curriculum and learning content • Five-component strategy (discovery, learning, practice, collaboration, assessment) • Dynamically adapt to the changing ecosystem of learning • Understand paradigm shifts in practices and instructional approaches • Research evidences the need to raise the bar for teacher training • Policymakers, educators, and researchers to work together • Resilient and neuro pedagogy • Build the capacity of qualified educators	• Unequal socioeconomic realities • Socio-emotional needs in students' engagement • Teacher-student agency and well-being • Compassionate goals • Reflective practitionership • Changing educators' role • Diverse students' realities and learning constraints • Care and concern to be integrated into higher education pedagogy	• Acceptance of technological interventions • Create supportive technological environments • Identify and address factors causing technostress • Provide training on global digital technologies • How to deal with it – embrace technology, set boundaries for its use, initiate work-life balance and implement a digital adoption platform • Digital teaching competence	• Translate vision across the institution • Have training initiatives as a policy • Have structured research and academic committees to work on learning design and changing dynamics of education • Have policy to build institutions of excellence • Have continuous project collaborations with industries • Have a leadership team to initiate practices to overcome uncertainties • Stock resources and finances	• Greater student autonomy and flexibility • Sustainability of emergent practices at universities • Keeping abreast with the learning challenges • Intensified demand for student-centred learning systems • Designing and facilitating learning in changing contexts • Globalization of higher education arena – the borderless phenomenon • Future of work

Source: Authors' own work.

To continuously enhance educators' qualifications and expertise, they need professional development opportunities.

Technostress can be addressed by promoting a culture of openness to technology adoption. Additionally, educators should receive resources that can assist them in effectively integrating technology into their classrooms. Technostress among educators can be significantly reduced by ensuring a robust and user-friendly technical infrastructure. In addition to conducting regular assessments, educators and students ought to be made aware of the factors that may contribute to technostress. In order to navigate the digital landscape effectively, educators and students must be provided with comprehensive training programmes. A useful strategy for managing technostress is to educate individuals about using technology, setting boundaries, developing resilience, being mindful, and maintaining work-life balance. As well as providing educators with resources to enhance their digital skills, it is significant to promote the development of digital teaching competencies.

Creating a more equitable learning environment requires appropriate strategies to address disparities among students in accessing support systems and resources. To foster student well-being and engagement, school environments that acknowledge and address students' socio-emotional needs are essential. Resources for professional development and self-care are essential for promoting agency and well-being among educators and students. Educational practices and policies can be enhanced by incorporating compassionate teaching and learning goals. Educators can improve their teaching methods and adapt to changing student needs by encouraging reflective practices. In addition, educators should be supported to transition to mentorship or facilitation roles that align with the evolving paradigms of education. To ensure an equitable learning environment, it is important to develop teaching strategies that accommodate different backgrounds, capabilities, and constraints. Pedagogy and institutional practices in higher education must incorporate care and concern for students' well-being.

In the future, educational institutions should develop systems to allow students to take charge of their education paths and offer them flexibility in scheduling. Emerging educational practices should be assessed regularly and adjusted as needed to ensure sustainability. For education to be effective, teachers must remain attentive to the challenges students face and adjust their teaching methods accordingly. To improve student engagement and success, it is necessary to shift the focus towards student-centred learning approaches. For educators to remain relevant, it is important to equip them with the skills and resources necessary to design and facilitate learning in a variety of changing contexts. Educators can enrich their educational experiences through international collaboration and exchange programmes. A fundamental component of preparing students for employment is aligning educational practices with the skills and knowledge needed for the rapidly changing and borderless job markets.

It is also imperative that educational institutions integrate technology in order to ensure that their students are knowledgeable of digital tools and prepared to compete in a changing work environment. By combining collaborative projects, online learning platforms, and virtual reality experiences, students are able to develop practical skills and solve real-world problems. Diversity and inclusivity in the educational environment are as important as technological advancements.

In order for students to be prepared for a globalized world where understanding and respecting different perspectives is crucial, schools and universities should actively promote diversity, equity, and inclusion. A supportive environment that celebrates cultural differences and incorporates diverse perspectives into the curriculum is part of this approach. Education should emphasize interdisciplinary learning to meet the demands of the workplace for critical thinking and creativity. A more holistic approach to problem-solving and innovation can be fostered by breaking down traditional silos between subjects. Furthermore, continuous assessment methods and project-based evaluations should be used to evaluate students' progress beyond traditional exams. It promotes lifelong learning and adaptability in students as well as a better understanding of their capabilities. By focusing on knowledge as well as skills and mindset, education becomes a dynamic, responsive system that prepares students for success in an ever-changing world.

Communication and upholding the institution's educational vision are critical for the achievement of institutional goals in terms of institutional practices and policies. All educators and staff should be required to participate in training and professional development. It is possible to drive innovation in education through the establishment of a research and academic committee that focuses on learning design and educational dynamics. Enhancing institutional reputation can be achieved through the development and implementation of policies designed to achieve excellence in education and research. Maintaining the relevance of educational programmes and curricula by collaborating with industries can be achieved through fostering continuous project collaborations. For an institution to succeed over the long term, it is vital to develop a dedicated leadership group that can address uncertainties and ensure institutional resilience. The optimal allocation and management of resources and finances are essential to the growth and sustainability of any institution.

References

Adekola, J., Dale, V. H. M., & Gardiner, K. (2017). Development of an institutional framework to guide transitions into enhanced blended learning in higher education. *Research in Learning Technology*, *25*. https://doi.org/10.25304/rlt.v25

Aguti, B., Wills, G. B., & Walters, R. J. (2014). An evaluation of the factors that impact on the effectiveness of blended e-learning within universities. In *International conference on information society (i-Society)* (pp. 117–121). IEEE.

Alammary, A., Sheard, J., & Carbone, A. (2014). Blended learning in higher education: Three different design approaches. *Australasian Journal of Educational Technology*, *30*(4).

Ali, W. (2020). Online and remote learning in higher education institutes: A necessity in light of COVID-19 pandemic. *Higher Education Studies*, *10*(3), 16–25.

Anthony, B., Kamaludin, A., Romli, A., Raffei, A. F. M., Eh Phon, D. N. A. L., Abdullah, A., & Ming, G. L. (2022). Blended learning adoption and implementation in higher education: A theoretical and systematic review. *Technology, Knowledge and Learning*, *27*, 531–578. https://doi.org/10.1007/s10758-020-09477-z

Ayyagari, R., Grover, V., & Purvis, R. (2011). Technostress: Technological antecedents and implications. *MIS Quarterly*, *35*(4), 831–858.

Bansal, P. (2014). Blended learning in Indian higher education: Challenges and strategies. *International Journal of Applied Research and Studies*, *3*(2), 1–13.

Boelens, R., De Wever, B., & Voet, M. (2017). Four key challenges to the design of blended learning: A systematic literature review. *Educational Research Review, 22*, 1–18.

Bohle Carbonell, K., Dailey-Hebert, A., Gerken, M., & Grohnert, T. (2013). Problem-based learning in hybrid, blended, or online courses: Instructional and change management implications for supporting learner engagement. In *Increasing Student Engagement and Retention in e-learning Environments: Web 2.0 and Blended Learning Technologies* (pp. 359–386). Emerald Group Publishing Limited.

Bonk, C. J., & Graham, C. R. (2012). *The handbook of blended learning: Global perspectives, local designs*. John Wiley & Sons.

Caner, M. (2012). The definition of blended learning in higher education. *Blended Learning Environments for Adults: Evaluations and Frameworks*, 19–34.

Cheung, S. K., & Wang, F. L. (2019). Blended learning in practice: Guest editorial. *Journal of Computing in Higher Education, 31*, 229–232. https://doi.org/10.1007/s12528-019-09229-8

Clark, D. (2003). Blended learning: An EPIC white paper. http://www.scribd.com/doc/84278560/Clark-D-Blended-Learning

Creswell, J. W., & Creswell, J. D. (2017). *Research design: Qualitative, quantitative, and mixed methods approaches*. Sage publications.

Cronje, J. (2020). Towards a new definition of blended learning. *Electronic Journal of e-Learning, 18*, 114–121. https://doi.org/10.34190/EJEL.20.18.2.001

De George-Walker, L., & Keeffe, M. (2010). Self-determined blended learning: A case study of blended learning design. *Higher Education Research & Development, 29*(1), 1–13.

Friesen, N. (2012, August). *Report: Defining blended learning* (p. 130). http://learningspaces.org/papers/Defining_Blended_Learning_NF.pdf

Galvis, Á. H. (2018). Supporting decision-making processes on blended learning in higher education: Literature and good practices review. *International Journal of Educational Technology in Higher Education, 15*(1), 1–38. https://doi.org/10.1186/S41239-018-0106-1

Garrison, D. R., & Kanuka, H. (2004). Blended learning: Uncovering its transformative potential in higher education. *The Internet and Higher Education, 7*, 95–105. https://doi.org/10.1016/j.iheduc.2004.02.001

Garrison, D. R., & Vaughan, N. D. (2008). *Blended learning in higher education framework, principles, and guidelines*. John Wiley and Sons.

Graham, C. R., Woodfield, W., & Harrison, J. B. (2013). A framework for institutional adoption and implementation of blended learning in higher education. *The Internet and Higher Education, 18*, 4–14. https://doi.org/10.1016/J.IHEDUC.2012.09.003

Heinze, A., & Procter, C. T. (2004). Reflections on the use of blended learning.

Hwang, I., & Cha, O. (2018). Examining technostress creators and role stress as potential threats to employees' information security compliance. *Computers in Human Behavior, 81*, 282–293.

Joksimović, S., Kovanović, V., Skrypnyk, O., Gašević, D., Dawson, S., & Siemens, G. (2015). The History and State of Blended Learning. *Preparing for the Digital University: A Review of the History and Current State of Distance, Blended, and Online Learning*, 55–92.

Joo, Y. J., Lim, K. Y., & Kim, N. H. (2016). The effects of secondary teachers' technostress on the intention to use technology in South Korea. *Computers & Education, 95*, 114–122.

Lawless, C. (2019). What is blended learning? https://www.learnupon.com/blog/what-is-blended-learning/

Lee, A. R., Son, S. M., & Kim, K. K. (2016). Information and communication technology overload and social networking service fatigue: A stress perspective. *Computers in Human Behavior, 55*, 51–61.

Li, L., & Wang, X. (2021). Technostress inhibitors and creators and their impacts on university teachers' work performance in higher education. *Cognition, Technology & Work, 23*(2), 315–330.

Lim, C. P., Wang, T., & Graham, C. (2019). Driving, sustaining and scaling up blended learning practices in higher education institutions: A proposed framework. *Innovation and Education, 1*(1), 1–12. https://doi.org/10.1186/S42862-019-0002-0

Lu, X., Zhao, G., & Jiang, J. (2012). Influential factors of blended learning in Chinese colleges: From the perspective of instructor's acceptance and students' satisfaction. In *Hybrid Learning: 5th International Conference, ICHL 2012, Guangzhou, China, August 13-15, 2012. Proceedings 5* (pp. 186–197). Springer Berlin Heidelberg.

McCarthy, S., & Palmer, E. (2023). Defining an effective approach to blended learning in higher education: A systematic review. *Australasian Journal of Educational Technology, 39*(2), 98–114.

Molino, M., Ingusci, E., Signore, F., Manuti, A., Giancaspro, M. L., Russo, V., ... & Cortese, C. G. (2020). Wellbeing costs of technology use during Covid-19 remote working: An investigation using the Italian translation of the technostress creators scale. *Sustainability, 12*(15), 5911.

Moskal, P., Dziuban, C., & Hartman, J. (2013). Blended learning: A dangerous idea? *The Internet and Higher Education, 18*, 15–23.

Mousa, M. (2021). COVID-19 and responsible management education (RME) among others: Why should public business schools feel threatened? *International Journal of Educational Management, 35*(3), 579–593.

Munyengabe, S., Yiyi, Z., Haiyan, H., & Hitimana, S. (2017). Primary teachers' perceptions on ICT integration for enhancing teaching and learning through the implementation of one laptop per child program in primary schools of Rwanda. *Eurasia Journal of Mathematics, Science and Technology Education, 13*(11), 7193–7204.

Mustapa, M. A. S., Ibrahim, M., & Yusoff, A. (2015). Engaging vocational college students through blended learning: Improving class attendance and participation. *Procedia-Social and Behavioral Sciences, 204*, 127–135.

Nguyen, V. A. (2017). Towards the implementation of an assessment-centred blended learning framework at the course level: A case study in a Vietnamese national university. *The International Journal of Information and Learning Technology, 34*(1), 20–30.

Nicolle, P. S., & Lou, Y. (2008). Technology adoption into teaching and learning by mainstream university faculty: A mixed methodology study revealing the "how, when, why, and why not". *Journal of Educational Computing Research, 39*(3), 235–265.

Nimrod, G. (2018). Technostress: Measuring a new threat to well-being in later life. *Aging & Mental Health, 22*(8), 1086–1093.

Norberg, A., Dziuban, C. D., & Moskal, P. D. (2011). A time-based blended learning model. *On the Horizon, 19*(3), 207–216.

Nimrod, G. (2022). Technostress in a hostile world: Older internet users before and during the COVID-19 pandemic. *Aging & Mental Health, 26*(3), 526–533.

Olitsky, N. H., & Cosgrove, S. B. (2014). The effect of blended courses on student learning: Evidence from introductory economics courses. *International Review of Economics Education, 15*, 17–31. https://doi.org/10.1016/j.iree.2013.10.009

Panisoara, I. O., Lazar, I., Panisoara, G., Chirca, R., & Ursu, A. S. (2020). Motivation and continuance intention towards online instruction among teachers during the COVID-19 pandemic: The mediating effect of burnout and technostress. *International Journal of Environmental Research and Public Health, 17*(21), 8002.

Poon, J. (2014). A cross-country comparison on the use of blended learning in property education. *Property Management, 32*(2), 154–175.

Rachmawati, R., Choirunnisa, U., Pambagyo, Z. A., Syarafina, Y. A., & Ghiffari, R. A. (2021). Work from home and the use of ICT during the COVID-19 pandemic in Indonesia and its impact on cities in the future. *Sustainability, 13*(12), 6760. https://doi.org/10.3390/su13126760

Ragu-Nathan, T. S., Tarafdar, M., Ragu-Nathan, B. S., & Tu, Q. (2008). The consequences of technostress for end users in organizations: Conceptual development and empirical validation. *Information Systems Research, 19*(4), 417–433.

Rahiem, M. D. (2020). Technological barriers and challenges in the use of ICT during the COVID-19 emergency remote learning. *Universal Journal of Educational Research*, *8*(11B), 6124–6133.

Riel, J., Lawless, K. A., & Brown, S. W. (2016). Listening to the teachers: Using weekly online teacher logs for ROPD to identify teachers' persistent challenges when implementing a blended learning curriculum. *Journal of Online Learning Research*, *2*(2), 169–200.

Salo, M., Pirkkalainen, H., Makkonen, M., & Hekkala, R. (2018). Distress, eustress, or no stress?: Explaining smartphone users™ different technostress responses. In *International Conference on Information Systems*. Association for Information Systems (AIS).

Sharma, S., & Gupta, B. (2022). Investigating the role of technostress, cognitive appraisal and coping strategies on students' learning performance in higher education: A multidimensional transactional theory of stress approach. *Information Technology & People*. *36*(2), 626–660.

Singh, H. (2021). Building effective blended learning programs. In *Challenges and opportunities for the global implementation of e-learning frameworks* (pp. 15–23). IGI Global.

Smith, K., & Hill, J. (2019). Defining the nature of blended learning through its depiction in current research. *Higher Education Research and Development*, *38*(2), 383–397.

So, H. J., & Brush, T. A. (2008). Student perceptions of collaborative learning, social presence and satisfaction in a blended learning environment: Relationships and critical factors. *Computers & Education*, *51*(1), 318–336.

Spring, K. J., Graham, C. R., & Hadlock, C. A. (2016). The current landscape of international blended learning. *International Journal of Technology Enhanced Learning*, *8*(1), 84–102.

Strielkowski, W. (2020). COVID-19 pandemic and the digital revolution in academia and higher education. *Preprints*, *1*, 1–6.

Subramaniam, S. R., & Muniandy, B. (2019). The effect of the flipped classroom on students' engagement. *Technology, Knowledge and Learning*, *24*(3), 355–372.

University Grants Commission. (2021). *Blended mode of teaching and learning: Concept note*. New Delhi.

Van Nuland, S., Mandzuk, D., Tucker Petrick, K., & Cooper, T. (2020). COVID-19 and its effects on teacher education in Ontario: a complex adaptive systems perspective. *Journal of Education for Teaching*, *46*(4), 442–451.

Vaughan, N., Reali, A., Stenbom, S., van Vuuren, M. J., & MacDonald, D. (2017). Blended learning from design to evaluation: International case studies of evidence-based practice. *Online Learning*, *21*(3), 103–114. https://doi.org/10.24059/OLJ.V21I3.1252

Wai, C. C., & Seng, E. L. K. (2015). Measuring the effectiveness of blended learning environment: A case study in Malaysia. *Education and Information Technologies*, *20*(3), 429–443.

Wang, L., Ertmer, P. A., & Newby, T. J. (2004). Increasing preservice teachers' self-efficacy beliefs for technology integration. *Journal of Research on Technology in Education*, *36*(3), 231–250.

Wang, Y., Han, X., & Yang, J. (2015). Revisiting the blended learning literature: Using a complex adaptive systems framework. *Journal of Educational Technology & Society*, *18*(2), 380–393. https://www.jstor.org/stable/jeductechsoci.18.2.380

Ward, J., & LaBranche, G. A. (2003). Blended learning: The convergence of e-learning and meetings. *Franchising World*, *35*, 22–23.

Weil, M. M., & Rosen, L. D. (1997). *Technostress: Coping with technology @work @home @play* (13, p. 240). John Wiley.

Yurkofsky, M. M., Blum-Smith, S., & Brennan, K. (2019). Expanding outcomes: Exploring varied conceptions of teacher learning in an online professional development experience. *Teaching and Teacher Education*, *82*, 1–13.

Chapter 10

Deglobalizing Education: Perspectives, Challenges, and Sustainability

Pratika Mishra[a] and Aurobindo Kiriyakere[b]

[a]*Welingkar Institute of Management Development and Research (WeSchool), Mumbai, Maharashtra, India*
[b]*Presidency University, Bangalore, Karnataka, India*

Abstract

The higher education industry has undergone major transformation because of the COVID-19, including a move away from globalization. Deglobalization is the process of reducing global interconnectedness and increasing self-reliance, often through the imposition of trade barriers and the localization of economic activity (Eftimie, 2017). Many nations have had to resort to placing travel restrictions and virtually closed their borders during the pandemic time, making it even more challenging for overseas students to pursue higher education abroad. Additionally, the pandemic has increased opportunities towards online education, making it simpler for students to receive quality education from their home countries making it possible for students who may not have been able to otherwise attend in-person classes (Ashour et al., 2021). This trend has also been influenced by political and economic forces like nationalism, protectionism, and international economic difficulties. Higher education institutions are consequently putting more emphasis on partnerships and collaborations at the local and regional levels (James, 2017; Pan, 2021).

Keywords: Deglobalization; post-pandemic higher education; online education; international students; mobility; internationalization

1. Introduction

COVID-19 has major impacts across the world, concerning every segment of the economy. As we know, the changes have been quite dramatic for education and business. The unexpected arrival of COVID-19 has led to temporary shutdowns of schools and shifting the entire set-up to a remote environment. The educators adapted to the changing circumstances to experiment with many teaching methods (Zhao & Watterston, 2021). Compared to traditional and inflexible models of education, educators worldwide took this as an opportunity to rethink the entire education system. At the same time, we can see that this leads to de-globalization or barriers between economies.

Many countries have started promoting local products or services and shortened their reliance on other countries for export, import, or outsourcing of services. According to policymakers and business leaders, alliances have become uncertain due to the absence of global cooperation. The economies are pondering on reducing their economic interdependence, while opening new channels in the fields of national security and public health. Before COVID-19, a historic mark was made by the Great Recession of 2008–2010, when global economic integration was slowly shifting away (Irwin, 2020). During this period, the policymakers reinforced the movement towards deglobalization as a part of their deliberate strategy.

Prior to COVID-19, the education sector was interconnected on a large scale across many parts of the world. We have seen many international schools and universities outperforming their competitors and meeting the education needs of the children (Nie, 2021). To limit the spread of COVID-19 virus, the schools have no option but to depend on internal resources, instead of dealing with international clients. The students and parents are also left with limited options while receiving an academic degree. We also cannot deny the fact that more than 1.7 billion children and youth could not attend academic institutions amid the COVID-19 (Weidmann, 2020).

2. Perspectives

To look at the broader picture of COVID-19, we can see that the incident has massively disrupted the education sector. The former Dean of Students in Harvard University once said that the institution will only close if God permits or it is the end of the world, yet the pandemic had forced the authorities to shut its doors temporarily. Fortunately, the world moved on with the help of webinars and online courses. Mostly, the young students are negatively affected due to remote learning as adult students have the required skills or intellectual capacity to grasp subjects even through remote teaching. You can clearly understand from this scenario that education plays a great role in personality and skill development. It also drives the income prospects of an individual in the existing business environment. According to Warren Baffet, the quotation says, 'The more you learn, the more you'll earn'. This statement applies throughout the career of a student.

Let us take a small example that shows the effects of de-globalization on the education sector back in the 1960s. During this time in West Germany, there was a concept of short school years, in which several West German States clubbed two school years into 16 months, so that the school year can start at the same time throughout the country. It was revealed that the affected students by this measure earned at least 5% less than their peers, who were not affected by the policy. From this example, it is clear to use that the policy was non-functional. Therefore, due to less integration or deglobalization, many students can be affected positively (Gratz, 2022).

However, deglobalization can be quite challenging in the coming years. As per the speech of Andreas Schleider, the learning loss has started coming into light since COVID-19 and is taking a toll on societies across the world. This is going to deteriorate the growth and productivity of the nation. We can easily see that the disruptions will not only affect the size of an economy but also its distribution network. Coming to the section of disadvantaged children, they are likely to have inadequate educational attainment and a slump in their average income levels.

Other common trends observed during the period of deglobalization were considerable erosion of international treaties; democratic backsliding in India, Brazil, or Turkey; and undermining of human rights conventions (Kornprobst & Wallace, 2022). All these economic and political regulations have indirect impacts on the education system of the country. In any case, problems are best solved when handled locally. The same principle was applied in the education sector. Localization of the education system can solve many questions of the students in an easy manner. They can easily interact with the faculties without facing any language issue. Developing countries acquainted with internal teaching techniques will be more benefitted than developed nations.

Farndale et al. (2021) examined the relationship between deglobalization and talent sourcing, with particular emphasis on cross-cultural evidence. As we can see from the previous sections, deglobalization is linked with various arenas of education, and its impacts have been realized accordingly. In the era of deglobalization, you might feel there is a shortage of corporate talent, concerning STEM (science, technology, engineering, and mathematics). This is true while dealing with activities related to STEM in the business setting. In this context, we can find variations in national government policy and political climates. During deglobalization, there have been excessive STEM talent shortages, and the institutional forces had to adapt to the changing environment and develop internal strategies effectively. After the steady growth of corporate globalization since World War II, the phase has come to a halt through the reduction in the level of global interdependence and disturbance in the chain of global trade.

Deglobalization reduces the ability of a firm to hire talents from the global market. The firms must rely only on the local workers to be a part of the business. Especially, firms belonging to the IT market require workers having STEM skills to meet the ever-growing demands of the clients. Data suggest that 25% of higher education (HE) students have scored two or less out five in numeracy skills. Strong skill imbalances have also been noticed in the Australian market, where the firms cannot easily meet the changing demands of clients (Kayan-Fadlelmula et al., 2022).

To take care of domestic skill shortages, the firms move to regions where talent is available or bring workers into the business, who are highly skilled and qualified. As qualification is an asset to any employer, a gap remains in filling the talent needs. A school of authors investigated that a growing source of STEM talent can be international students transfer to work visas after completing postgraduation. Before deglobalization, the STEM talent shortage was compensated for through the supply of STEM talent from other countries. Post deglobalization, mobility of talent pool has become a cumbersome task for the employers.

We can understand other perspectives of deglobalization through the study of pandemic lockdowns (Sanjana, 2022). After the consecutive phases of lockdown, the global market faced a recession, unemployment, and reduction in global trade activities. In this era, the world was going through the process of deglobalization, and each nation-state was completely involved with their personal growth and profitability. Under this new normal state, a well-structured and refined globalization method is required for embedding globalization into the economy. Keeping the effects of the pandemic at the forefront, we must dig deeper into the process of deglobalization, which brought about an alarming change in the global economy.

Having the greatest change effect on society, the COVID-19 was able to uplift the world technologically. Being constrained at home, many perceived lives in a new way. The dynamics of the world economy drastically transformed, leading to a restructuring of the world through deglobalization. E-commerce business segments like online education application, remote work, online entertainment, and online shopping became prominent in the aftermath of the pandemic. The biggest blow of the pandemic was experienced by the education sector, which adopted the virtual mode, also known as the e-learning mechanism. Steps were taken to switch to an online mode of education.

Let us see another critical aspect of the post-pandemic world, that is, international student mobility (ISM). ISM is characterized by the cacophony of international students, who experience movement across borders to receive further education or get enrolled for a scholarship. Other factors added to the condition were trade or geopolitical tensions, xenophobic politics, and intensification of globalization. Contrary to these narratives, the author has drawn attention to the resilience and tenacity showcased by the international students in dealing with these challenges. As the nation slowly bounces back to its original state, youths have been going abroad for study.

After suffering sharp losses in the student enrolment for the years 2020 and 2021, the US universities have regained their position with a surge in applications in 2022/2023. In the Asia-Pacific region, the maximum number of enrolments has been observed in Australia. A closer look at the evidence tells us that the Indian students have surged the demand in Australia. In the Asian city-state of Singapore, Chinese students appear to be increasing in the last few months. A common question in our mind is to find out the instrument for measuring student mobility in the dying state of globalization.

To measure the resilience of ISM, it should be considered the locus of social promise and hope. Let's take an example. Twenty years ago, many foreign students visited China when it was undergoing globalization. ISM emerged due to favourable factors like flexible citizenship and cosmopolitanism. Two decades later, the same country became a nightmare for the youth to study and complete their degrees. A 'zero COVID' policy crippled in China, which degraded the faith of students in the country as they searched for potential escape routes (Sanjana, 2022). Many South Asian international students who went abroad could not return to China during the 'zero COVID' phase.

2.1. Case Study

To study the impact of globalization on HE, Lam (2010) empirically found out the education policy required for planning and designing education in Hong Kong. In the domain of HE, the new policy stated the roles of senior management, course leader, and design trainer in the process of building a remote educational set-up. Examples of strategies include development of a knowledge-based factory by upskilling the students in the segments of language proficiency and IT skill development. The students must possess intellectual curiosity to work under a tight schedule and according to the curriculum. Hong Kong is committed to embrace all the issues persisting in different educational levels.

The Government of Hong Kong Special Administrative Region (HSKAR) regards educational reforms as a hugely complex exercise, where sectors and agencies can be involved. At the onset of deglobalization, the country aimed to upgrade its general standard of academic performance. HSKAR recognized this education reform as a hugely complex exercise, which may affect different sectors and agencies. The goal was to enable 60% of the senior-secondary school goers to continue studying so that they can attain a competitive edge in the market. Another goal was to encourage Hong Kong people to enhance their knowledge and skills for meeting the requirements of a knowledge-based economy.

3. Challenges

Deglobalization is viewed as a long-term, historical response to people's loss of agencies. In the 20th and 21st centuries, the paradoxes of deglobalization unfolded. In the realm of deglobalization, we see people and communities forming a singular perspective, either to judge philosophies, practices, or cultures. Deglobalization might be used as a harbinger of an era, which can redress the historical misdeeds (Yang & Tian, 2023). It might also be used as a model of horizontal solidarity, which recognizes the rights of nature in a natural and cosmological world. The roots of deglobalization were observed during the period when rising powers like China, India, and Russia created their own histories, cultures, and philosophies.

International relations became a common field of study in Euro-American academic communities. Two schools of thought became very common during this phase, that is, scholars who exemplified Chinese school of international relations and others who drew a more eclectic, non-western, de-colonial thought. In China, there had been many universities that taught social sciences, which included China's ruling regimes in the service of the state. However, in 1952, political science was abolished from the HE system by referring to it as 'the pseudo-ideology of the bourgeois'. During the same period, the Ministry of HE was also abolished, bringing a stagnation in the teaching of social sciences.

The prominence of international relations (IR) was also observed in America and Europe at the beginning of the 21st century. There was a prevailing vision in Europe that the non-Europeans were not capable of producing abstract knowledge categories (Behera, 2021). The scholars in the Southern Hemisphere used local expertise and data to theorize IR. On the contrary, the theory of IR was viewed as 'socialism with Chinese characteristics', by the Chinese scholars. We can also see that a large proportion of Western knowledge tradition has been improvised within the training sessions conducted by Chinese at the American universities.

Another set of authors (Rapanta et al., 2021) highlighted the post-pandemic challenges of HE, which can occur while balancing technology, pedagogy, and the new normal lifestyle. In the light of COVID-19 crisis, the emergency remote teaching (ERT) norms have become common worldwide. Educators from primary and secondary educational levels felt the necessity to rethink their roles and support students through learning tasks (Monitor, 2015). Many believe that the emphasis should be given to 'pedagogy-ization' instead of digitalization. It is also noteworthy that the teachers, educational administrators, and other institute authorities suffered from lack of readiness in handling the situation.

To rush and shift to a fully online teaching and learning platform, many educators tried to replicate the face-to-face mechanism of physical teaching through lengthy pre-recorded lectures and video conferencing websites. In most cases, synchronous technology experienced challenges related to connectivity, accessibility, and time zone. Distance educators feared that they would not be able to impart the maximum value to the students by teaching through these platforms. Many post-secondary instructors were familiar with the technology and felt comfortable in teaching through online platforms. Early education theories and practices related to traditional distance offered a starting point for the faculties, who wished to completely replicate the face-to-face teaching methods.

Murphy (2020) brought into light all the consequences of securitization of HE during the emergency e-learning of the COVID-19 period. At the spread of the novel coronavirus, there are profound changes in the interaction between the teachers and students. Primary student population appeared to be at a lower mortality risk category as compared to the elderly people. Reduction in interpersonal contacts has minimized community transmission, which might have taken place in the university campus. Measures like social distancing have limited the face-to-face interactions in the classrooms and brought in additional costs in the realm of normal discourse.

The study follows securitization theory, where the state or its key actors can claim a special right whenever there is a security issue. Anything can become a security issue when securitized through the Speech Act. In the *magnum opus* of the Copenhagen school, the securitization framework is well explained. As an immediate measure to the crisis, the emergency e-learning programme has been started across the world. A similar situation was observed during Fall 2009 when 61% of H1N1 contingency plans had substituted physical teaching with online classes. Before this period, Hurricane Katrina's occurrence physically damaged about 27 colleges in Texas.

Emergency e-learning was the immediate measure proposed to protect the community from the deadly virus. The public health officials warned people against the dangers of community transmission but guaranteed the rights to university officials for enacting exceptional measures. According to the joint consensus of disease specialists, epidemiologists, and other public health officials, the decision was taken to limit face-to-face interaction as reduction of close-proximity interaction was justifiable. Preference was given to the emergency e-learning mechanisms as declared by Harvard and Yale Universities. The spread of asynchronous online learning has grabbed the attention of the scholars as they researched on the full-scale attainment of online education in the COVID-19 period. These events can prompt colleges to make online classes as their own.

Other authors (Ashour et al., 2021) shed light into the challenges of HE as viewed by university leaders and educational experts in the United Arab Emirates. One of the eminent challenges has been aligning education across different modes. Distance education is strikingly different from that of face-to-face education, and the two modes must be equivalent to one another to derive the same outcome. Orr et al. (2020) came to a viewpoint that all the perspectives of HE must be jammed to a single frame so that the society understands the cultural benefits of digitalization.

To analyse these challenges, the authors have predicted major changes in the educational curriculum as well as academic programmes to meet the future requirements of the labour market. Other changes will be brought about by automation, Big Data movement, and artificial intelligence. More emphasis has been put into tasks that require advanced professional skills along with social and emotional intelligence. With the decline of routine jobs, there will be a period of crunch for all the companies, where many workers will be dismissed from their jobs. Administrative jobs will decrease by 26% as reported by British Council.

Other stated issues of the respondents have been inappropriate handling of the new software related to teaching or learning and inadequate enrichment of educational experience from all the students. Many students did not score high as the transition from HE to e-learning happened in the middle of a semester. Few academicians believe that online education can be used in a much better sense so that it is customized according to specific requirements of students and solves their individual queries. Many other respondents talked about the advantages of a recorded lecture, which is extremely needed when they are physically absent on campus.

A school of authors (Pichardo et al., 2021) delved into the use of technological innovation to combat challenges of HE during pandemic and post-pandemic phases. It was a trigger from the pandemic to develop digital skills so that the academic institutions can adapt to online teaching. To find out the solution, the authors have joined 400 students across 12 academics. Both qualitative and quantitative data were collected that showed student participation in both face-to-face and online discussions in synchronous or asynchronous ways. These online discussions improve collaborative learning, interaction, and engagement among the students. Their concentration also developed, and immediate feedback was received so that the teachers can easily monitor the learning progress of the students. Educators around the world highlighted the inclusive potential of online learning so that students from diverse backgrounds and capacities can be engaged. Education should be equitable for all as opined by the authors.

The authors also discovered all the trivial and severe factors that made it increasingly urgent to consider information and communication technology (ICT) as an important resource of education. Use of audience response system (ARS) and gamification tools have enhanced knowledge and competences of the teachers and students. These methods will reshape the learning techniques at universities. Mentimeter will slowly emerge onto the scene and increase concentration of students as per the level of face-to-face classes. This is because lack of attention is one of the fundamental problems of students during online classes. With the help of Mentimeter, the students can also participate in quizzes or real-time gameplays.

Another pertinent issue reported in the online classroom is the inability to express due to personal characteristics or any other factor. There might be lack of confidence, shyness, diversity factors, or any other trait that limit student engagement. Sometimes, few students take the leadership and speak up fluently or confidently. Such a situation undermines other students' ability to express their thoughts. They take time in doing so. In such cases, Mentimeter can come to their rescue as it does not set any time limit, and nobody can see who has or has not answered. There is no added pressure from peers or teachers to perform at their best.

4. Sustainability

At the present state of deglobalization, it is now clear to us that the education system needs an innovative and sustainable model to improve the educational attainment of children. We have already revised through some of the proposed solutions of past researchers. Now, let us come to the concept of mobile learning (ML) in the post-pandemic world, which can be an important component of HE. As opined by Drwish et al. (2023), digital transformation has been an integral aspect of HE in the post-pandemic era. Studying 400 undergraduate and postgraduate students from Saudi Arabia, a novel hybrid model was proposed and subsequently tested.

During COVID-19, all academic institutions resorted to distance education, which was believed to be the ideal solution for them. Formal education was suddenly replaced by distance education, and changes were made in the lesson plans to integrate digitalization within the system. Extending this approach in the modern environment, we can notice that the advancement in technology and the cheaper prices of mobile phones have provided several benefits for the learners. The students can use mobile phone applications and have access to unlimited learning platforms. The shift is slowly happening from e-learning to m-learning.

M-learning can provide innumerable features to the learners, such as versatility of information-sharing methods and easy channels of interaction between learners and teachers.

Studies have proven that 67% of learners can organize interesting learning activities through ML. In Saudi Arabia, an aspirational federal plan has been proposed by the Crown Prince, which encouraged the use of ML in the education sector by opening corridors for hardware and software advancement. The first educational application, Kofu, was launched in 2022 by King Faisal University that supports both inside and outside classroom learning activities. In the sphere of e-learning, the Information System Success Model (ISSM) incorporates six factors of learning, that is, information quality, system quality, service quality, positive experience of the learner, and increasing number of end users.

Studies across similar domains (Deák et al., 2021) have shown that there is an evolution of new approaches in pedagogy in the era of post-pandemic. In relation to this, the new approaches in pedagogy have been STEM integration and classroom engagement. Many analytical tools have been suggested that complement the new strategies of pedagogy. Examples of these methods can be integration flow, matrix analysis, and balancing of skill sets.

In Texas, a model of pedagogical approach has been launched, that is, T-STEM, which improved the readiness of college and high-school students towards the ongoing change of the educational landscape. Most of the schools in the Middle East have already adapted to ICT. Among the K-12 teachers, the skill development process has become very crucial so that they are able to acquire skills related to pedagogy. Other authors (Nadelson et al., 2012) investigated the utility of short-term residential summer schools for the professional growth of teachers. These collaborative activities showed gains in efficacy and comfort among the participants.

Fig. 10.1 shows the trends in STEM publication between 2001 and 2018. There is a significant rise in the modern pedagogical approaches through the application of several models among education practitioners. One of these models is inquiry-based learning, which is highly effective for science subjects and is a recommended technique in science pedagogy. In the area of science, educators focus on the development of online lab skills through digital platforms like GoLabs.

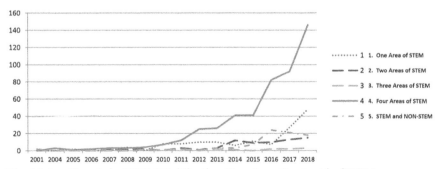

Fig. 10.1. Trends in STEM Publication Based on Content in STEM Education. *Source*: Li et al. (2020).

Gowin's modified Vee diagram (see Fig. 10.2) is a popularly used method to assess the outcomes of inquiry-based learning. This is the idea of converting initial ideas into final claims through a complete cycle. The difference between the two makes the knowledge gap.

Keshavarz (2020) proposed another sustainable model for post-pandemic HE. The global impact of COVID-19 has been vividly felt across the education sector. In this context, the different types of educational models have been reviewed, followed by a comparative study between the traditional face-to-face classroom education and online education. In the world of ICT, education has got a new name. The biggest advantage of online education is the wide scope and accessibility of the system. It provides an opportunity to the private universities to earn attractive incentives. It is cost-effective for both students and institutions and solves the problem of addressing individual candidate needs.

Research findings indicate that the academic institutions have switched to virtual mode of lecture delivery by preparing the lessons in advance. At the same time, they uploaded the reading materials in the online portals and shared them either through slides or texts. For some students, online teaching can be a favourable option as they can study sitting in the comfort of their home without commuting to school. Total reliance on distance education can have many disadvantages, such as absence of human interaction, laziness or procrastination, and lack of discipline.

To solve most problems, blended learning is facilitated, which encompasses the advantages of both traditional and online teaching methods. In this arrangement, students will attend computer lab classes and other critical classes based on the instructions given by the respective faculty. The hybrid campus model can work productively if implemented in the right way. It is economical for both the institutions and students and saves a great deal of time, energy, and money. Many small universities suffer from shortage of space, and they can adopt this scheme to avoid building new infrastructure.

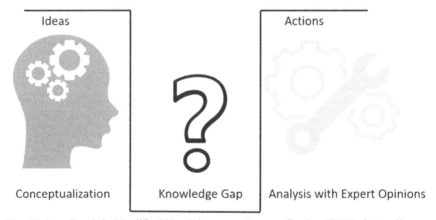

Fig. 10.2. Gowin's Modified Vee Diagram. *Source*: Caglar (2015). https://www.sciencedirect.com/science/article/pii/S1569190X1500101X

The changing landscape of HE is conspicuous at the age of COVID-19 and neo-liberal paradigm (Pan, 2021). The paper deploys conceptual mapping as the analytical tool to study the global news update to generate a real-time update of the fast-spreading pandemic. Key findings of the paper were shrinking of public funding in Western Universities which changed roles of HE, increased reliance on students' tuition fees and user-pay philosophy during the outbreak of the pandemic. Testing of International HE resilience showed that there was a 75% drop in the international enrolment of students due to travel restrictions.

Neo-liberal paradigm is one of the dominant ideologies followed by the HE sectors. It assumes the concept of 'West's Triumph', which means expansion of capitalism from economic dimension to other core areas of the economy, such as public policymaking and HE. It is a market-driven ideology, which states the global capitalization and commercialization of HE along with regional responses to globalization and integration of the financial markets. Some of the educational models followed under this paradigm are cross-border educational services, state-supervising models, market mechanisms, and 'user-pays' philosophy. Organizations involved in providing a neo-liberal direction to HE are the Organization for Economic Cooperation and Development (OECD) and World Bank.

Before the development of future education models, we can have a glimpse of lessons learnt from the COVID-19 as applicable in the education sector. Two weaknesses of university management have been found, that is, lack of institutional support for the international students in terms of financial aid and mental care and overcoming mental stress along with budgetary constraints. In a survey conducted by Erasmus Student Network, about 41.2% students reported higher levels of stress and anxiety after the outbreak of the pandemic. Many international students felt lost and isolated on a foreign land and were not able to come back to their own countries.

4.1. Case Study

A way forward to post-pandemic online teaching has been shown by the HE system of Pakistan. According to Thomas et al. (2022), the spread of COVID-19 led to the adoption of Anderson's online learning model, which solved many issues and in an ad hoc manner. The paper also digs deeper into the theory of reasoned action along with the technology acceptance model (TAM), which reflects instructor's perceived usefulness during online teaching and ease of using technology. Universities in Pakistan maintained an ad hoc policy to battle the crisis, instead of developing a systematic procedure for quality education.

Notable issues regarding the online educational process at both public and private sectors can be conducive learning environment at home, issues of affording and accessing the internet, challenges of taking lab practices, online examination, and assignment submission. Many universities installed a learning management system but are still at the grassroot levels concerning areas like disseminating lectures, online interactions, resources, or professional expertise of teachers. Many students are non-tech savvy and financially unstable to arrange for an online learning set-up. In response to this, all the institutions have adopted Anderson's online teaching model, which involves two major human actors, that is, instructor and learner.

Anderson's learning model integrates collaborative learning with a group of inquiry models. A few independent learning models have also been considered in this theory. In this environment, the learners can directly find the content on the web when they are unable to follow any online lecture. They can directly chat with the web portals to acquire new knowledge. The conceptual framework used in the research is Theory of Reasoned Action (TRA), which is used to predict people's attitudes towards online teaching, whether they find it useful or destructive. Personal variables like teaching experience, exposure to technology, and financial support are considered to figure out the relation.

5. Conclusion

From the above discussion, we can conclude that de-globalization is a very critical phase for the education industry, whereby the interconnectedness between economies is getting shrunk and there are restrictions across borders. Post-COVID-19, many academic institutions have employed online teaching methods to continue the sessions of the students. Studies across all the sectors have shown that online teaching methods have proven useful only under restricted conditions. Many students have perceived it to be a luxury to sit back at home and enjoy the classes, without commuting to the institution. On the contrary, some of the students still find it very difficult to handle online learning procedures.

Proposed solutions to all the challenges of online teaching have been blended learning platforms and mobile-based learning. Among all other measures, these two have shown the highest positive results. Blended learning platforms refer to a hybrid model, whereby students will commute to schools as and when instructed by the faculty. In this model, the students can come to school to take notes or do practical classes. During the rest of the period, they can attend online classes and submit the test paper online. Mobile-based learning applications are very useful during online classes.

References

Ashour, S., El-Refae, G. A., & Zaitoun, E. A. (2021). Post-pandemic higher education: Perspectives from University leaders and educational experts in the United Arab Emirates. *Higher Education for the Future*, 8(2), 219–238. https://doi.org/10.1177/23476311211007261

Behera, N. C. (2021). Globalization, deglobalization and knowledge production. *International Affairs*, 97(5), 1579–1597. https://doi.org/10.1093/ia/iiab119

Caglar, F., Shekhar, S., Gokhale, A., Basu, S., Rafi, T., Kinnebrew, J., & Biswas, G. (2015). Cloud-hosted simulation-as-a-service for high school STEM education. *Simulation Modelling Practice and Theory*, 58, 255–273. https://www.sciencedirect.com/science/article/pii/S1569190X1500101X

Deák, C., Kumar, B., Szabó, I., Nagy, G., & Szentesi, S. (2021). Evolution of new approaches in pedagogy and STEM with inquiry-based learning and post-pandemic scenarios. *Education Sciences, 11*(7), 319. https://www.mdpi.com/2227-7102/11/7/319

Drwish, A. M., Al-Dokhny, A. A., Al-Abdullatif, A. M., & Aladsani, H. K. (2023). A sustainable quality model for mobile learning in post-pandemic higher education: a structural equation modeling-based investigation. *Sustainability, 15*(9), 7420. https://www.mdpi.com/2071-1050/15/9/7420

Eftimie, S. (2017). Challenges for education – From globalization to deglobalization. *Jus et Civitas – A Journal of Social and Legal Studies (former Buletinul Universității Petrol Gaze din Ploiești, Seria Științe Socio-Umane și Juridice), 68*(2), 21–28.

Farndale, E., Thite, M., Budhwar, P., & Kwon, B. (2021). Deglobalization and talent sourcing: Cross-national evidence from high-tech firms. *Human Resource Management, 60*(2), 259–272. https://publications.aston.ac.uk/id/eprint/41884/6/GTM_Paper_Final_Aug_25_2020.pdf

Gratz, F. (2022). Does schooling affect socioeconomic inequalities in educational attainment? Evidence from a natural experiment in Germany. file:///C:/Users/Pratika%20Misra/Downloads/SchoolingGraetz2022.pdf

Irwin, D. A. (2020). The pandemic adds momentum to the deglobalization trend. *Peterson Institute for International Economics, 23.* https://cepr.org/voxeu/columns/pandemic-adds-momentum-deglobalisation-trend

James, H. (2017). *Deglobalization as a global challenge.* CIGI Paper No. 135. Centre for International Governance Innovation.

Kayan-Fadlelmula, F., Sellami, A., Abdelkader, N., & Umer, S. (2022). A systematic review of STEM education research in the GCC countries: trends, gaps and barriers. *International Journal of STEM Education, 9*, 2. https://doi.org/10.1186/s40594-021-00319-7

Keshavarz, M. H. (2020). A proposed model for post-pandemic higher education. *Budapest International Research and Critics in Linguistics and Education (BirLE) Journal, 3*(3), 1384–1391. https://doi.org/10.33258/birle.v3i3.1193

Kornprobst, M., & Wallace, J. (2022). What is deglobalization? Chat Ham House. https://www.chathamhouse.org/2021/10/what-deglobalization

Lam, Y. Y. (2010). Impact of globalization on higher education: an empirical study of education policy & planning of design education in Hong Kong. *International Education Studies, 3*(4), 73–85. https://files.eric.ed.gov/fulltext/EJ1065882.pdf

Li, Y., Wang, K., Xiao, Y., & Froyd, J. E. (2020). Research and trends in STEM education: A systematic review of journal publications. *International Journal of STEM Education, 7*, 11.

Monitor, I. C. E. F. (2015). The state of international student mobility in 2015. https://monitor.icef.com/2015/11/the-state-of-international-student-mobility-in-2015/

Murphy, M. P. (2020). COVID-19 and emergency e-learning: Consequences of the securitization of higher education for post-pandemic pedagogy. *Contemporary Security Policy, 41*(3), 492–505. https://doi.org/10.1080/13523260.2020.1761749

Nadelson, L. S., Seifert, A., Moll, A. J., & Coats, B. (2012). i-STEM summer institute: An integrated approach to teacher professional development in STEM. *Journal of STEM Education: Innovation and Outreach, 13*(2), 69–83. https://scholarworks.boisestate.edu/cifs_facpubs/92/

Nie, W. (2021). Deglobalisation – What does it mean for the education industry? https://futureofeducation.my/deglobalisation-in-education-industry

Orr, D., Luebcke, M., Schmidt, J. P., Ebner, M., Wannemacher, K., Ebner, M., & Dohmen, D. (2020). *Higher education landscape 2030: A trend analysis based on the ahead international horizon scanning* (p. 59). Springer Nature. https://library.oapen.org/handle/20.500.12657/39550

Pan, S. (2021). COVID-19 and the neo-liberal paradigm in higher education: changing landscape. *Asian Education and Development Studies*, *10*(2), 322–335. https://doi.org/10.1108/AEDS-06-2020-0129

Pichardo, J. I., López-Medina, E. F., Mancha-Cáceres, O., González-Enríquez, I., Hernández-Melián, A., Blázquez-Rodríguez, M., Jiménez, V., Logares, M., Carabantes-Alarcon, D., Ramos-Toro, M., Isorna, E., Cornejo-Valle, M., & Borrás-Gené, O. (2021). Students and teachers using mentimeter: Technological innovation to face the challenges of the Covid 19 and post-pandemic in higher education. *Education Sciences*, *11*(11), 667. https://www.mdpi.com/2227-7102/11/11/667

Rapanta, C., Botturi, L., Goodyear, P., Guardia, L., & Koole, M. (2021). Balancing technology, pedagogy and the new normal: post-pandemic challenges for higher education. *Postdigital Science and Education*, *3*, 715–742. https://doi.org/10.1007/s42438-021-00249-1

Sanjana, S. (2022). Deglobalization: The new normal or the need of the hour. *International Journal of Law Management and Humanities*, *5*(4), 738. https://heinonline.org/HOL/LandingPage?handle=hein.journals/ijlmhs18&div=63&id=&page=

Thomas, M., Khan, A. H., & Ahmad, N. (2022). Way forward for post pandemic online teaching: A case of higher education in Pakistan. *Journal of Humanities, Social and Management Sciences (JHSMS)*, *3*(1), 1–15. https://www.ideapublishers.org/index.php/jhsms/article/view/559

Weidmann, J. (2020). Deglobalisation, disrupted education and debt: economic policy challenges following the pandemic. https://www.bis.org/review/r201020a.pdf

Yang, P., & Tian, Y. (2023). International student mobility in a deglobalizing and post-pandemic world: resilience, reconfiguration, renewal. *Journal of International Students*, *13*(1), i–v. https://www.ojed.org/index.php/jis/article/view/5538

Zhao, Y., & Watterston, J. (2021). The changes we need: Education post COVID-19. *Journal of Educational Change*, *22*(1), 3–12. https://link.springer.com/article/10.1007/s10833-021-09417-3?trk=public_post_main_feed-card_feed-article-content

Chapter 11

Technology-Enabled Education Innovation: The Hybrid Teaching-Learning Process

J. Meenakumari[a], Ramakrishnan N.[b] and Sriharish Ramakrishnan[c]

[a]Surana Educational Institutions, India
[b]School of Business and Management, Christ University, India
[c]Bosch Global Software Technologies, India

Abstract

Hybrid teaching-learning unlocked the potential to shape the world of education through disruptive innovation, emerging as an innovative, resilient, and viable model of the teaching-learning process. The model meets the evolving needs of teachers and students by providing wider accessibility, better engagement levels, and opportunities for a sustainable and flexible learning model. Playing the role of change-agent and catalyst in enabling transformation in every sector especially in education, the proliferation of technology in the teaching-learning process has brought tremendous changes into the teaching-learning activities. Technology-enabled hybrid learning approaches have resulted in a transformation from the traditional chalk-and-talk methodology towards experience-based learning, leading to 'improved academic achievement' and 'enhanced industry-readiness'. Made feasible through artificial intelligence (AI), virtual reality, augmented reality, and other immersive learning techniques, a heterogeneous combination of technologies is essential for effective implementation. There is a high degree of involvement of audio-video technologies, collaborative software, interactive whiteboards, and wireless presentation displays which could vary based on the requirement and budget. Hybrid learning approaches have leveraged AI, helping teachers ascertain learning capabilities of students and provide feedback in a convenient manner. A hybrid teaching-learning model facilitates upskilling and reskilling in a flexible mode. Elements needing consideration in a hybrid teaching-learning model include experiential learning, experimental learning, assessment-related transformation, elevated levels of creative thinking, and potential for improved employability. This chapter focuses on various enablers that drive the hybrid teaching-learning process, and the role of technology as an important pillar in educational transformation, introducing a technology-enabled framework for a systematic and sustainable solution.

Keywords: Technology; transformation; educational innovation; hybrid teaching-learning process; sustainable and flexible learning; framework

Introduction

Educational transformation refers to systematic changes that are applied to the existing educational model. In the present scenario, transformation in the education system is in the forefront for many educationalists and policymakers. It is all about how the education system could be strengthened, reformed, and redesigned for better sustainability. Transformation in the education system should ideally begin with the review of goals of the systems and mapping them with the current needs. It is preferred to have the transformation oriented towards tackling inequality and building resilience in the dynamic world. It is equally important to position various attributes of the education system for logically and consistently contributing to the revised set of goals. Innovative and inclusive educational practices are essential for successful transformation. This requires identification and implementation of new and creative approaches that align to the objectives. Inclusion deals with education for all such that it reaches everyone without any discrimination.

Role of Technology in Education Transformation

Proliferation of technology into various facets of education especially into the classroom set-up has brought tremendous changes to the ways in which teachers and students acquire knowledge. Technology has been a catalyst in the education transformation and has also played an integral part in every aspect of the knowledge cycle. Technology helps the learners to learn at ease and at their own pace. Similarly, it has changed the way in which a teacher teaches too. Technology helps in a collaborative teaching-learning scenario. The role of teachers in the present era has transformed to a 'facilitator'. There are many tools that provide experiential and experimental learning platforms enabled by augmented reality (AR) and virtual reality (VR). The classroom engagements have become more effective with the deployment of technology. Technology helps teachers in course-level planning and assessments. According to the World Bank report, to reduce digital inequalities, education systems must focus on the following: good digital platforms, stakeholder performance and satisfaction in terms of teacher's capacity, developing the student's skill set, etc. It also recommended good backend support systems to maintain the required technical aspects. At present, technologies have entirely reshaped the education system. The classrooms with digital empowerment have made education possible anytime and anywhere across various geographical areas.

According to Schindler et al. (2017), the application of technology in education has proved to be more engaging in terms of students' and faculty involvement. The study also indicated that usage of technology helps in other aspects like critical thinking, communication skills, and presentations along with enhancing their digital competency. Mistler-Jackson and Songer (2000) established that integration of suitable technologies in the classroom has enhanced motivation of the student to understand and accomplish the tasks better. According to Saad and Surendran (2020), proficiency in technology has been considered a vital tool for learning in the 21st century. John Dewey, the great educator, had said, "if we teach today's students as we taught yesterday we rob them of tomorrow." This emphasizes the significance of technology in the education system.

Innovation in Education

Innovation is the process of organizing and sustaining an aggregation of concepts, actors, and practices for addressing specific problems (Smith, 2006). Innovation in education comes in different ways. Innovation in the education sector is not limited to programmes, processes, products, partnerships, services, and people management. In a broader sense, innovative practices need to focus on achieving equitable and quality-oriented education for all. Embracing innovation in education encourages critical thinking, a sense of exploration, and an openness to adapt for better teaching-learning experience.

Need for Innovation

Innovation plays a significant role in the growth of any domain, and the education sector is no exception. It facilitates constant and systematic evolution of people and educational processes. Innovation enables relevant stakeholders to apply evolving trends in the education sector. The teaching-learning process could be enhanced through deployment of innovative practices and approaches for changing 'how educators teach' and 'how students learn'.

It helps the concerned to select suitable tools for completing their tasks efficiently and effectively. It also provides confidence and adaptive skills for tackling challenges in their present and future teaching-learning environments.

Key Elements of Educational Innovation

Innovation in the education sector across the globe is considered very important. Innovation is required to make the teachers and students love teaching and learning all through life. Innovation also helps to have better and effective classroom engagements. Innovation in education could be used to support unique approaches in techniques for instruction.

According to Popescu and Crenicean (2012), innovations in education can be categorized as 'Technical innovation, Conceptual innovation, and Relational innovation'. Technical innovations consider the applications of various new technologies in education. Technology is considered as a catalyst for educational innovation according to the study conducted by Serdyukov (2017). In addition to this study, Findikoglu and Ilhan (2016) stated that 'innovation does not necessarily mean the adoption of the latest technology rather it is more about utilisation of the technology'. Technology facilitates the innovation process to achieve the desired results. In the education sector, technology-driven innovative processes will help in setting up hybrid teaching-learning environments. The introduction of new courses, new educational methodologies, and new educational programmes is the inclusion of conceptual innovations. Relational innovation mainly deals with the relationship aspects and with the better way of establishing communication and interactions that are internal and external to educational institutions. It is evident from various literature available that innovation with appropriate technologies could bring in significant changes in the overall education system.

Learning Models

In general, a learning model defines the mechanism of learning. Every mechanism has a process of absorption of information. This when applied while learning new skills and techniques makes the process easy and effective.

Sustainable Learning Model

The focus of a sustainable learning model in education is not limited to imparting knowledge and skills to the learners but relates to the positive impact on learners, economy, society, and the learning environment. A sustainable learning model in education has an orientation towards holistic development of the learners by enhancing critical thinking and problem-solving. It also provides personalization to meet the needs of the learning styles of individual learners. The integration of technology and innovative teaching-learning approaches increases the adaptability of learners in an environment involving dynamic changes. A sustainable learning model intends to create an environment of continuous improvement. Further, it facilitates learners to be equipped with knowledge and skills apart from positively influencing individual growth and societal progress. A sustainable learning model in education is depicted in Fig. 11.1.

A sustainable learning model in education provides a positive impact on the following four key dimensions:

- Learners
- Learning Environment
- Society
- Economy

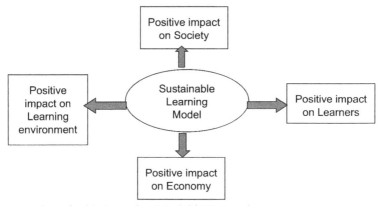

Fig. 11.1. Sustainable Learning Model in Education.

The positive impact on the above-mentioned four dimensions is facilitated through interactivity, independent learning, collaboration, transferability, process orientation, situational experience, and a futuristic perspective.

Flexible Learning Model

'Flexible learning' as the name implies provides a high degree of flexibility in terms of learning, and it is a highly learner-centric model in the 21st century. A flexible learning model caters to the needs and preferences of the individual learners. It is flexible in terms of what, how, and when to learn and has no geographical barriers or not many challenges associated with it. It is facilitated by technology wherein it combines the aspects of both traditional and remote learning features. It has a huge repository of online resources, interactive platforms, and personalized learning tools. The goal of a flexible learning system is to accommodate diverse learning styles, paces, and schedules, ultimately enhancing the overall educational experience and outcomes for students. The usage of new technologies and their implementation in online and blended learning designs facilitate more flexibility and individualization in higher education institutions (Müller & Mildenberger, 2021).

Key Aspects of Flexible Learning Model

Few key aspects of flexible learning model that are different from the traditional set-up are discussed below but not limited to the following:

- *Accessible Education*: This model mainly provides access to education for all types of learners irrespective of geographical, physical, and other barriers that are inherent in traditional learning models.
- *Continuous Education*: Flexible learning model encourages the culture of continuous learning at learner's pace there by making it highly convenient for professionals and all individuals.

- *Personalized Education*: Flexible learning model helps the learners to select the topic of their choice, learning style, resources, etc. based on their requirement. Wide range of resources is also available to the learners to select according to their requirements.
- *Collaborative Education*: Flexible learning model allows the learners to collaborate via online forum discussions, group projects, and by other virtual set-ups. These aspects help students to share knowledge with a wider group and learn accordingly.
- *Assessment Variety*: This system again has various aspects of assessment activities which includes online quizzes, multimedia-based presentations, projects, etc. that allow students to demonstrate their understanding that best suits their strengths.
- *Teachers as Facilitators*: Teachers often take the role of mentors and provide support as and when needed.

Hybrid Teaching-Learning Process

Overview

As the hybrid teaching-learning process is intended to bring in flexibility to the process, understanding the stakeholders' views and the theory behind hybrid learning becomes essential. The major stakeholders are the teachers and students in the process along with administrators who would be deciding the right technology at the right time for the right process. Key dimensions of hybrid learning are largely understood as the educational model in which some teachers deliver, and students attend classes in-person while others join the class virtually, or where both undertake a mix of in-person and online/remote learning. In a hybrid teaching-learning environment, 'Online/remote learning is meant to replace an element of the in-person class'. The online material is designed as a substitute to in-person material and is meant to bring in flexibility to the entire teaching-learning experience. Students in a hybrid learning environment receive individualized attention and learn at their own pace, leading to greater understanding and engagement with the subject content. Blended pedagogical approach would best suit a hybrid environment. In a hybrid environment, it is always better to use both synchronous and asynchronous modes of teaching. A synchronous delivery mode includes live sessions such as virtual class rooms, webinars, video conferencing, etc. In this, students and teachers can interact in real-time giving a flavour of traditional classroom sessions. A asynchronous mode includes but is not limited to pre-recorded lectures, online discussion forums, and self-paced assignments giving a greater flexibility. The asynchronous learning tools must be balanced with synchronous learning tools to facilitate learning by learners having varied learning preferences and located in different countries.

Need for Hybrid Teaching-Learning

Hybrid teaching-learning process is mainly facilitated by technology, and it is very important to understand the underlying technological aspects that are part of this process. Thought leaders in the education domain along with other stakeholders have taken the challenge to redesign the education experience, by keeping successful and proven pedagogical concepts intact. At the same time, digitalization that influences technology-enabled transformation is equally important to be considered for sustainability.

Phases in Educational Innovation for a Hybrid Teaching-Learning Model

The phases in educational innovation through a hybrid teaching-learning model is proposed based on McKinsey's innovation model and is depicted in Fig. 11.2.

Phase 1: Goal Setting

A long-term vision is a key factor to initiate action towards innovative approaches and methodologies in the teaching-learning process.

Innovation could have greater accountability if tangible goals which align to futuristic growth perspectives are specified and incorporated as a part of the educational strategy. The objectives for achieving the specified goals need to be quantified and considered during educational process redesign. These would subsequently be included during the curriculum planning/design phase. The quantifiable goals would need to be apportioned to the various 'process owners' as applicable and drilled down to the level of specific measures.

This type of tangible goals setting and drilling down quantifiable measures from an innovation dimension would help in recognizing the contributions made by various stakeholders.

The goals need to be defined such that they align to the SMART framework, namely Specific, Measurable, Achievable, Relevant, and Timebound.

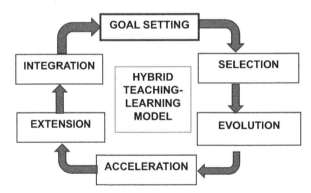

Fig. 11.2. Educational Innovation Phases for a Hybrid Teaching-Learning Model. *Source*: Adapted from the eight essentials of innovation, McKinsey Quarterly, April 2015.

- *Specific:* An educational goal that is clear to the learner as well as the person imparting learning.
- *Measurable:* A quantifiable goal which could be tracked by the educator and performance measured to ensure achievement by the learner.
- *Achievable:* A goal related to the teaching-learning process that is not too hard but propels one to improve.
- *Relevant:* A short-term goal that facilitates meeting the long-term educational goal/strategic objectives.
- *Timebound:* A timeline to mark the progress of activities and achievement of the specified educational goals.

Phase 2: Selection

When too many innovative ideas emerge from different perspectives, it becomes difficult to finalize the appropriate idea in terms of implementation and scalability.

The various approaches to select the best possible option among multiple alternatives are as follows:

Experience-based approach

The educator relies on past experiences relating to the teaching-learning process and the related learning while selecting the option.

Experiment-based approach

The educator conducts experiments and the learning based on the outcome of the experiments used to select the most relevant option.

Research-based approach

The educator performs research studies on educational processes and uses analytical techniques to select the best possible option out of the available alternatives. A decision matrix could be used to identify the best possible option from among the available alternatives.

The selection of a hybrid learning approach could be based on the following parameters:

1. Degree of flexibility in the teaching-learning process
2. Scope of interactivity in the teaching-learning process
3. Level of personalized attention to learners
4. Extent of learner's engagement with the content
5. Adherence to quality standards
6. Effectiveness of assessments
7. Adequacy of support in teaching and learning
8. Richness of learning experience for students
9. Excellence of instructional materials
10. Cost of instructional delivery

Table 11.1. Decision Matrix for Hybrid Learning.

Parameter	Weight	Choice 1 Score	Choice 1 Total	Choice 2 Score	Choice 2 Total	Choice 3 Score	Choice 3 Total
Degree of flexibility in the teaching-learning process							
Scope of interactivity in the teaching-learning process							
Level of personalized attention to learners							
Extent of learner's engagement with the content							
Adherence to quality standards							
Effectiveness of assessments							
Adequacy of support in teaching and learning							
Richness of learning experience for students							
Excellence of instructional materials							
Cost of instructional delivery							
Overall score			Overall score (Opt. 1)		Overall score (Opt. 2)		Overall score (Opt. 3)

A decision matrix as depicted in Table 11.1 could be prepared to evaluate the best option for hybrid learning considering the above-mentioned parameters.

The final decision is arrived at based on the overall scores. This would also help in visualizing the right expectations and planning for the resource requirements for the chosen hybrid learning approach.

Phase 3: Evolution

It is important to perform a systematic analysis of the following aspects:

a) Solution provided by the identified hybrid learning approach
b) Technology involved in the identified solution
c) Implementation requirements
d) Value generated by the hybrid learning process model

An exploration of the insights with reference to the above provides clarity and a better perspective on the way forward. This is an iterative process and involves development, testing, validation, and refinement of the innovation on a continuous basis. It is required to arrive at a well-developed innovative learning process model by considering all the phases involved in the educational innovation approach.

Phase 4: Acceleration

After completion of pilot testing of the innovative hybrid teaching-learning process, it is required to accelerate the adoption to reap the benefits as initially envisaged. It is required to monitor the progress with reference to the budget, timelines, benefits realization, etc. The existence of a feedback mechanism would help in fine-tuning the implementation process and to realize the expected benefits in an accelerated manner.

Phase 5: Extension

This involves extension of the innovative approach across other programmes and locations, as applicable. It would also involve enhancing the approach by discovering different ways of value creation for the stakeholders.

Phase 6: Integration

This requires the innovative approach for hybrid learning to be embedded in the system. It is also required to establish tight inter-connections among the educational strategy, innovative approach, and performance/realization of benefits. Many individual initiatives could be taken up across the institution to integrate the innovative approach into the entire ecosystem. The process of integration could involve change in the operational structures, enhanced focus on internal collaboration and experimentation, and setting up of 'innovation centres' or 'innovation cells'. This could facilitate intrapreneurship within the overall institutional governance framework. A comprehensive assimilation and integration could help in innovating effectively within the institutional culture and structure.

Feedback could be obtained during integration and utilized to analyse and apply improved practices towards achievement of the innovation objectives. The outcome and learning from the integration phase could help in institutionalizing the innovative approach pertaining to hybrid learning. Further, it could also serve as an input for goal setting as a part of the next cycle. The best practices adopted, lessons learnt, and feedback obtained in the various phases of the current cycle are considered while setting goals for the next cycle. Hence, this facilitates an ongoing process of continuous improvement.

Integrated Technology-Enabled Hybrid Teaching-Learning Framework

A technology-enabled framework with reference to hybrid teaching-learning incorporates the integration of multiple technologies and tools. This helps to provide a blended in-person and online learning experience. An integrated technology-enabled hybrid learning system blends the advantages of in-person learning with the flexibility and convenience of online learning.

Various strategies, processes, technologies, and tools could be used to provide an enriching experience for the learners in a hybrid learning approach. This is possible through a seamless integration of face-to-face and online elements. The integrated technology-enabled hybrid teaching-learning framework is provided in Fig. 11.3.

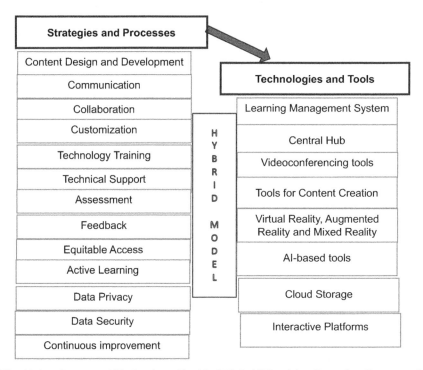

Fig. 11.3. Integrated Technology-Enabled Hybrid Teaching-Learning Framework.

Strategy and Processes

- **Content design and development**

The course content must be designed and developed such that it enables active learning and a good learning engagement for learners in an interactive online mode. Further, accessibility and compatibility of content across various devices should be ensured.

- **Communication**

Relevant communication guidelines for a hybrid learning model are required to be established. Appropriate video conferencing tools need to be utilized for effective communication during online learning and discussions.

- **Collaboration**

The tool utilized should effectively support collaboration activities such as group discussions, virtual study teams, and document sharing.

- **Customization**

The content and activities are to be customized for meeting the needs and preferences of individual learners. Personalization is also required for providing suggestions on additional learning materials and resources for learners.

- **Technology training**

Course facilitators and learners need to attain proficiency in the utilization of technologies. Hence, it would be important to organize relevant training programmes.

- **Technical support**

In a hybrid learning environment, adequate technical support is to be provided for addressing the technical challenges faced by course facilitators and learners. This could be done through online tutorials, help desks, online FAQs, etc.

- **Assessment**

In a hybrid learning model, a blend of online assignments, quizzes, and traditional assessment activities in an in-person environment is required. Tools would also be required to check for plagiarism and generate analytical reports pertaining to assessments.

- **Feedback**

The hybrid learning model should facilitate providing constructive feedback through the digital platform on time to the learners.

- *Equitable access*

It should be ensured that access to the technology and related resources is available in an equitable manner to all learners. This would facilitate equitable opportunities for learning. Further, alternative approaches need to be made available for those learners who face connectivity challenges.

- *Active learning*

Approaches that facilitate techniques for active learning need to be considered. Examples of techniques for active learning include group discussion, problem-solving exercises/activities, and case studies. Various tools for conducting opinion polls, brainstorming activities, and problem-solving would be required. Active learning also involves exploration and self-learning by the learners.

- *Data privacy and security*

The information provided by students as needed for the hybrid learning process is required to be protected by adhering to data privacy regulations and data security processes/procedures. Further, the trainers and learners need to be trained on the best practices related to data privacy and data security.

- *Continuous improvement*

As part of a continuous improvement exercise, feedback on the teaching-learning processes needs to be obtained from the trainers and learners. The hybrid learning model is required to be assessed for its effectiveness on a continuous basis. This would help to identify improvement areas and to fine-tune the hybrid learning model. The improvement or enhancement of the hybrid learning model could pertain to technology or pedagogy-related aspects.

Relevant Technologies and Tools

A hybrid teaching-learning process is considered as a technology-driven process to a large extent. There are many technologies and tools that are in the forefront driving the hybrid mode of teaching and learning.

Learning management system (LMS)

The LMS that is intended to be used should effectively support delivery of content, assessment, communication, and collaboration. It should facilitate notifications, discussion forums, and interactions among peer learners.

Central hub

Central hub is a kind of warehouse where all course materials, assignments, different forms of assessments like quiz, presentations, online tests, etc. are made available as in the case of any LMS. This helps the instructors to plan and organize the content and engage the students effectively.

Video conferencing tools

Various platforms like Zoom, Microsoft Teams, Google Meet, Webex, etc. are used for communication and virtual class sessions, discussions, and collaborative projects, thereby facilitating the hybrid mode.

Tools for content creation

Tools like Camtasia, Captiva, and PowerPoint are widely used to engage the students with multimedia contents to make the sessions more interactive.

VR, AR, and mixed reality (MR)

Tools based on these aspects help to simulate the learning scenarios to facilitate experiential learning. It provides an immersive experience for the learners and helps in understanding the concepts well. This also enhances classroom engagements in a virtual mode to a larger extent.

Artificial intelligence (AI)-based tools

Tools having AI-based features could be used in providing students with enhanced learning opportunities and the facility to take up assessments in a hybrid mode.

Cloud storage

Services like Dropbox, OneDrive, Google Drive, etc. help in easy sharing of voluminous data, thereby making the learning resources available to the learners easily.

Interactive platforms

Tools such as Kahoot, Mentimeter, etc. help to conduct interactive quizzes, polls, and surveys for effective classroom engagements.

Applications of Hybrid Teaching-Learning

Hybrid teaching-learning is ideally positioned to aid the learning needs of a diverse range of students. This model is used widely in K-12 education systems to create personalized set-up mainly in terms of remedial classes to facilitate all types of learners. Training and development divisions of the organizations make use of this model to help their employees to upskill and re-skill as part of their professional development. It also helps in continuing education for the individuals seeking to pursue their education along with work and in technical and vocational training by means of simulation.

Benefits and Challenges of Hybrid Teaching-Learning

There are plenty of benefits that could be accounted for in a hybrid mode, mainly flexibility in learning, availability of resources, personalized learning, lifelong learning, collaborative environment, and effective engagements. However, there are few challenges that are associated in implementing a flexible mode. Technological barriers, design, and delivery of contents effectively, maintaining teacher–student relationship, and online assessments.

Conclusion

A hybrid model seems to be the future of teaching-learning. It leverages various technologies to create a dynamic yet flexible learning environment for continuous learners. This mode is highly suitable for learners with diverse needs and varied learning styles. Hence, this model has the potential to shape the future of education.

This chapter has a focus on educational system transformation and a redesigned learning experience through a hybrid teaching-learning model. Educational system transformation involves application of technology while redesigning processes for enhanced sustainability. Innovative methods in education constitute a key aspect in the transformation of education. Learning models provide a mechanism of learning and could pertain to either sustainable learning or flexible learning. A hybrid teaching-learning model involves a blend of synchronous and asynchronous learning. The most effective blend could be chosen based on evaluation of various parameters using a decision matrix. The various phases in a hybrid teaching-learning approach include goal setting, selection, evolution, acceleration, extension, and integration. The integrated technology-enabled hybrid teaching-learning framework has been proposed considering various aspects such as strategy, processes, technologies, and tools, which if implemented appropriately could provide engaging and adaptable learning experiences while catering to the needs and preferences of diverse learners. This chapter also highlights the applications, benefits, and challenges of hybrid teaching-learning.

References

Ben-Eliyahu, A. (2021), Sustainable learning in education. *Sustainability, 13*, 4250. https://doi.org/10.3390/su13084

Fındıkoğlu, F., & Ilhan, D. (2016). Realization of a desired future: Innovation in education. *Universal Journal of Educational Research, 4*, 2574–2580. https://doi.org/10.13189/ujer.2016.041110.

Mistler-Jackson, M., & Songer, N. B. (2000). Student motivation and Internet technology: Are students empowered to learn science? *Journal of Research in Science Teaching, 37*(5), 459–479.

Müller, C., & Mildenberger, T. (2021). Facilitating flexible learning by replacing classroom time with an online learning environment: A systematic review of blended learning in higher education. *Educational Research Review, 34*, 1–16. https://doi.org/10.1016/j.edurev.2021.100394

Popescu, M., & Crenicean, L. C. (2012). Innovation and change in education–economic growth goal in Romania in the context of knowledge-based economy. *Procedia-Social and Behavioral Sciences, 46*, 3982–3988.

Saad, N., & Sankaran, S. (2020). *Technology proficiency in teaching and facilitating*. https://doi.org/10.1093/acrefore/9780190264093.013.591.

Schindler, L. A., Burkholder, G. J., Morad, O. A., & Marsh, C. (2017). Computer-based technology and student engagement: A critical review of the literature. *International Journal of Educational Technology in Higher Education*, *14*, 25. https://doi.org/10.1186/s41239-017-0063-0

Serdyukov, P. (2017). Innovation in education: what works, what doesn't, and what to do about it? *Journal of Research in Innovative Teaching & Learning*, *10*(1), 4–33. https://doi.org/10.1108/JRIT-10-2016-0007

Smith, C. (2006). The future of a concept: The case for sustaining 'innovation' in education. In P. Jeffery (Ed.), *AARE 2006: Conference papers, abstracts, and symposia* (pp. 1–11). Australian Association for Research in Education.

Chapter 12

Incorporation of Deep Learning-Based AI Tools in Education: A Statistical Evaluation of the Perceptions of Gen-Z and Millennials

Remya Nair[a,b]

[a]*University of Mysore, India*
[b]*Welingkar Institute of Management Development and Research, Bangalore, Karnataka, India*

Abstract

The Millennials (1981–1995) witnessed conceptualization, adaptation, incorporation, and improvement of numerous technological aspects like the first personal computers by IBM in 1981 as well as the ARPANET adoption of the TCP/IP protocol which is the fundamental basis for the internet. The Generation Z (Gen-Z) (1996–2010) are born in a period that practically amalgamated a wide range of technologies in various realms – cloud computing, machine learning, introduction of e-commerce, big data analysis, mobile technology, automations, etc. Some of the existing deep learning-based tools are ChatGPT, TensorFlow (open-source library developed by Google), PyTorch (deep learning-based digital library), Keras (TensorFlow and allows users to quickly prototype and experiment with deep learning models), and OpenCV (open-source computer vision library that includes a wide range of image and video processing algorithms). In the academic sector, the Millennials (42–28 years of age) are currently the educators, and the Gen-Z (13–27 years of age) can be from any stage of life – students to educators. The study is to statistically evaluate the perceptions of Gen-Z as well as the Millennials in the incorporation of deep learning-based AI tools in education. The research framework used is the unified theory of acceptance and use of technology-3 (UTAUT-3) model. The research methodology is a qualitative analysis based on the data collected in a questionnaire from 200 participants; 100 each from Gen-Zs and Millennials. The study is limited to the understanding of perceptions regarding application of the deep learning-based AI tools in education. The technical aspects and knowledge required to create deep learning tools are not in the scope.

Keywords: Deep learning; artificial intelligence; Gen-Zs, Millennials; UTAUT-3

Introduction

In the rapidly evolving landscape of artificial intelligence (AI), deep learning-based tools have emerged as a driving force behind various breakthroughs in technology. These tools leverage intricate neural networks to simulate human-like learning processes, enabling them to excel at tasks that require pattern recognition, complex decision-making, and data analysis. Among the prominent deep learning tools are ChatGPT, TensorFlow, PyTorch, Keras, and OpenCV, each contributing uniquely to the advancement of AI applications.

ChatGPT represents a significant stride in natural language processing. Developed by OpenAI, it employs a generative pre-trained transformer (GPT) architecture to generate coherent and contextually relevant text. With applications ranging from chatbots to content generation, ChatGPT showcases AI's ability to simulate human-like conversations and understand intricate language nuances. TensorFlow stands out as one of the most influential open-source libraries for deep learning. Created by Google, it provides a comprehensive framework for building and training neural networks. Its flexibility and scalability enable researchers and practitioners to tackle a wide spectrum of AI tasks, from image and speech recognition to natural language processing. PyTorch, a deep learning library, has gained substantial popularity due to its user-friendly nature and dynamic computation graph. Created by Facebook's AI research lab, it allows developers to create complex neural network architectures more intuitively. Its flexible design has made it a preferred choice for researchers experimenting with novel deep learning techniques. Keras, although a distinct library, is tightly integrated with TensorFlow and serves as a high-level interface for building deep learning models. Known for its user-friendly Application Programming Interfaces (APIs), Keras enables rapid prototyping and experimentation, making it ideal for beginners and researchers seeking quick model development. OpenCV is a critical tool for computer vision applications. This open-source library offers a comprehensive suite of image and video processing algorithms, simplifying tasks such as object detection, image segmentation, and facial recognition. Its versatility and extensive documentation make it an invaluable resource for AI practitioners working in the visual domain. These deep learning-based tools collectively represent the convergence of advanced algorithms, computational power, and big data. They drive innovation across industries, revolutionizing fields like healthcare, finance, manufacturing, and entertainment. Hence, the incorporation of deep learning-based AI tools in education is significant.

The Key Areas of Incorporation of Deep Learning-Based AI Tools in Education

Personalized Tutoring, Monitoring, and Continuous Assessment

AI-driven tutoring systems can act as virtual tutors, providing real-time feedback, assistance, and answering questions for students. These systems offer personalized tutoring and continuous monitoring of student progress. AI algorithms can efficiently grade assignments, quizzes, and exams, saving teachers valuable time and providing faster feedback to students. This automation enables teachers to focus on more strategic aspects of teaching (see Fig. 12.1) (Zachari Swiecki, 2022).

Inclusive Education

AI-powered virtual classrooms facilitate seamless communication between students and teachers from diverse linguistic backgrounds. AI language translation tools help break down language barriers, promoting inclusive education. AI-powered tools, such as language translation and speech recognition, break communication barriers, enabling students from different linguistic backgrounds to participate fully (Mohammed & Nell'Watson, 2019). Additionally, AI-driven adaptive learning platforms cater to individual learning styles, ensuring equitable educational opportunities. By promoting inclusivity, AI fosters an environment where all students can thrive academically and socially.

Data-Driven Curriculum Design

AI enables educators to gather and analyse vast amounts of data, allowing them to identify trends, predict student performance, and make data-driven decisions to enhance teaching methods and curriculum design. Data-driven curriculum design using AI and deep learning leverages large datasets and sophisticated algorithms to analyse educational data, student performance, and learning patterns (Guan et al., 2020). AI and deep learning models can identify learning gaps, assess the effectiveness of instructional materials, and tailor curriculum content

Fig. 12.1. Diagram on the Advantages of Using AI in Education. *Source*: Image courtesy (self).

to individual students' needs. By continuously refining the curriculum based on real-time data, educators can enhance teaching methodologies and optimize student outcomes. This data-driven approach ensures that educational content is relevant, engaging, and aligned with students' progress, leading to more effective and personalized learning experiences.

Prognostic Analytics

Deep learning models can forecast student performance and identify potential challenges, allowing educators to intervene proactively and offer timely support to struggling students (Doleck et al., 2020). By harnessing the power of machine learning algorithms, these tools can analyse vast amounts of educational data, including student performance, engagement, and behaviour, to identify patterns and trends. With predictive analytics, educators can forecast student outcomes, detect early warning signs of academic struggles, and provide timely interventions to support at-risk students. This proactive approach helps in reducing dropout rates and improving overall student success. AI-based predictive analytics aids in curriculum design and resource allocation, optimizing educational content and ensuring efficient use of resources. It assists in identifying areas that require improvement, allowing educators to continuously refine teaching methodologies.

Future Trends

Institutions can leverage predictive analytics to predict future enrolment trends, facilitating effective planning and resource management (Agrusti et al., 2020). Predicting future enrolment trends using deep learning-based AI tools in education has become increasingly feasible due to their data analysis capabilities. These tools can process large amounts of historical enrolment data, student demographics, and other relevant factors to identify patterns and make accurate forecasts. By leveraging deep learning algorithms, educational institutions can anticipate future enrolment numbers, understand fluctuations in demand for courses, and plan resource allocation accordingly. This predictive ability empowers institutions to optimize their course offerings, staffing, and infrastructure, ensuring better preparation for changing student enrolment patterns and fostering more efficient and effective educational planning.

Theoretical Background

Baker and Smith (2019) categorize AI tools in education into three distinct groups: (a) those that engage learners directly, (b) those designed for teachers to enhance their efficiency, and (c) tools aimed at system-level management. (a) Learner-centric AI tools encompass software that empowers students in their learning of various subjects. (b) Teacher-centric systems assist educators in automating tasks like administration, assessment, feedback, and plagiarism detection, ultimately streamlining their workflow and enhancing effectiveness. (c) AI tools geared towards system management offer insights to administrators and managers at an institutional level, aiding in the monitoring of attrition patterns across faculties or colleges.

Farooq et al. (2017) proposed the UTAUT-3 framework as an extension of the UTAUT-2 model, incorporating eight key determinants of technology acceptance: performance expectancy (PE), effort expectancy (EE), social influence (SI), facilitating conditions (FC), hedonic motivation (HM), habit (HB), price value, and personal innovativeness in information technology (IT). According to the authors, the UTAUT-3 model demonstrates a significant explanatory power of 66% in predicting technology adoption. In the paper by Gunasinghe et al. (2020), the study aims to assess the adequacy of unified theory of acceptance and use of technology-3 (UTAUT-3) model in understanding academician's adoption to e-learning, with intent of getting more academicians to accept e-learning.

In previous studies (Van Raaij & Schepers, 2008), personal innovativeness in IT has been identified as a crucial factor in comprehending teachers' adoption of educational technology. As per the research article by Fitria (2021), in the future advancements of science and technology, various aspects of teachers' work, such as grading, taking attendance, conducting daily tests and exams, managing administrative tasks, and other routine activities, can be delegated to technology devices. This automation of systemic work can enable teachers to conserve energy and dedicate more time to non-systemic tasks, fostering the development of a generation with enhanced character and higher quality of natural intelligence, which robots are incapable of replicating. Technology will play a crucial role in streamlining and automating systematic processes based on human commands, while teachers will continue to be the essential drivers of imparting new knowledge and facilitating meaningful learning experiences (Fitria, 2021).

In the paper by Chen et al. (2020), the authors explain a qualitative research approach, leveraging the use of literature review as a research design. This study clearly signifies the role of AI in education. In the research paper by Mikropoulos and Natsis (2011), 10 years research data from 1999 to 2009 are analysed regarding the educational virtual environments. This paper is based on 53 research studies found by using specific search criteria. The research paper by Pokrivcakova (2019) centres on the integration of AI into foreign language learning and teaching. This encompasses a diverse array of technologies and methodologies, including machine learning, adaptive learning, natural language processing, data mining, neural networks, algorithms, and even crowdsourcing.

Conceptual Model

Research Methodology

Research design: The research methodology is a qualitative analysis based on the data collected in a questionnaire from 200 participants; 100 each from Gen-Zs and Millennials. The collected data are statistically analysed to understand the perceptions of both Gen-Zs and millennials in terms of performance expectancy, effort expectancy, social influence, facilitating conditions, hedonic motivation, price value, habit, personal innovativeness, as well as orientation towards continuous learning (see Fig. 12.2).

Data sample: The sampling method is simple random sampling.

Research device: The questionnaire is circulated among the Gen-Zs and Millennials. The variables to measure the constructs like performance expectancy, effort expectancy, social influence, facilitating conditions, hedonic motivation, price value, habit, personal innovativeness, as well as orientation towards continuous learning are included in the questionnaire.

Data collection: A total of 200 responses are collected; 100 each from Gen-Zs as well as Millennials. In the academic sector, the Millennials (42–28 years of age) are currently the educators and the Gen-Z (13–27 years of age) can be from any stage of life – students to educators. The study statistically evaluates the perceptions of Gen-Z as well as the Millennials in the incorporation of deep learning-based AI tools in education.

Research framework: The research framework used is the UTAUT- 3 model. The key constructs in this proven model are performance expectancy, effort expectancy, social influence, facilitating conditions, hedonic motivation, price value, habit, and personal innovativeness. Orientation towards continuous learning is also analysed in this study.

Data analysis and interpretations: See Tables 12.1–12.7.

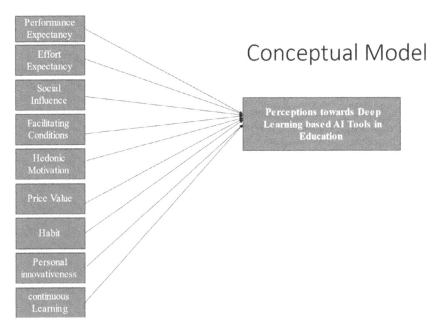

Fig. 12.2. Conceptual Model. *Source*: Image courtesy (self).

Table 12.1. Reliability of Data (Cronbach's Alpha).

Question	Cronbach's Alpha
How confident are you that using the AI-based educational tools will improve your performance in completing tasks or achieving goals?	0.8296
Rate on a scale of 1–7, the contribution of AI-based tools to the quality of your education or the outcomes you produce?	0.8287
How will AI-based tools facilitate your ability to learn and acquire new skills or knowledge?	0.8289
On a scale of 1–7, how much impact do AI-based tools have on your productivity and efficiency?	0.8343
How much effort do you think was reduced after you learn and become proficient in using the AI-based tools in education?	0.8352
How much effort is saved in the educational activities/research after the introduction of AI-based tools?	0.8327
Do your peers use AI-based tools for education?	0.8310
Do your teachers/peers recommend AI-based tools for learning and other educational activities?	0.8352
Do you get a positive impact during conversations related to educational activities after using AI-based tools?	0.8311
Does your educational institution have the required faculties with relevant experience in using AI-based tools?	0.8369
Does your educational institution encourage the use of AI-based tools?	0.8314
Does your educational institution support innovative approaches towards learning?	0.8353
Rate the role AI-based tools play in enhancing your motivation and enthusiasm for your education?	0.8314
Do the AI-based tools make you feel excited, entertained, and innovative?	0.8317
How much do the AI-based tools contribute to make the educational experience enjoyable?	0.8331
Do you think the price of the AI-based educational tools is reasonable and justified considering its features and functionalities?	0.8252
Would you be willing to pay a premium price for the AI-based tools/apps if it offers unique and valuable features that meet your needs?	0.8249
How important is the price factor in your decision-making process when considering the adoption or purchase of AI-based tools in education?	0.8289

(*Continued*)

Table 12.1. (*Continued*)

Question	Cronbach's Alpha
How often do you find yourself using the AI-based educational tools in your daily life?	0.8370
Do you have a habit of depending on the latest tools and technology for the educational/research activities?	0.8308
Do you find yourself using AI tools as the default primary option for educational activities without consciously thinking about it?	0.8254
Are you comfortable with experimenting and learning new technologies on your own?	0.8266
How often do you proactively explore and adopt new technologies before others in your social or professional circles?	0.8270
How often do you actively seek out opportunities to learn new technological skills?	0.8263
Do you continuously upgrade yourself with information related to the latest relevant updates in technology?	0.8309
Are you ready to upskill yourself if required to use a new tool/app?	0.8336
To what extent do you believe that learning new technologies is important for your professional growth?	0.8313
Cumulative Cronbach's alpha	0.8362

Table 12.2. Summary of Fit.

Sample Size	200
−2 Log likelihood	18,416.592686
Iterations	370
Number of parameters	126
Akaike information criterion (AIC)	19,107.003645
Bayesian information criterion (BIC)	19,084.180674
Chi square	1,033.2455558
df	279
Probability > chi square	4.287008e−87
Comparative fit index (CFI)	0.562628232
Root mean square error of approximation (RMSEA)	0.1162623991
Lower 90%	0.1087289523
Upper 90%	0.1238866009

Table 12.3. Descriptive Statistics.

	How Confident are You That Using the AI-based Educational Tools Will Improve Your Performance in Completing Tasks or Achieving Goals?	Rate on a Scale of 1–7, the Contribution of AI-based Tools to the Quality of Your Education or the Outcomes You Produce?	How Will AI-based Tools Facilitate Your Ability to Learn and Acquire New Skills or Knowledge?	On a Scale of 1–7 How Much Impact Does AI-based Tools Have on Your Productivity and Efficiency?	How Much Effort Do You Think was Reduced After You Learn and Become Proficient in Using the AI-based Tools in Education?	How Much Effort is Saved in the Educational Activities/ Research After the Introduction of AI-based Tools?	Do Your Peers Use AI-based Tools for Education?
Mean	5.685	5.175879	5.277778	4.708543	4.835	4.92	4.92
Standard error	0.096569	0.091356	0.090536	0.110728	0.114913	0.114163	0.101832
Median	6	5	5	5	5	5	5
Mode	7	5	5	6	6	6	5
Standard deviation	1.365687	1.288732	1.273953	1.56201	1.625109	1.614507	1.440128
Sample variance	1.865101	1.660829	1.622955	2.439876	2.64098	2.606633	2.07397
Kurtosis	0.008806	0.09485	−0.14002	−1.02904	−0.8961	−0.86036	−0.35958
Skewness	−0.9685	−0.60447	−0.52004	−0.30075	−0.36184	−0.44072	−0.39911
Range	5	6	5	5	6	6	6
Minimum	2	1	2	2	1	1	1
Maximum	7	7	7	7	7	7	7
Sum	1137	1030	1045	937	967	984	984
Count	200	199	198	199	200	200	200
Confidence level (95.0%)	0.190429	0.180155	0.178544	0.218357	0.226603	0.225124	0.200809

Table 12.4. Descriptive Statistics.

	Do your Teachers/Peer Recommend AI-based Tools for Learning and Other Educational Activities?	Do You Get a Positive Impact During Conversations Related to Educational Activities After Using AI-based Tools?	Does Your Educational Institution Has the Required Faculties with Relevant Experience in Using AI-based Tools?	Does Your Educational Institution Encourage the Use of AI-based Tools?	Does Your Educational Institution Support Innovative Approaches Towards Learning?	Rate the Role AI-based Tools Play in Enhancing Your Motivation and Enthusiasm for Your Education?	Does the AI-based Tools Make You Feel Excited, Entertained and Innovative?
Mean	5.16	5.455	4.99	4.71	5.27	5.311558	5.14
Standard error	0.112852	0.094788	0.115395	0.10505	0.11269	0.097515	0.111193
Median	5	6	5	5	6	6	6
Mode	7	6	7	6	6	6	6
Standard deviation	1.595975	1.340507	1.631936	1.48558	1.593675	1.375624	1.572502
Sample variance	2.547136	1.79696	2.663216	2.20693	2.539799	1.89234	2.472764
Kurtosis	−0.74948	0.988576	−0.92422	−0.49591	−0.33039	0.031002	−0.63258
Skewness	−0.5046	−1.01557	−0.35516	−0.5218	−0.76663	−0.8471	−0.64123
Range	6	6	6	6	6	6	6
Minimum	1	1	1	1	1	1	1
Maximum	7	7	7	7	7	7	7
Sum	1032	1091	998	942	1054	1057	1028
Count	200	200	200	200	200	199	200
Confidence level (95.0%)	0.22254	0.186918	0.227555	0.20715	0.222219	0.192302	0.219267

Deep Learning-Based AI Tools in Education 209

Table 12.5. Descriptive Statistics.

	How Much Do the AI-based Tools Contribute to Make the Educational Experience Enjoyable?	Do You Think the Price of the AI-based Educational Tools is Reasonable and Justified Considering its Features and Functionalities?	Would You Be Willing to Pay a Premium Price for the AI-based Tools/Apps If it Offers Unique and Valuable Features That Meet?	How Important is the Price Factor in Your Decision-making Process When Considering the Adoption or Purchase of AI-based?	How Often Do You Find Yourself Using the AI-based Educational Tools in Your Daily Life?	Do You Have a Habit of Depending on Latest Tools and Technology for the Educational/ Research Activities?	Do You Find Yourself Using AI Tools as Default Primary Option for Educational Activities without Consciously Thinking About it?
Mean	4.975	5.38	5.01005	5.205	4.84	5.03	4.845
Standard error	0.103564	0.101387	0.106628	0.104736	0.112406	0.095346	0.100526
Median	5	6	5	5	5	5	5
Mode	6	7	6	6	6	6	5
Standard deviation	1.464616	1.433834	1.504169	1.481197	1.589665	1.348403	1.421647
Sample variance	2.145101	2.055879	2.262525	2.193945	2.527035	1.818191	2.02108
Kurtosis	−0.40365	−0.09775	0.15305	−0.70514	−0.66711	−0.52534	−0.49772
Skewness	−0.54767	−0.73246	−0.81777	−0.48925	−0.48495	−0.42768	−0.46503
Range	6	6	6	6	6	5	6
Minimum	1	1	1	1	1	2	1
Maximum	7	7	7	7	7	7	7
Sum	995	1076	997	1041	968	1006	969
Count	200	200	199	200	200	200	200
Confidence level (95.0%)	0.204224	0.199931	0.210272	0.206536	0.22166	0.188019	0.198232

Table 12.6. Descriptive Statistics.

	Are You Comfortable with Experimenting and Learning New Technologies on Your Own?	How Often Do You Proactively Explore and Adopt New Technologies Before Others in Your Social or Professional?	How Often Do You Actively Seek Out Opportunities to Learn New Technological Skills?	Do You Continuously Upgrade Yourself with Information Related to the Latest Relevant Updates in Technology?	Are You Ready to Upskill Yourself If Required to Use a New Tool/App?	To What Extent Do You Believe That Learning New Technologies is Important for Your Professional Growth?
Mean	4.89	5.225	5.155	4.725	4.945	5.61
Standard error	0.108621	0.10501	0.106591	0.109116	0.112575	0.086178
Median	5	5	5	5	5	6
Mode	5	7	6	6	6	6
Standard deviation	1.536131	1.48506	1.507427	1.54314	1.592058	1.21874
Sample variance	2.359698	2.205402	2.272337	2.381281	2.534648	1.485327
Kurtosis	−0.66023	−0.92432	−0.17301	−0.74407	−0.57498	−0.6034
Skewness	−0.33436	−0.34641	−0.74687	−0.34242	−0.611	−0.59531
Range	6	6	6	6	6	4
Minimum	1	1	1	1	1	3
Maximum	7	7	7	7	7	7
Sum	978	1045	1031	945	989	1122
Count	200	200	200	200	200	200
Confidence level (95.0%)	0.214196	0.207074	0.210193	0.215173	0.221994	0.169939

Table 12.7. Performance Expectancy.

Regression Statistics

Multiple R	0.142423178
R^2	0.020284362
Adjusted R^2	0.015336303
Standard error	0.933287661
observations	200

ANOVA

	df	SS	MS	F	Significance F
Regression	1	3.57073434	3.570734	4.099458	0.044239929
Residual	198	172.4631198	0.871026		
Total	199	176.0338542			

	Coefficients	Standard Error	t Stat	P-value	Lower 95%	Upper 95%	Lower 95.0%	Upper 95.0%
Intercept	4.597982498	0.311605928	14.75576	9.97E-34	3.983490162	5.212474834	3.983490162	5.212474834
To what extent do	0.109911022	0.05428477	2.024712	0.04424	0.002860507	0.216961537	0.002860507	0.216961537

Role of Performance Expectancy in Incorporation of Deep Learning-Based AI Tools in Education

Interpretation (See Table 12.8)

Multiple R is the correlation coefficient that indicates the strength and direction of the linear relationship between the predictor variables (independent variables) and the response variable (dependent variable). Here, the multiple R value is 0.1424, which is a relatively weak positive correlation.

R^2 represents the proportion of the variance in the dependent variable (behavioural intention) that can be explained by the predictor variables (performance expectancy in this case). An R^2 value of 0.0203 indicates that only about 2.03% of the variability in behavioural intention can be explained by performance expectancy.

In summary, the regression statistics suggest that the performance expectancy has a weak positive relationship with incorporation of deep learning-based AI tools in education.

Role of Effort Expectancy in Incorporation of Deep Learning-Based AI Tools in Education

Interpretation (See Table 12.9)

In the analysis of variance (ANOVA), the F-statistic is 0.0848 with a p-value of 0.7712, which indicates that the effort expectancy in this model is not statistically significant. The study examined the perceptions of Gen-Z and Millennials using the UTAUT-3 model. Notably, the statistical evaluation revealed that 'effort expectancy' lacked significant influence on their intentions. This implies that the perceived ease of use might not be a primary driving factor for these generations when considering the adoption of AI tools in education.

Role of Social Influence in Incorporation of Deep Learning-Based AI Tools in Education

Interpretation (See Table 12.10)

The regression model indicates a moderate positive relationship between the social influence and the incorporation of deep learning-based AI tools in education. The

Table 12.8. Effort Expectancy.

ANOVA					
	df	SS	MS	F	*Significance F*
Regression	1	0.140530567	0.140531	0.084804	0.771193933
Residual	198	328.1082194	1.657112		
Total	199	328.24875			

Table 12.9. Social Influence.

Regression Statistics

Multiple R	0.243063032
R^2	0.059079638
Adjusted R^2	0.054327515
Standard error	0.988047841
observations	200

ANOVA

	df	SS	MS	F	Significance F
Regression	1	12.13685305	12.13685	12.43226	0.000524268
Residual	198	193.2952303	0.976239		
Total	199	205.4320833			

	Coefficients	Standard Error	t Stat	P-value	Lower 95%	Upper 95%	Lower 95.0%	Upper 95.0%
Intercept	3.849048199	0.329889248	11.6677	2.8E-24	3.198500837	4.499595562	3.198500837	4.499595562
To what extent do	0.202635496	0.057469901	3.525941	0.000524	0.089303847	0.315967146	0.089303847	0.315967146

Table 12.10. Facilitating Conditions.

Regression Statistics

Multiple R	0.20175089
R^2	0.040703422
Adjusted R^2	0.035858489
Standard error	0.966105606
observations	200

ANOVA

	df	SS	MS	F	Significance F
Regression	1	7.841378483	7.841378	8.401237	0.004172427
Residual	198	184.8052882	0.93336		
Total	199	192.6466667			

	Coefficients	Standard Error	t Stat	P-value	Lower 95%	Upper 95%	Lower 95.0%	Upper 95.0%
Intercept	4.373437485	0.223418917	19.57505	3.51E-48	3.932851475	4.814023494	3.932851475	4.814023494
Are you ready to u	0.124684027	0.04301691	2.898489	0.004172	0.039853928	0.209514127	0.039853928	0.209514127

R^2 value of 0.0591 indicates that around 5.91% of the variability in the dependent variable can be explained by the predictor variable. The ANOVA results confirm the significance of the regression model, as indicated by the low p-value associated with the F-statistic (0.0005). This proves that social influence has a deep impact on the incorporation of deep learning-based AI tools in education.

Role of Facilitating Conditions in Incorporation of Deep Learning-Based AI Tools in Education

Interpretation (See Table 12.11)

The regression model indicates a moderate positive relationship between the facilitating conditions and the incorporation of deep learning-based AI tools in education. The model explains about 4.07% of the variability in the dependent variable. The ANOVA results confirm the significance of the regression model, with a small p-value (0.0042), indicating that the relationship between the facilitating conditions and the incorporation of deep learning-based AI tools in education is statistically significant. This suggests that the facilitating conditions are having a meaningful impact on incorporation of deep learning-based AI tools in education.

Role of Hedonic Motivation in Incorporation of Deep Learning-Based AI Tools in Education

Interpretation (See Table 12.12)

The regression model suggests a moderate positive relationship between the predictor variable(s) and the dependent variable. The model explains about 6.40% of the variability in the dependent variable. The ANOVA results indicate that the model is statistically significant, and the coefficients provide insights into the magnitude and significance of the impact of the predictor variables on the dependent variable.

Role of Price in Incorporation of Deep Learning-Based AI Tools in Education for Gen-Zs and Millennials

The paired two-sample t-test is used to determine whether there is a significant difference between the means of the attitudes of the two groups, Millennials (1) and Gen-Zs (2), towards the price factor. In this case:

- The calculated t-statistic is −41.4355, indicating a very large difference between the means.
- The extremely small p-values indicate a highly significant difference.
- The results suggest that there is a significant and substantial difference in the attitudes of the two groups towards price. The negative sign of the t-statistic suggests that Group 2's (Gen-Zs) attitude towards price (mean: 5.61) is significantly higher than Group 1's (Millennial's) attitude (mean: 1.5).

Table 12.11. Hedonic Motivation.

Regression Statistics

Multiple R	0.253055274
R^2	0.064036972
Adjusted R^2	0.059309886
Standard error	1.010137753
observations	200

ANOVA

	df	SS	MS	F	Significance F
Regression	1	13.82287841	13.82288	13.54682	0.000299961
Residual	198	202.0348994	1.020378		
Total	199	215.8577778			

	Coefficients	Standard Error	t Stat	P-value	Lower 95%	Upper 95%	Lower 95.0%	Upper 95.0%
Intercept	3.926821842	0.337264624	11.64315	3.32E-24	3.261730109	4.591913575	3.261730109	4.591913575
To what extent do	0.216252791	0.058754763	3.6806	0.0003	0.100387371	0.332118211	0.100387371	0.332118211

Table 12.12. Price.

Mean	1.5	5.61
Variance	0.251256281	1.485327
Observations	200	200
Pearson correlation	−0.189193108	
Hypothesized mean difference	0	
df	199	
t-statistic	−41.43554991	
$p\ (T \le t)$ one-tail	4.1132E−100	
t critical one-tail	1.652546746	
$p\ (T \le t)$ two-tail	8.2264E−100	
t critical two-tail	1.971956544	

In summary, based on the provided results, it appears that Gen-Z's incorporation of deep learning-based AI tools in education has a significant relation to the price of the tool.

Attitudes of the Gen-Zs and Millennials Towards Personal Innovativeness in the Context of Their Proactive Exploration and Adoption of New Technologies

The paired two-sample t-test is used to determine whether there is a significant difference between the means of the attitudes of the two groups towards personal innovativeness in the context of their proactive exploration and adoption of new technologies (see Table 12.13).

In this case:

- The calculated t-statistic is −32.7187, indicating a substantial difference between the means.
- The extremely small p-values indicate a highly significant difference.

The results suggest that there is a significant and substantial difference in the attitudes of the two groups towards personal innovativeness. The attitudes of Gen-Z towards personal innovativeness in the context of their proactive exploration and adoption of new technologies are significantly higher compared to Millennials (see Table 12.14).

- The calculated t-statistic is −29.8403, indicating a substantial difference between the means.
- The p-value is extremely small, indicating strong evidence to reject the null hypothesis that the means are equal.

Table 12.13. Attitude Comparison.

Mean	1.5	5.225
Variance	0.251256281	2.20540201
Observations	200	200
Pearson correlation	−0.091133562	
Hypothesized mean difference	0	
df	199	
t-statistic	−32.71866478	
$p\,(T \leq t)$ one-tail	2.57995E−82	
t critical one-tail	1.652546746	
$p\,(T \leq t)$ two-tail	5.1599E−82	
t critical two-tail	1.971956544	

Table 12.14. Attitudes of the Gen-Zs and Millennials Towards Continuous Learning.

Mean	1.5	4.725
Variance	0.251256	2.381281
Observations	200	200
Pearson correlation	0.191648	
Hypothesized mean difference	0	
df	199	
t-statistic	−29.8403	
$p\,(T \leq t)$ one-tail	1.07E−75	
t critical one-tail	1.652547	
$p\,(T \leq t)$ two-tail	2.13E−75	
t critical two-tail	1.971957	

The results suggest that there is a significant and substantial difference in the attitudes of Millennials and Gen Z individuals towards continuous learning. The extremely small p-values indicate a highly significant difference.

In summary, based on the provided results, it appears that the attitudes of Gen Z individuals towards continuous learning are significantly higher compared to Millennials. The extremely small p-values indicate a highly significant difference (see Fig. 12.3).

Deep Learning-Based AI Tools in Education 219

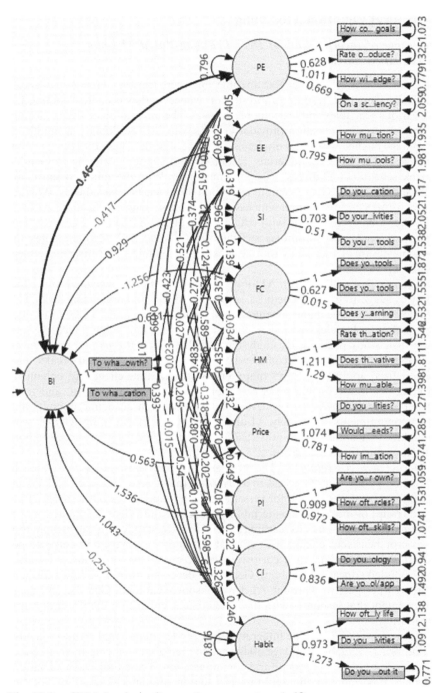

Fig. 12.3. SEM Analysis. *Source*: Image courtesy (self).

Structural Equation Modelling

Relevance of Incorporation of Deep Learning-Based AI Tools in Education for Gen-Zs

24/7 Availability: AI tools enable anytime, anywhere learning. Gen-Zs can access educational content, resources, and support whenever they need it, accommodating various schedules and learning preferences. The integration of deep learning-based AI tools in education provides Gen-Zs with 24/7 availability, a significant advantage aligned with their on-demand digital lifestyle. These tools ensure constant access to learning materials, resources, and support, catering to Gen-Zs' flexible schedules and diverse learning preferences. With the ability to learn anytime and anywhere, Gen-Zs can fit education into their fast-paced lives. Whether it's revisiting concepts, completing assignments, or seeking clarification, AI tools empower Gen-Zs to engage with educational content at their convenience. This perpetual availability promotes self-directed learning and accommodates the dynamic nature of their daily routines, fostering a seamless and enriching educational experience.

Efficient time management: AI tools can help students manage their time effectively by suggesting study schedules, setting reminders, and organizing tasks. This promotes better time management and reduces academic stress. These tools offer personalized schedules, reminders, and task organization, helping Gen-Zs optimize their study routines. By analysing their learning patterns and preferences, AI tools provide tailored recommendations for study sessions and breaks. This personalized approach ensures that Gen-Zs allocate time effectively, enhancing productivity and reducing procrastination. With the ability to plan and track their progress, Gen-Zs can achieve a balance between academic pursuits and other commitments. Ultimately, AI-driven time management equips Gen-Zs with vital skills that align with their fast-paced lives, preparing them for success in both education and future endeavours.

Access to diverse resources: The integration of deep learning-based AI tools in education grants Gen-Zs access to a diverse array of resources, a crucial advantage aligned with their thirst for versatile learning experiences. These tools curate a wide range of multimedia materials, from articles and videos to interactive simulations, catering to various learning styles and interests. Gen-Zs can explore topics comprehensively, engage with content in multiple formats, and delve deeper into subjects that pique their curiosity. This access to diverse resources fosters a well-rounded education, enabling Gen-Zs to develop critical thinking skills and a broader perspective. Through AI-driven resource curation, Gen-Zs can engage with content that resonates with their preferences, enhancing their overall learning journey.

Language assistance: The integration of deep learning-based AI tools in education brings valuable language assistance to Gen-Zs, enhancing their language learning journey and cross-cultural communication. These tools harness natural language processing to offer real-time translation, grammar suggestions, vocabulary building exercises, and pronunciation assistance. Gen-Zs engaging in foreign language studies receive instant feedback and guidance, promoting accurate language acquisition. AI-driven language tools also encourage self-expression, enabling Gen-Zs to confidently engage in multilingual interactions. This language support fosters cultural awareness, facilitates global communication, and prepares Gen-Zs for an interconnected world. Through AI-powered language assistance, Gen-Zs can navigate language barriers and expand their linguistic horizons with confidence.

Support for special needs: The incorporation of deep learning-based AI tools in education offers invaluable support for Gen-Zs with special needs, fostering inclusivity and personalized learning experiences. These tools can be tailored to provide assistive features such as text-to-speech, speech-to-text, visual aids, and adaptive interfaces. Gen-Zs with diverse learning abilities receive targeted support, enabling them to access and engage with educational content more effectively. AI tools analyse their progress and preferences, adjusting materials to accommodate individual needs. This ensures that Gen-Zs with special needs have equal access to education, empowering them to learn, participate, and thrive within a supportive and inclusive learning environment.

Preparation for future careers: AI tools provide Gen-Zs with essential preparation for their future careers, aligning their learning experiences with the demands of the evolving job landscape. These tools expose Gen-Zs to cutting-edge technologies and skills relevant to their desired professions. AI-powered platforms offer insights into emerging industries, trends, and job requirements, helping Gen-Zs make informed decisions about their educational and career paths. Through hands-on experiences with AI-driven tools, Gen-Zs develop critical skills such as data analysis, problem-solving, and digital literacy. This forward-looking education equips Gen-Zs with the competitive edge they need to excel in a rapidly changing workforce, ensuring their readiness for the challenges and opportunities of the future.

Global collaboration: AI-powered communication platforms connect students from around the world, fostering cross-cultural collaboration and expanding their perspectives.

Continuous education: AI tools promote a culture of continuous learning by offering recommendations for further study, keeping students engaged even beyond formal education. AI-powered platforms curate diverse resources, from articles and videos to interactive simulations, fostering curiosity and exploration. Gen-Zs can engage with learning materials that align with their interests, enabling them to stay updated on emerging trends and acquire new skills. Through AI-driven continuous education, Gen-Zs develop a growth mindset, honing their abilities to learn, unlearn, and relearn as they navigate a dynamic world, ensuring their sustained intellectual growth and professional success.

Relevance of Incorporation of Deep Learning-Based AI Tools in Education for Millennials

The deep learning-based AI tools in education enhance Millennials (teachers) capacity to provide personalized, effective, and engaging learning experiences while alleviating administrative burdens. Ultimately, teachers are better equipped to nurture students' growth and success in the dynamic educational landscape.

Personalized instruction: AI tools analyse students' learning patterns and progress, enabling teachers to tailor instruction to individual needs. This personalized approach helps address learning gaps and challenges more effectively. Educators can optimize their instructional methods, fostering a dynamic and adaptive classroom environment that caters to diverse student abilities, ultimately elevating the quality of education and nurturing student success.

Time efficiency: AI tools automate routine tasks such as grading, assessment, and data analysis. This streamlines routine processes, allowing educators to allocate more time to impactful teaching, curriculum development, and student support. With reduced administrative burden, educators can focus on higher-value activities that enhance the learning experience. AI tools also offer data-driven insights into student performance, aiding instructional planning and interventions. This increased time efficiency enables educators to create dynamic and engaging lessons, fostering a more productive and enriched educational environment for both educators and students.

Data-driven insights: AI-powered analytics provide teachers with valuable insights into students' performance, learning behaviours, and areas of struggle. These data help teachers make informed decisions about instructional strategies and interventions. By analysing student performance, engagement, and learning patterns, these tools provide educators with actionable information to tailor their instructional strategies. Educators gain a comprehensive understanding of individual and group progress, enabling timely interventions for struggling students and challenges. AI-powered analytics identify trends, informing curriculum enhancements and resource allocation. This data-centric approach empowers educators to make informed decisions, resulting in more effective teaching and improved student outcomes. Through AI-generated insights, educators can optimize their instructional methods, creating a dynamic and responsive learning environment that fosters growth and achievement.

Effective feedback: AI tools offer instant feedback on assignments and assessments. Teachers can supplement this feedback with personalized guidance, helping students understand their mistakes and improve their performance.

Resource curation: AI tools curate a wide variety of learning resources, making it easier for teachers to access relevant materials that align with their curriculum. This streamlines lesson planning and content creation. These tools analyse vast amounts of educational content, curating relevant and diverse resources tailored to educators' needs. Through data-driven insights, AI assists in selecting materials aligned with curriculum goals, student preferences, and learning styles. This automation streamlines the process of finding high-quality resources, saving educators valuable time and ensuring up-to-date content. By providing a curated pool of materials, AI tools empower educators to create dynamic and engaging lessons, fostering enriched learning experiences that cater to diverse student needs while staying current with the latest educational trends.

Early intervention: AI analytics can identify students at risk of falling behind early on. Teachers can intervene promptly to provide additional support and prevent learning gaps from widening. These tools analyse students' progress, behaviour, and engagement to detect signs of struggling or falling behind. Educators receive data-driven insights that help them intervene proactively, offering personalized assistance and targeted resources. By addressing issues early, Gen-Zs can overcome learning obstacles and maintain their academic momentum. This approach ensures that every student receives the support they need, fostering a nurturing and inclusive learning environment that maximizes Gen-Zs' potential and sets them on a path to success.

Reduced administrative load: AI automates administrative tasks like attendance tracking and scheduling, reducing the administrative burden on teachers and allowing them to focus on teaching. These tools streamline routine processes, enabling educators to focus more on teaching, mentorship, and curriculum development. By handling administrative tasks efficiently, AI tools enhance productivity and time management for educators. This reduction in administrative load not only increases their capacity for impactful teaching but also improves the overall learning experience for students. As a result, educators can dedicate more energy to fostering meaningful connections and creating engaging learning environments, ultimately elevating the quality of education.

Effective communication: AI-powered communication platforms facilitate efficient interaction with students, parents, and colleagues. These tools facilitate seamless interaction with students, parents, and colleagues through notifications, updates, and messaging systems. AI-driven platforms analyse communication patterns to suggest optimal timing and content, ensuring clear and timely information dissemination. Educators can focus more on fostering meaningful connections and educational content, as routine communication tasks are streamlined. This improved communication fosters collaboration, engagement, and transparency, ultimately enhancing the overall learning experience and strengthening the relationships between educators, students, and stakeholders.

Professional collaboration: AI-powered platforms enable teachers to collaborate with peers globally, sharing best practices, resources, and insights to enhance their teaching methodologies. AI-driven platforms automate communication, streamline collaboration on curriculum development, and offer data-driven insights that inform pedagogical strategies. Through virtual networks, teachers can access a diverse range of perspectives, fostering a culture of continuous learning. As educators engage in collaborative problem-solving and knowledge exchange, AI tools catalyse innovation and elevate the collective expertise of the teaching community, ultimately enhancing the quality of education.

Strategic planning: AI tools offer data-driven insights that help teachers identify trends and patterns in student performance. This informs long-term curriculum planning and instructional strategies. Educators can make informed decisions about curriculum design, instructional methods, and resource allocation. AI-driven analytics identify emerging educational needs, enabling timely adaptation of teaching strategies. This data-centric approach enhances long-term planning, ensuring alignment with evolving educational goals and industry demands. By harnessing AI's predictive capabilities, educators can proactively shape educational pathways, creating a dynamic and responsive learning environment that prepares students for future challenges and opportunities.

Scope for Future Research

Personalized Student Models – Not the One Shoe Fits All

Deep learning can be used in intelligent tutoring systems. Deep learning can be used to analyse student data, such as performance on exercises, quizzes, and interactions with the system, to build comprehensive student models. These models can capture individual learning preferences, strengths, weaknesses, and knowledge gaps, enabling the interrupted time series (ITS) to personalize the learning content accordingly.

Advanced Inclusive Education

Natural language processing (NLP) can be used to convert educational materials into different formats, such as audio, braille, or simplified text, to cater to students with visual impairments or reading difficulties. NLP can aid in translating educational content into different languages, ensuring that students from diverse linguistic backgrounds can access learning materials in their native languages. NLP-powered speech recognition systems can be integrated into learning platforms, allowing students with writing difficulties or motor impairments to interact with the system and submit responses using voice commands. NLP-based sentiment analysis can help detect emotional states in students' written responses, discussions, or chats. This information can enable educators to provide appropriate emotional support and interventions to students experiencing stress or anxiety. NLP can be employed to develop tools that support students with learning disabilities like dyslexia and dysgraphia. These tools can offer word prediction, grammar checking, and text-to-speech functionalities.

Technological Integration

This involves aligning technology with pedagogy to create a harmonious learning environment that harnesses the potential of AI to enhance teaching, learning, and student outcomes. Testing AI tools through pilot programmes allows educators and students to familiarize themselves with the tools, identify challenges, and provide insights for refinement before full-scale integration. AI tools should be integrated into existing learning management systems (LMS) and platforms used by educators and students. This ensures a cohesive user experience and minimizes disruption. Integration requires a robust data management strategy to handle the influx of student data. This involves ensuring data security, privacy, and compliance with relevant regulations. Close collaboration between educational institutions and AI tool developers ensures that tools are tailored to meet specific educational needs, fostering a synergistic relationship.

Long-Term Tracking, Prediction, and Suggestions Based on Performance

AI tools continuously gather and analyse data on student performance over time. This data-driven approach enables educators to monitor academic growth, identify learning trends, and track progress towards learning objectives. Deep learning algorithms can predict future academic performance based on historical data. By considering factors such as past grades, engagement levels, and study habits, AI tools provide educators with insights into students' potential achievements. Deep learning-based AI tools dynamically adjust learning paths based on students' strengths and weaknesses. As students progress, the tools adapt content difficulty and pace to ensure optimal learning experiences. AI tools help students set realistic academic goals based on their historical performance and potential. This promotes a proactive approach to learning and encourages students to strive for continuous improvement. AI tools can analyse students' academic trajectories to provide guidance on college and career choices. Students receive insights into which paths align with their strengths and interests. Institutions can use AI-generated data to refine curricula, instructional methodologies, and programmes. This data-driven approach ensures ongoing improvement of the overall educational experience.

Conclusions

The incorporation of deep learning-based AI tools in education has emerged as a transformative trend that holds immense potential to revolutionize the learning landscape. In this modern era, the utilization of advanced technologies such as deep learning and AI is reshaping various industries, and education is no exception. This study delved into the perceptions of Gen-Z and Millennials towards the integration of these AI tools in the educational realm, employing the UTAUT-3 model as a lens to understand the factors influencing their attitudes and intentions.

The results of this statistical evaluation shed light on the attitudes of these two distinct generational cohorts towards AI in education. The findings revealed that while both Gen-Z and Millennials exhibited a degree of positive perception, there were notable variations in their responses. The UTAUT-3 framework, which encompasses constructs like social influence, facilitating conditions, hedonic motivation are the major contributing factors in incorporating deep learning-based AI tools in education.

It is also identified that Gen-Z's and Millennial's perception towards the factor price, personal innovativeness, as well a continuous education also vary. Gen-Z individuals exhibit a stronger inclination towards personal innovativeness and continuous learning in comparison to Millennials. This highlights a generational difference in their proactive exploration of new technologies and their commitment to ongoing skill development. The findings underscore Gen-Z's propensity for embracing innovation and their eagerness to engage with new learning opportunities, which may have significant implications for education and workplace environments seeking to cater to these distinct generational preferences.

The findings provide valuable insights into the perceptions of Gen-Z and Millennials regarding the integration of deep learning-based AI tools in education. The utilization of the UTAUT-3 model allowed for a multifaceted exploration of the factors shaping their attitudes and intentions. As educational institutions and policymakers strive to embrace technological advancements, the findings underscore the importance of tailoring approaches to cater to the distinctive preferences of these generational cohorts.

References

Agrusti, F., Mezzini, M., & Bonavolontà, G. (2020). Deep learning approach for predicting university dropout: A case study at Roma Tre University. *Journal of E-learning and Knowledge Society*, *16*(1), 44–54.

Baker, T., & Smith, L. (2019). Educ-AI-tion rebooted? Exploring the future of artificial intelligence in schools and colleges. https://media.nesta.org.uk/documents/Future_of_AI_and_education_v5_WEB.pdf

Chen, L., Chen, P., & Lin, Z. (2020). Artificial intelligence in education: A review. *Ieee Access*, *8*, 75264–75278.

Dolcek, T., Lemay, D. J., Basnet, R. B., & Bazelais, P. (2020). Predictive analytics in education: A comparison of deep learning frameworks. *Education and Information Technologies*, *25*, 1951–1963.

Farooq, M.S., Salam, M., Jaafar, N., Fayolle, A., Ayupp, K., Radovic-Markovic, M., & Sajid, A. (2017). Acceptance and use of lecture capture system (LCS) in executive business studies: Extending UTAUT2. *Interactive Technology and Smart Education*, *14*(4), 329–348.

Fitria, T. N. (2021, December). Artificial intelligence (AI) in education: Using ai tools for teaching and learning process. *Prosiding Seminar Nasional & Call for Paper STIE AAS*, *4*(1), 134–147.

Guan, C., Mou, J., & Jiang, Z. (2020). Artificial intelligence innovation in education: A twenty-year data-driven historical analysis. *International Journal of Innovation Studies*, *4*(4), 134–147.

Gunasinghe, A., Hamid, J. A., Khatibi, A., & Azam, S. F. (2020). The adequacy of UTAUT-3 in interpreting academician's adoption to e-Learning in higher education environments. *Interactive Technology and Smart Education*, *17*(1), 86–106.

Mikropoulos, T. A., & Natsis, A. (2011). Educational virtual environments: A ten-year review of empirical research (1999–2009). *Computers & education*, *56*(3), 769–780.

Mohammed, P. S., & Nell'Watson, E. (2019). Towards inclusive education in the age of artificial intelligence: Perspectives, challenges, and opportunities. In J. Knox, Y. Wang, & M. Gallagher (Eds.), *Artificial intelligence and inclusive education: Speculative futures and emerging practices* (pp. 17–37).

Pokrivcakova, S. (2019). Preparing teachers for the application of AI-powered technologies in foreign language education. *Journal of Language and Cultural Education*, *7*(3), 135–153.

Swiecki, Z., Khosravi, H., Chen, G., Martinez-Maldonado, R., Lodge, J. M., Milligan, S., Selwyn, N., & Gašević, D. (2022). Assessment in the age of artificial intelligence. *Computers and Education: Artificial Intelligence, 3*, 100075. https://doi.org/10.1016/j.caeai.2022.100075

Van Raaij, E. M., & Schepers, J. J. L. (2008). The acceptance and use of a virtual learning environment in China. *Computers and Education, 50*(3), 838–852.

Chapter 13

Integrating AI Tools in Academic Curriculum: A Study on the Effectiveness of AI Tools in Higher Education

Santosh Rupa Jaladi, Hema Doreswamy and Radhika Uttam

Prin. L. N. Welingkar Institute of Management Development and Research, Bangalore, Karnataka, India

Abstract

The COVID-19 pandemic pushed academic institutions to rapidly transition from tradition classroom teaching to online teaching methods globally, leading to huge disruption in the academic world. Online teaching makes education accessible to people who may have struggled to attend the traditional classes. This transition is facilitated by advancement in technology, fuelled by tools like artificial intelligence (AI) and machine learning (ML). Higher education institutions are leveraging on these tools to enhance student learning process and student engagement. However, stakeholders are raising genuine concerns about ethical issues surrounding these platforms like plagiarism, reduced attention span of students. Reliance on these tools may limit the creativity of faculty and students. Usage of tools for regular administrative and academic tasks like grading and marking attendance can increase the process effectiveness at the same time. This will help in identifying strengths and areas for improvement of every student and offers feedback also based on those observations. Though concerns about the usage of AI tools in the classroom persist, the benefits offered by these tools cannot be undermined. It is important to study various ways of integrating these tools in the teaching pedagogy by being conscious of the ethical aspects. The study focuses on detailed analysis of AI tools applicable in education and research domain and the innovative methods of integrating the same in the classroom teaching.

The study is based on qualitative data collected from secondary sources. Findings can be used by high education institutions for leveraging technology for better student engagement and improving performance.

Keywords: Classroom teaching; student engagement; online teaching; AI, ML

Introduction

> I never teach my pupils; I only attempt to provide the conditions in which they can learn. (Albert Einstein)

Teaching is the world's largest profession. Educational institutions are the cornerstones for creating a just, equitable, and inclusive society. Teachers inspire and motivate students to perform, be successful, and become responsible citizens in a society. Quality teachers and a good teaching pedagogy are the most important requirements to build impactful educational institutions. Total number of teachers across the globe stands close to 85 million, out of which 39.7 million represent pre-primary and primary section, 18.1 million lower secondary teachers, 14 million teachers in upper secondary, and 12.5 million teachers in territory education or higher education (https://www.worldbank.org/en/topic/teachers).

Higher education is considered as the last step in formal education. Opting for higher education promises stable careers, growth opportunities, good salary, and other benefits. Overall, it helps in leading a good quality life. With higher education, people will be well informed in various fields, and they engage in intellectual pursuits like reading, writing, research, and exploration. This in turn will lead to various kinds of inventions and innovations which will transform human life in many ways. Higher education is not just about reading, writing, and earning a degree. It involves new levels of thinking, analysis, and finding solutions to problems and challenges. Learners are expected to go out of their comfort zone and develop critical thinking when analysing different scenarios. They must enhance their reading, writing, and presentation skills to put across their thought process and new ideas. On many occasions, it will involve a high level of interactions with the peer group and other stakeholders like faculty. To enable a favourable learning experience and output, higher education institutions (HEIs) must use effective and vibrant teaching pedagogy. Pedagogy can be explained as tools and techniques of teaching and learning. It refers to how a curriculum is being taught. There are different pedagogical tools used by educators. It depends on subjects being taught and on the educator himself or herself. In case of higher education, pedagogy plays a very important role as the goal is to train learners towards enhancing cognitive abilities and to develop problem-solving capabilities. Educators are expected to be facilitators, and they should help learners in acquiring knowledge on their own after thorough reading, discussions, and research. Higher education pedagogical tools are continuously evolving over a period and attaining new levels of sophistication. Ultimately, the objective of a pedagogy is to present the curriculum in such a way that the learner finds it interesting and easy to understand the concepts and theories being taught.

This chapter delves into the realm of teaching practices within higher education, particularly highlighting the evolving landscape influenced by the emergence of artificial intelligence (AI) and machine learning (ML). The discussion is structured into four key sections:

- *Conventional Pedagogical Approaches in Higher Education*: This section explores the traditional methods and practices commonly employed in higher education for teaching.
- *The Influence of the COVID-19 Pandemic on Higher Education*: Here, we discuss the impact of the global pandemic, COVID-19, on the higher education sector, leading to significant transformation in teaching and learning methods.
- *Utilizing AI Tools in Higher Education*: This section attempts discussion on the integration and application of AI tools in the landscape of higher education, shedding light on the transformative power of AI in revolutionizing teaching methodologies.
- *Conclusion*: This chapter concludes by summarizing the key takeaways and insights garnered from the discussion, providing a complete view of emerging dynamics of teaching pedagogy particularly in higher education, especially in the context of AI and ML advancements.

Traditional Pedagogical Methods in Higher Education

1. Constructivism learning approach: This method seeks active participation from the learners rather than just receiving the information passively. Constructivism is 'an approach to learning that holds that people actively construct or make their own knowledge and that reality is determined by the experiences of the learner' (Elliott et al., 2000, p. 256). This approach believes that 'Knowledge is constructed rather than innate or passively absorbed'. The theory strongly advocates that human beings construct their new knowledge based on their previous learnings. Previous understanding and knowledge that a learner has will influence what new knowledge he or she is going to acquire based on the new learning experiences (Phillips, 1995). Constructivism learning approach believes that learning is an active process. Know, What you Know, Have learned, Learned (KWH(L)) charts can be used to assess students' learning process throughout the term. This type of chart helps in documenting what learners already know, what they want to learn, how they can learn, and finally what they have learnt (Mokhtar et al., 2021). Such charts can be used to assess the learning process before, during, and after the teaching and felicitation schedules. The teaching tools that can be applied here can be observation and understanding of concepts being taught by the teacher, student journalizing, conferring, and preparing a chart or an organizer for reference post the assessment.
2. Enquiry-based learning: It is a teaching pedagogy in which students are posed with a lot of questions, situations, challenges, problems, and scenarios. It is an active learning process and contrasts with the traditional teaching pedagogy where the teacher/facilitator presents theories, concepts, facts, and figures in a lecture mode.

Process of enquiry-based learning:

- Develop a problem statement on the topic to be taught which requires reading and research.
- Exploring various sources for the information and conducting research, in this process faculty can guide and help the students.
- Presenting the research outcomes to peer groups to facilitate exchange of ideas.
- End of session by asking students to reflect on new topics learnt, what worked and steps to improve the learning process.

Teaching tools which can be applied in this method include case-based teaching. A case can be either real or hypothetical which will present a scenario with a specific problem statement. Students are expected to read the case, analyse, and come up with different solutions. Assigning projects on different topics and asking students to come up with findings is also another important way of adopting enquiry-based learning in the classroom.

3. Collaborative pedagogy: In this method, it is believed that students learn and acquire knowledge in a better way if collaborative learning process is adopted. Isolated learning may not be effective in all situations, and learning in groups through discussions/exchange of ideas with the peers will always lead to better understanding. Dividing students into smaller groups and assigning them a scenario/topic to study/a case or challenge to analyse/assigning a project to work on are the different methods through which collaborative teaching methods can be adopted. This is a very popular method of teaching tools in higher education. In the end, students will be asked to exchange the learning outcomes which will help in larger dissemination of knowledge.
4. Integrative learning method: This method of teaching and learning can be adopted when concepts/theories are interrelated and needs a consolidation of different areas to understand a new topic or a theory. For example, if the overall performance of a business is to be assessed, inputs from various units in a business such as finance, marketing, human resource, operations, corporate social responsibility, sustainability, etc. are needed. This method of teaching is very popular in higher education as discussion on many topics will be interrelated with other fields or areas. Veronica Boix, cofounder of integrative teaching methods, says, 'when [students] can bring together concepts, methods, or languages from two or more disciplines or established areas of expertise in order to explain a phenomenon, solve a problem, create a product, or raise a new question', they are demonstrating interdisciplinary understanding.
5. Reflective and critical pedagogy: These two types of teaching tools can be adopted alongside a main pedagogical tool discussed above. In reflective pedagogy, students are asked to reflect on their learnings by having a conversation with their peers and teachers. Once the faculty completes the explanation on a topic, students need to be divided into smaller groups and topics/cases on the concepts taught must be distributed. Students will apply the concepts learnt to the scenario provided and discuss on the same. In the end, faculty can take reflections on learnings from each group.

In critical pedagogy, students are expected to challenge the existing theories and beliefs. This type of pedagogy is very important when social science topics like democracy, social justice, law, and regulation, etc. are being taught. Such areas are continuously evolving and hence needs students to challenge the existing rules and regulations. It helps students in reading, research, and finally acquire a critical consciousness. This teaching pedagogy can be adopted through tools such as debates, essay competitions, panel discussions, and round tables in the classrooms.

Impact of COVID-19 on Higher Education

The COVID-19 pandemic has caused an unprecedented impact on the global education leading to significant disruptions in the traditional teaching-learning systems. Disruption caused by the pandemic has enforced a shift to online learning due to social distancing measures and lockdowns imposed by governments. This transition posed substantial challenges since many institutions were unprepared for such a sudden change. Remarkably, underprivileged students faced the greatest difficulties, lacking the necessary resources for online education. The long-term impact on education remains uncertain, but it is evident that learning methods will be permanently altered.

Examples of the pandemic's impact on education include the closure of schools in India, affecting approximately 250 million students, and a McKinsey study revealing students falling behind by five months in mathematics and four months in reading by the end of the school year. Existing disparities in educational opportunities were exacerbated, disproportionately affecting historically marginalized students. In the United States, nearly half of college students encountered difficulties in accessing online learning resources. Additionally, the pandemic has heightened student anxiety and stress. This crisis underscores the imperative for equitable and accessible education, emphasizing the need for preparedness in the face of future disruptions. By investing in digital infrastructure and supporting educators and students, we can mitigate the impact of future crises and ensure that everyone has access to a high-quality education (McKinsey & Company, 2021). In April 2020, a UNESCO report highlighted that HEIs experienced extraordinary closures on a global scale, with 185 countries implementing full shutdowns of these institutions (see Table 13.1). This action had a profound effect, significantly disrupting the education of more than 1 billion learners, marking it as the largest closure of HEIs in history (Marinoni et al., 2020).

The 'new normal' designed by the COVID-19 pandemic has paved the way for an unfathomable transformation in education and training. Global higher education has undergone a significant digital transition (Dwivedi et al., 2020). The unexpected shift away from traditional offline teaching has pushed educators and students into unacquainted territory, necessitating a swift adaptation to fully online learning environments (Carolan et al., 2020). This sudden change has forced universities to quickly transition to online teaching, making use of existing technology resources and involving faculty and researchers who may not have shown natural inclination towards online education. Universities must now deliver high-quality education within a context of digital transformation,

Table 13.1. The Global Impact of the Pandemic on Higher Education.

Country	Impact
United States	Decline in enrolment, increase in financial assistance, mental health concerns
India	Devastating impact on higher education, loss of learning, decline in enrolment
Brazil	Rise in the cost of higher education, digital divide
United Kingdom	Shift to online learning, financial impact
China	Increased investment in online learning, mental health concerns
South Africa	Digital divide, financial impact
Germany	Shift to online learning, support for mental health
France	Financial impact, rethinking the curriculum
Canada	Shift to online learning, support for mental health
Australia	Shift to online learning, financial impact

Source: Authors' compilation based on secondary sources – Novel coronavirus (COVID-2019) pandemic (2020); Carolan et al. (2020); Govindarajan and Srivastava (2020); Crompton and Song (2021).

disruptive technological innovation, and rapid changes in the educational landscape. The emergence of disruptive innovation presents both opportunities and risks, inoculating talent and innovation into the education system.

Disruption, when applied to education, signifies a significant departure from established models of knowledge dissemination (Carolan et al., 2020; Mishra et al., 2020). Innovative changes alter the course of education by supplanting or displacing existing methods. They disrupt traditional educational practices in unexpected ways, initially enhancing the existing model and subsequently offering fresh perspectives on its continual evolution. Disruptive educational innovation substitutes established approaches to knowledge transmission with new learning options. It also introduces advancements in education systems through information and communication technologies. This educational disruption takes into account both students and educators as catalysts for learning, promoting an open curriculum enabled by digital education. It encompasses innovative teaching methods, the creation of novel learning materials, mechanisms, and environments, as well as the transformation of the student's role and how they acquire and apply educational knowledge. Disruptive innovations cater to the needs of current customers and existing services (Christensen et al., 2006). However, a successful educational transformation must also prioritize sustainability, reach, and magnitude (Carolan et al., 2020). Transforming universities from traditional learning systems should cultivate a participatory culture, engage stakeholders, and encourage evidence-based decision-making and transparent evaluation of outcomes.

Higher educational institutions faced challenges in shifting to online learning, addressing digital disparities, and managing financial challenges. Universities across the globe have implemented various strategies (see Table 13.2). In the United States, financial aid and mental health services were prioritized (Krishnamurthy, 2020). India stressed on dual-credit programmes and accessible online platforms. In Brazil, reduced fees and improved access to online resources were key initiatives. The pandemic's lasting impact is ongoing, prompting universities to reassess their educational approaches, embrace new technologies, and innovate (Govindarajan & Srivastava, 2020).

AI and ML can address many of these challenges and provide personalized learning experience to the students. Table 13.3 provides details of how AI addresses some of the challenges posed by the pandemic. Undoubtedly, the pandemic has disrupted the traditional education system. Innovative teaching

Table 13.2. Impact of the Pandemic on Higher Education and the Measures Taken by Universities in Different Countries.

Impact	Measures	Country
Shift to online learning	Investing in new technologies and teaching methods, providing financial assistance, supporting mental health, rethinking the curriculum, collaborating with other institutions.	United States, India, Brazil, United Kingdom, China, South Africa, Germany, France, Canada, Australia
Digital divide	Providing laptops and internet access to students, offering financial assistance to students who need it, and creating online learning platforms that are accessible to all students.	India, Brazil, South Africa, Mexico, Indonesia
Financial impact	Providing financial assistance to students and faculty, reducing costs, and increasing fundraising efforts.	United States, United Kingdom, Canada, Australia
Mental health concerns	Providing counselling services, mindfulness workshops, and peer support groups.	United States, India, Brazil, United Kingdom, China, South Africa, Germany, France, Canada, Australia

Source: Authors' compilation based on secondary sources – Novel coronavirus (COVID-2019) pandemic (2020); Carolan et al. (2020); Govindarajan and Srivastava (2020); Crompton and Song (2021).

Table 13.3. How AI Can Address the Challenges of the COVID-19 Pandemic in Higher Education.

Challenge	How AI Can Address It
Shift to online learning	AI can be used to create personalized learning experiences for students, by tailoring the content and pace of instruction to each student's individual needs. This can help students to learn more effectively and efficiently, even in an online environment.
Digital divide	AI can be used to develop and distribute educational resources to students who do not have access to technology or the internet. This can help to ensure that all students have the opportunity to learn, regardless of their socio-economic status.
Financial impact	AI can be used to automate tasks, such as grading and assessment, which can free up teachers' time so that they can focus on more important activities, such as providing feedback to students. This can help to reduce the financial impact of the pandemic on universities.
Mental health concerns	AI can be used to develop chatbots and virtual assistants that can provide students with support and guidance. This can help students to cope with the stress and anxiety caused by the pandemic.

Source: Authors' compilation based on secondary sources – Novel coronavirus (COVID-2019) pandemic (2020); Carolan et al. (2020); Govindarajan and Srivastava (2020); Crompton and Song (2021).

pedagogy with new teaching-learning methods will change the pace of higher education. AI will emerge as an indispensable part of higher education. The next section of this chapter will highlight various AI tools in higher education.

AI Tools in Higher Education

AI tools utilize AI algorithms to accomplish particular tasks or address issues. They have been extensively used in healthcare, marketing, finance, etc. for automation, data analysis, and decision-making. Recently, the higher education sector seems to focus on bringing in transformation through usage of AI. AI has assumed a prominent role in the field of education due to its convenience and adaptability, which are embraced by both educators and students. Educators increasingly value AI for its effectiveness in evaluating students' performance, while students are significantly benefiting from the opportunity to harness their creativity through collaborative innovation with AI strategies (Jain & Jain, 2020). In their research, Crompton and Song (2021) highlighted the potential of AI in creating a learning system that caters to learners' requirements and fosters collaboration among faculty. They also emphasized the implementation of integrated collaborative systems, encompassing student models, teacher models, domain models, diagnosis models, and many more. The absence of educational theories and models has become the biggest concern for many researchers from the past two decades (Zhang & Aslan, 2021). Some of the AI tools popularly used in higher education is discussed below:

1. Cognii (2023): This is an innovative virtual learning assistant for undergraduate (UG)/postgraduate (PG) students. Cognii offers a wide variety of options for both faculties and students to explore and adapt to Ed-Tech. Here few of them are mentioned:

   - Utilizing AI for the creation of online courses.
   - An assessment instrument that enhances faculty's capabilities.
   - On-demand, round-the-clock tutoring through AI.
   - Instant and precise assessment of student-written content.

   The application assists students and teachers from the background of arts/humanities, business, life sciences, health sciences, engineering, etc.

2. Grammarly (2020): Another well-liked AI tool is Grammarly, which aids in academic writing in an effective way. It supports students in HEIs to be involved in academic writing without making grammatical errors. A student can also brainstorm topics for essays or assignments, and faculties can brainstorm ideas for writing a research paper (Sivarajah et al., 2019) Grammarly employs the method of suggesting appropriate words and also rephrasing sentences to enhance the effectiveness of the content.
3. Gradescope (2014): This tool has been used extensively in educational institutions for valuing student assignments online. Using this tool, the student's assignments can be scanned, graded, and the same can be extracted into reports based on which the faculty can get detailed analytics of students' performance in the test.
4. Plaito (2018): This personal AI tutor offers a wealth of intriguing capabilities, blending advanced AI technology with language expertise to deliver customized lessons that assist students in their learning journey by adapting to their individual needs, ensuring they progress at an optimal level and speed. Plaito replicates the behaviour of a friend by speaking in four different languages and thus makes learning more fun.
5. Ivy chatbot (Ivy.ai., 2016): Ivy is a tailored AI chatbot suite exclusively designed for educational institutions, offering comprehensive assistance throughout the university application and enrolment journey, including crucial aspects like application submission, enrolment procedures, tuition information, and deadline management. What sets Ivy apart is its remarkable ability to harness collected data for crafting targeted recruitment initiatives. Moreover, it serves as a valuable resource for students by furnishing essential information on financial aid options such as loans, scholarships, grants, and tuition payments.

In addition to the previously discussed tools, there is QuillBot (2017), an AI tool that assists in paraphrasing the content; Fetchy (2016) that helps educators in preparing the teaching lesson plans; Knowji (2011) that works on creating multiple learning modes; and Eklavvya (n.d.), an AI proctoring system that monitors students during their online exams and many more.

Opportunities, Challenges, and Disruptions

Let us now explore some of the potential advantages, obstacles, and transformative impacts associated with the application of AI within the field of education. Pisica et al. (2023) examined the perspectives of Romanian academics regarding the integration of AI in higher education (Mynbayeva et al., 2018). The research highlights the ongoing debate surrounding AI's impact, emphasizing its potential benefits in learning and administrative efficiency, alongside concerns related to psycho-social effects, data security, and ethical considerations. The study suggests that HEIs should make smart policies and plans when using AI to benefit society. Similarly, another study conducted by Jain and Jain (2020) investigates how students perceive the perspectives of their teachers on AI-based learning methods in Rajasthan's selected universities. It underscores the potential for AI to enhance learning in higher education but also highlights the need for substantial investments in funding and time. According to the authors, institutions contemplating AI adoption should carefully assess various factors to ensure it positively impacts students, teachers, and the institutions themselves.

The integration of AI in higher education presents numerous opportunities. One prominent advantage is the ability to provide a personalized learning experience tailored to individual student needs (World Economic Forum, 2020). Furthermore, institutions can enhance efficiency by automating administrative tasks, allowing for more effective resource allocation. The implementation of a data-driven approach enables the assessment of student performance, facilitating timely interventions to address challenges. AI also plays a pivotal role in increasing accessibility to education, particularly for students in remote or underdeveloped regions. Additionally, it fosters continuous learning, contributing significantly to career development (UNESCO, 2017).

However, the adoption of AI in education is not without challenges. Data privacy and security concerns necessitate stringent regulations to safeguard sensitive information. Ethical dilemmas arise in ensuring unbiased AI-generated content, posing questions about fairness and inclusivity. The potential decrease in human touch in lesson delivery may impact the overall quality of education. Infrastructure issues within educational institutions can pose barriers to the seamless implementation of AI systems (Bates, 2019). Moreover, there is a notable investment of time and resources required for training faculty members in the effective utilization of AI tools.

Despite these challenges, the disruptive potential of AI in education is noteworthy. AI has the capacity to redefine the roles of educators, shifting them from traditional lecturers to facilitators of personalized learning journeys. Institutions offering AI-powered online courses have the potential to disrupt traditional education models by appealing to a global student audience, intensifying global competition. The adaptability of AI in adjusting curricula based on industry demands ensures that graduates are better positioned in the job market. Moreover, the acceleration of research output through the use of AI tools among both faculty and students is a notable outcome. The emergence of AI-driven platforms also raises questions about the changing dynamics of education, with a shift towards learning outside traditional classroom settings.

Conclusion

This chapter has explored the landscape of teaching pedagogy within higher education, with a specific emphasis on the transformative influence of AI and ML. We began by highlighting the traditional methods and practices that have long been prevalent in higher education, setting the stage for a deeper examination of recent developments. The COVID-19 pandemic has had a significant impact on higher education, necessitating rapid adaptations to remote and online learning. This unforeseen challenge has augmented the implementation of technology and digital tools, providing a catalyst for the integration of AI and ML into educational practices. The discussion then curdled to the role of AI tools in higher education and discussed various tools that can be leveraged in higher education to make teaching more effective and improve student outcomes.

In summary, the convergence of traditional pedagogical methods, the disruptive power of the COVID-19 pandemic, and the advent of AI and ML technologies has reshaped higher education. Educators and institutions must remain agile, embracing innovative approaches to teaching and learning while leveraging emerging technologies as a powerful tool in the pursuit of academic excellence.

References

Bates, T. (2019). *Teaching in a digital age: Guidelines for designing teaching and learning.* BCcampus Open Education.
Carolan, G., Adie, T., & Corrigan, P. (2020). The impact of COVID-19 on higher education: A rapid review of the evidence. *Research Papers in Education, 35*(3), 289–308. https://doi.org/10.1080/02671522.2020.1759495
Christensen, C. M., Raynor, M. E., & McDonald, R. (2006). *The innovator's dilemma: When new technologies cause great firms to fail.* Harvard Business Review Press.
Cognii. (2023). Solutions for higher education. https://www.cognii.com/solutions#higher-ed
Crompton, H., & Song, D. (2021). The potential of artificial intelligence in higher education. *Revista Virtual Universidad Católica Del Norte, 62*, 1–4. https://doi.org/10.35575/rvucn.n62a1
Dwivedi, Y. K., Chen, H., Vaidya, S., Srivastava, S. K., & Kumar, V. (2020). The transformation of higher education after the COVID disruption: Emerging challenges in an online learning scenario. *Frontiers in Psychology, 11,* 616059. https://doi.org/10.3389/fpsyg.2020.616059
Eklavvya. (n.d.). AI EdTech tools – A list of AI tools for EdTech. https://www.eklavvya.com/blog/ai-edtech-tools/
Elliott, S. N., Kratochwill, T. R., Littlefield Cook, J., & Travers, J. (2000). *Educational psychology: Effective teaching, effective learning* (3rd ed.). McGraw-Hill College.
Fetchy. (2016). Fetchy. https://www.fetchy.com/
Govindarajan, S., & Srivastava, S. K. (2020). The impact of COVID-19 on higher education: A rapid review of the evidence. *Research Papers in Education, 35*(3), 289–308. https://doi.org/10.1080/02671522.2020.1759495

Gradescope. (2014). Gradescope. https://www.gradescope.com/
Grammarly. (2020). Grammarly for education. https://www.grammarly.com/edu
Ivy.ai. (2016). Ivy.ai. https://ivy.ai/
Jain, S., & Jain, R. (2020). Role of artificial intelligence in higher education-an empirical investigation. *IJRAR-International Journal of Research and Analytical Reviews*, 6, 144–150. http://ijrar.com/
Knowji. (2011). Knowji. https://www.knowji.com/
Krishnamurthy, S. (2020). The impact of artificial intelligence on education: A systematic review. *Education and Information Technologies*, 25(4), 3753–3769. https://doi.org/10.1007/s10639-020-09974-8
Maddumapatabandi, T. D., & Gamage, K. A. (2020). Novel coronavirus (COVID-2019) pandemic: Common challenges and response from higher education providers. *Journal of Applied Learning and Teaching*, 3(2), 1–11.
Marinoni, G., Khosla, R., & Altbach, P. G. (2020). *COVID-19: Higher education in crisis*. UNESCO.
McKinsey & Company. (2021). COVID-19 and education: The lingering effects of unfinished learning. https://www.mckinsey.com/industries/education/our-insights/covid-19-and-education-the-lingering-effects-of-unfinished-learning#:~:text=Many%20students%2C%20however%2C%20chose%20to,or%20fully%20in%2Dperson%20learning.&text=Our%20analysis%20shows%20that%20the,low%2Dincome%20schools%20with%20seven.
Mishra, P., Mehta, S., & Mehta, S. (2020). Disruptive innovation in higher education: A response to COVID-19 pandemic. *Education and Information Technologies*, 25(4), 3753–3769. https://doi.org/10.1007/s10639-020-09974-8
Mokhtar, M. M., Jamil, M., Rahman, F. A., Baki, R., Yaakub, R., & Amzah, F. (2021). Assimilation of the KWHL model: A review of learning and facilitation (LaF) of HOTS for argumentative essay writing. *Asian Social Science*, 17(11), 159. ISSN 1911-2017. E-ISSN 1911-2025.
Mynbayeva, A., Sadvakassova, Z., & Akshalova, B. (2018). Pedagogy of the twenty-first century: Innovative teaching methods. *New Pedagogical Challenges in the 21st Century. Contributions of Research in Education*, 7, 564–578.
Novel coronavirus (COVID-2019) pandemic: Common challenges and response from higher education providers. (2020). *Canadian Philosophy of Education Society*, 2(2). https://doi.org/10.37074/jalt.2020.3.2.20
Phillips, D. C. (1995). The good, the bad, and the ugly: The many faces of constructivism. *Educational Researcher*, 24(7), 5–12.
Pisica, A. I., Edu, T., Zaharia, R. M., & Zaharia, R. (2023). Implementing artificial intelligence in higher education: Pros and cons from the perspectives of academics. *Societies*, 13(5). https://doi.org/10.3390/soc13050118
Plaito. (2018). Plaito. https://www.plaito.ai/
QuillBot. (2017). QuillBot. https://quillbot.com/
Sivarajah, R. T., Curci, N. E., Johnson, E. M., Lam, D. L., Lee, J. T., & Richardson, M. L. (2019, January 1). A review of innovative teaching methods. *Academic Radiology*, 26(1), 101–113.
UNESCO. (2017). *Guidelines for the development and implementation of open educational resources*. UNESCO.
World Economic Forum. (2020). *The future of jobs report 2020*. World Economic Forum.
Zhang, K., & Aslan, A. B. (2021). AI technologies for education: Recent research & future directions. In *Computers and education: Artificial intelligence* (Vol. 2, p. 100025). Elsevier B.V. https://doi.org/10.1016/j.caeai.2021.100025

Chapter 14

Post-COVID Scenario and E-Learning: Fate of Student Academia at Tertiary Level

Obaid Ullah[a], Shehnaz Tehseen[b], Khalid Sultan[a], Syed Arslan Haider[c] and Azeem Gul[a]

[a]*National University of Modern Languages, Pakistan*
[b]*Sunway University Business School, Malaysia*
[c]*Capital University of Science and Technology, Pakistan*

Abstract

The post-COVID-19 scenario has presented significant learning challenges for university students worldwide. The swift shift from face-to-face to online classes posed greater difficulties because students were not mentally, financially, or physically prepared for this change, nor were they provided with adequate training to operate the learning management system (LMS). Online learning necessitates a school-like environment at home, which is challenging for students to replicate. This study aimed to determine the effect of online learning on students' academic achievement and to explore the challenges they faced in adapting to this new mode of learning. A quantitative research approach was employed, gathering primary data from 230 respondents in the Faculty of Social Sciences at the National University of Modern Languages, Islamabad. This was done using a validated closed-ended questionnaire featuring a five-point Likert scale. The collected data underwent analysis via the Friedman test using SPSS 20v. The results revealed that online learning negatively impacted students' academic achievement due to factors such as lack of internet accessibility, decreased motivation towards academics, low satisfaction levels, and difficulties in understanding academic concepts, particularly in the natural sciences. The study recommends

---

Global Higher Education Practices in Times of Crisis:
Questions for Sustainability and Digitalization, 241–254
Copyright © 2025 by Obaid Ullah, Shehnaz Tehseen, Khalid Sultan, Syed Arslan Haider and Azeem Gul
Published under exclusive licence by Emerald Publishing Limited
doi:10.1108/978-1-83797-052-020241015

a focus on implementing new teaching methods such as reciprocal teaching, digitalizing classrooms, offering remedial classes, and enhancing student motivation through teacher engagement.

Keywords: Online learning; motivation; computing education; satisfaction; academic achievement

Introduction

COVID-19, a novel virus causing respiratory ailments among people, was discovered in Wuhan, China, and swiftly spread across the globe. For most individuals, initial contact with this virus results in mild respiratory illness, and they can recover without requiring special treatment. However, individuals with compromised immune systems may experience chronic ailments such as cardiovascular disease, diabetes, or chronic respiratory conditions. The spread of this disease can be prevented by practising social distancing, avoiding touching one's face, and frequently washing hands for at least 20 seconds (World Health Organization (WHO), 2021). These circumstances have significantly disrupted daily life, including the education system at all levels.

The WHO advocated for a new educational approach, e-learning, which, although previously practised at a lower scale, became the primary mode of instruction during the pandemic. E-learning, also known as electronic learning, refers to education facilitated through electronic means or acquired via electronic media or the internet (Tamm, 2019). Throughout the pandemic, it served as an invaluable tool to remotely engage students and has demonstrated significant efficiency. Like other electronic media-related innovations, e-learning has its drawbacks; however, it has notably contributed to enhancing students' academic achievements.

The emergence of e-learning and its implementation in teaching has seen an exponential acceleration during the COVID-19 pandemic (Haider et al., 2021). A critical consideration arises regarding whether students and teachers prefer e-learning environments or traditional face-to-face interactions in classrooms. Sasa (2020) conducted a study aimed at determining the impact of the COVID-19 pandemic on student enrolment across various educational levels. The study revealed a notable decrease in student enrolment, particularly at the college level, by 8%. The primary reason reported for this decline was the perceived burden caused by e-learning and teaching, impacting students' ability to create conducive learning environments at home.

Rationale of the Study

The present study aimed to underscore the significance of, and enhance, the e-learning process at the tertiary level, focusing primarily on two crucial educational components: course content and teaching strategies. Recognizing the urgency, all stakeholders in higher education aspire to instigate an educational emergency at the national level. The lack of serious attention from students towards e-teaching and e-learning has led to diminished motivation and adversely impacted students' academic achievements. This study delved into the factors influencing or hindering quality education and proposed methods for improvement. Additionally, it evaluated the extent of both positive and negative impacts of e-learning on students' academic achievements. It further identified the factors crucial for enhancing e-learning, intending to provide policymakers and relevant stakeholders with actionable measures to attain the desired educational objectives.

Research Objectives

The objectives of the study were:

1. Effect of e-learning on students' academic achievement
2. Factors to improve e-learning process towards students' academic achievement

Research Hypothesis

Based on research objectives, the research hypotheses were as follows:

i) H_o = Online learning does not influence students' academic achievement at the tertiary level.

H_1 = Online learning influences students' academic achievement at the tertiary level.

ii) H_o = The satisfaction level of students was high towards online learning.

H_1 = The satisfaction level of students was low towards online learning.

Statement of Problem

In the post-COVID scenario, there has been a significant shift in the mode of education, causing considerable unrest among the masses. The multitude of changes in educational systems during the COVID-19 pandemic has resulted in numerous unknown and confounding factors related to learning. Researchers have concentrated their efforts on evaluating students' learning concerning their academic achievements. The advent of digitalization and e-learning stands out as a major change, sparking widespread discussion among stakeholders. Consequently, researchers aim to ascertain whether the new mode of learning through digital or online platforms positively or negatively impacts students' academic achievements at the tertiary level.

Literature Review

According to Chalise et al. (2021), Bughio et al. (2014), and Ullah et al. (2017), the positive aspects of e-learning and teaching include the ease with which students can access course materials with just a click and save them for future reference.

Additionally, students have the convenience of joining classes by clicking on links provided by their teachers well in advance, streamlining the academic process. However, students with lower incomes encounter significant challenges in accessing academic gadgets such as laptops or personal computers (PCs), often relying solely on smartphones. Using small screens for academic purposes adversely affects students' performance. Issues like limited access to internet connectivity, high costs imposed by network companies for internet services, and the lack of access to these facilities in remote areas significantly impede e-learning and teaching. Consequently, students experience demotivation towards their studies, which can have adverse effects, sometimes even leading to the freezing of a semester.

In a parallel study conducted at a private medical college, results indicated that students harboured negative perceptions regarding e-learning, with approximately 76% of respondents resorting to using cell phones for online classes, which proved to be an uncomfortable source for academic enrichment (Abbasi et al., 2020). To address these challenges, a four-D model (Define, Design, Develop, and Disseminate) was introduced, aiming to explore effective techniques for e-learning. The model aimed to alleviate the students' difficulties in grasping essential content. Instructional development proved instrumental in aiding students' academic understanding at the tertiary level. This model was deemed suitable and effective in enhancing student comprehension, fostering interaction among peers and teachers, and elevating student satisfaction and motivation levels (Tehseen & Haider, 2021).

Research conducted by Kwary and Fauzie (2018) and Aung and Khaing (2015) has highlighted numerous positive aspects of e-learning. However, several limitations have also been identified, such as a lack of information and communication technology (ICT) knowledge, weak technological and physical infrastructure, limited experience in using the internet, and computer self-efficacy issues (Kanwal & Rehman, 2017). Additionally, challenges like student isolation, inadequate teacher–student interaction, and connectivity issues have been observed (Chalise et al., 2021; Maheshwari, 2021). In Indonesia, e-learning has been a topic of interest since 2011 and continues to seek improvement. Despite these challenges, students have shown a positive attitude towards e-learning. Before the COVID-19 pandemic, e-learning received insufficient attention. However, in the post-COVID-19 scenario, universities launched a learning management system (LMS), transitioning all academic processes purely online (Almaiah et al., 2020).

According to Bughio et al. (2014) and Mata et al. (2021), teachers are exerting strong efforts to ensure the effectiveness of e-learning, suggesting that e-learning might become the predominant mode of education in future academics. In 2005, the Kingdom of Saudi Arabia established the National Centre of E-learning and Distance Learning (NCEDL) involving nine universities, aiming to enhance the e-learning experience and implement effective practices. The NCDEL facilitates quick remote access to learning materials for students and trains teachers to adapt to technology-oriented teaching-learning processes (Alqahtani & Rajkhan, 2020). Additionally, a study conducted by Konyefa and Nwanze (2020) revealed that using social media as a medium of instruction in the subject of chemistry yielded positive outcomes, providing a suitable platform for effective interaction between teachers and students.

E-learning has significantly expanded in recent times across academic institutions, providing a comfortable environment for students. However, evaluating students' progress on a daily basis becomes essential to monitor their academic performance (Strong et al., 2012). This study explores the integration of social media tools in online classes to enhance students' engagement in e-learning. Additionally, it examines the impact of various variables, such as demographic traits and the conducive learning environment, on students' satisfaction with e-learning. The findings revealed a low level of satisfaction among students regarding e-learning. Despite the growing concept of e-learning in the UAE, there are limited studies on its acceptance at the tertiary level. Siron et al.'s (2020) study, supported by the Technology Acceptance Model (TAM) model, contributes to understanding the acceptance of e-learning in this context.

The potential of online education significantly expands the opportunities for students by enabling them to identify and explore new learning paradigms for academic concepts. This approach ensures reliability in the learning process and reduces stress levels for both students and teachers (Koehler et al., 2004; Platt et al., 2014; UNESCO, 2020). Numerous studies suggest that assessing students' academic performance and outcomes in online and traditional learning can occur through formative or summative assessments. However, online learning lacks the formal interaction found in physical classroom environments (Bali & Liu, 2018; Ocak, 2020). Contrarily, a study conducted by Fortune et al. (2011) revealed that there was no significant difference in the learning preferences between students taught through online modes and those taught in traditional in-person classroom environments.

Online learning has significantly expanded new paradigms, offering not only enhanced learning opportunities but also effective networking platforms connecting students with experts in their respective fields. It provides flexibility and a wide array of opportunities, allowing students to easily access experts and numerous educational courses. However, online learning also presents drawbacks, including limited access to necessary resources, institutional staff downsizing leading to economic instability, challenges related to low internet speed, and technical issues encountered during the learning process (Arkorful & Abaidoo, 2014; Healy et al., 2014).

Methodology

Research Design

A quantitative study was conducted, focusing on descriptive research. This design was opted because of getting in-depth data from a wide array of respondents.

Population and Sample

The study encompassed the entire student body of 625 individuals from the Department of Education, Faculty of Social Sciences, NUML, Islamabad. Employing standardized sampling techniques (Krijice & Morgan, 1970), a sample of 230 students was randomly selected from this population.

Research Instrument

A survey with 40 closed-ended questions, utilizing a five-point Likert scale, was used to gather data from the respondents. The Likert scale ranged from 1 to 5, with 1 representing 'strongly disagree', 2 as 'disagree', 3 as 'neutral', 4 as 'agree', and 5 as 'strongly agree'. The questionnaire was developed based on an empirical approach and relevant literature. It was categorized into four themes: accessibility/availability of internet, student satisfaction with online classes, student motivation, and student understanding in online classes.

Validity of the Instrument

The questionnaire was validated using the Focus Group Design method, involving an assessment by three experts in the relevant field. These experts evaluated both the content validity of the questionnaire and the construct of its items. Initially, Q-technique was used to validate the questionnaire, and the average extract variance (AEV) was found to be 0.81, with a composite reliability of 0.67, indicating a higher level of construct validity (Fornell & Larcker, 1981).

Pilot Study and Reliability of the Questionnaire

A pilot study was conducted with 12 selected students based on general guidelines. Using an adaptive trial design through a retrospective approach, these respondents were not included in the main study. Post the pilot study, the questionnaire's reliability was evaluated using Cronbach's alpha, which returned a value of 0.96. This value falls within the 0.4–0.9 range, indicating a high level of questionnaire reliability.

Data Collection

The data were collected empirically during the months of September and October 2020, coinciding with the reopening of universities after a prolonged lockdown due to the COVID-19 pandemic. Respondents were approached under strict observation of COVID-19 standard operating procedures (SOPs).

Ethical Considerations

Before data collection, the sample size was randomly selected from the population, and formal consent was obtained for collecting research data. The majority of respondents agreed to provide data, and appointments were scheduled at their convenience. Measures were taken to ensure that data would not be shared with any third party without respondents' consent. However, for publication and research dissemination purposes, respondents had no objections. Furthermore, respondents' details were not disclosed to any party to guarantee anonymity.

Rapport Development

It's beneficial to establish coordination with respondents before data collection to build rapport, allowing for more comprehensive and candid responses. This approach ensured that respondents felt comfortable sharing their insights and perspectives.

Results

The collected data underwent analysis using the Friedman test within SPSS. This test was chosen due to the dependent nature of the variable, the ordinal scale of measurement, and the presence of more than two samples. Since the questionnaire comprised four themes – accessibility/availability of internet, student satisfaction with online classes, student motivation, and student understanding in online classes – each theme was independently analysed to prevent the distortion of null hypotheses. The themes related to accessibility/availability of internet and student satisfaction with online classes aligned with *Hypothesis 1*, indicating that online learning negatively influences students' academic achievement at the tertiary level. Similarly, the themes of student motivation and student understanding in online classes aligned with *Hypothesis 2*, suggesting that the satisfaction level of students was low towards online learning.

Theme A

Table 14.1 displays the mean ranks of statements concerning internet access and availability at home. The statement 'Student is well familiar with operating educational apps' obtained the highest mean rank of 6.42, while 'Student has a printer at home' received the lowest mean rank of 3.89.

Table 14.1. Access and Availability of Internet.

Ranks Statements	Mean Rank
Student has internet connection at home	4.03
Student always has the access to use computer at home to do university work	5.97
Student has access to printer at home	3.89
Student always has the smartphone with data plan	5.66
Student has personal smartphone	5.81
Student has 4G service provider for the data plan	5.01
Student can easily afford internet connection at home	6.20
Student can easily afford data packages for an online class	5.91
Student is well familiar with operating educational apps	6.42
Student feel connectivity issues in their data plan	6.10

Table 14.2. Test Statistics.

Test Statistics	
N	230
Chi-square	260.451
df	9
Asymptotic significance	0.000
Significance	0.000

The statistical test rejects the null hypothesis, i.e., 'the access and availability of internet to students is good' with df and p value, i.e., $x^2(9) = 260.451$ (Table 14.2). The rejection of the null hypothesis is supported by the findings of the studies of Abbasi et al. (2020) and Chalise et al. (2021).

Theme B

Table 14.3 illustrates the mean ranks of statements regarding student satisfaction in the domain of online classes. The statement 'Availability of assistance on how to use the learning management system' received the highest mean rank of 6.40, whereas the lowest mean rank of 3.32 was for the statement 'Availability of E-library resources'.

The statistical test rejects the null hypothesis, i.e., the satisfaction level of students is high in online learning at the university level with df and p value, i.e., $x^2(9) = 279.878$ (Table 14.4). The rejection of the null hypothesis is supported by the studies of Al Kurdi and Salloum (2021) and Ullah et al. (2017).

Table 14.3. Student Satisfaction with Online Classes.

Ranks Statements	Mean Rank
Availability of assistance on how to use the LSM	6.40
Availability of virtual agent's assistance instructor use of technology	5.60
Availability of E-library resources	3.32
Availability of course martial online	5.52
Availability of online tutoring	4.67
Availability of supplemental online academic support	6.07
Availability of information about technical skills required for course	5.95
Availability of book source service	6.06
Comfortable in interacting online with teachers	5.74
Comfortable with interacting online with fellows	5.67

Table 14.4. Test Statistics.

Test Statistics	
N	230
Chi-square	279.878
df	9
Asymptotic significance	0.000
Significance	0.000

Theme C

Table 14.5 displays the mean ranks of statements regarding student motivation in the domain of online classes. The statement 'Students are confident to attend online classes' received the highest mean rank of 6.12, while the lowest mean rank of 4.90 was for the statement 'Students are willing to attend online classes'.

The study rejects the null hypothesis, i.e., online learning does not influence students' motivation towards their academics at the university level with df and *p* value, i.e., $x^2(9) = 80.475$ (Table 14.6). The rejection of the null hypothesis is not supported by the study conducted by Vitoria and Nurmasyitah (2018).

Table 14.5. Student Motivation.

Ranks Statements	Mean Rank
Students are willing to attend online classes	4.90
Students always try to attend all online classes	5.72
Students like to attend online classes	5.16
Students are confident to attend online classes	6.12
Students are confident to get good jobs after online classes	5.96
Students experience pleasures and motivation with online learning	5.20
Students think online course will help better prepare for the career	5.22
Students feel that online study is wasting their time	5.99
Students can set goals and deadlines for themselves	5.73
Students' motivation level is same in online class as physical class	4.99

Table 14.6. Test Statistics.

	Test Statistics
N	230
Chi-square	80.475
df	9
Asymptotic significance	0.000
Significance	0.000

Theme D

Table 14.7 indicates the highest mean rank is 5.97 for the statement 'Teacher encourages student's participation in online classes', while the lowest mean rank is 5.13 for the statement 'Students can complete all the topics of the course through online classes'.

The study rejects the null hypothesis, i.e., online learning does not influence students' academic achievement at the university level with df and p value, i.e., $x^2(9) = 43.944$ (Table 14.8). The rejection of the null hypothesis is not supported by the studies conducted by Bughio et al. (2014), Alqahtani and Rajkhan (2020), and Konyefa and Nwanze (2020). On the other hand, a study conducted by Kingsbury (2021) reveals that in online learning, the schools contributed well and provided teaching with high quality.

Table 14.7. Student Understanding of Course Work.

Ranks Statements	Mean Rank
Student completely understand what's been taught in online classes	5.15
Student can complete all the assignments homework and activities prescribed	5.33
Students can complete all the topics of the course through online classes	5.13
Students are completely satisfied with online lectures	5.19
Teachers clear my queries in online classes as before	5.60
Students feel independent and creative in online classes	5.57
Teacher encourages student's participation in online classes	5.97
Teacher supports student-centred strategies in online classes	5.89
Online discussion is useful to student learning	5.24
Online learning is helpful in improving my computer skills with other skills	5.94

Table 14.8. Test Statistics.

	Test Statistics
N	230
Chi-square	43.944
df	9
Asymptotic significance	0.000
Significance	0.000

Conclusion

The study's findings concluded that e-learning had a negative impact on the academic achievement of tertiary-level students primarily due to decreased motivation. Additionally, findings from Han et al. (2022) indicated that students often freeze their semester or drop courses due to exam fear and anxiety. These factors significantly affect the e-learning process, resulting in low satisfaction among students, leading to reduced comprehension and motivation, consequently contributing to a decline in students' academic achievements (Gupta & Mili, 2017).

Several factors significantly impact students' e-learning processes and, consequently, their academic achievements. These factors include students' lack of internet access, inadequate access to suitable gadgets for online classes, difficulties in understanding course content in e-learning, high taxes and prices for cell phone recharges, students relocating to remote areas, frequent electricity load shedding, challenges related to downloading heavy lecture notes, presentations, and videos, students experiencing anxiety due to COVID-19, and those suffering from the virus. These factors collectively contribute to a decline in students' academic performance.

Recommendations

The following recommendations were drawn based on conclusion.

Motivation of Students

The study suggests that teachers should endeavour to maintain high morale among students in online classes, akin to face-to-face sessions. A teacher's elevated motivation towards academics positively influences students' performance. Additionally, engaging students through effective teaching methods is crucial. Encouraging an inquisitive approach among students facilitates the learning of complex concepts.

Reciprocal Teaching

Introducing the concept of reciprocal teaching in online learning is recommended. In this method, the teacher teaches a specific topic and subsequently motivates students to give presentations on that topic, effectively becoming teachers themselves. The teacher then assesses the weaker aspects of students' understanding that require improvement.

Digitalization of Classroom

The study recommends transforming traditional classrooms into digital classrooms, offering students ample opportunities to enhance their learning. Digital classrooms facilitate access to lecture notes and enable students to revise concepts at their convenience, catering to their individual learning needs.

Provision of Remedial Classes

Educational planners can arrange additional remedial classes for students struggling with low understanding. Moreover, integrating e-skill programmes into the tertiary-level curriculum can help students navigate these skills more smoothly, ensuring they are better prepared for the demands at the tertiary level.

Provision of Laptops to Low-Income Students

Educational bodies could appeal to the government for additional funding to supply laptops to students from low-income families. With many parents facing financial constraints and inflation due to the impact of COVID-19 on the economy, government support could significantly alleviate the burden of educational expenses, potentially enhancing the academic capabilities of these students.

Future Research

There is a need to assess the quality, scalability, and application of learned content through e-learning at the higher education level. Additionally, it is crucial to evaluate the effectiveness of teaching and learning processes, focusing on outcomes-based strategies in online education.

References

Abbasi, S., Ayoob, T., Malik, A., & Memon, S. (2020). Perceptions of students regarding E learning during COVID-19 at a private medical college. *Pakistan Journal of Medical Sciences, 36*(COVID19-S4), COVID19-S57–S61. https://doi.org/10.12669/pjms.36.COVID19-S4.2766

Al Kurdi, B., & Salloum, B. S. (2021). An empirical investigation into examination of factors influencing university students' behavior towards elearning acceptance using SEM approach. *International Journal of Interactive Mobile Technologies, 14*, 19–41. https://www.online-journals.org/index.php/i-jim/article/view/11115

Almaiah, M. A., Al-Khasawneh, A., & Althunibat, A. (2020). Exploring the critical challenges and factors influencing the E-learning system usage during COVID-19 pandemic. *Education and Information Technologies, 25*, 5261–5280.

Alqahtani, A. Y., & Rajkhan, A. A. (2020). E-learning critical success factors during the COVID-19 pandemic: A comprehensive analysis of e-learning managerial perspectives. *Education Sciences, 10*(9), 216.

Arkorful, V., & Abaidoo, N., (2014). The role of e-learning, advantages and disadvantages of its adoption in higher education. *International Journal of Educational Research, 2*, 397–410.

Aung, T. N., & Khaing, S. S. (2015, August). Challenges of implementing e-learning in developing countries: A review. In T. Zin, J. W. Lin, J. S. Pan, P. Tin, & M. Yokota (Eds.), *International conference on genetic and evolutionary computing* (pp. 405–411). Springer.

Bali, S., & Liu, M., (2018). Students' perceptions toward online learning and face-to-face learning courses. *Journal of Physics: Conference Series, 1108*, 012094.

Bughio, I. A., Abro, Q. M. M., & Rashdi, P. R. S. (2014). Effective online distance learning in Pakistan and challenges. *International Journal of Management Sciences, 2*(6), 274–279.

Chalise, G. D., Bharati, M., Bajracharya, J., Kc, A., Pradhan, S., Adhikari, B., & Shrestha, M. (2021). Undergraduate medical science students positive attitude towards online classes during COVID-19 pandemic in a medical college: A descriptive cross-sectional study. *Journal of Nepal Medical Association, 59*(234), 134–140. https://doi.org/10.31729/jnma.5413

Fornell, C., & Larcker, D. F. (1981). Evaluating structural equation models with unobservable variables and measurement error. *Journal of Marketing Research, 18*(1), 39–50.

Fortune, M., Spielman, M., & Pangelinan, D. (2011). Students' perceptions of online or face-to-face learning and social media in hospitality, recreation and tourism. *MERLOT Journal of Online Learning and Teaching, 7*, 1–16.

Gupta, P. K., & Mili, R. (2017). Impact of academic motivation on academic achievement: A study on high schools students. *European Journal of Education Studies, 3*(3), 44–49. https://zenodo.org/record/321414#.YG8KK-gzbIU

Haider, S. A., Gul, A., Anwar, B., Tehseen, S., & Iqbal, S. (2021). The impacts of the COVID-19 outbreak on the education sector: Evidence from Pakistan. In M. W. Bari, & E. Alaverdov (Eds.), *Impact of infodemic on organizational performance* (pp. 311–328). IGI Global.

Han, S., Li, Y., & Haider, S. A. (2022). Impact of foreign language classroom anxiety on higher education students academic success: Mediating role of emotional intelligence and moderating influence of classroom environment. *Frontiers in Psychology, 13*, 945062.

Healy, S., Block, M., Judge, J., (2014). Adapted physical educators' perceptions of advantages and disadvantages of online teacher development. *Palaestra Sagamore Journal, 28*, 4.

Kanwal, F., & Rehman, M. (2017). Factors affecting e-learning adoption in developing countries–empirical evidence from Pakistan's higher education sector. *IEEE Access, 5*, 10968–10978.

Kingsbury, I. (2021). Online learning: How do brick and mortar schools stack up to virtual schools? *Education and Information Technologies, 26*, 6567–6588. https://doi.org/10.1007/s10639-021-10450-1

Koehler, M. J., Mishra, P., Hershey, K., & Peruski, L. (2004). With a little help from your students: A new model for faculty development and online course design. *Journal of Technology Education, 12*, 25–55.

Konyefa, B. I., & Nwanze, A. C. (2020). Integrating WhatsApp application into learning process: Effects on pre-service teacher's interest in chemistry in colleges of education. *International Journal of Innovative Research and Advanced Studies (IJIRAS), 7*(9), 121–125.

Krijice, R. V., & Morgan, D. W. (1970). Determining sample size for research activities. *Educational and Psychological Measurement*, *30*, 607–610.

Kwary, D. A., & Fauzie, S. (2018). Students' achievement and opinions on the implementation of e-learning for phonetics and phonology lectures at Airlangga University. *Educação e Pesquisa*, *44*(0), 1–16. https://doi.org/10.1590/s1678-4634201710173240

Maheshwari, G. (2021). Factors affecting students' intentions to undertake online learning: An empirical study in Vietnam. *Education and Information Technologies*, *26*, 6629–6649. https://doi.org/10.1007/s10639-021-10465-8

Mata, M. N., Anees, S. S. T., Martins, J. M., Haider, S. A., Jabeen, S., Correia, A. B., & Rita, J. X. (2021). Impact of non-monetary factors on retention of higher education institutes teachers through mediating role of motivation. *Academy of Strategic Management Journal*, *20*, 1–17.

Ocak, M. (2020). What we learned about distance education during COVID-19? EPALE Electronic plat form for adult learning in Europe. Retrieved July 12, 2020, from https://epale.ec.europa.eu/en/blog/what-we-learned-about-distance-education-during-covid-19

Platt, C.A., Raile, A., & Yu, N. (2014). Virtually the same? Student perceptions of the equivalence of online classes vs. face-to-face classes. *MERLOT Journal of Online Learning and Teaching*, *10*, 489–494.

Sasa, R. (2020). *Students speak up about eLearning amid COVID-19* (pp. 1–8). QCC eLearning Newsletter. Retrieved from: https://www.qcc.cuny.edu/governance/academicSenate/elearning/docs/eLearning-Newsletter-Fall-2020.pdf

Siron, Y., Wibowo, A., Narmaditya, B.S. (2020). Factors affecting the adoption of e-learning in Indonesia: Lesson from COVID-19. *JOTSE: Journal of Technology and Science Education*, *10*(2), 282–295.

Strong, R., Irby, T. L., Wynn, J. T., & McClure, M. M. (2012). Investigating students' satisfaction with eLearning. *Journal of Agricultural Education*, *53*(3), 98–110.

Tamm, S. (2019, December 21). *What is E-learning?* E-Student.Org. https://e-student.org/what-is-e-learning/

Tehseen, S., & Haider, S. A. (2021). Impact of universities' partnerships on students' sustainable entrepreneurship intentions: A comparative study. *Sustainability*, *13*(9), 5025.

Ullah, O., Khan, W., & Khan, A. (2017). Students' attitude towards online learning at tertiary level. *PUTAJ-Humanities and Social Science*, *25*(1–2), 63–82.

UNESCO. (2020). COVID-19 and higher education: Today and tomorrow. Impact analysis, policy responses and recommendations. Retrieved July 2, 2020, from http://www.iesalc.unesco.org/en/wp-content/uploads/2020/04/COVID-19-EN-090420-2.pdf

Vitoria, M., & Nurmasyitah, L. M. N. (2018). Students' perceptions on the implementation of e-learning: Helpful or unhelpful? *Journal of Physics: Conference Series*, *1088*(012058), 1–6. https://iopscience.iop.org/article/10.1088/1742-6596/1088/1/012058

World Health Organization. (2021). *Coronavirus disease (COVID-19) pandemic*. Www.Who. Int. https://www.google.com/search?q=WHO.±(2021).±coronavirus.±Retrieved±from±www.who.int%3A±https%3A%2F%2Fwww.who.int%2Fhealth-topics%2Fcoronavirus%23tab%3Dtab_1&oq=WHO.±(2021).±coronavirus.±Retrieved±from±www.who.int%3A±https%3A%2F%2Fwww.who.int%2Fhealth-topics%2Fcoronavirus%23tab%3Dtab_1&aqs=chrome.69i57.931j0j7&sourceid=chrome&ie=UTF-8

Chapter 15

Recent Trends in Deployment of Multi-Protocol Label Switching (MPLS) Networks in Universities

Siddhartha Goutam and Aradhana Goutam

Prin. L. N. Welingkar Institute of Management Development and Research (WeSchool), Matunga, Mumbai, Maharashtra, India

Abstract

Multi-protocol label switching (MPLS) networks are basically packet-based networks. There are various advantages of MPLS, such as better utilization of the network, reduction in the network latency, and the ability to adhere to the strict and stringent quality of service (QoS) criteria of incoming traffic. Since most of the applications are moving towards the packet-based networks, this move is mounting a pressure on the network providers for changing and upgrading their existing systems. There are various innovations and upgrades which are under progress and being improvised. These innovations and improvements will ensure that the networks can provide the ever-growing and rising demand of bandwidth. This research study captures the review of the concepts of MPLS networks and innovative technologies like traffic engineering, differentiated services, protection, and restoration. This research study also captures MPLS transport profile and its applications. As per the recent literature review, new protocols and designs of MPLS should be handled with care, and designers should exercise caution while recommending and proposing new designs and protocols. Most of the universities need to converge their networks to a single infrastructure in order to reduce operational costs and provide better network with improvised QoS to the students and faculties. Most of the universities and colleges are migrating to internet protocol (IP)/MPLS-based infrastructure. This will help in providing better networks to students studying and staying in universities.

Global Higher Education Practices in Times of Crisis:
Questions for Sustainability and Digitalization, 255–269
Copyright © 2025 by Siddhartha Goutam and Aradhana Goutam
Published under exclusive licence by Emerald Publishing Limited
doi:10.1108/978-1-83797-052-020241016

IP/MPLS is highly scalable and can be deployed end to end to accommodate the needs of any network size.

Keywords: Multi-protocol label switching (MPLS); quality of service (QoS); latency; packet loss; jitter; fault notification

1. Introduction

There has been a continuous and ever-growing demand for high data rate due to usage of various mobile applications. This has led to the exponential increase in the traffic which cannot be handled by circuit-based networks. The applications such as videos on demand, voice over internet protocol (VOIP), etc. are gaining popularity among the smart phone users. The smart phone users want the highest data rate coupled with the least possible cost (Goudarzi et al., 2015; Goutam & Unnikrishnan, 2019). Hence, the communication networks must be continuously improved and upgraded for obtaining better traffic management and fulfilling the service-level agreements (SLAs). The challenges and difficulties are observed while network designing and dimensioning for optimization of the network performance for achievement of the high rate of efficiency (Al-Qudah et al., n.d.; Girao-Silva et al., 2014).

Multi-protocol label switching (MPLS) can be defined as the switching technology which helps in regulating the data traffic and packet forwarding in complex networks. It is a technology which can be termed as connection-oriented methodology that traverses packets from source to destination node across networks which leads to faster transmission of packets. MPLS was created in the late 1990s as an efficient alternative to traditional internet protocol (IP) routing. It continued to evolve with growth and development of backbone network technologies. In the year 2000, MPLS traffic engineering was developed (Ridwan et al., 2020).

MPLS can be used for enhancing network optimization and providing better quality of service (QoS) to the traffic. It is a scalable technology which is connection oriented and is independent from packet forwarding technology. It attains reduction in IP address look up at each router and leads to minimization in network latency (Adeyinka et al., 2016; Bartos & Raman, 2001). These features of MPLS are extremely important considering digital universities (Ridwan et al., 2020; Thu et al., 2019). Fig. 15.1 describes the basic MPLS network for the university.

The organization of this chapter is as follows: Section 2 describes the literature review, Section 3 provides details of MPLS technologies, and Section 4 describes the need of MPLS at the time of crisis followed by conclusion in Section 5.

2. Literature Review

In this section, the authors have presented the work done by earlier researchers and academicians. In Ridwan et al. (2020), the authors have reviewed various

Recent Trends in Deployment of MPLS 257

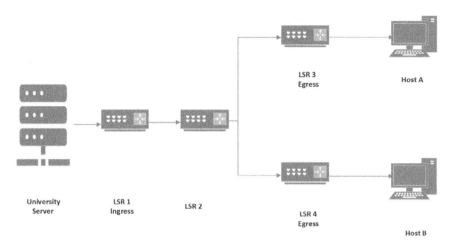

Fig. 15.1. Basic MPLS Network for the University.

issues with respect to MPLS networks and have also discussed the deployment of MPLS transport profile (TP) networks. The deployment with respect to power grid and smart grid is captured in the research paper. In Zhang and Ionescu (2007), the authors have done performance analysis of QoS for various types of services which includes VOIP, online demand for videos, etc. It has been observed that the better QoS is observed for real-time traffic when data rate is guaranteed. Also, it has been highlighted that with the change of video traffic, the QoS gets degraded. In Bensalah et al. (2018), the authors have performed the comparative analysis of the performance of MPLS and MPLS/DiffServ using the optimized network engineering tool (OPNET) Modeller v14.5. The approach followed in the research paper is designing an operator network-type backbone for simulation of a real scenario which conveys various types of traffic. The various types of traffic which have been considered are voice traffic, data traffic, and video traffic. In Raju et al. (2013), the authors have conducted a comparative study of interior gateway protocol (IGP)-based routing and MPLS-based traffic engineered routing. It is observed in the research paper that there are significant improvements for the traffic when it follows MPLS-enabled paths.

In Al-Qudah et al. (n.d.), the authors investigated the stability and diversity of the internet paths and the variation in round trip time (RTT). This variation is measured with respect to the change in path between source and destination pair. In Park et al. (2008), the authors have proposed a dynamic MPLS path management strategy. The path management strategy sustains the link failures. In Adeyinka et al. (2016), the authors have performed a study for investigating the technology which is involved in the packet delivery mechanism. The packet delivery process is studied for MPLS and MPLS traffic engineering (TE). The study has found that MPLS TE provides better performance in terms of packet loss and latency. In Suhaimy et al. (2018), the authors have performed the analysis of the various applications for MPLS TP which have been utilized for protection and Operations, Administration and Maintenance (OAM). The standard switching time for protection is 50 ms.

In Zhang et al. (2009), the authors have performed a comparison of open shortest path first (OSPF) and traditional MPLS. The comparison is performed on the basis of link utilization and traffic management. In Sun and Wu (n.d.), the authors have performed a comparative analysis of features and functions of MPLS virtual private network (VPN) and traditional VPN. In Thu et al. (2019), the authors have captured the details of the addressing table and router configuration for the deployment of the campus area networks of the university using MPLS, virtual local area network (VLANs), and the internet. In Virk and Boutaba (2004), the authors have proposed an economical global protection framework. The proposed model is cost-effective and fast. In Agrawal et al. (2005), the authors have modeled the mixed integer linear problem for design of label switched paths for MPLS networks. The evaluation of the performance of the models has been done and presented in the paper. In Suryasaputra et al. (n.d.), the authors have presented the paper considering two main objectives for MPLS routing models. The first objective is minimization of the network cost, and the second objective is maximization of residual link capacity. In Bhalla (2015), the design, simulation, and capability of MPLS have been presented by the author. The simulation has been done using the OPNET simulator.

In Haddaji et al. (2017), the authors have presented the challenges which are faced by service providers during the transformation for E2-IOPN. A long-term strategy which is based on software defined networks (SDN) is presented in the paper. The cost and benefit analysis is presented in the paper. In Tokuhisa et al. (n.d.), the software for optical path design has been developed in laboratories. An overview of the software has been presented in the document. In Zhang and Ionescu (2008), the authors have proposed a framework for providing an integrated provisioning of QoS. The simulation has been performed on the HyperChip PBR 1280 router system.

In Craveirinha et al. (2007a), the authors have presented a new hierarchical routing model which is based on two path traffic splitting routing methods in MPLS networks. The model has two levels of the objective functions and multiple constraints. In Bigos et al. (2007), the authors have studied and presented various options for the implementation in MPLS over OTN. The various options in terms of utilization of network resources and cost are studied. In Craveirinha et al. (2007b), the authors have presented various issues in the methodology for multi-objective routing optimization models for MPLS n/w. The research paper also focuses on the stochastic tele traffic modelling approach. In Rafamantanantsoa et al. (2021), the authors have studied the performance metrics for MPLS. The evaluation of the performance is done and analysed. In Lopez et al. (2009), the authors have presented the study on the data transmission and analysis of the results. The performance of the MPLS is best under the network congestion. NS2 has been used as a simulator tool. In Martins et al. (2009), the authors have presented a simplistic version of multi-objective dynamic routing. The results in the condition of the overload of traffic are analysed and presented.

3. MPLS – Technological Details

3.1. QoS

QoS is dependent upon the three network parameters which are as follows:

i. Latency (L)
ii. Jitter (J)
iii. Packet loss (PL) (Goutam & Unnikrishnan, 2019, 2021; Goutam, Unnikrishnan, & Karandikar, 2020, 2021)

Fig. 15.2 describes the parameters for QoS and Fig. 15.3 describes the relationship between the parameters and QoS.

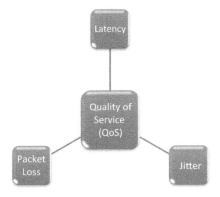

Fig. 15.2. Parameters for QoS.

Quality of service (QoS) = f^n (latency, jitter, and packet loss)

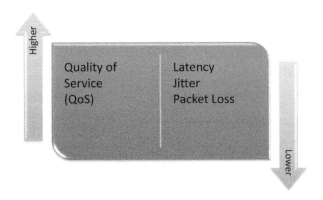

Fig. 15.3. Relationship Between the Parameters and QoS.

Table 15.1 describes the description of each parameter impacting QoS (Goutam et al., 2019, 2021, 2022; Goutam, Unnikrishnan, & Kudu, 2020).

3.2. Segments in MPLS Header

Fig. 15.4 describes the details of headers in MPLS segments. As described in Fig. 15.4, there are four significant sections in the header. The 20-bit label is the initial segment, and it will be indexed into the MPLS forwarding table. The next section is experimental (Exp) bits which defines the class of service for each packet. The QoS treatment that will be given to the traffic is dependent on the Exp section. The next section is the bottom-of-stack (S) bit. When more than one label is assigned to the packet, this field is utilized. The term 'TTL' refers to the 'Time-To-Live segment', which is used for path tracing and in which the value drops off until it reaches the desired location. When the TTL value drops to 0, the packet is deleted. MPLS works by prefixing packets with an MPLS header, containing one or more labels. This is called a label stack. Each entry in the label stack contains four fields (Ridwan et al., 2020):

- 20-bit label value
- 3-bit *traffic class* field for QoS priority and explicit congestion notification (ECN)
- a 1-bit *bottom of stack* flag. If this is set, it signifies that the current label is the last in the stack.
- an 8-bit TTL field
- Label – 20 bits
- Exp – 3 bits
- S – 1 bit
- TTL – 8 bits

Table 15.1. Description of Parameters.

S. No.	Parameter	Unit of Measurement (UoM)	Description
1	Latency	Milliseconds (ms)	It describes the mean time which is required by data packet while traversing from source to destination.
2	Jitter	Milliseconds (ms)	It measures the relative inconsistency while delivering the data packets between two end points of the network providing the access.
3	Packet loss	Percentage (%)	It refers to the loss of the packets while transmission in access networks.

Recent Trends in Deployment of MPLS 261

Layer 2 Header	MPLS Header				Layer 3 Header
	Label (20 bits)	EXP (3 bits)	S (1 bit)	TTL (8 bits)	

Fig. 15.4. Details of Headers in MPLS Segment.

3.3. Important Features of MPLS

The main and important features of MPLS are as follows:

- Optimization of network resources
- Provide QoS
- Scalability
- Connection oriented
- Minimizes network latency
- Data protection (Bhalla, 2015; Virk & Boutaba, 2004)

Fig. 15.5 describes the important features of MPLS.

3.4. Evolution of Technologies

Fig. 15.6 describes the evolution of technologies starting from plesiochronous digital hierarchy (PDH).

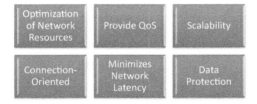

Fig. 15.5. Features of MPLS.

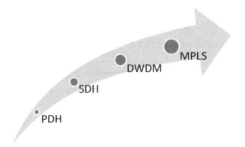

Fig. 15.6. Evolution of Technologies.

3.5. PDH and Synchronous Digital Hierarchy (SDH)

PDH is a technology used in telecommunications networks to transport large quantities of data over digital transport equipment such as fibre optic and microwave radio systems.

SDH is a multiplex technology. SDH is suitable as a transmission system for broadband integrated services digital network (ISDN) and for transporting asynchronous transfer mode (ATM) cells, PDH signals, Ethernet aggregations, storage area network (SAN) signals, and other communication signals (Bartos & Raman, 2001; Virk & Boutaba, 2004).

3.6. Advantages of MPLS Over SDH

- SDH captures the mechanism for movement and carriage voice traffic across the carrier-built fibre optic networks deployed throughout the world.
- As Layer 1, physical-level protocol, synchronous optical networking (SONET) establishes link connections along and between these fibre networks.
- SONET evolved over time to include data services. Because SONET was originally designed for voice and not variable-sized data packets.
- MPLS are data transport protocols, meaning that both reside above the physical data layers in the open systems interconnections (OSI) model and aid in moving data from one point to another (Ridwan et al., 2020; Virk & Boutaba, 2004).

Fig. 15.7 describes the key advantages of MPLS deployment, i.e., improvement in QoS and reduction in operational cost (expenditure).

Fig. 15.7.   Key Advantages of MPLS Deployment.

4. Need of MPLS in Time of Crisis

The main requirement is that the delivery of the packets in MPLS networks should have least latency and no packet loss. Fig. 15.8 describes the requirement in MPLS networks.

Equation 1 describes the condition of zero packet loss in MPLS networks.

$$\text{Packet loss (PL)} = 0 \qquad (1)$$

This requirement exists due to the high data rate applications which are also sensitive to the delays.

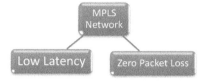

Fig. 15.8. Requirement of MPLS Networks.

The delays with reference to the protection data are not acceptable and must be avoided. It is also to be ensured that there is no discrepancy between the source data and destination data. This essentially means that source data must be equal to the destination data. This is described by Equation 2.

$$\text{Source data} = \text{Destination data} \tag{2}$$

The above requirement is very critical at the time of crisis and is required for handling any failure. It is essential that a recovery must be done in case of any failure. Hence, the restoration and data protection becomes extremely critical in a crisis. The data traffic, for which the adherence to strict and tight SLAs is essential, should have reliability and resiliency compulsorily.

For MPLS networks, the requirement is that post the occurrence of failure, the recovery and restoration should be done on an immediate basis. In order to achieve the requirement of immediate restoration of services in a situation of a crisis, MPLS fast reroute (FRR) was introduced. The main aim for introduction of MPLS FRR is to ensure for MPLS tunnels at the time of a crisis (also denoting the event of failure). While the underlying principle for MPLS FRR is same as SONET, yet there is a difference between FRR and SONET in terms of recovery time (Adeyinka et al., 2016; Rafamantanantsoa et al., 2021; Virk & Boutaba, 2004).

In FRR, the time required for recovery in case of crisis is less since the recovery decision is done locally. The efficiency for the network recovery is dependent on two important parameters, i.e.

i. Rate of detection of failure of network
ii. Switching of the traffic to the alternative route

Fig. 15.9 describes the parameters describing the efficiency of the network recovery in time of crisis.

The protection by MPLS in case of crisis can be achieved by faster detection of the network failure. The most important step in case of recovery is detection of the occurrence of failure. This detection can be either hardware based (SONET) or software based (implementing the algorithm on a higher layer) (Ridwan et al. 2020; Suryasaputra et al., n.d.). Fig. 15.10 describes the methods of the detection of failure in the event of crisis.

Fig. 15.9. Parameters for Efficiency of Network Recovery in Crisis.

Fig. 15.10. Methods of Detection of the Failure.

Fig. 15.11 describes the MPLS protection at the time of crisis. MPLS protection can be achieved by the following two steps:

i. Detection of the fault
ii. Implementation of the fault notification (Lopez et al., 2009; Park et al., 2008)

As described in Fig. 15.12, the classification of the MPLS-based recovery mechanism can be of two types:

i. Local protection
ii. Global protection

Fig. 15.11. MPLS Protection in Crisis.

Recent Trends in Deployment of MPLS 265

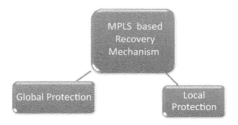

Fig. 15.12. MPLS-based Recovery Mechanism.

The global protection is done in a centralized fashion. The main objective of the global protection is providing protection against the failure of the link or node for the complete path or the segment of the path. In case of the failure or occurrence of crisis, the switching of the traffic to the available back-up path is done. The requirement of the global protection is that the notification of failure has to be sent faster for switching over to the available back-up path (Bartos & Raman, 2001; Ridwan et al., 2020; Zhang & Ionescu, 2007).

As shown in Fig. 15.13, there are four variants for the local protection. All the variants have their own benefits and disadvantages.

The link failure is the most common type of failure which happens in an organization. The link failure may occur in case of the link itself having a problem or an issue. The link failure may also occur in case of the issue at the other link end node. This may cause disruption in the traffic and finally leading to the failure of services.

In the event of the occurrence of crisis, a protection on an immediate basis can be ensured only if the back-up path is readily available to the traffic as soon as detection of the failure happens.

For attaining the rapid and immediate protection in the event of the occurrence of crisis, the computations pertaining to the back-up paths must be performed in advance. Also, it is important to set up the forwarding state for switching (Craveirinha et al., 2007b; Ridwan et al., 2020; Virk & Boutaba, 2004). Fig. 15.14 describes the requirements for immediate protection in case of the occurrence of crisis.

The deployment of MPLS networks leads to the significant improvement in QoS and reduction in the signalling and packet delivery cost.

Fig. 15.13. Variants of Local Protection.

Fig. 15.14. Requirements of Immediate Protection in Crisis.

In case of the occurrence of the failure, the traffic is transferred to the back-up path. Once the failure is rectified, then the traffic is transferred back to the working path. This phenomenon is known as restoration. As shown in Fig. 15.15, the restoration may be automatic or manual (Bartos & Raman, 2001; Bhalla, 2015; Craveirinha et al., 2007b; Virk & Boutaba, 2004).

The protection from MPLS may be dynamic or pre-negotiated as per the case. In case of pre-negotiated protection, the back-up paths are pre-established.

There is no reservation of resources in dynamic protection. There is improvement of resource utilization in dynamic protection, but it is at the cost of recovery time. Fig. 15.16 shows the comparison of the approaches for MPLS protection ((Ridwan et al., 2020; Virk & Boutaba, 2004).

Fig. 15.15. Types of Restoration of Traffic.

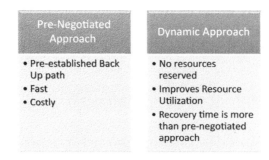

Fig. 15.16. Comparison of MPLS Protection Approach.

5. Conclusion

There exists a major requirement of convergence of networks in organizations for reduction of operational expenditure (OPEx). This convergence will also support and aid new networking services (which are IP based in nature) and traditional Layer 2 transport services. Most of the organizations are migrating to the IP/MPLS-based infrastructure. The main feature of IP/MPLS is its scalability and deployment in order to accommodate the needs of any network size.

MPLS TP can be termed as L2.5 technology which is superior to SDH and is associated with low cost. IP/MPLS is the most advanced version and meets the requirements of Industry 4.0. The requirements of current business scenarios and future goals can be easily managed by deployment of an end-to-end IP/MPLS communication network. IP/MPLS has become the technology of choice for communication networks pertaining to digital universities.

The deployment of MPLS will provide a single physical infrastructure for operational and communication requirements and will also lead to an increase in operational efficiency, network resiliency, and enabling advanced QoS. This is particularly important for online and digital universities which intend to have zero tolerance towards network failure.

References

Adeyinka, A., Emmanuel, R., Samuel, N., & Charles, N. (2016). A comparative simulation study of IP,MPLS, MPLS-TE for latency and packet loss reduction over a WAN. *International Journal of Networks and Communications, 6*(1), 1–7.

Agrawal, G., Huang, D., & Medhi, D. (2005, October). Network protection design for MPLS networks. In *Proceedings of 5th international workshop on design of reliable communication networks (DRCN 2005)*, Naples, Italy.

Al-Qudah, Z., Alsarayreh, M., Jomhawy, I., & Rabinovich, M. (n.d.). Internet path stability: Exploring the impact of MPLS deployment. In *2016 IEEE global communications conference (GLOBECOM)*, Washington, DC, USA.

Bartos, R., & Raman, M. (2001). A heuristic approach to service restoration in MPLS networks. In *ICC 2001. IEEE international conference on communications. Conference record (Cat. No.01CH37240)*, Helsinki, Finland.

Bensalah, F., Kamoun, N. E., & Bahnasse, A. (2018). Study of QoS efficiency in deployment of MPLS and MPLS/DiffServ. *International Journal of Pure and Applied Mathematics, 119*(10), 1171–1186.

Bhalla, J. (2015). Multiprotocol label switching. *International Journal of Advanced Research in Management, Architecture, Technology and Engineering (IJARMATE), 1*(4), 31-35.

Bigos, W., Cousin, B., Gosselin, S., Foll, M. L., & Nakajima, H. (2007). Survivable MPLS over optical transport networks: Cost and resource usage analysis. *IEEE Journal on Selected Areas in Communications, 25*(5), 949–962.

Craveirinha, J. M. F., Climaco, J. C. N., Pascoal, M. M. B., & Martins, L. M. R. A. (2007a). Traffic splitting in MPLS networks – A hierarchical multicriteria approach. *Journal of Telecommunications and Information Technology, 4*, 3–10.

Craveirinha, J. M. F., Girao-Silva, R., & Climaco, J. (2007b). A meta-model for multiobjective routing in MPLS networks. *Central European Journal of Operations Research, 16*, 79–105.

Girao-Silva, R., Craveirinha, J., & Climaco, J. (2014). Stochastic hierarchical multiobjective routing model in MPLS networks with two service classes: an experimental study on imprecision and uncertainty issues. *Journal of Uncertainty Analysis and Applications, 2*(3), 1–31.

Goudarzi, S., Hassan, W. H., Anisi, M. H., & Soleymani, A. (2015, September). A comparative review of vertical handover decision-making mechanisms in heterogeneous wireless networks. *Indian Journal of Science & Technology, 8*(23), 1–20.

Goutam, S., & Unnikrishnan, S. (2019a). Analysis & comparison of decision tree algorithms for vertical handover in wireless networks. *Grenze International Journal of Engineering and Technology, 5*(2), 83–89.

Goutam, S., & Unnikrishnan, S. (2019b). Decision for vertical handover based on naive Bayes algorithm. In *International conference on advances in computing, communication and control (ICAC3'19)*. IEEE, Mumbai.

Goutam, S., & Unnikrishnan, S. (2019c). QoS based vertical handover decision algorithm using fuzzy logic. In *2019 International conference on nascent technologies in engineering (ICNTE 2019)*. IEEE, Mumbai.

Goutam, S., & Unnikrishnan, S. (2021). Design, implementation & analysis of vertical handoff decision algorithm. *International Journal of Interdisciplinary Telecommunications and Networking, 13*(3), 33–53.

Goutam, S., Unnikrishnan, S., & Karandikar, A. (2020). Algorithm for vertical handover using multi attribute decision making techniques. In *2020 IEEE International conference on communication, networks and satellite (Comnetsat)*. IEEE, Batam, Indonesia.

Goutam, S., Unnikrishnan, S., & Karandikar, A. (2021). *Algorithm for vertical handover using network fitness function*. IEEE, Indian Institute of Information Technology Design and Manufacturing (IIITDM).

Goutam, S., Unnikrishnan, S., Karandikar, A., & Goutam, A. (2022). Algorithm for vertical handover decision using geometric mean and MADM techniques. *International Journal of Information Technology, 14*, 2691–2699.

Goutam, S., Unnikrishnan, S., & Kudu, N. (2020). *Decision for vertical handover using k-means clustering algorithm*. IEEE.

Goutam, S., Unnikrishnan, S., Prabavathy, S. S., & Karandikar, A. (2021). Algorithm for vertical handover decision using least cost function. *IEIE Transactions on Smart Processing and Computing, 10*(1), 44–54.

Goutam, S., Unnikrishnan, S., Prabavathy, S., Kudu, N., & Goutam, A. (2019). Assessment and prediction of quality of service of wireless networks using support vector machines. *Grenze International Journal of Engineering and Technology, 5*(2), 119–126.

Haddaji, N., Nguyen, K., & Cheriet, M. (2017). Towards end-to-end integrated optical packet network: empirical analysis. *Journal of Optical Switching and Networking, 27*, 18–39.

Lopez, D., Octavio, S., & Cesar, H. (2009). Performance evaluation in MPLS/IP data networks. *Revista Facultad de Ingeniería-Universidad de Antioquia, 50*, 181–187.

Martins, L., Francisco, C., Redol, J., Craveirinha, J., Climaco, J., & Monteiro, P. (2009). Evaluation of a multiobjective alternative routing method in carrier IP/MPLS networks. NETWORKING 2009, IFIP International Federation for Information Processing, LNCS 5550.

Park, J. T., Nah, J. W., & Lee, W. H. (2008). Dynamic path management with resilience constraints under multiple link failures in MPLS/GMPLS networks. *IEEE Transactions on Dependable and Secure Computing, 5*(3), 143–154.

Rafamantanantsoa, F., Aubert, R. C., & Haja, R. L. (2021). Analysis and evaluation of MPLS network performance. *Communications and Network, 23*, 25–25.

Raju, S. V., Premchand, P., & Govardhan, A. (2013). Improving routing performance in wide area networks using MPLS. *International Journal of Computer Science and Information Technologies (IJCSIT), 4*(4), 640–641.

Ridwan, M. A., Radzi, N. A. M., Ahmad, W. S. H. M. W., Abdullah, F., Jamaludin, M. Z., & Zakaria, M. N. (2020). Recent trends in MPLS networks: Technologies, applications and challenges. *IET Communications, 14*(2), 177–185.

Suhaimy, N., Ahmad, W. S. H. M. W., Radzi, N. A. M., Abdullah, F., Jamaludin, M. Z., & Zakaria, M. N. (2018). Analysis of MPLS-TP network for different applications. *International Journal of Engineering & Technology, 7*, 892–898.

Sun, M. S., & Wu, W. H. (n.d.). Engineering analysis and research of MPLS VPN. In *2012 7th International forum on strategic technology (IFOST)*. IEEE, Tomsk, Russia.

Suryasaputra, R., Kist, A. A., & Harris, R. J. (n.d.). Verification of MPLS traffic engineering techniques. In *2005 13th IEEE international conference on networks jointly held with the 2005 IEEE 7th Malaysia international conference on communications*, Kuala Lumpur, Malaysia.

Thu, K. A., Mon, S. S., & Soe, T. (2019). Camtus area networks of the university using MPLS, VLANs and the internet. *International Journal of Trend in Scientific Research and Development (IJTSRD), 3*(5), 1467–1470.

Tokuhisa, M., Nogami, S., Abe, T., Ngatsu, N., & Takigawa, Y. (n.d.). Optical path design software for photonic MPLS networks. *Letters, NTT Technical Review, 1*(6), 76–81.

Virk, A. P. S., & Boutaba, R. (2004). Economical protection in MPLS networks. *Computer Communications, 29*, 402–408.

Zhang, D., & Ionescu, D. (2007). QoS performance analysis in deployment of DiffServ-aware MPLS traffic engineering. In *Eighth ACIS international conference on software engineering, artificial intelligence, networking, and parallel/distributed computing*. IEEE Computer Society.

Zhang, D., & Ionescu, D. (2008). Providing guaranteed packet loss probability service in IP/MPLS-based networks. In *ICC 2008 proceedings*. IEEE Communications Society.

Zhang, M., Lui, B., & Zhang, B. (2009). Multi-commodity flow traffic engineering with hybrid MPLS/OSPF routing. In *IEEE "GLOBECOM" proceedings*. IEEE.

Chapter 16

Educational Innovation and Digitalization During the Crisis

Sridhar Chakravarthi Mulakaluri

XIM University, Bhubaneswar, Odisha, India

Abstract

Access to education has been globalized and democratized to a certain extent through massive open online courses (MOOCs) and other open-access platforms and content databases. In a recent study by Inayatullah and Milojević (2014), the recommendations were to establish a pilot project, enhance digital pedagogy and learning, customize degrees, create a culture of change in higher education, enhance collaboration, support research activities, redefine frames of reference, and anticipate and prepare for futures trends. The need for democratization of education has been increasing to meet the need of individuals and groups to assert and highlight their identity and role in society. Education is the means to facilitate this through a practical and active approach through wider stakeholder participation. Religious belief was identified as the main cause of conflicts among multi-ethnic cohorts. Adding socio-cultural differences to the mix and uncontrolled access to various opinions through social media makes the task much more complex. Educational policies must consider mother-tongue learning to improve learning outcomes. However, making the vast learning content accessible in multiple languages could be daunting. This chapter explores these emerging challenges and changing stakeholder expectations from the formal education system. The policy implications, possible technology-driven solutions, and their effectiveness in addressing the growing challenges of a global learning village have been explored.

Keywords: Higher education; Ed-Tech; digitalization of pedagogy; accessibility; technology; globalization of higher education

Introduction – Global Learning Village

This chapter explores the dynamics of higher education (HE) across the world, reviewing the different perspectives from both developed and developing countries. A view from 30,000 ft rather than a deep dive into specific issues and challenges has been presented, with an honest attempt to cover all the contemporary challenges. Any omission is unintentional.

World is changing and so is the education landscape across the world. Technology has made information, knowledge, and education accessible to everyone everywhere, provided they are able to cross the barriers of infrastructure and language. Yes, these two continue to be huge barriers for learning. Staley and Trinkle (2011) noted a few tectonic shifts, comparing the American HE landscape to a seismic zone. They have noted increasing differentiation leading to a highly diversified system. While the intent of education has been equality, we have ended up with multiple systems based on the diversified customers and their goals for seeking education. With the emergence of accredited programmes from companies like McDonald's, students were expected to prefer them over conventional college education. Staley and Trinkle (2011) have also noted the transformation of general education curriculum, where despite the hiring managers looking for generic skills, students have been focusing on their majors, with the faculty failing to see these courses as tools for building vocational skills. This has created a neglect of liberal arts and other generic curriculum leading to the conflict among the stakeholder expectations. Information technology expanded the academic networks beyond boundaries and borders, exploding the availability, sharing, and collaboration among the academicians. There is an increasing pressure to show the value from a formal degree in terms of securing gainful employment. This has created a tremendous pressure on the institutions in terms of campus placements, more than quality of education. As per the latest report from www.statista.com, the employability of engineering graduates in India is at 57.44%, showing only about 6% increase from 2014. Middle-skill jobs were expected to continue to be in demand while the institutions have started lifelong association and partnership with the alumni.

Koch (2015) compared the American HE market to the restaurant market, full of choices and across a wide price range. Sharma et al. (2017) explored the impact of e-learning on education, through social media networks and platforms. Virtual campuses offering massive open online courses (MOOCs) have become popular. Learners are more focused on utilizing different learning opportunities to build competencies for better employment.

Knight (2018) posited that the HE landscape around the world had transformed due to internationalization leading to dramatic changes. Some of the unintended consequences were 'commercialisation, diploma mills, international rankings and the great brain race'. They argued that focusing on the 'collaboration, mutual benefit, capacity building, and exchange aspects' could lead to optimal benefit for individuals, institutions, region, and the country as well.

Saykili (2019) posited that digital connective technologies have facilitated new knowledge creation and discrimination through social interactions and collaboration.

Changing Stakeholder Expectations

Learner Expectations

Technological advancements are dramatically changing workforce qualifications, and an estimated 65% of the children today will work in jobs that would be created in future (Şahin & Alkan, 2016). In the digital age, learners should develop futuristic skills like learning and innovation, information, media and technology skills, life and career skills (Dede, 2009), along with soft skills like flexibility, adaptability, and information processing (Doyle, 2016). Along with these, knowledge of human culture, physical and natural world, liberal arts, personal and social responsibility, ethical and action, and integrated learning skills are also recommended by American Association of College & Universities (AAC&U, 2007). The question is whether the higher education institutions (HEIs) are equipped and aligned to impart these skills through their existing curricula and pedagogy.

Learners are actively creating online learning communities and play active roles there (Lonka, 2015). Thus, such learning communities should be an integral part of their learning environment and experience. According to some educators, traditional teaching methods are not attractive to digital age learners (Şahin & Alkan, 2016).

Educause Horizon Report for teaching and learning (2023) highlighted changing expectations of students towards more flexible and convenient learning models, with increased focus on micro credentials. They are also looking for more equitable and inclusive education. Need and demand for lifelong, continuous education is on the rise. Learners are more focused on affordability and return on investment (ROI).

Teacher Expectations

The role of the teacher has changed from being the sage on the stage to a guide on the side. From being a source of knowledge, the teacher has become a learning facilitator, enabling the learners to develop thinking and analytical skills. The instructor is expected and required to use all the latest technologies and tools to meet the learner's expectations as well as create an effective experience (Lonka, 2015). This makes the instructor a learning engineer who designs an effective learning environment using digital innovations (Saykili, 2019).

The American Association of Colleges of Teacher Education (AACTE) and The Partnership for 21st Century Learning (P21) published a joint report highlighting the instructor skills for the 21st century (AACTE & P21, 2010). These include aligning technologies with content and pedagogy, creatively mapping technologies to learner needs, meeting futuristic standards, project-oriented teaching, using diverse assessment strategies, actively participating in learning communities, coaching and mentoring, supporting peers, and pursuing continuous learning. All these expectations need a huge amount of time that limit the classroom time and teaching load. Yet, the current operations of the HEIs don't facilitate these new roles and skills (Saykili, 2019).

Naylor and Nyanjom (2021) explored the nature and significance of educators' emotions in the HE context, while adapting to online teaching. Driven by a combination of institutional support and the type of emotional response, they identified four emergent orientations: futuristic, ambivalent, disillusioned, and cautious. This indicates a major role for administration to provide necessary support and orientation, along with the infrastructure.

The following transitions were suggested by Saykili (2019). From standardized to individualized learning, standardized to specialized evaluation, internalizing knowledge to leveraging external resources, covering the content to discovering knowledge, and learning through information to learning by doing. Lonka (2015) recommended hybrid learning environments using a combination of the digital, mobile, virtual, online, social, and physical spaces.

Minett-Smith and Davis (2019) showed that the changing HE landscape is promoting innovation into existing team-teaching models, suggesting exploring and developing academic leadership at every level of employment. Their work throws light on the changing role of academic leadership, increasing workloads and emerging teacher identity. These emerging changes are to be cautiously integrated into every academic role in HE to ensure leadership development across the board to tackle the emerging demands and opportunities.

Rapanta et al. (2021) found that when teaching with digital technologies is forced through emergency remote teaching, it could lead to a smooth integration of teaching methods, physical tools, and digital tools resulting in a more active, flexible, and effective learning. This brings out the challenges faced by the teachers in adapting the technology tools and how that can be facilitated. However, appropriate training and handholding should be provided to ensure efficiency and effectiveness.

Parent Expectations

Immerwahr (2000) reported that most of the parents thought that HE was important as well as of significant value. While they understood the individual challenges of the students, they expected each student to be supported. This is where the role of individualized learning and attention comes into play where the current processes and practices of HEIs fall short. Goyette and Xie (1999) as well as Beutel and Anderson (2008) explored the relation between race and educational expectations of parents and children and established that irrespective of the race, there were high expectations associated with education among the parents. The main expectations were building family social capital and status attainment, driven by socio-economic backgrounds. Kim (2002) from South Korea and Guo (2014) from China reported similar expectations where the students expected a diverse college experience, while the parents expected protection from economic disadvantages without HE, driven by socio-economic realities. From across the globe, the expectations of the parents seem to remain consistent, so that HE would help their children live better lives.

Role of Technology-Driven Solutions

Saykili (2019) posited that the digital age had re-engineered every aspect of life, including education. The paradigm of school has fallen short to meet the needs of the digital age student. Technology disrupted learning processes with open educational resources (OERs), MOOCs, and learning analytics, breaking the traditional boundaries of learning and pushing for a new paradigm shift in education. Learning experience has become informal and enriched through online communities using social media, making it independent of time. Knowledge is being created through social interaction and collaboration, creating immense opportunities for HE.

Ganesh (2023) experimented with peer-to-peer anonymous reviews and assessments in a flipped classroom set-up, using an open edX platform. The experiment involved case analysis by students outside the classroom and giving anonymous feedback to their classmates within specific timeframes. The process led to an increase in student interest, engagement, and achievement. It freed up the faculty member to utilize classroom time effectively through facilitated discussions, exploring key concepts.

Cranfield et al. (2021) explored the impact of sudden shift to online classes across different universities and geographies and measured the level of disruption to student learning experience. They reported that the disruption varied depending on the country and the lockdown logistics. They evaluated student experience with online e-learning across four dimensions, 'home learning environment, engagement, participation preference, and impact on learning skills', and identified significant differences, depending on the economic and digital development of the country.

Bates et al. (2020) suggested that artificial intelligence (AI) is a sleeping giant in HE and is unlikely to come from mainstream institutions. Companies like LinkedIn and Coursera with access to huge datasets would build them, threatening the existence of traditional institutions. They posed a critical question whether technology should replace the teacher or enable both teacher and learner.

Ferrer et al. (2020) studied the learners' attitude to online learning and found that it influenced both motivations to know and engage, indicating that the learning environment design can enhance learning experiences. However, attitudes to online learning did not motivate learners to build relationships.

Horizon Report (2023) highlighted the rising influence of AI, online learning and low code/no-code technologies in the learning space. However, Reich (2020) summarized these technology trends and posited that technology would not work for every learner and in every context. The new age tools will be as effective as the teachers who would be using them. He explored three ways of online learning, instructor guided, algorithm guided, and peer guided and concluded that the effectiveness of online learning was dependent on the learner's commitment. Hockly (2023) explored the role of AI and chatbots in English Language teaching and opined that while AI facilitated some advantages, privacy issues were a concern, particularly in the case of children. Alamri et al. (2021) reported an increased personalized learning in HE, using three technological models in blended learning environments. However, they have also found that data-driven independent studies were lacking to establish their effectiveness in student learning.

Role of Religion

Religion has been playing a pivotal role in education from the time immemorial. Most of the Christian missionaries have been running schools and colleges across the world. Furniss (1995) documented the unfortunate incidents at a residential missionary school that led to the demise of two boys. During her research, many old students told her that it was just a tip of the iceberg. Gilliat-Ray (2019) explored the changing religious dynamics in HEIs and related politics. While some institutions tried to project a secular campus to attract overseas students, there was a lot of de-secularization and polarization on the campuses based on religious diversity, which has been on the rise. Two extreme scenarios were usually present, a generic apathy towards the spiritual needs of the students and staff and at the other end disturbances created by some extremists to gain visibility. However, many HEIs have been trying to meet the spiritual needs of their students from diverse religious backgrounds, across the world. The different faiths have developed their local communities to meet these needs, outside the HEI.

Jogezai et al. (2021) explored how the teachers' attitudes towards the use of social media were influenced by the usage of social media by religious leaders. This indicated the external influence of religion on the teacher and learner behaviour about adopting and integrating new technology and tools into education. Hidayaturrahman et al. (2021) explored the integration of science and religion implemented by Islamic universities in Malaysia and Indonesia and found that they opened programmes without any religious claims or restrictions for admission, making education more inclusive, leading to successful advancement of the institutions. Jamaludin (2022) explored the process of religious moderation as a concept as well as practice in Indonesia and found that based on centrally defined indicators from the Ministry of Religion, it was practised every day for developing and implementing the measures of moderation. This is an interesting approach by policymakers to ensure that the right practices are developed and percolated across the system. Baratta and Smith (2019) studied the clash of academic and religious identities of the students and found that many students experienced conflicts ranging from disconnect between religious beliefs and assessment, to feeling safe on campus. Coupled with identity politics, these issues warrant more work to better understand student experience to formulate better policies.

Role of Social Media

Social media has become an integral part of our daily lives across the world, and education is not spared from this phenomenon. This omnipresent bouquet of tools can be a hindrance to learning or can also become an effective learning aid. Manca (2020) analysed 46 studies to explore the role of WhatsApp, Instagram, Pinterest, and Snapchat in pedagogy, focusing on 'mixing information and learning resources, hybridization of expertise, widening of the context of learning, and the benefits for learning'. It was found that the use of WhatsApp was well documented. However, not enough research about Instagram, Pinterest, and Snapchat was found. Most of the studies focused on the preferences of the general population and integration of social media into pedagogy was partial and at varied levels. This study indicates that HE systems and faculties are yet to fully adopt and leverage social media platforms.

Kumar and Nanda (2019) discussed how most of the HEIs have embraced social media for promotional purposes, due to cost-effectiveness as well as interactive engagement with the young people. This brings out another way social media is influencing HE. There are student posts and ratings about almost all HEIs. Sobaih et al. (2020) showed that students' extensive usage of social media paved the way for its effective usage in formal teaching and learning. However, the research found significant differences between teachers and students for using social media to support students and building an online learner community. While students focused on building an online learner community for support, faculty members focused mostly on teaching and learning. The research showed that social media could be effectively used to promote social learning, and social presence, providing an alternative learning platform.

Mishra (2020) showed how the networks of students, their family, friends, ethnic and religious groups, and faculty influence academic success. A framework showed how network members provide necessary social support and information, complementing one another. This is a significant insight as these networks are easily built and accessed using social media, essentially highlighting that it is not the social media tools per se, but the social capital being built through these platforms that contributes to the success.

Manu et al. (2021) established the openness of students and teachers to use social media in education, along with pedagogical significance. Motivations for use were identified as interaction and information. A student engagement framework was proposed where behavioural, emotional, and cognitive indicators were identified, and the role of social media in facilitating these indicators was established. The research showed how social media tools could be strategically integrated into the classroom, positively influencing learners' perception of the teachers and the institution. However, all the students may not use all the tools similarly, and this should be considered while integrating these tools into pedagogy. Similar findings were reported by Lacka and Wong (2021). Bouton et al. (2021) found that students used social media tools mainly for sharing learning artefacts and information. This indicates that the present use is quite rudimentary and can be enhanced to create an effective learning environment as suggested by Mishra (2020) and Manu et al. (2021), driving social support and collaborative learning.

Jogezai et al. (2021) explored how the teachers' attitudes towards use of social media were influenced by the physical distancing, knowledge of social media, increased social media use, and usage by religious leaders. The paper captured the interplay of constraints, capabilities, behaviours, and external influences, to shape the attitude of teachers to adopt social media tools in education. This also indicates the need for HEIs to invest in enhancing teacher capabilities to adopt new age technology tools into education. Tang and Hew (2017) explored the use of Twitter in education and concluded that while it helped the sharing of information and communication among the students, no causation could be established for a positive influence on improved learning outcomes. They suggested five guidelines for improving the learning effectiveness by providing technology training, clarifying the tool-related learning activities, mandating the tool usage, providing regular support, and expanding the learner community. While these suggestions were in the context of Twitter, they can be applied to all social media tools.

Learning in Mother Tongue

Phatudi (2013) acknowledged that mother tongue was both a significant medium of learning and identity formation. However, due to the globalization of education across the world, the medium of instruction has become English in most of the HEIs. This, while creating the workforce of the future, is also leading to an identity crisis, creating a distance between the ethnic identity and the student identity of the student.

Brückner et al. (2015) established the influence of native language on learning performance in HE. Phatudi (2013) studied the student perception about the use of mother tongue in HEIs and found that students acknowledged the role of mother tongue in HE, but the usage differed based on the institutional culture. This perception encourages and helps the success of mother-tongue education and the teacher training process. However, the administrators should ensure that the institutional culture does not hinder this process. Preece (2009) discussed the impact of English writing courses on non-native English learners, where they use their native language for establishing social networks for support. Mansoor (2010) found a language shift among the regional speakers in Pakistan, leading to low competency of their mother-tongue/regional languages in both formal and informal settings. They also showed negative attitudes towards their own languages and preferred to study in English and Urdu medium at every level of school. The research recommended a language policy in HEIs promoting cultural pluralism along with the provision of state support to the minority languages. This seems to be a global concern where the youth is slowly drifting away from their mother tongue and their native culture.

Nishanthi (2020) posited that most of the children in the Global South were learning very little in school, due to non-native medium of instruction. Ignoring the mother tongue in the early years can negatively impact children's learning. This is leading to limited learning of knowledge and skills resulting in alienating experiences, leading to high drop-out rates. The research suggests that language policies should accommodate mother-tongue learning to improve learning quality. Mother-tongue education at least in early years can enable teachers to teach and learners to learn more effectively. However, Nyika (2015) posited that poor performance of university learners who studied in non-native language of instruction may not be solely due to the language proficiency in the medium of instruction, as there were several other factors including quality of basic education, teacher quality, socio-economic status, and the learning environment. Involving all the pertinent stakeholders in policymaking was recommended along with ensuring primary education in mother tongue and integrating the international language slowly could help.

While the AI and natural language processing technologies can help bridge the gap, particularly between the content in English and native language learners, caution is recommended in implementation.

Emerging New Models and Solutions

Short boot camps have emerged as an interesting alternative for skill development. Price and Dunagan (2019) studied boot camps using disruption theory and identified its disruptive potential to HE. While being inferior to traditional degrees, boot camps are simpler and cheaper, improving the consumption among an overserved market. Boot camps focus on skill building, leverage technology, and spread their online presence, with no competition from traditional institutions. The authors suggested a major role of government funds to decide the future of boot camps. It also depends on boot camps offering lifelong learning across all sectors. Even if the traditional institutions start offering professional and technical skill programmes, as they have already started, boot camps would still disrupt them. However, if boot camps continue to innovate and expand, they could completely change the education and training landscape. The proposed multi-level graduation model in national education policy (NEP) 2020 in India is an indicator for responding to the changing learner demands for short-term programmes that would enable them to secure jobs early and continue education along their professional growth. This also aligns the learner investments to their career growth, leading to a better ROI.

The increasing connectedness and learners becoming location agnostic has opened new challenges of ensuring inclusivity and protecting learners from racism. Ash et al. (2020) along with Chun and Feagin (2019) explored the impact of racism, diversity, equity, and inclusion in HE and suggested solutions and frameworks for the non-dominant groups to cope up with the challenges, while suggesting mechanisms for distribution of leadership and authority. Using critical race theory proposed in the 1970s and further researched (Collins & Jun, 2017; Delgado & Stefanic, 2012), the authors proposed a framework for power sharing and re-education of white leaders.

Antonaci et al. (2019) showed that gamification design of a MOOC enhanced social presence and sense of community of users, improving their learning performance, though not directly proportional to engagement levels. This research indicates that newer curriculum designs using gamification and building a sense of community are necessary in the changing HE landscape.

Oussous et al. (2023) evaluated the existing open-source Ed-Tech solutions, comparing them using the OpenBRR assessment methodology leveraging its flexibility and ease of use. They have identified three adaptive learning approaches: learner system that provides the traditional sequence of content for every learner, macro-adaptive approach that customizes the content using a few parameters like learners' goals and current knowledge, and micro-adaptive approach that involves real-time diagnostics of learner progress and needs and customizing the content accordingly. The study compared the platforms in terms of functionality, adaptive learning, operational characteristics, support services, technology, and community adoption. They found Moodle to be the best, compared to Canvas, Open edX, Sakai, Chamilo, and Ilias. This study highlights the various aspects of learning platforms that are critical to learners' success and should be focused on.

Based on their empirical research, Vale et al. (2021) concluded that people were appreciative of the need for collaborative work using suitable technologies to ensure effective learning and evaluation processes, even during lockdown. People could see a new paradigm of education emerging across the globe, through extensive use of technology, leading to innovative teaching and learning. However, the lack of development in the fundamental interpersonal skills was also identified. Similar findings were reported from across the world – from Malaysia and Indonesia (Pramono et al., 2021) and Poland (Stecuła & Wolniak, 2022).

Policy Implications

Saykili (2019) suggested that with the advent of the digital age, education policymakers should consider the new challenges and opportunities for advancing the educational processes and adding more value to the stakeholders. Odabaşi et al. (2010) suggested that challenges of the HEIs are managed through three types of changes: service delivery and financing, administration, and learning and teaching. Erdem (2006) highlighted how the responsibilities of the government, society, and universities have changed, stressing on the changing dynamics between HEIs and the government due to increased accountability of HEIs.

Increased learner mobility has created a diverse mix of learners from different ethnic and cultural backgrounds. Integrating them into a learning cohort for collaborative learning is another major classroom challenge (Saykili, 2019). Today, HEIs are expected to play multiple roles including education, leading technology development, research and development, industry collaboration, thus contributing to regional development (Şahin & Alkan, 2016).

Provision of laptops to American school children (Hu, 2007) and tablets to children in Turkey (*Hürriyet*, 2015) did not prove effective. Finland reported a lack of understanding about using such devices (Lonka, 2015). Saykili (2019) posited that effective utilization of technology innovations was hampered by strict organizational culture, traditional pedagogy, lack of leadership and suitable policies, and regulatory framework. From the learner's perspective, issues like distraction, cheating, plagiarism, and academic misconduct were delaying adoption.

Zuiderwijk and Yin (2018) explored the open-access philosophy for transforming education. They explored the potential of virtual research environments (VREs), connected to open-source datasets and MOOCs, and established their immense potential for advancing education and research across the world. VREs are online environments making data, software, and resources accessible (Bornschlegl et al., 2016; Candela et al., 2013; Zuiderwijk et al., 2016), offering advanced tools for collaboration between researchers (Carusi & Reimer, 2010; Sarwar et al., 2013).

Education is generally understood to play a major role in reducing social inequalities. Horizon Report (2023) suggested that reduced public funding for educational institutions added more pressure on the institutions to become efficient and frugal. Balbachevsky et al. (2019) explored the expansion process of education into HE in Brazil and concluded that it could not reduce the social inequalities due to a conservative approach following the traditional models, while allowing the private sector to absorb most of the demand. This is an important insight for the policymakers, who must ensure necessary expansion of the public funding and infrastructure in HE so that all sections of the society would have access.

Considering all the above aspects, policymakers need to engage with multiple stakeholders including the students, parents, academics, administrators of tertiary education, politicians, donors, industry, and local communities. They need to consider both technological challenges and short- and long-term implications on society as well as students.

Conclusions and Future Directions

Having considered the current scenario and the global landscape of HE, along with the changing expectations and perceptions of learners as well as teachers, we can summarize the following aspects:

- The learners are mainly using the technology for sharing information and building social learning networks.
- The teachers are struggling to adopt and leverage the new age technologies, including social media tools and platforms to improve effective learning.
- The parents are expecting HE to improve their children's socio-economic status.
- The HEIs are leveraging social media and technological advancements more for marketing purposes.
- The increasing diversity on the campus is bringing more diversity-, equity-, and inclusivity-related challenges.
- The role of religion in HE seems to be increasing due to the influence it wields on both teachers and learners.
- While the role of mother tongue in early education is significant, integrating international medium of instruction in a systematic way should be addressed through policy.

With these conclusions, the following future directions are suggested:

- Teacher training, enabling, and support is of paramount importance for integrating technology and social media tools into the classroom for improving learning outcomes.
- Instructional design and pedagogy should be reviewed for better integration and group learning using technology platforms and tools, familiar to the learners.
- Learner engagement should be designed to ensure cognitive, behavioural, and emotional indicators, using technology.
- Course design should include micro-credential opportunities to ensure lifelong and continuous learning.

- HEIs should review their policies, both pedagogical and cultural, to address diversity, equity, and inclusivity, while keeping the changing workplace demands in view.
- Policymakers should facilitate effective learning outcomes while ensuring that HE meets the expectations of social capital and socio-economic well-being of future generations.

References

AACTE & P21. (2010). *21st century knowledge and skills in education preparation*. AACTE & P21.

Alamri, H. A., Watson, S., & Watson, W. (2021). Learning technology models that support personalization within blended learning environments in higher education. *TechTrends, 65*, 62–78.

Antonaci, A., Klemke, R., Lataster, J., Kreijns, K., & Specht, M. (2019). Gamification of MOOCs adopting social presence and sense of community to increase user's engagement: An experimental study. In M. Scheffel, J. Broisin, V. Pammer-Schindler, A. Ioannou, & J. Schneider (Eds.), *European conference on technology enhanced learning* (pp. 172–186). Springer International Publishing.

Ash, A. N., Hill, R., Risdon, S., & Jun, A. (2020). Anti-racism in higher education: A model for change. *Race and Pedagogy Journal: Teaching and Learning for Justice, 4*(3), 2.

Association of American Colleges and Universities. (2007). *College learning for the new global century: A report from the National Leadership Council for Liberal Education and America's Promise*. Association of American Colleges and Universities.

Balbachevsky, E., Sampaio, H., & de Andrade, C. Y. (2019). Expanding access to higher education and its (limited) consequences for social inclusion: The Brazilian experience. *Social Inclusion, 7*(1), 7–17.

Baratta, A., & Smith, P. V. (2019). The confrontation of identities: How university students manage academic and religious selves in higher education. *Educational Studies, 45*(6), 771–786.

Bates, T., Cobo, C., Mariño, O., & Wheeler, S. (2020). Can artificial intelligence transform higher education? *International Journal of Educational Technology in Higher Education, 17*(1), 1–12.

Beutel, A. M., & Anderson, K. G. (2008) Race and the educational expectations of parents and children: The case of South Africa. *The Sociological Quarterly, 49*(2), 335–361. https://doi.org/10.1111/j.1533-8525.2008.00118.x

Bornschlegl, M. X., Manieri, A., Walsh, P., Catarci, T., & Hemmje, M. L. (2016). Road mapping infrastructures for advanced visual interfaces supporting big data applications in virtual research environments. Paper presented at the Workshop on Advanced Visual Interfaces AVI.

Bouton, M. E., Maren, S., & McNally, G. P. (2021). Behavioral and neurobiological mechanisms of Pavlovian and instrumental extinction learning. *Physiological Reviews, 101*(2), 611–681.

Brückner, S., Förster, M., Zlatkin-Troitschanskaia, O., & Walstad, W. B. (2015). Effects of prior economic education, native language, and gender on economic knowledge of first-year students in higher education. A comparative study between Germany and the USA. *Studies in Higher Education, 40*(3), 437–453.

Candela, L., Castelli, D., & Pagano, P. (2013). Virtual research environments: An overview and a research agenda. *Data Science Journal, 12*, GRDI75-GRDI81. http://dx.doi.org/10.2481/dsj.GRDI-013

Carusi, A., & Reimer, T. (2010). Virtual research environment collaborative landscape study. JISC, Bristol, 106.
Chun, E., & Feagin, J. (2019). *Rethinking diversity frameworks in higher education*. Routledge.
Collins, C. S., & Jun, A. (2019). Introduction to belief systems in higher education. *Higher education and belief systems in the Asia Pacific region: Knowledge, spirituality, religion, and structures of faith* (pp. 1–12).
Cranfield, D. J., Tick, A., Venter, I. M., Blignaut, R. J., & Renaud, K. (2021). Higher education students' perceptions of online learning during COVID-19 – A comparative study. *Education Sciences, 11*(8), 403.
Delgado, R., & Stefanic, J. (2012). *Critical race theory: An Introduction*. New York University Press.
Dede, C. (2009). *Comparing frameworks for '21st century skills'*. Harvard Graduate School of Education. http://sttechnology.pbworks.com/f/Dede_(2010)_Comparing%20Frameworks%20for %2021st%20Century%20Skills.pdf
Doyle, A. (2016). *Hard skills vs. soft skills*. The balance.
Educause Horizon Report for teaching and learning. (2023).
Erdem, A. R. (2006). Dünyadaki yükseköğretimin değişimi. *Selçuk Üniversitesi Sosyal Bilimler Enstitüsü Dergisi, 15*, 299–314.
Ferrer, J., Ringer, A., Saville, K., A Parris, M., & Kashi, K. (2020). Students' motivation and engagement in higher education: The importance of attitude to online learning. *Higher Education, 83*(2), 1–22.
Furniss, E. (1995). *Victims of benevolence: The dark legacy of the Williams Lake Residential School*. Arsenal Pulp Press.
Ganesh, S. S. (2023). *Peer learning experiment*. Open edX platform. https://openedx.org/blog/transforming-education-the-open-edx-platform/
Gilliat-Ray, S. (2019). *Religion in higher education: The politics of the multi-faith campus*. Routledge.
Goyette, K., & Xie, Y. (1999). Educational expectations of Asian American youths: Determinants and ethnic differences. *Sociology of Education, 72*(1), 22–36. https://doi.org/10.2307/2673184
Guo, J. (2014). Educational expectations of parents and children: Findings from a case of China. *Asian Social Work and Policy Review, 8*(3), 228–242.
Hidayaturrahman, M., Sudarman, S., Husamah, H., & Kusumawati, I. R. (2021). Integrating science and religion at Malaysian and Indonesian higher education. *Al-Ta Lim Journal, 28*(1), 55–66.
Hockly, N. (2023). Artificial intelligence in English language teaching: The good, the bad and the ugly. *RELC Journal, 54*(2), 445–451.
Hürriyet. (2015). Fatih Projesi'ni çok yanlış anladılar.
Hu, W. (2007). Seeing no progress, some schools drop laptops. *The New York Times*. http://www.nytimes.com/2007/05/04/education/04laptop.html
Immerwahr, J. (2000). Great expectations: How the public and parents – White, African American, and Hispanic – View higher education. ERIC. ERIC – ED444405.
Inayatullah, S., & Milojević, I. (2014). Augmented reality, the Murabbi and the democratization of higher education: Alternative futures of higher education in Malaysia. *On the Horizon, 22*(2), 110–126. https://doi.org/10.1108/OTH-08-2013-0029
Jamaludin, A. N. (2022). Religious moderation: The concept and practice in higher education institutions. *AL-ISHLAH: Jurnal Pendidikan, 14*(1), 539–548.
Jogezai, N. A., Baloch, F. A., Jaffar, M., Shah, T., Khilji, G. K., & Bashir, S. (2021). Teachers' attitudes towards social media (SM) use in online learning amid the COVID-19 pandemic: The effects of SM use by teachers and religious scholars during physical distancing. *Heliyon, 7*(4), E06781.

Kim, D. (2002) What do high school students and their parents expect from higher education? A case study of South Korea. *Journal of Higher Education Policy, and Management, 24*(2), 183–196. https://doi.org/10.1080/1360080022000013509

Knight, J. (2018). The changing landscape of higher education internationalisation– for better or worse? In D. Law & M. Hoey (Eds.), *Perspectives on the internationalisation of higher education* (pp. 13–19). Routledge.

Koch, J. V. (2015). The multifurcation of American higher education. In G. A. Olson & J. W. Presley (Eds.), *Future of higher education* (pp. 21–30). Routledge.

Kumar, V., & Nanda, P. (2019). Social media in higher education: A framework for continuous engagement. *International Journal of Information and Communication Technology Education (IJICTE), 15*(1), 97–108.

Lacka, E., & Wong, T. C. (2021). Examining the impact of digital technologies on students' higher education outcomes: The case of the virtual learning environment and social media. *Studies in Higher Education, 46*(8), 1621–1634.

Lonka, K. (2015). *Innovative schools: Teaching & learning in the digital era*. European Union.

Manca, S. (2020). Snapping, pinning, liking, or texting: Investigating social media in higher education beyond Facebook. *The Internet and Higher Education, 44*, 100707.

Mansoor, A. (2010). Teaching creative writing to university level second language learners in Pakistan. *New Writing, 7*(3), 201–218.

Manu, B. D., Ying, F., Oduro, D., & Boateng, S. A. (2021). Student engagement and social media in tertiary education: The perception and experience from the Ghanaian public university. *Social Sciences & Humanities Open, 3*(1), 100100.

Minett-Smith, C., & Davis, C. L. (2019). Widening the discourse on team-teaching in higher education. *Teaching in Higher Education, 25*(5), 579–594.

Mishra, S. (2020). Social networks, social capital, social support, and academic success in higher education: A systematic review with a special focus on 'underrepresented' students. *Educational Research Review, 29*, 100307.

Naylor, D., & Nyanjom, J. (2021). Educators' emotions involved in the transition to online teaching in higher education. *Higher Education Research & Development, 40*(6), 1236–1250.

Nishanthi, R. (2020). Understanding of the importance of mother tongue learning. *International Journal of Trend in Scientific Research and Development, 5*(1), 77–80.

Nyika, A. (2015). Mother tongue as the medium of instruction at developing country universities in a global context. *South African Journal of Science, 111*(1–2), 1–5.

Odabaşı, H. F., Fırat, M., & İzmirli, S. (2010). Küreselleşen dünyada akademisyen olmak. *Anadolu Üniversitesi Sosyal Bilimler Dergisi, 10*(3), 127–142.

Oussous, A., Menyani, I., Srifi, M., Lahcen, A. A., Kheraz, S., & Benjelloun, F. Z. (2023). An evaluation of open-source adaptive learning solutions. *Information, 14*(2), 57.

Phatudi, N. C. (2013). Perspectives of black students on the use of the mother tongue at higher education institutions in South Africa. *Journal of Educational Studies, 12*(1), 1–15.

Pramono, S. E., Wijaya, A., Melati, I. S., Sahudin, Z., & Abdullah, H. (2021). COVID-driven innovation in higher education: Analysing the collaboration of leadership and digital technology during the pandemic in UiTM Malaysia and UNNES Indonesia. *Asian Journal of University Education, 17*(2), 1–15.

Preece, S. (2009). Multilingual identities in higher education: Negotiating the 'mother tongue', 'posh' and 'slang'. *Language and Education, 24*(1), 21–39. https://doi.org/10.1080/09500780903194036

Price, R., & Dunagan, A. (2019). *Betting on bootcamps: How short-course training programs could change the landscape of higher education*. Clayton Christensen Institute for Disruptive Innovation.

Rapanta, C., Botturi, L., Goodyear, P., Guàrdia, L., & Koole, M. (2021). Balancing technology, pedagogy and the new normal: Post-pandemic challenges for higher education. *Postdigital Science and Education, 3*(3), 715–742.

Reich, J. (2020). *Failure to disrupt: Why technology alone can't transform education*. Harvard University Press.
Şahin, M., & Alkan, R. M. (2016). Yükseköğretimde değişim dönüşüm süreci ve üniversitelerin değişen rolleri. *Eğitim ve Öğretim Araştırmaları Dergisi, 5*(2), 297–307.
Sarwar, M. S., Doherty, T., Watt, J., & Sinnott, R. O. (2013). Towards a virtual research environment for language and literature researchers. *Future Generation Computer Systems, 29*(2), 549–559.
Saykili, A. (2019). Higher education in the digital age: The impact of digital connective technologies. *Journal of Educational Technology and Online Learning, 2*(1), 1–15.
Sharma, S. K., Palvia, S. C. J., & Kumar, K. (2017). Changing the landscape of higher education: From standardized learning to customized learning. *Journal of Information Technology Case and Application Research, 19*(2), 75–80.
Sobaih, A. E. E., Hasanein, A. M., & Abu Elnasr, A. E. (2020). Responses to COVID-19 in higher education: Social media usage for sustaining formal academic communication in developing countries. *Sustainability, 12*(16), 6520.
Staley, D. J., & Trinkle, D. A. (2011). The changing landscape of higher education. *Educause Review, 46*(1), 15–32.
Stecuła, K., & Wolniak, R. (2022). Influence of COVID-19 pandemic on dissemination of innovative e-learning tools in higher education in Poland. *Journal of Open Innovation: Technology, Market, and Complexity, 8*(2), 89.
Tang, Y., & Hew, K. F. (2017). Using Twitter for education: Beneficial or simply a waste of time? *Computers & Education, 106*, 97–118.
Vale, A., Coimbra, N., Martins, A., & Oliveira, J. (2021). *Education and innovation: Impacts during a global pandemic in a higher education institution*. SHS Web of Conferences.
Zuiderwijk, A., Jeffery, K., Bailo, D., & Yin, Y. (2016). Using open research data for public policy making: Opportunities of virtual research environments. Paper presented at the Conference for E-democracy and open government, Krems an der Donau, Austria.
Zuiderwijk, A., & Yin, Y. (2018). Open education global 2018 conference-transforming education through open approaches open science, open government, and open data: Creating an impact through open online education and virtual research environments. In *Open Education Global Conference 2018*: OEGlobal2018.

Chapter 17

Deconstructing Value Creation in Indian Management Education: A Learner Journey Perspective

Bharath Rajan and Sujatha Natarajan

Prin. L. N. Welingkar Institute of Management Development and Research (WeSchool), Mumbai, Maharashtra, India

Abstract

Value creation in management education has been argued to happen throughout an academic programme. This study adopts a learner-centric value-perspective approach that advances the view that value creation is not a unitary occurrence but accrues in different forms in each phase of the learner journey process. As learners progress through a management programme, we focus on four key phases in the learner's journey – pre-admission, pre-programme commencement, programme duration, and post-programme completion. These phases correspond to the learner's transitioning from a prospect to having secured admission to actively attending classes to having graduated. Accordingly, in each phase of the learner journey in an Indian management education programme, this study (a) maps the institute's actions, (b) identifies the learner touchpoints, and (c) evaluates the potential learner engagement levels from the respective touchpoints. This study categorizes the emergent value in each phase in the learner journey as the exploration of value, the commencement of value, the formation and augmentation of value, and the accrual of value. The study then concludes with identifying future research areas. Such an approach to deconstructing value can aid management institutions in nurturing talented and engaged learners.

Keywords: Value creation; value deconstruction; Indian management education; learner journey; learner experience

Introduction

India has the second-largest pool of MBAs in the world, and a growing number of MBA candidates are choosing to attend Indian management schools (Bhattacharyya, 2022; Khatun & Dar, 2019). On the supply side, however, we observe a drop in the total number of AICTE[1]-approved management institutes as well as a gap between enrolment levels and sanctioned intake (AICTE Dashboard, 2023; Rana et al., 2020). By addressing this imbalance between supply and demand, possibilities can arise in the future for Indian management education.

A large number of approved Indian management institutes (3,000+) operate in a highly competitive landscape and face several challenges such as minimal visibility in global rankings (*The Economic Times*, 2023). Additionally, Indian management institutes are also grappling with the short-term problems posed by the pandemic, paucity of qualified talent and resources, changing needs of learners, technological disruptions that have forced institutions to reevaluate their internal and external partnerships, teaching pedagogies, and student pathways while creating long-term plans for institutional transformation (Marmolejo & Groccia, 2022; Rana et al., 2020).

From a learners' viewpoint, a few of the post-pandemic difficulties affecting learners include shorter attention spans, behavioural, and mental health challenges (Avanse, n.d.; Malik et al., 2020), and social media fatigue that has adversely impacted their academic performance (Kuhfeld et al., 2022). From an overall student satisfaction viewpoint, studies have shown that the student's motivation, retention, and building of an engaged alumni community are influenced by the delivery of a high-quality student educational experience (Bruce & Edgington, 2008; Elliott, 2002; Elliott & Shin, 2002). Similarly, student engagement is one of the key factors that can increase MBA students' intention to remain loyal to the institution after graduation (Lee, 2008).

The above-mentioned issues that learners and management institutes face can be viewed as a value problem. To address this, we take inspiration from businesses that have realized that it is no longer enough to compete based on their products and services but rather based on how well they serve their consumers. Herein, designing customer journeys that begin from a customer needs perspective instead of what the organization can or wants to provide is important (Duncan et al., 2016). Also, looking beyond touchpoints to focus on the consumer's end-to-end experience can maximize customer satisfaction (Maechler et al., 2016).

Therefore, this study aims to investigate value creation in an Indian management institute that focuses on the entire learner's journey and the learner's touchpoints. Also, it deconstructs the created value to identify value typologies emerging in each learner journey phase. Such a focus could enhance learner satisfaction and engagement levels while creating opportunities for sustained value generation for both the institute and the learner.

---

[1] AICTE – All India Council for Technical Education – a statutory national-level body for technical education and management education, functioning under the Department of Higher Education in India.

This study is organized as follows: First, we present the related literature upon which the study is developed. Next, we explain the study background and approach. Then, we present the conceptual model that explains the value creation and value deconstruction in Indian management education. Here, we identify the specific institute actions taken in each of the four learner phases, namely (a) pre-admission phase, (b) pre-programme phase, (c) programme duration phase, and (d) post-programme completion phase. Further, we categorize the resultant value typology in each of the learner phases. Finally, we conclude by offering an agenda for future research.

Related Literature

Studies have examined value creation in higher education from diverse perspectives – a relational viewpoint that examines how trust, the university's reputation, and the quality of student–faculty interactions affect student perceived value (Fernández et al., 2010); the use of social media platforms for value creation (Voropai et al., 2019); the focus on consumer behaviour and identifying needs and desires as a means for value creation (Silva et al., 2020a); and that value of management education is realized over time, i.e., some of the benefits accrue upon programme completion (Kumar & Rajan, 2017; Salunkhe et al., 2022), among others.

According to research, value creation and student satisfaction are both results of individual or group efforts (by an institution, a teacher, and a student) (Silva et al., 2020b). In this regard, the studies on student satisfaction have identified that (a) student centeredness and instructional effectiveness are key determinants of how satisfied a learner is with his/her overall educational experience (Elliott, 2002), and (b) factors that influence student satisfaction are not only academic quality but also include university core services, information technology services, and skill building. These factors are interrelated and recommend a holistic approach rather than addressing each factor in isolation (Lai et al., 2015).

Additionally, studies have revealed that (a) students tend to evaluate their course based on their experience (Centoni & Maruotti, 2021); (b) student satisfaction is influenced by non-academic aspects such as students' feelings of belonging and views of the institution's responsiveness and concern (Gibson, 2010); (c) student satisfaction impacts the students' motivation and retention (Elliott & Shin, 2002); and (d) student satisfaction can result in positive word-of-mouth communication and the willingness to give back to the institute after they graduate (Bruce & Edgington, 2008). Table 17.1 presents the selected related literature regarding value creation.

Building on prior literature, this chapter proposes a conceptual framework that tracks the value creation in management education while paying specific attention to deconstructing how and when the value has emerged. Therefore, the study focuses on the learner and the phases in the learner journey in a two-year full-time MBA programme in India. Here, we consider the end-to-end learner journey that begins from the learner being a prospective applicant to an enrolled student and finally becoming a graduate and an alum. In this regard, this study advances that value emerging from each learner phase can be characterized differently.

Table 17.1. Selected Related Literature.

Study	Background	Concepts covered					Study Context	Study Approach	Key Findings
		Learner Journey	Learner Engagement	Learner Touchpoint	Value Creation	Value Deconstruction			
Fernández et al. (2010)	Analyses the effects of the quality of the student-professor interaction, trust, and university image on student perceived value.	No	No	No	Yes	No	Spain	Empirical	Perceptions of value in the educational service encounter are influenced by the quality of the student–professor interaction, the student's trust, and the university's image. Findings also reveal that perceived value contributes to students' satisfaction and loyalty.
Judson and Taylor (2014)	Evaluate the marketization of education from a service science perspective.	No	No	No	Yes	No	USA	Empirical	Evidence of a substantial disconnect developing between what institutions of higher learning are trying to achieve (learning) in their value propositions and those attributes important to students' means-end evaluations of specific courses (relevance).

Study	Background	Concepts covered					Study Context	Study Approach	Key Findings
		Learner Journey	Learner Engagement	Learner Touchpoint	Value Creation	Value Deconstruction			
Horwitch and Stohr (2012)	Examine the major environmental changes that must be addressed by technology management and the skills that future technology management graduates will require.	No	No	No	Yes	No	Global	Analytical	Suggests that the capabilities of technology management graduates are the primary source of value of technology management programmes to industry and society. Also proposes that the designers of technology management programmes recognize four general classes of students in the technology arena: managers, analytics, entrepreneurs, and integrators.
Stankeviciene and Vaiciukevičiūtė (2016)	Investigate value creation from the perspective of internationalization and employee engagement.	Yes	No	Yes	Yes	No	Lithuania	Analytical	Professors' internationality and the institution's service and administration resource environment influenced the overall value creation the most.

(*Continued*)

Table 17.1. (*Continued*)

Study	Background	Concepts covered					Study Context	Study Approach	Key Findings
		Learner Journey	Learner Engagement	Learner Touchpoint	Value Creation	Value Deconstruction			
Dingyloudi et al. (2019)	Examine expected and experienced values of participation in learning communities in higher education.	No	No	No	Yes	No	Germany	Empirical	Identified the key values attributed by students to their community participation and identified the key values attributed by students to the community as a social learning context.
Silva et al. (2020b)	Examine the students' quality of life through a value-creation perspective.	No	No	Yes	Yes	No	Brazil	Empirical	The students' quality of life is directly linked to student satisfaction and value creation, emerging from individual or joint actions of the institution, faculty, and students.
Correia and Santos (2021)	Examine (a) the public perception of value produced by public higher education, (b) the indicators that can promote the importance of public higher education, and (c) criticisms about the public value concept.	No	No	Yes	Yes	No	Global/ developing countries	Analytical	Better use of communication channels in public management is necessary to communicate the creation of public value by universities. Spillover of value creation must be communicated outside the academic community to positively impact the perception of value creation.

Study	Background	Concepts covered					Study Context	Study Approach	Key Findings
		Learner Journey	Learner Engagement	Learner Touchpoint	Value Creation	Value Deconstruction			
Naheen and Elsharnouby (2021)	Investigate the effects university brand personality and student–university identification has on student participation and citizenship behaviour.	No	Yes	No	Yes	No	Qatar	Empirical	The sincerity and lively facets of university brand personality play a vital role in informing student–university identification. Also found that students who identify with their university engage in various forms of participation and citizenship behaviours.
Salunkhe et al. (2022)	Investigate value creation by (a) identifying nine value categories in which value can be created and managed, (b) advancing a stakeholder engagement approach in creating and managing value, (c) identifying and categorizing value measures as contiguous and future measures, and (d) recognizing the resources and capabilities needed to create and manage value.	No	Yes	No	Yes	No	India	Conceptual	Defines value, identifies nine value categories and recognizes resources and capabilities required for creating and managing value.

(Continued)

Table 17.1. (Continued)

Study	Background	Concepts covered					Study Context	Study Approach	Key Findings
		Learner Journey	Learner Engagement	Learner Touchpoint	Value Creation	Value Deconstruction			
Current study	Investigate value creation that focuses on the entire learner's journey and the learner's touchpoints. Also deconstructs the created value to identify value typologies emerging in each learner journey phase.	Yes	Yes	Yes	Yes	Yes	India	Conceptual	Advances the view that value creation accrues in different forms in each phase of the learner journey process and not as a unitary occurrence. Classifies the emergent value in each phase in the learner journey as the exploration of value, the commencement of value, the formation and augmentation of value, and the accrual of value.

Source: Compiled by the authors.

Additionally, we contend that value creation cannot be viewed as a unitary occurrence, as it occurs continuously throughout a learner's journey. Recognizing this, we deconstruct the value created in each of the four key learner journey phases.

Conceptual Framework

To develop the conceptual framework, we consider a typical Indian management institute that has the following attributes – (i) has a governing board/trust led by a dean/director; (ii) has the requisite resources (i.e., financial, technical, human, infrastructure (physical and digital); (iii) offers AICTE-approved programmes that are nationally accredited; (iv) promotes stakeholder engagements for teaching, research, training, and consultancy; (v) undertakes various marketing campaigns to promote its programmes for recruitment of students; (vi) requires applicants to fulfil the necessary eligibility requirements and pass a nationally recognized competitive test; and (vii) requires enrolled students to pursue internships during the two-year MBA programme (Salunkhe et al., 2022).

In such a management institute, we identify the four key phases in the learner's journey as (a) pre-admission phase, (b) pre-programme phase, (c) programme duration phase, and (d) post-programme completion phase. Within each phase of the learner journey, this study (a) traces the institute actions, (b) identifies the learner touchpoints, (c) evaluates the potential engagement levels for the learners from the respective learner touchpoints, (d) impacts the institute, and (e) classifies the emergent value from each of the phases in the learner's journey. Fig. 17.1 illustrates the approach we adopt to develop the conceptual framework.

As illustrated in Fig. 17.1, we propose that the potential engagement responses in learners resulting from the institute's actions (in each of the phases) can be classified into the following – know, do, and feel. Here, 'know' refers to the learners

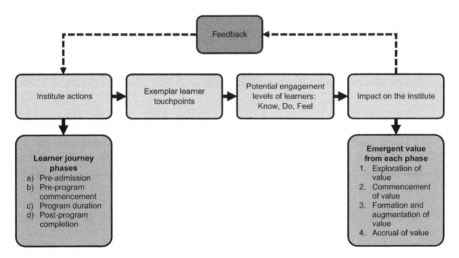

Fig. 17.1.   Approach to Conceptual Framework. *Source*: Authors' own.

acquiring information/knowledge distinct to the phases, 'do' relates to the actions of learners using information/knowledge acquired, and 'feel' refers to the learner's sense of belonging exhibited towards the institute. Here, we assume that all institute actions will result in a certain level of know, do, and feel. Our advancement of the know-do-feel classification is based on prior studies in engagement across various study contexts that have advanced the notion of engaged users exhibiting qualities of knowing, doing, and feeling (Kahn, 2010; O'Shea et al., 2015; Whitmarsh et al., 2013). Further, we advance that the acts of knowing, doing, and feeling can result in three levels of potential engagement among learners namely high, moderate, and low. The institute's attention to understanding the levels of learner engagement in each of the phases in the learner's journey can allow them to take necessary institutional interventions to ensure continuous value generation.

Following the classification of engagement response categories, we then identify the corresponding impact on the institute. After the creation of value, we propose that the created value can be deconstructed (from each of the four phases) as follows – exploration of value, commencement of value, formation and augmentation of value, and accrual of value. If the institute fails to perform any of the above critical actions in the four phases, we expect it to lead to value destruction. Finally, we complete this process by tracing a feedback loop to inform the institute of further refinements. Table 17.2 presents the four phases of the learners' journey and the respective learner touchpoints along the value realizations in each of the phases.

According to Table 17.2, in the pre-admission phase, the institute's actions are primarily focused on the following two aspects:

1. Brand-building initiatives. Involves the institute's actions towards increasing awareness of its offerings and reaching out to the largest number of aspirants. Additionally, attention is given to matching its programme with the appropriate target groups. Here, we believe that these actions can result in learners' potential engagement level being moderate in know, low in do, and moderate in feel. Here, the institute undertakes actions such as hosting information sessions/webinars and student admission fairs and launching marketing campaigns (using traditional and digital platforms) to promote its brand and offerings.
2. Social media marketing. Involves leveraging media analytics (e.g., search engine optimization, click-through rate, conversion rate, website traffic, etc.) and using new-age technologies (e.g., chatbots, augmented reality (AR)/virtual reality (VR)). We believe that these actions can result in learners' potential engagement level being high in know, low in do, and high in feel. The potential impact on the institute includes enhanced brand image, more awareness of its programme, a better understanding of the prospective learner and their needs, and a higher lead-to-conversion rate, to name a few.

Based on this, we refer to the value emerging from this phase as 'exploration of value' as the institute is exploring avenues to initiate value creation for the learner

Table 17.2. Learners' Journey, Learner Touchpoints, and Value Realizations.

Phases in the Learner Journey	Institute Actions	Exemplar Learner Touch-points Through …	Potential Engagement Levels of Learners in …			Impact on institute	Value Typology
			Know	Do	Feel		
Pre-admission phase	Branding and social media marketing	• Information sessions and student fairs • Marketing campaigns (includes traditional and digital media)	Moderate	Low	Moderate	• Enhancement in the brand image of the institute. • Improved visibility of the programme • Ability to know the prospective students.	Exploration of value
		• Social media analytics (e.g., target marketing) • Search engine optimization (SEO) • Digital aids (e.g., apps, kiosks) • New-age technologies (e.g., chatbots, AR, etc.) • Webinars • Virtual campus tours	High	Low	High	• Improved conversion-to-lead generation. • Attract the right candidates for the institute. • Ability to focus on high-quality applications. • Better understanding of the learner's needs and profiles through feedback.	
Pre-programme phase	Campus life connect	• Welcome kits. • Administrative/campus assistance (scholarship support, hostel facilities) • Peer group inclusion	Moderate	Low	Moderate	• Fulfilment of intake capacity. • Better retention of admitted students. • Enhanced brand image.	Commencement of value

(Continued)

Table 17.2. (*Continued*)

Phases in the Learner Journey	Institute Actions	Exemplar Learner Touch-points Through …	Potential Engagement Levels of Learners in …			Impact on institute	Value Typology
			Know	Do	Feel		
		• Personalized support through people and technology (e.g., welcome kits, inquiry sessions, boarding options)	High	Moderate	High	• Highly engaged admitted students. • Stronger brand identification. • Higher ease and efficiency of onboarding. • Better understanding of the incoming class profile.	
	Select stakeholder interactions	• Interactive sessions (e.g., with potential recruiters, alumni, and partners) • Alumni-led sessions • Industry competitions	Moderate High	Moderate Moderate	Moderate High	• Better informed student base. • Establishment of stakeholder connections. • Increase in early opportunities for internships, placement, mentoring, and grooming. • Stronger connection with stakeholders.	
	Preparatory interventions	• Foundational preparatory courses/material • Course materials and e-learning content	High	Moderate	Moderate	• Even the distribution of academic workload. • Well-equipped student base.	

Phases in the Learner Journey	Institute Actions	Exemplar Learner Touchpoints Through …	Potential Engagement Levels of Learners in …			Impact on institute	Value Typology
			Know	Do	Feel		
		• Bridge courses • Pre-boot camps • Buddy programmes	High	High	High	• Early start to spotting and developing talent. • Nurturing awakened learners. • Establishing opportunities for higher-order learning and engagement.	
Programme duration phase	Student orientation	• Orientation sessions • Foundational programmes • 'Expert talk' series • Immersion programmes with partner organizations • Boot camps • Social immersion programmes • Sponsored/customized SWAYAM and MOOCs	High	High	High	• Gain stakeholder connections (e.g., industry and alumni). • Continuous revenue stream. • Higher stakeholder engagement. • Involved student base. • Higher brand visibility. • Enhanced potential for establishing collaborative initiatives.	Formation and augmentation of value
	Curricular delivery	• Courses (teaching, learning assessment) • Projects • Competitions • Conferences • Student portal • LMS • Various pedagogical approaches • Exchange programmes				• Achievement of programme outcomes. • Improvement in placement performance. • Strengthening of revenue streams. • Ability to attract the right talent (students and faculty). • Better ranking and recognition.	

(Continued)

Table 17.2. (Continued)

Phases in the Learner Journey	Institute Actions	Exemplar Learner Touch-points Through …	Potential Engagement Levels of Learners in …			Impact on institute	Value Typology
			Know	Do	Feel		
		• Anytime, anywhere learning • Simulations • Virtual labs • Virtual company visits, virtual internships • Personalized online self-paced modules. • Omnichannel delivery • Dashboards to inform students about their academic progress				• Ability to track student progression (academic and non-academic). • Ability to establish overall efficient and effective systems. • Enhancements to brand image. • Positive word of mouth.	
	Co/extra-curricular delivery	• Real-world projects • Research competitions • Grooming • Certifications • Sports & cultural festivals (domestic and global) • Development labs (e.g., leadership labs, functional/domain-specific labs, behavioural labs, innovation/entrepreneurship labs) • Hackathons • Institute's Innovation Council (IIC)				• Develop knowledgeable students. • Ability to offer better career prospects for students. • Establishing competitive advantage. • Holistic development of students. • Ability to create an entrepreneurial ecosystem. • Ability to attract talent, funding, and opportunities.	

Phases in the Learner Journey	Institute Actions	Exemplar Learner Touch-points Through …	Potential Engagement Levels of Learners in …			Impact on institute	Value Typology
			Know	Do	Feel		
Post-programme completion phase		• Alumni portal • Alumni meets/reunions. • Alumni awards • Participation in the student selection process, academic/advisory boards, and recruitment panels • Providing internships and placement opportunities • Mentoring and grooming support • Alumni fundraiser • Continuing education • Upskilling and mentoring programmes for alumni • Alumni-led campaigns • Alumni-led recruitment • Alumni start-ups	Moderate	High	High	• Establish alumni connect. • Leverage through alumni successes. • Receive alumni endowments. • Develop brand ambassadors.	Accrual of value

Source: Authors' own.

Note: SWAYAM (Study Webs of Active-Learning for Young Aspiring Minds) is a digital platform initiated by the Government of India designed to promote access, equity and quality in education.

community. Also, in the pre-admission phase, aspirants are exploring and evaluating multiple options for study but have not yet applied to the institute.

The pre-programme period is the phase between student enrolment and the start of the programme. Here, the institute's actions can be categorized in the following three areas:

1. Establishing campus life connections. Here, the institute provides enrolled learners with welcome kits, and administrative and campus onboarding support (e.g., for hostels, scholarships, connecting with peers). Such institute actions establish connections with the enrolled students, enhance their engagement levels with the institute and its brand, and thereby fulfil the intake capacity. We contend that the potential engagement levels of learners are moderate for know, low for do, and moderate for feel. In addition, the institute provides personalized support by leveraging people and technology platforms. For example, clarifying individual doubts and providing additional information to facilitate the smooth onboarding process. We contend that the potential engagement levels in learners are high in know, moderate in do, and high in feel.
2. Interactions with select stakeholders. The institute provides interaction opportunities with stakeholders such as industry experts via online and offline sessions to raise awareness and provide early opportunities to enrolled students (for instance, companies that provide scholarship support to deserving students). As a result, we believe that the potential learner engagement levels are moderate in know, do, and feel. Furthermore, the interactions with alumni allow (a) the talent of the enrolled learners to be showcased and noticed and (b) the seeking of summer internships/placement opportunities by the learners. Here, we contend that the potential learner engagement is high in know, moderate in do, and high in feel.
3. Preparatory interventions. These interventions include foundational courses/materials and provide bridge courses/e-learning content to orient students from diverse backgrounds. As a result, we believe that the potential learner engagement levels are high in know, moderate in do, and moderate in feel. Additionally, hosting pre-boot camps and buddy programmes for enrolled learners that provide opportunities to connect with their peers and faculty members and get a glimpse of campus life. Such institute actions provide valuable inputs for identifying early talent and their needs, which can help curate higher-order learning and engagement. As a result, we contend that the potential learner engagement levels in know, do, and feel are high.

Hence, we name the value emerging from this pre-programme phase as the 'commencement of value' as the institute can begin to realize the value in this phase. In this phase, the institute engages with the learners to ensure a smooth onboarding experience into the programme and campus life. Here, the institute's actions can help retain the enrolled learners.

The third phase of the learner journey is the programme duration phase, which is an integral component in the learner's journey. We have identified three broad areas in this phase.

1. Student orientation. Here, the institute conducts a student induction programme to orient enrolled students to the institute's culture, values, and programmes. As part of this, eminent speakers from diverse disciplines are invited to share their leadership insights. In addition, industry/social immersion programmes, experiential learning programmes, and boot camps provide learners with practical exposure and learning as well as opportunities for team bonding opportunity with peers/seniors. This strengthens the institute's brand and stakeholder connections with the industry, the alumni, and the enrolled students. By fulfilling its intake capacity, the institute can realize continuous revenue streams.
2. Curriculum delivery. The management institute with its experienced faculty (which includes industry experts and international faculty) offers an industry-oriented curriculum, thereby creating a conducive learning environment. To nurture learners with the necessary knowledge, skills, and behaviours, the institute uses innovative pedagogies and technology platforms such as simulation, gamification, learning management system (LMS), apps, massive open online courses (MOOCs), self-paced modules, virtual labs, virtual immersions, and assessment tools to track student progression individually. Through such actions in the curriculum delivery, the institute achieves its programme outcomes and strengthens its placement performance and overall positioning of the programme and the institute.
3. Co-curricular activities. Typical co-curricular activities such as competitions, hackathons, labs, exchange programmes, and conferences are made available to learners. Additionally, extracurricular initiatives (e.g., clubs, sports, and cultural activities) are also offered to promote the holistic development of learners. The Institute Innovation Council (IIC), entrepreneurship cells, and incubation labs help nurture innovative and entrepreneurial mindsets among learners. In addition, assessment and development centres (which help learners identify their strengths and areas for development), leadership labs, and behavioural labs prepare learners for their professional careers. Furthermore, the placement cells of management institutes actively work to support students for their summer internships and final placements through the institute's industry connections.

In this phase, the institute has several learner touchpoints to engage with the learners and thereby generate more opportunities to create and consolidate value. As a result of such institute actions during this phase, we contend that the learners' potential level of engagement is high for know, do, and feel. The overall outcomes of such institute actions in this phase lead to higher stakeholder engagement, better ranking and recognition, greater collaborative opportunities, and the ability to attract future talent (i.e., students and faculty). We name the resultant value from this phase as 'formation and augmentation of value'.

In the fourth and final step, i.e., the post-programme completion phase, learners successfully graduate and achieve the status of alumni. Alumni are regarded as key stakeholders for the institute, and numerous accrediting and ranking agencies use alumni progression as one of the yardsticks to assess the institute's performance. In this phase, the institute and its alumni actively interact with each other over time. The institute's actions are focused on creating platforms for periodic engagement with its alumni, such as a dedicated alumni portal, periodic alumni meetings, a registered alumni body, and alumni involvement in institute initiatives (e.g., serving on academic/advisory boards, participating in recruitment processes, providing internships, placement, and mentoring support). Alumni involvement leads to the implementation of several alumni-led initiatives such as fundraising, endowments, consulting, and executive education. In addition, the institute provides access to its entrepreneurial ecosystem to promote alumni-led start-ups. Among the population of alumni that choose to remain engaged with the institution, we expect the alumni to have a moderate level of potential engagement regarding know and a high level of potential engagement regarding do and feel. Such alumni-focused initiatives help the institute build a strong alumni network where alumni serve as brand ambassadors, which further creates opportunities in the future. We term the value emerging in this phase as 'accrual of value', as the institute can continue to create and realize value for its alumni.

Finally, we propose that management institutes have a shorter and real-time feedback loop from each of the learner phases that can unlock useful insights and provide future value-creating opportunities. Consistent and focused efforts are required in pursuing the areas emerging from the learning journey that can reinvent the learner journey and maximize the value-creation potential for management institutes. Such feedback loops can help management institutes quickly adapt their approach to address any challenges and leverage opportunities. For this, the alignment of the leadership vision with the overall organization is critical for sustained value creation.

Agenda for Future Research

In this study so far, we have deconstructed value and identified the emergent value from each of the learner phases in an Indian management institute. The four value typologies identified are the exploration of value, the commencement of value, the formation and augmentation of value, and the accrual of value.

Based on this typology, Table 17.3 advances a research agenda that future researchers can consider. This table is structured to identify the various value typologies in the four learner phases, identify the areas of immediate attention for Indian management institutes, and advance questions for future research. Researchers and management institutes could identify additional areas that can be explored in each of the learner phases.

Therefore, with a learner-focused value perspective, Indian management institutes can unlock several areas that can be pursued to create value. From a policy perspective in India, this study also aligns with the 2020 National Education Policy that revolves around promoting learner-centric education (*Hindustan Times*, 2021).

Table 17.3. Agenda for Future Research.

Learner Phase	Deconstructed value Typology	What We Need to Know	Potential Research Questions (RQs) for the Indian Context
Pre-admission	Exploration of value	• The approach to personalized targeting of management education aspirants • Curating a social media campaign for brand management	• *RQ1*: What personalized and targeted marketing initiatives can management institutes design and implement to attract applicants from a learner skill-set perspective? • *RQ2*: How can management institutes leverage social media analytics and new-age technologies to promote their brand? • *RQ3*: What metrics can be used in real time to increase the conversion rate of aspirants to applicants?
Pre-programme	Commencement of value	• Establishing and managing stakeholder relationships • Personalized support	• *RQ4*: How can management institutes use stakeholder relationships to ensure that the applicants convert into enrolled learners? • *RQ5*: How can management institutes develop applicant personas that can guide the delivery of personalized support?

(Continued)

Table 17.3. *(Continued)*

Learner Phase	Deconstructed value Typology	What We Need to Know	Potential Research Questions (RQs) for the Indian Context
Programme duration	Formation and augmentation of value	• Assessing learner skillset • Personalized learning and development	• *RQ6*: How can management institutes develop dynamic processes to assess and monitor the holistic development of each learner? • *RQ7*: How can management institutes curate a personalized learning path for each enrolled learner? • *RQ8*: What factors should management institutes consider that can lead to the creation of an ecosystem that nurtures entrepreneurial mindset and start-ups?
Post-programme completion	Accrual of value	• Managing alumni engagement	• *RQ9*: How can management institutes design a continuous individualized alumni interaction strategy that can balance alumni needs with the institute's needs? • *RQ10*: What factors influence voluntary alumni financial and non-financial contributions?

Source: Authors' own.

Conclusion

For value to emerge from each of the identified learner phases, the management institute must have the requisite resources (i.e., financial, technical, human, infrastructure (physical and digital)), leadership/board commitment, and active stakeholder networks that can be leveraged to create new offerings that can generate additional resources for the future initiatives. Hence, management institutes must pay close attention to each of the learner touchpoints in the learner journey. While all learner phases are important, management institutes may prioritize specific learner phase(s) and touchpoints based on the learner's need, the institute's context, and priorities.

Additionally, it must be noted that to leverage value-creating opportunities, continuous and close attention is required in the design, implementation, monitoring, and measurement of outcomes of such interventions. Here, new-age technology platforms (e.g., machine learning-based adaptive learning tools, persona mapping techniques for aspirants and learners, etc.) can be leveraged in the launch and rollout of new initiatives to redesign learner journeys. The alignment of leadership vision and employee buy-in is required as the mere launch of such initiatives may not guarantee value as an outcome. Notably, value destruction can happen due to compromised efforts, a lack of effective monitoring and measurement processes, a discontinuity in efforts, resistance to change, a slow response time to learner demands, a lack of leadership buy-in, and a misalignment between management and employees. Such value destruction can adversely impact learner engagement and jeopardize management institutes' future ability to create value (Kumar & Rajan, 2017).

Acknowledgements

We thank the Editors of this book for allowing us to submit this manuscript. We thank the panel and the participants of the *2nd Lincoln International HE Practices Conference*, held on 2–3 November 2023, in Bengaluru for their constructive comments and feedback on this manuscript. Both authors contributed equally to the preparation of this manuscript.

References

AICTE Dashboard. (2023). https://facilities.aicte-india.org/dashboard/pages/dashboardaicte.php

Avanse. (n.d.). *COVID's impact on India's higher education*. Avanse Financial Services. Retrieved September 22, 2023, from https://www.avanse.com/blog/covids-impact-indias-higher-education

Bhattacharyya, R. (2022, April 23). More and more students are opting to study in local business schools. *The Economic Times*. https://economictimes.indiatimes.com/industry/services/education/more-and-more-students-are-opting-to-study-in-local-business-schools/articleshow/91018266.cms?from=mdr

Bruce, G., & Edgington, R. (2008). Factors influencing word-of-mouth recommendations by MBA students: An examination of school quality, educational outcomes, and value of the MBA. *Journal of Marketing for Higher Education*, *18*(1), 79–101. https://doi.org/10.1080/08841240802100303

Centoni, M., & Maruotti, A. (2021). Students' evaluation of academic courses: An exploratory analysis to an Italian case study. *Studies in Educational Evaluation*, *70*, 101054. https://doi.org/10.1016/j.stueduc.2021.101054

Correia, A. B., & Santos, A. M. (2021). Drivers for public value creation in universities and community awareness. *International Journal of Entrepreneurship*, *25*(4), 1–9.

Dingyloudi, F., Strijbos, J.-W., & Laat, M. de. (2019). Value creation: What matters most in communities of learning practice in higher education. *Faculty of Social Sciences – Papers (Archive)*, *62*, 209–223. https://doi.org/10.1016/j.stueduc.2019.05.006

Duncan, E., Fanderl, H., Maechler, N., & Neher, K. (2016). *Customer experience: Creating value through transforming customer journeys* (pp. 3–7). McKinsey Practice Publication. https://www.mckinsey.com/capabilities/growth-marketing-and-sales/our-insights/customer-experience-creating-value-through-transforming-customer-journeys

Elliott, K. M. (2002). Key determinants of student satisfaction. *Journal of College Student Retention: Research, Theory & Practice*, *4*(3), 271–279. https://doi.org/10.2190/B2V7-R91M-6WXR-KCCR

Elliott, K. M., & Shin, D. (2002). Student satisfaction: An alternative approach to assessing this important concept. *Journal of Higher Education Policy and Management*, *24*(2), 197–209. https://doi.org/10.1080/1360080022000013518

Fernández, R., Bonillo, M., Schlesinger, W., & Rivera, P. (2010). Analysis of the value creation in higher institutions: A relational perspective. *Theoretical and Applied Economics*, *10*, 25–36.

Gibson, A. (2010). Measuring business student satisfaction: A review and summary of the major predictors. *Journal of Higher Education Policy and Management*, *32*(3), 251–259. https://doi.org/10.1080/13600801003743349

Hindustan Times. (2021, March 17). NEP aims to overhaul existing education regime, making it more learner-centric. *Hindustan Times*. https://www.hindustantimes.com/ht-school/nep-aims-to-overhaul-existing-education-regime-making-it-more-learnercentric-101615983037779.html

Horwitch, M., & Stohr, E. A. (2012). Transforming technology management education: Value creation-learning in the early twenty-first century. *Journal of Engineering and Technology Management*, *29*(4), 489–507. https://doi.org/10.1016/j.jengtecman.2012.07.003

Judson, K., & Taylor, S. (2014). Moving from marketization to marketing of higher education: The co-creation of value in higher education. *Higher Education Studies*, *4*, 51–67. https://doi.org/10.5539/hes.v4n1p51

Kahn, W. A. (2010). The essence of engagement: Lessons from the field. In S. L. Albrecht (Ed.), *Handbook of employee engagement: Perspectives, issues, research and practice* (pp. 20–30). Edward Elgar Publishing. https://doi.org/10.4337/9781849806374.00008

Khatun, A., & Dar, S. N. (2019). Management education in India: The challenges of changing scenario. *Entrepreneurship Education*, *2*(1), 19–38. https://doi.org/10.1007/s41959-019-00010-7

Kuhfeld, M., Soland, J., Lewis, K., & Morton, E. (2022). *The pandemic has had devastating impacts on learning. What will it take to help students catch up?* Brookings. https://www.brookings.edu/articles/the-pandemic-has-had-devastating-impacts-on-learning-what-will-it-take-to-help-students-catch-up/

Kumar, V., & Rajan, B. (2017). What's in it for me? The creation and destruction of value for firms from stakeholders. *Journal of Creating Value*, *3*(2), 142–156. https://doi.org/10.1177/2394964317723449

Lai, M. M., Lau, S. H., Mohamad Yusof, N. A., & Chew, K. W. (2015). Assessing antecedents and consequences of student satisfaction in higher education: Evidence from Malaysia. *Journal of Marketing for Higher Education*, *25*(1), 45–69. https://doi.org/10.1080/08841241.2015.1042097

Lee, J. (2008). Effects of leadership and leader-member exchange on innovativeness. *Journal of Managerial Psychology*, *23*(6), 670–687. https://doi.org/10.1108/02683940810894747

Maechler, N., Neher, K., & Park, R. (2016). *To maximize customer satisfaction, companies have long emphasized touchpoints. But doing so can divert attention from the more important issue: The customer's end-to-end journey.* McKinsey & Company.

Malik, A., Dhir, A., Kaur, P., & Johri, A. (2020). Correlates of social media fatigue and academic performance decrement: A large cross-sectional study. *Information Technology & People*, *34*(2), 557–580. https://doi.org/10.1108/ITP-06-2019-0289

Marmolejo, F. J., & Groccia, J. E. (2022). Reimagining and redesigning teaching and learning in the post-pandemic world. *New Directions for Teaching and Learning*, *2022*(169), 21–37. https://doi.org/10.1002/tl.20480

Naheen, F., & Elsharnouby, T. (2021). You are what you communicate: On the relationships among university brand personality, identification, student participation, and citizenship behaviour. *Journal of Marketing for Higher Education*, *34*(2), 1–22. https://doi.org/10.1080/08841241.2021.1992814

O'Shea, S., Stone, C., & Delahunty, J. (2015). "I 'feel' like I am at university even though I am online." Exploring how students narrate their engagement with higher education institutions in an online learning environment. *Distance Education*, *36*(1), 41–58. https://doi.org/10.1080/01587919.2015.1019970

Rana, S., Anand, A., Prashar, S., & Haque, M. M. (2020). A perspective on the positioning of Indian business schools post COVID-19 pandemic. *International Journal of Emerging Markets*, *17*(2), 353–367. https://doi.org/10.1108/IJOEM-04-2020-0415

Salunkhe, U., Rajan, B., & Natarajan, S. (2022). Creating and managing value in Indian management education. *Journal of Creating Value*, *8*(2), 253–283. https://doi.org/10.1177/23949643221118153

Silva, M., Silva, L., & Brambilla, F. (2020a). A bibliographical analysis in the literature of value co-creation in private higher education between the years 2006 to 2016. *Independent Journal of Management & Production*, *11*, 1323. https://doi.org/10.14807/ijmp.v11i4.1136

Silva, M., Silva, L., & Brambilla, F. (2020b). Value co-creation: A study of life quality at an university in the south Brazil. *Independent Journal of Management & Production*, *11*, 833. https://doi.org/10.14807/ijmp.v11i3.1026

Stankeviciene, J., & Vaiciukevičiūtė, A. (2016). Value creation for stakeholders in higher education management. *E+M Ekonomie a Management*, *19*, 17–32. https://doi.org/10.15240/tul/001/2016-1-002

The Economic Times. (2023, February 13). Six B-schools from India in this year's financial times list of global top 100 MBA institutes. *The Economic Times*. https://economictimes.indiatimes.com/industry/services/education/six-b-schools-from-india-in-this-years-financial-times-list-of-global-top-100-mba-institutes/articleshow/97857141.cms?from=mdr

Voropai, O., Pichyk, K., & Chala, N. (2019). Increasing competitiveness of higher education in Ukraine through value co-creation strategy. *Economics & Sociology*, *12*(4), 228–240. https://doi.org/10.14254/2071-789X.2019/12-4/14

Whitmarsh, L., O'Neill, S., & Lorenzoni, I. (2013). Public engagement with climate change: What do we know and where do we go from here? *International Journal of Media & Cultural Politics*, *9*(1), 7–25.

Chapter 18

Business Education: COVID-19 and Beyond

Swapna Pradhan

Welingkar Institute of Management Development and Research (WeSchool), Mumbai, Maharashtra, India

Abstract

> Increasingly, we believe, B schools are at a crossroads and will have to take a hard look at their value propositions. (Datar et al., 2011)

While this was said more than a decade ago, it could not be further from the truth even today. In early 2020, the pandemic, a black swan-like event, struck suddenly, forcing educational institutions to adapt in the blink of an eye. Business schools (B-Schools) too had to transition and adapt to a new learning normal. Platforms like Webex, Zoom, Microsoft Teams, Google Meet, etc. became the new classrooms across the globe. The pandemic forced the industry to change and enabled the adoption of technology much faster than what was estimated. The metaphor of the chrysalis is apt in the context of B-Schools as they emerged out of the pandemic. The new order required B-Schools to relook at teaching pedagogy, learning mechanisms, methodologies for evaluation, collaborations, and industry connect. While digital literacy gave way to digital citizenship, there was a need to nurture it responsibly. As students move forward in their journey of becoming digital citizens, it becomes necessary to evolve norms and practices that will be acceptable.

Keywords: Business education; COVID-19; technology; pedagogy; collaboration

---

Global Higher Education Practices in Times of Crisis:
Questions for Sustainability and Digitalization, 311–325
Copyright © 2025 by Swapna Pradhan
Published under exclusive licence by Emerald Publishing Limited
doi:10.1108/978-1-83797-052-020241019

Introduction

In March 2020, the world and its citizens woke up to the harsh reality of the pandemic. Most countries went into a lockdown which meant limiting human interaction and other restrictions on movement and conduct of day-to-day chores and businesses. This was a scenario not faced by most in their lifetime. It required a change in the way people lived and worked. The education sector too was severely impacted with the closing down of schools and colleges. The only option available was to conduct their businesses online. Platforms like Webex, Zoom, Microsoft Teams, Google Meet, etc. became the new classrooms. The pandemic forced the education industry to change and adopt technology much faster than what was estimated.

This chapter is reflective in nature and draws upon published secondary data sources from authenticated resources and readily available databases. Data from World Bank, World Economic Forum, and International Monetary Fund; select research papers from the ProQuest database; and journal articles have been referred to build the synthesis.

This chapter broadly traces the evolution of business education and the changes that have taken place therein and the triggers for the change. The next section of this chapter brings out the views that have been articulated by educationists and thinkers – in terms of what ails business education. It is observed that the need for a change in business school (B-School) education was articulated much before the pandemic. How B-Schools dealt with the pandemic is covered next, followed by the dynamic changes in the industry. These changes necessitate new skills in B-School graduates. What B-Schools can do to adapt to the changing future makes the penultimate section of this chapter.

Business Education Over the Years: Looking Back

In the context of this chapter, business education is considered as defined in the Merriam Webster dictionary as 'an education designed for use in business, training in subjects such as business administration, finance, which are useful in developing general business knowledge and training in subjects which are useful in developing commercially useful skills'.

Education for management or management education as we know it today took root at multiple centres across Europe and America at similar points in time. The world today follows either the American or the European thought process in management education. It is believed that the first institution for commerce was the Escola do Comercio, founded in Lisbon in 1755 after the earthquake. The school was set up to train public administrators to manage taxes and disbursements. The origins of B-School education can be traced back to the establishment of Ecole Spéciale de Commerce (ESCP) in 1819 in Paris. The first American B-School was the Wharton School of Finance and Economy at the University of Pennsylvania, established in 1881 with an endowment from Philadelphia businessman Joseph Wharton. Taking the lead from Wharton, many universities over the next two decades forayed into management education. The Harvard School of Business and Administration was established in 1908 and focused on postgraduate education. Thus, business education and B-Schools emerged from a basic need for professionals who understood specific domains. These are related to the economy, finance, and areas of general management.

Post-World War II, the changes in the methods manufacturing and the overall organizational structures in the industry led to a change in the managerial issues that needed to be addressed. During the period 1819–1945, the Industrial Revolution played a key role in influencing the type of business enterprises which evolved. This was in terms of size of business, number of people, etc. as compared to a small business. Thus, the kind of person needed to manage the same was different, and this played a role in how business education evolved at that time. This was typically seen as an age when the B-Schools were being set up and *the creation of the discipline of management or business education*.

As the number of B-Schools increased in America and across the world, the need for monitoring quality led to the setting up of Association to Advance Collegiate Schools of Business (AACSB) – in 1916. The importance of accreditations gradually came in. This was also a period when the curriculum in many B-Schools became codified in terms of what would be taught. Henri Fayol, the classical management thinker in the early 20th century, put forth the idea that a large part of the manager's job was to plan, organize, direct, and control. The discipline of management revolved around this thinking.

The period post-1945 till 2000 is often termed as a span when business education became more definitive. In America, reports by the Bennis (2014) played a key role in shaping what would emerge as a scientific and a stand-alone discipline. The emphasis on research at the faculty end and the dictum of publish or perish led to a clamour for publishing in so-called A category journals. The emergence of B-School rankings impacted the kind of students that were drawn to them. The introduction of the World Wide Web in 1991, initiated multiple changes in the world, one such change was the start of computer-based learning and online courses. This offered an opportunity to working professionals and adult learners to enhance their skills.

The period between 2000 and 2020 saw many dynamic changes in the environment which pushed B-School to evolve and adapt (see Fig. 18.1). The financial crisis of 2008 raised questions on ethics and morality in the context of B-School curriculum. Notable changes were caused by the spread of globalization and the rapid evolution of technology. Globalization enabled many B-Schools in America and Europe to spread their wings, by setting up campuses in parts of Asia and the Middle East. As competition became intense, the need for accreditation grew in significance.

At this point in time, all MBA programmes largely looked the same. Europe saw the launch of one-year MBA programmes which focused on students with prior work experience. It was predicted by many that massive open online courses (MOOCs) like Khan Academy, Coursera, Udemy, among others would be the next big thing in business education. However, the same did not really happen. Since inception, business education has undergone multiple iterations. Environmental factors have triggered a change and influenced the evolution of B-Schools and in turn business education.

```
┌─────────────────────┐    ┌─────────────────────┐    ┌─────────────────────┐
│      1819 – 1945    │    │     1946 – 2000     │    │     2000 – 2020     │
│ Industrial Revolution│    │ More definitive with│    │   Financial Crisis  │
│  Monitoring quality │    │  wide web - Online  │    │Globalization, Compe-│
│ (AACSB) Accreditation│    │       Courses       │    │tition Rankings of   │
│   More Definitive   │    │   Multiple Campuses │    │      bschools       │
│                     │    │        MOOC's       │    │  Changing skill     │
│                     │    │                     │    │  requirements       │
│                     │    │                     │    │Understanding of     │
│                     │    │                     │    │global markets and   │
│                     │    │                     │    │culture              │
│                     │    │                     │    │  Sustainability     │
└─────────────────────┘    └─────────────────────┘    └─────────────────────┘
```

Fig. 18.1. Factors Which Have Influenced a Change in B-School Curriculum. *Source*: Created by the author.

What Ails Business Education?

Many academics and researchers over the years have flagged the need for a change in business education. It has been described as

> An industry that, if not actually in crisis, is certainly suffering from a bad case of existential angst. (Thomas et al., 2014)

As early as April 2002, the Management Education Taskforce of AACSB had raised a flag on the relevance of B-School curriculum in the context. As early as April 2002, the Management Education Taskforce of AACSB had raised a flag on the relevance of B-School curriculum. AACSB recommended teach 'basic management skills, such as communications, interpersonal skills, multicultural skills, negotiations, leadership development, and change management … and prepare managers for global responsibility'.

Several academics and thinkers have been vocal on what ails business education much before the outbreak of the pandemic. Mintzberg (2004) stressed the need for a different approach to management education, whereby practising managers learn from their own experience. He emphasized the need to build the art and the craft back into business education. Select views articulated by other authors are presented in Table 18.1.

Thus, it can be summarized that what ails management education had come to the fore much before the outbreak of the pandemic.

Business Education and the Pandemic

Persons in academia and those associated with higher education have found the transition to online teaching[1] a life-changing experience. Changes have been

---

[1] Online teaching may be defined as a learning experience that uses a variety of internet-based supporting technologies (e.g., virtual learning platforms, videoconferencing packages, smart phones, and laptops, etc.) for use in synchronous or asynchronous environments.

Table 18.1. Select Literature on Changes in Business Education.

Author	Title of the Paper	Discussion	Contribution
Friga P et al. (2003)	Changes in Graduate Management Education and New Business School Strategies for the 21st Century	Strategic options for business schools are examined, considering that within the next 10-20 years, major changes in the demand and supply of education are likely. The paper emphasises the need that management educators need to develop careful strategies that consider the drivers of change such as globalization, disruptive technologies, demographic shifts, and deregulation.	The research presents an overview of management education value chain. Although dominant now, over the next decade, U.S. business schools are likely to share the spotlight with strong international schools. The value chain is used to examine the past 50 years of management education. The paper emphasises that rather than abandoning progress made in business school processes. over the past 50 years and returning completely to the "Corporate-Based Era," suggests moving to the "Student-Based Era."
Bennis W and O'Toole (2005)	How Business Schools Lost their way Article	Delves into multiple causes of what is wrong with business school education.	Highlights the lack of **practical aspects in business school curriculum.** The need for reforming business education by **adding areas which are multi-disciplinary in nature and include other forms of knowledge.**
Schoemaker Paul (2008)	Future challenges of business: Rethinking management education	The traditional paradigm of business schools, with its strong focus on analytical models and reductionism, is not well suited to **handle the ambiguity and high rate of change facing many industries today.**	The paper highlights the domain changes that have taken place in the world and those who were blindsided as a consequence of ignoring these changes. It highlights implications for business schools in terms of teaching, research and at an institutional level.

(Continued)

Table 18.1. (*Continued*)

Author	Title of the Paper	Discussion	Contribution
Thomas H, and Cornuel E (2012)	The Business schools in transition? Issues of impact, legitimacy, capabilities and re-invention	The paper examines the impact and **environmental influences on management education including issues of globalization, global sustainability and advances in digital and social media.** It also examines the challenges and criticisms of management education covering issues of legitimacy, business model sustainability and the need for change in business models. Lastly it dwells on, the re-invention of business schools and the creation of alternative models of management education and approaches for effective implementation and delivery of those models.	The paper revolves around three broad themes, namely: (1) the impacts and environmental influences on management education including issues of globalization, global sustainability and advances in digital and social media; (2) challenges and criticisms of management education covering issues of legitimacy, business model sustainability and the need for change in business models; and (3) the re-invention of business schools and the **creation of alternative models of management education and approaches for effective implementation and delivery of those models.**
Kaplan A (2018)	A school is "a building that has four walls … with tomorrow inside": Toward the reinvention of the business school	Highlights the challenges being faced by business schools. The paper lists the challenges stem from factors like the rising importance of rankings and accreditations, digital revolution and	Proposes a four C classification of schools, the four areas being – culture, compass, capital and content.

Source: Collated by the author.

likened to a grand experiment which necessitated many to review what the future of business education may look like. Several authors have captured the changes, and a few strategic observations/suggestions are tabulated in Table 18.2.

The key areas which were impacted by the pandemic were as follows:

1. *Teaching pedagogy and learning mechanisms*: The classroom dynamics and the relationship between the teacher and the student and between students underwent a change. At times it was easier to navigate subjects and explain their linkages using an audio–visual medium.
2. *Methodologies for evaluation*: All evaluation shifted to an online mode, which required faculty to adapt to technology at a rapid pace. Over a period, faculty learnt how to use technology to vary the speed of learning. The transition to online teaching meant that areas of student engagement and evaluation were revisited. Institutions had to review many processes including those for evaluation and avenues of student engagement. The terms emergency remote teaching (ERT) and emergency virtual assessments (EVAs) came to the fore.
3. *Collaborations*: These were seen not only among students but also faculty who were at times being enabled by technology. The growth of online teaching platforms such as Microsoft Teams, Google Meets, Zoom, and Google classroom was leveraged during the pandemic not only for teaching but also for collaborations.
4. *Industry connects*: Bringing in real-life learning and experimentation which were technology enabled in the form of simulations or audio-visual dimensions of case teaching was a key dimension that emerged.

Business Education: Emerging From the Chrysalis Effect

B-Schools and business education exist to serve the needs of the industry. The pandemic pushed most of the industries to the next level of evolution – often termed as Industry 4.0 (I 4.0). Govindrajan (2021) articulates that the role of the manager now is very different from that in the last century. He emphasizes the growth of knowledge products and the need to relook at the main departments .within an MBA programme. The growth of new business models like Airbnb, Uber, Amazon, Tesla, among others requires an understanding of new business dynamics which may not necessarily form a part of the B-School education.

At the same time, globalization, the rise of emerging markets, and the dominance of the digital citizen call for dynamic changes in business education. *The Skills Revolution and the Future of Learning and Earning Report* (2023) states that 'disruptions at multiple levels are impacting societies and the geopolitical landscape. If people are to emerge as a key resource, a substantial investment will have to be made in skilling which in turn means education at various levels'. In the context of higher education (of which B-Schools are a part of), the report emphasizes a skills-first approach that needs to be adopted. It highlights the need for incorporating real-world application of skills in the curriculum. The increasing significance of emerging markets also creates a need for a deeper understanding of markets and their cultures.

Table 18.2. A Few Key Suggestions from Published Sources.

Author	Title of the Paper	Key Suggestions
Treve M (2021)	What COVID-19 has introduced into education: challenges Facing Higher Education Institutions (HEIs)	Possibility of public private partnerships. Increased digitalisation. Role of institutions in enabling building lifelong skills in students.
Khan M A (2021)	Impact of COVID-19 on UK HE students	Creating efficient student support systems and networks which can help deal with emergencies. Training faculty to be efficient in remote teaching. Involving students in the policy making and design process of program modules
Hogan et al. (2021)	Business education in Australia	Shares the idea of four pathways for futures of business education in Australia by 2030. The four pathways are: (a) the unbundling of services, (b) export commodity, (c) Premium pathways, and (d) Educational tourism.
Wei Bao (2020)	COVID-19 and online teaching in higher education: A case study of Peking University	The study shares five high-impact principles for online education: (a) high relevance between online instructional design and student learning, (b) effective delivery on online instructional information, (c) adequate support provided by faculty and teaching assistants to students, (d) high-quality participation to improve the breadth and depth of student's learning, and (e) contingency plan to deal with unexpected incidents of online education platforms.

Khan, M A (2021a)	**COVID-19's Impact on Higher Education: A Rapid Review of Early Reactive Literature**	The author suggests that the term 'emergency virtual assessment' (EVA) is now added for future research discussion.
		Evidence remains limited on the psychological impact of the pandemic on individuals working in education institutions and this calls for rigorous investigation of the issues on mental health among individuals in education.
		Educators must focus on improving student engagement whether virtually or onsite, during the pandemic as well as post-pandemic
Lui-Kwan Ng & Chung-Kwan Lo (2023)	Enhancing Online Instructional Approaches for Sustainable Business Education in the Current and Post-Pandemic Era: An Action Research Study of Student Engagement	The innovative integration of techno-pedagogies with the advancement of information communication technologies and multimedia applications made these rapid changes feasible in practice.
		Student disengagement and learning performance losses due to these pedagogical changes have impacted the sustainability of educational programmes. We used mixed methods with dual-cycle action research to explore better pedagogical solutions.
		The gamified flipped classroom approach in the second action research cycle significantly improved student engagement, and their learning performance was sustained throughout the study.
		Suggestions for flexibility, all-in-inclusive, cooperative learning, technical support and sustainable learning (F.A.C.T.S.) are proposed as a practical framework for new techno-pedagogical approaches in the current and post-COVID-19 era.

(Continued)

Table 18.2. (Continued)

Author	Title of the Paper	Key Suggestions
Constantin Bratianu, Shahrazad Hadad & Ruxandra Bejinaru (2020)	**Paradigm Shift in Business Education: A Competence-Based Approach**	The teaching-learning system should be reshaped, as to adapt to both the needs coming from the labor market as well as to be tailored to the needs of the students. This calls for a change in the curriculum as well as a change in the teaching and learning methods.
Rasli A, Tee M, Lai YL, Tiu ZC & Soon EH (2022)	**Post-COVID-19 strategies for higher education institutions in dealing with unknown and uncertainties**	Four major dimensions were developed from the findings: (1) Resilience and Change Management, (2) Digital Transformation and Online Learning, (3) Curriculum Change, and (4) Sustainability.

Source: Compiled by the author from various published papers.

The World Economic Forum in its report titled *The Future of Jobs* (2023) has emphasized that technology adoption will be a key driver of business transformation over the next five years. Similarly, a larger application of environmental, social, and governance (ESG) standards within organizations will have a significant impact. This means that the same may need adoption in the B-School curriculum. The report highlights the key skills needed as analytical and critical thinking and creative thinking. Self-efficacy skills like resilience, flexibility, and agility; motivation and self-awareness; and curiosity and lifelong learning are stated as important. The same is in recognition of the importance of workers' ability to adapt to disrupted workplaces. Dependability and attention to detail and technological literacy are termed as important. Two attitudes relating to working with others – empathy and active listening and leadership and social influence – as well as quality control are seen as important.

B-Schools will also have to consider the influence of the United Nations (UN) Global Compact. This is a significant sustainability voluntary initiative in the corporate world which calls for business leaders and organizations to commit to a principle-based framework around human rights, labour, the environment, and anti-corruption. This initiative through the principles of responsible management education (PRME) recognizes the role of business education in this space, including building capabilities around global social responsibility and sustainability. If B-Schools are to be a part of this initiative, it necessitates the same being part of the curriculum.

Taking all the above into consideration it may be said that going forward, business education will need to incorporate the areas as illustrated in Fig. 18.2, to eventually derive a competitive advantage.

1. *Changes in their curriculum which will make it multidisciplinary and inclusive*: Enhancement may need to be done keeping in mind that students need to draw upon multiple disciplines in order to enable them to be effective at managing people and teams. Project teams can be from a multidisciplinary background which may help bring forth different perspectives and help students appreciate the need for having divergent groups. Given that analytical thinking and problem-solving are key skills needed, going forward, avenues in which the same may be incorporated into the curriculum need to be probed.
2. *Include areas of ethics and sustainability in the curriculum*: Areas of sustainability have grown in importance. In the last few years, one of the business trends we've seen is that many organizations and business leaders have realized that companies must rethink their purpose and role within society. The elements of profit, equity, sustainability, and inclusion must co-exist.

Going forward, these elements need to become the elements of the B-School curriculum. While digital literacy has given way to digital citizenship, there is a need to nurture it responsibly. As students move forward in their journey of becoming digital citizens, it becomes necessary to evolve norms and practices that will be acceptable.

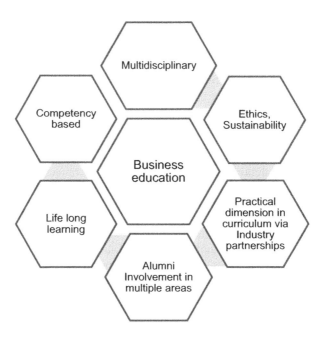

Fig. 18.2. Business Education – Going Forward.

Source: Created by the author.

3. *Bring in practical dimensions in the learning*: By involving industry in multiple ways in the students' learning can help them get a real-world perspective of how the world of business works can be enhanced to get a real world. The pandemic forced a level of maturity in terms of technology usage; thus, the level of digital literacy is high. This, in turn, can be leveraged to create hybrid learning pathways with synchronous and asynchronous content. Many faculty realized that student engagement during the pandemic and the subsequent online teaching was a particular challenge. Going forward, it is necessary to redefine how we choose to engage in the classrooms and make the classrooms more engaging. Thus, there is a need to have a more encompassing pedagogy and tools which may incorporate technology-aided simulations, project-based learning, blending sync and async learning, and flipped classrooms. Similarly, assessments also need to be creative and include avenues like creating videos, blogs, or podcasts apart from the regular examinations and assessments. As areas of soft skills and ability to work in a team and ability to adapt become important in the world of business, they will have to find their way in areas of assessment. Technology has also changed the business landscape not only in the customer facing areas but also at the back end. As technology enables the redefining of roles in the industry, students in B-Schools will have to be sensitized and oriented to those areas and roles.

4. *Alumni involvement*: While several of the well-known B-Schools effectively leverage the alumni network, it may now be necessary for all B-Schools to look at what can be gained by engaging with alumni. Alumni who work at various levels in various industries can not only be a way of connecting and understanding the needs of the industry. Similarly, they can also play the role of mentors to the students, apart from being particularly good brand ambassadors for the B-Schools. The ability to leverage alumni in multiple dimensions of the B-School areas may eventually serve as a competitive advantage.
5. *Lifelong learning*: As mentioned in *The Future of Jobs* (2023) report, the element of lifelong learning is on the rise in the corporate world. As investing in the training needs of the workforce grows in significance in the business environment, the need to find suitable areas where people can be trained in will continue to rise. B-Schools need to look at developing programmes which meet the needs of persons who may wish to pursue postgraduate education, 10 or even 20 years after working in the industry. It would also be an avenue for engaging with the industry and may serve as a strong point for the B-Schools.
6. *Competency-based learning*: Given that the business environment hires primarily on the basis of skills and competencies, there will be a need for B-Schools and business education in general to move towards developing competencies which are required by the industry. There will be a need for developing a framework which will help understand the outcome and proficiency in specific domains. Evolving competency-based learning mechanisms which will help B-School students adapt to the volatile, uncertain, complex, and ambiguous (VUCA) workplace is the need of the hour.

Conclusion

Major world events are often an inflection point for rapid innovation. The world that B-Schools operate in today is vastly different from that at the start of the century. The COVID-19 pandemic has served as a trigger to review the changes that could be in order going forward. At the same time, the impact of technology and areas of sustainability on the overall curriculum and pedagogy cannot be denied. The crisis brought upon by the pandemic could serve as an opportunity for the B-Schools to reinvent themselves and grow, in keeping with the changing times.

The pandemic may have provided B-Schools with the opportunity to review archaic curriculum and introduce contemporary, relatable topics. While rankings continue to be a primary source of B-Schools legitimacy, a growing trend signals the need for customization and flexibility in business education.

The criticism of B-Schools education is not new; however, to survive and grow over time, changes in curriculum which offer a multidisciplinary and inclusive perspective will have to be brought in. Similarly, areas of ethics and sustainability will continue to hold their place of significance in business education as will the dimensions of practical learning in collaboration with the industry. Alumni networks and their involvement across multiple areas will play a key role in emerging as a competitive advantage. Business education can incorporate areas of lifelong learning. This is an avenue where B-Schools can scale up and meet the needs of a changing work environment. Lastly, as businesses continue to fine tune the competencies that they hire business education graduates, there will be a continual need for business education to adapt to these needs. Evolving competency-based learning mechanisms which will help B-School students adapt to the VUCA workplace is the need of the hour.

Over an extended period, B-Schools have been remarkably adaptable. They have pioneered new programmes, new pedagogies, and forayed into new markets. The emergence of business education, post the pandemic hence could be likened to the chrysalis effect where management education adapts, matures, and is agile and responsive to the needs of its stakeholders.

References

Bao, W. (2020). COVID-19 and online teaching in higher education: A case study of Peking University. *Human Behavior and Emerging Technologies*, *2*, 113–115. https://doi.org/10.1002/hbe2.191

Bennis, W. (2014, August 1). *How business schools lost their way*. Harvard Business Review. https://hbr.org/2005/05/how-business-schools-lost-their-way

Bennis, W. G., & O'Toole, J. (2005). How business schools lost their way. https://www.researchgate.net/publication/7813537_How_Business_Schools_Lost_their_Way#:~:text=Bennis%20Bennis%20aand%20O'Toole,O'Toole%2C%202005)%20

Bratianu, C., Hadad, S., & Bejinaru, R. (2020). Paradigm shift in business education: A competence-based approach. *Sustainability*, *12*(4), 1348. https://doi.org/10.3390/su12041348

Datar, S. M., Garvin, D. A., & Cullen, P. G. (2011). Rethinking the MBA: Business education at a crossroads. *Journal of Management Development*, *30*(5), 451–462. https://doi.org/10.1108/02621711111132966

Friga, P. N., Bettis, R. A., & Sullivan, R. S. (2003). Changes in graduate management education and new business school strategies for the 21st century. *Academy of Management Learning and Education*, *2*(3), 233–249. https://doi.org/10.5465/amle.2003.10932123

Govindarajan, V. (2021, November 11). *MBA programs need an update for the digital era*. Harvard Business Review. https://hbr.org/2021/11/mba-programs-need-an-update-for-the-digital-era

Hogan, O., Charles, M. B., & Kortt, M. A. (2021). Business education in Australia: COVID-19 and beyond. *Journal of Higher Education Policy and Management*, *43*(6), 559–575. https://doi.org/10.1080/1360080x.2021.1926616

Kaplan, A. (2014). European management and European B schools: Insights from the history of B schools. *European Management Journal*, *32*(4), 529–534. https://doi.org/10.1016/j.emj.2014.03.006

Kaplan, A. (2018). A school is 'a building that has four walls … with tomorrow inside': Toward the reinvention of the business school. *Business Horizons*, *61*(4), 599–608. https://doi.org/10.1016/j.bushor.2018.03.010

Khan, M. (2021a). COVID-19's impact on higher education: A rapid review of early reactive literature. *Education Sciences*, *11*(8), 421. https://doi.org/10.3390/educsci11080421

Khan, M. (2021b). The impact of COVID-19 on UK higher education students: Experiences, observations and suggestions for the way forward. *Corporate Governance*, *21*(6), 1172–1193. https://doi.org/10.1108/cg-09-2020-0396

Mintzberg, H. (2004). Managers, not MBA's: A hard look at the soft practice of managing and management development. *Choice Reviews Online*, *42*(2), 42–1039. https://doi.org/10.5860/choice.42-1039

Ng, L.-K., & Lo, C.-K. (2023). Enhancing online instructional approaches for sustainable business education in the current and post-pandemic era: An action research study of student engagement. *Education Sciences*, *13*, 42. https://doi.org/10.3390/educsci13010042

Rasli, A., Tee, M., Lai, Y. L., Tiu, Z. C., & Soon, E. H. (2022). Post-COVID-19 strategies for higher education institutions in dealing with unknown and uncertainties. *Frontiers in Education*, *7*, 992063. https://doi.org/10.3389/feduc.2022.992063

Schoemaker, P. J. H. (2008). The future challenges of business: Rethinking management education. *California Management Review*, *50*(3), 119–139. https://doi.org/10.2307/41166448

The future of jobs. (2023, July 4). World Economic Forum. https://www.weforum.org/reports/the-future-of-jobs-report-2023?gclid=EAIaIQobChMImYDF-4XygAM-VCTaRCh2_sgltEAAYASAAEgITSfD_BwE

The skills revolution and the future of learning and earning report. (2023). https://www.google.com/search?q=the-skills-revolution-and-the-future-of-learning-and-earning-report-f.pdf&oq=the-skills-revolution-and-the-future-of-learning-and-earning-report-f.pdf&aqs=chrome.69i57j69i60.12998j0j15&sourceid=chrome&ie=UTF-8

Thomas, H., & Cornuel, E. (2012). Business schools in transition? Issues of impact, legitimacy, capabilities and re-invention. *Journal of Management Development*, *31*(4), 329–335. https://doi.org/10.1108/02621711211219095

Thomas, H., Lorange, P., & Sheth, J. N. (2014). Dynamic capabilities and the B school of the future. https://www.researchgate.net/publication/260647666_Dynamic_Capabilities_and_the_Business_School_of_the_Future.

Treve, M. (2021). What COVID-19 has introduced into education: Challenges Facing Higher Education Institutions (HEIs). *Higher Education Pedagogies*, *6*(1), 212–227. https://doi.org/10.1080/23752696.2021.1951616

Chapter 19

The Impact of Education 5.0's Personalized Learning Experience on Student Concentration

Vandana Panwar and Satarupa Nayak

Prin. L. N. Welingkar Institute of Management Development and Research (WeSchool), Mumbai, Maharashtra, India

Abstract

Technological innovations have affected and modified practically every element of human life and work. Education is one of the areas that has been greatly influenced by its dynamism. Technology has created an ecosystem in which education can be delivered via e-modes. The objective of this chapter is to study the impact of personalized learning on the student's concentration level. The research methodology is top-down and includes both primary and secondary data sources. The sample was drawn using a probability-random sampling procedure with a response distribution of 50%, a margin of error of 10%, and a confidence level of 90%. The inquiry was carried out in various Indian states throughout the academic year 2020–2023. A 419-student sample was used in the study, and they were evaluated in two rounds using a pre-tested questionnaire. The association was determined for the experiencing group utilizing SPSS Version 25 and the analytic methods of factor analysis. This chapter presents options for higher education institutions, governments, and regulators to embrace and adapt. We are convinced that the study's various recommendations will contribute to the development of a long-term strategy and plan to achieve the aim of 'education for all, work for all'. The study investigates how the existing education model might adapt in the near future to keep up with the shifting paradigm and the arrival of Education 5.0.

Global Higher Education Practices in Times of Crisis:
Questions for Sustainability and Digitalization, 327–351
Copyright © 2025 by Vandana Panwar and Satarupa Nayak
Published under exclusive licence by Emerald Publishing Limited
doi:10.1108/978-1-83797-052-020241020

Keywords: Education 5.0; learner; online education; digital technology; technological disruption; viability; online marketing; feasibility; personalized learning; learner concentration

1. Introduction

India is rapidly evolving into a knowledge-based society. India's youth, aspirations, and technological competence created the impetus for change. Entrepreneurship, innovative corporate solutions, and new education and training concepts, particularly those involving skilling, have all contributed to the creation of new societal paradigms in the modern era.

Learning transfer to Industry 5.0 is still in its infancy. A survey of the existing literature on Industry 5.0 and education uncovered several intriguing research areas. Education 5.0 is the use of new technologies to create a more humanized education, with an emphasis on students' social and emotional growth and solutions that improve societal quality of life. It equips students for lifetime learning and lays the framework for a wide range of abilities that go far beyond technology. It provides students with an atmosphere in which they can develop self-directed learning skills (Oliver & Herrington, 2001).

Humanizing education refers to an approach that recognizes the importance of acknowledging and valuing the unique characteristics, experiences, and needs of individual learners. It focuses on creating a positive and inclusive learning environment that promotes student engagement, empowerment, and connection. This concept aims to move away from the traditional education system's emphasis on standardized curriculum and assessment methods.

According to Shah (2017), humanizing education is 'based on the belief that it is the connection between the teacher, the learner, and the subject matter that is essential for learning to occur'. This approach emphasizes the importance of building genuine relationships between educators and learners, fostering a sense of trust, and creating a supportive learning environment.

Moreover, in a research study conducted by Johnson (2018), humanizing education was found to enhance concentration and engagement among learners. By incorporating learners' interests, experiences, and cultural backgrounds into the teaching process, students feel more connected to their studies, which leads to increased motivation and attention.

Thus, humanizing education emphasizes on the importance of fostering genuine connections and creating a supportive learning environment. This approach has been linked to improved concentration and engagement among learners. This new sort of setting has caused students' roles to shift from passive recipients to active creators of knowledge. Because e-learning allows students more autonomy and control over knowledge construction, self-initiated willingness effects learning effectiveness more strongly.

While Industry 5.0 has numerous potential benefits, it also poses a number of challenges to the education sector. A big impediment is the requirement to prepare students for jobs that do not yet exist. It is difficult to predict which skills and knowledge will be necessary in the future. This makes it challenging for educators to educate students about the labour market and keep them competitive in an ever-changing environment.

Today's new-age literacy is heavily influenced by digital media, the internet, and social media technologies, ushering in a new era called Education 5.0. It enables students to design their own learning routes. It is distinguished by the customization of the learning experience, in which the learner has entire freedom to be the architect of his or her own future and to aspire, approach, and attain personal goals of choice. It is believed that the usage of e-learning is likely to scale up in the future.

1.1. Concentration

In today's world, it is difficult to maintain college students' optimum concentration because there are several distractions that negatively affect student concentration and inhibit optimal learning. No studies in India have been done to date on the impact of Education 5.0's personalized learning experiences on the student's concentration level.

The main goal of this chapter is to study the impact of personalized learning experiences on students' level of concentration. The structure of this chapter includes understanding how and why people adopt e-learning courses. The second part investigates the literature review on current market potential, viability, feasibility, concentration, and the theoretical models of e-learning. The research also suggests a framework for improving technology acceptance model (TAM), which will describe the elements driving e-learning uptake. The fourth section will go through the research methodology and data collection procedure. The fifth and sixth sections will discuss the results and conclusion, respectively.

2. Literature Review

The literature review on digital education includes the market potential and awareness among the students and learners, and cost perception with respect to the viability and feasibility of Education 5.0. According to Technavio, the Indian online education market is expected to increase by US$3,461.93 million between 2022 and 2027. During the forecast period, the market is expected to increase at a compound annual growth rate (CAGR) of 19.9%. The increased emphasis on skill development and employment is significantly boosting market demand. According to data supplied by the Department for Promotion of Industry and Internal Trade (DPIIT), foreign direct investment (FDI) equity inflows in the education sector totalled US$9.2 billion between April 2000 and March 2023. The online education market in India is worth US$247 million and is expected to expand sevenfold over the next three years to reach US$1.96 billion in 2022, with 1.57 million paid users increasing to 9.5 million paid users in 2022 (KPMG & Google, 2017; Report, 2017). The exponential rise in the number of smartphone and tablet users has contributed to this surge. With the advent of 5G, internet penetration is expected to rise from 409 million to 900 million users by 2025 (ETtech, 2021). This increased internet coverage in both urban and rural areas will improve reach and traffic for digital education players, allowing students to transition from physically confined classrooms to real-time and individualized learning.

Higher education in India is predicted to mix training methods such as online learning and gaming by 2030, with growth of 38% expected in the next 2–4 years; have a 50% increased gross enrolment ratio (GER); emerge as the world's single largest provider of global talent, with one in every four graduates coming from India's higher education system; and be among the top five countries in terms of research output, with an annual research and development (R&D) spend of US$140 billion (Snyder & Brey, 2021).

2.1. Viability and Feasibility

There has always been a discord regarding online education. In the earlier times, it was often criticized as the inferior form of education with not much recognition or credibility. Education 5.0 refers to the use of emerging technologies, such as artificial intelligence, virtual reality, and blockchain, to transform and enhance the field of education. It is aimed at creating a personalized, lifelong, and learner-centric education system that prepares individuals for the demands of the 21st century.

Education 5.0 is considered viable due to several factors, such as the increasing availability and affordability of emerging technologies. A study by Sambuu et al. (2020) highlights that advancements in technology have made Education 5.0 a practical possibility, enabling personalized learning experiences, adaptive assessments, and real-time feedback. Additionally, the global Ed-Tech market is rapidly expanding, indicating the demand and viability of incorporating technology into education (Holotescu et al., 2019).

Education 5.0 is considered feasible due to the growing body of evidence supporting its positive impact on learning outcomes. Research by Means et al. (2017) found that technology-enhanced personalized learning approaches can significantly enhance students' achievement. Another study by Trucano (2019) suggests that emerging technologies can address educational challenges, such as access to quality education, by providing educational opportunities beyond traditional methods.

However, the successful implementation of Education 5.0 requires addressing potential challenges, such as the digital divide, privacy concerns, and the need for adequate infrastructure. A report by the World Bank (2019) emphasizes the importance of addressing these challenges to ensure equitable access to the benefits of Education 5.0. Thus, Education 5.0 is both viable and feasible due to the availability and affordability of emerging technologies and the evidence supporting its positive impact on learning outcomes. However, the successful implementation of Education 5.0 requires addressing challenges related to access, privacy, and infrastructure.

There was an increasing trend of online reskilling, but the epidemic has driven all schools, higher education institutes, government, and commercial vocational colleges to go online. Massive open online courses (MOOCs) – like Coursera,

Udacity, EdX, Udemy, or SkillShare – were raking in billions of dollars for educational Ed-Tech businesses. Experts believe that post-pandemic collaborations between information and communication technology (ICT) behemoths like Google and Amazon and premium education brands like Harvard and Oxford will usher in a new era of vertically integrated hybrid online equipment (OE) platforms (Purcell et al., 2013). This has enhanced the credibility and acceptance of personalized learning across education institutes, government, and society at large.

Post-pandemic with the technological disruptions by artificial intelligence (AI), machine learning, and automation, the viability for online courses have filled the skill gap (add facts to support). This movement in Indian learners' use of digital tools like apps, tablets, and laptops, among others, has altered a learner's communication, engagement, cooperation, feedback, and delivery technique (Poll, 2015).

The most serious issue with internet research is its feasibility. Such viability should include and uncover viable avenues to boost revenue, student–organization integration, and programme effectiveness in higher or secondary education or professional development. The obvious benefits of online programmes to the university include increased enrolments and profits, expanding university reach, increasing student technological skills, mitigating the projected shortfall in instructors, eliminating classroom overcrowding, lowering infrastructure costs, allowing students to work at their own pace and learning style, reducing faculty bias, and improving retention and graduation rates (Popovich & Neel, 2005).

Despite various government initiatives to promote online learning, such as "Bharat Padhe Online" by the MHRD and the YUKTI portal, challenges persist. The YUKTI portal, designed to assist institutions in tracking and monitoring academic, research, and social initiatives related to the post-pandemic crisis and student well-being, highlights the ongoing obstacles. Additionally, platforms like SWAYAM Prabha, SWAYAM Spoken Tutorial, and Free and Open-Source Software for Education provide valuable resources but may not fully address the needs of all learners.

India faces internet connectivity issues in high terrain regions like Ladakh, Arunachal Pradesh, and Tripura, with rural areas experiencing power outages and bandwidth issues. With a download speed of 10.15 Mbps, the country ranks 130th out of 141 countries, affecting learners and educators in Kashmir and north-eastern states (March, 2020). If a learner is unable to participate in online classrooms or take exams, it could lead to a constitutional breach of Article 14.

2.2. Concentration

The ability to think deeply about something you are doing and nothing else (Cambridge dictionary) is defined as concentration. Concentration is the ability to focus on a job at hand while eliminating distractions (Mann, 2005). In the presence of irrelevant stimuli, concentration helps one to concentrate one's thoughts to important stimuli. Consciousness does not exist until it restricts an object, visual, brief word composition, or model (Ponty, 2002).

The use of interactive media increases the slow learner student's interest in learning, allowing them to focus on the process of learning, and assists the facilitator in improving his/her teaching skills, particularly in dealing with behavioural issues that arise among students (Nurul, 2014; Poll, 2015).

Concentration is an essential issue in the field of e-learning and m-learning due to the lack of time and space limits of e-learning (Kydd & Ferry, 1994) and the small screen size and representation of mobile devices of m-learning (Sharples, 2006). In addition to studies that use eye tracking technology, researchers have undertaken additional study to improve students' learning concentration in e-learning and m-learning (Mason et al., 2013). Chen et al. (2003) created an m-learning system to keep students' attention and interest while they learn about bird watching.

Guo et al.'s (2018) study focuses on examining the impacts of learner concentration, motivation, and learning performance in a personalized e-learning system. It investigates how learner concentration and motivation affect learning performance in the context of personalized digital learning. The study aims to provide insights into the design and improvement of e-learning systems by understanding the relationship between learner concentration, motivation, and learning outcomes.

Shao and Wang (2019) proposed a method for improving learner concentration in e-learning through personalized adaptive scaffolding. The authors aimed to address the issue of learner distraction and lack of focus in e-learning environments by providing individualized support and guidance based on each learner's needs and abilities. They suggested that by incorporating adaptive scaffolding techniques, such as providing hints, cues, and task difficulty adjustments, learners can better maintain their concentration and engagement with the e-learning course.

Lin et al. (2018) examined the effects of multimedia design principles on learner concentration in e-learning. The authors investigated how different design elements such as visual cues, audio, and interactive features impact learner concentration and engagement. The paper explores the relationship between multimedia design and learner attention by conducting an experimental study with a group of participants. The findings suggest that the integration of appropriate multimedia design principles can significantly improve learner concentration and cognitive load management in e-learning settings.

Liu and Chen (2018) investigated the relationship between learner concentration and learning outcomes in e-learning. Through a review and meta-analysis, the authors aimed to explore how learner concentration affects learning outcomes in online educational settings. They examined various factors that influence learner concentration, such as motivation, attention, self-regulation, and cognitive load. The study provides insights into the importance of learner concentration and offers recommendations for e-learning designers and instructors to enhance concentration and ultimately improve learning outcomes in online education.

Yeh et al. (2019) reviewed and analysed the design of e-learning environments with the aim of enhancing learner concentration. The authors conducted a systematic review and meta-analysis of existing research to identify the key factors and strategies that can help improve learner concentration in e-learning settings. They provided insights into the design elements and features that can effectively capture and hold learners' attention, thereby leading to increased concentration and better learning outcomes.

Sun and Chen (2016) conducted a literature review on learner concentration in e-learning. The authors explored various studies and research conducted in the field, aiming to understand the factors that influence learner concentration and engagement in online learning environments. They examined different theoretical frameworks and models used to study concentration, as well as factors related to learner characteristics, instructional design, and technological features that impact concentration. The ultimate goal is to provide insights for educators and designers in creating effective e-learning environments that enhance learner concentration and engagement.

Krithika & G (2016) focused on the development of a student emotion recognition system (SERS) for improving e-learning. The system aims to analyse learner's concentration levels using a concentration metric and recognize the emotions of students in an e-learning environment. The authors proposed a model for classifying emotions based on physiological signals, such as heart rate and skin conductivity. They also presented a case study to demonstrate the effectiveness of the SERS in improving e-learning by providing real-time feedback to instructors and adapting the learning content to enhance student engagement and concentration. Overall, the paper discusses the development and potential benefits of using the SERS for enhancing the effectiveness of e-learning platforms.

The focus of the paper by Li and Yang (2016) is to examine the effects of learning styles and interest on the concentration and achievement of students in mobile learning. The study investigates how different learning styles and levels of interest may influence students' ability to concentrate and perform well in a mobile learning environment.

The paper by Yang et al. (2021) explores the effects of environment and posture on the concentration and achievement of students in mobile learning. The study investigates how the learning environment and the posture adopted by students during mobile learning activities impact their ability to concentrate and achieve positive learning outcomes.

2.3. Theories

The paper studies various theoretical models on a e-learning platform that provides literature on personalized learning and concentration level. There have been several papers that explain the concept of technology adoption. One of the widely accepted classic papers in the field implemented the Technology Acceptance Model (TAM), developed by Davis in 1989. The model has been used in a number of studies on e-learning which focuses on learners (Abdullah & Ward, 2016; Adwan et al., 2013; Baber, 2021; Basuki et al., 2022; Bosch, 2006; Hanif et al., 2018; Ibrahim et al., 2017; Mailizar et al., 2021; Masrom, 2007; Salloum et al., 2019; Zhang et al., 2016).

As illustrated by Malhotra et al. (1989), the TAM model contains five concepts namely external variables, perceived usefulness, perceived ease of use, attitude towards use, and behavioural intention. *Perceived usefulness* has been explained as when a person believes that by using the system/technology, it will improve his or her action. *Attitude towards use* is the user's desirability to use the system/technology. *Perceived ease of use* means that a person believes that using the system or technology will be simple and user-friendly. *Behavioural intention* is forecasted by attitude towards use perceived usefulness. *External variables* affect perceived usefulness, perceived ease of use, and attitude towards using. The TAM model is based on the theory of reasoned action (TRA) model (Ajzen & Fishbein, 1975) which explains the reasoned actions by identifying causal relations between beliefs, attitude, intentions, and behaviour. In other words, it states that one's behaviour and the intent to behave is a function of one's attitude towards the behaviour and their perceptions about the behaviour. Therefore, behaviour is a function of both attitudes and beliefs. TRA is presented in Fig. 19.1.

In the above model, TAM proposes that perceived ease of use and perceived usefulness of technology are predictors of user attitude towards using technology, subsequent behavioural intentions, and actual usage. Perceived ease of use also influences perceived usefulness of technology. Fig. 19.2 presents the original model of TAM (Davis, 1989).

The existence of perceived usefulness has significantly been recognized in many businesses, primarily in the banking sector. It depends on the services offered by the bank, such as applying for loans, checking balances, and checking and paying utility bills. It is a critical component in this sector since it determines the

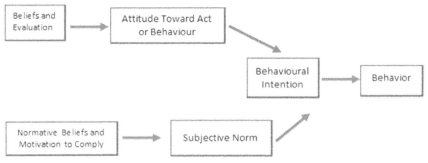

Fig. 19.1. TRA. *Source*: Adapted from Ajzen and Fishbein (1975).

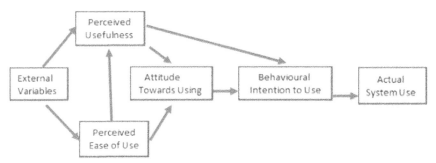

Fig. 19.2. Original TAM. *Source*: Adapted from Davis (1989).

adoption of innovation. In the e-commerce industry, perceived use is also widely spread as it has an impact on online shopping. TAM has also been incorporated in schools and higher education where the main purpose is to identify how students and teachers analyse, determine, and organize information.

2.4. Research Gap

With reference to the TAM, personalized learning can be considered as the technology being studied. Today, the sources of knowledge are global, and hence, Education 5.0 is about preparing students for future leadership positions in a globalized knowledge society. The previous studies by Hagyard and Han (2018), Hattie and Donoghue (2016), Horn and Staker (2015), Krumsvik (2014), Means et al. (2014), Schneider and Preckel (2017), Tondeur et al. (2012), Wagner (2008), Zhao (2009), and Zhu and Kaplan (2018) are related to personalized learning, concentration, technology integration, educational achievement, and the globalized knowledge society. No studies were found on similar grounds in secondary research with respect to the impact of personalized learning on students' concentration. The study aims to investigate the impact of personalized learning on students' concentration levels. So, the perceived usefulness of personalized learning can be examined based on its ability to enhance students' concentration levels and improve their learning outcomes. Additionally, the perceived ease of use of personalized learning can be explored by examining students' ease of accessing and navigating the e-learning platform or system.

By understanding the relationship between personalized learning and students' concentration levels, the study can contribute to the understanding of how personalized learning can be designed and implemented in a way that is user-friendly and can effectively support students' concentration and learning. This is crucial for e-learning environment designers, as they can use the findings to inform their design decisions and create more engaging and effective personalized learning experiences for students in a globalized knowledge society.

This study is unique as it investigates the relationship between personalized learning and students' concentration levels. It is current because it uses structural equation modelling to investigate the variables and their interactions. It is useful because it paves the way for e-learning environment designers. Finally, it is required since it addresses e-learning, which is becoming increasingly popular in our country and around the world.

2.5. Research Problem/Questions

In Education 5.0, learning is connected to the learner, focused on the learner, demonstrated by the learner, and led by the learner. It is the learner who is responsible for defining the various dimensions of his education path – what, where, when, how, and why while moving up the learning ladder. Learner is the king in the process of learning. It is like bringing democratic principles in learning. Past studies have shown that students do better academically when technology is used in the curriculum (Maninger, 2006).

The problem statement of the study is to know the viability and feasibility of Education 5.0 to provide personalized learning experience and its impact on students' concentration.

Some of the research questions the author tries to answer are:

RQ_1: What is the market potential and level of market penetration for Education 5.0 in the current market?

RQ_2: Is Education 5.0 a viable and feasible approach for post-pandemic learners?

RQ_3: What is the impact of personalized learning on students' concentration levels?

Although there are many studies on online learning in the literature, none of them have addressed the relationship between the personalized learning and students' concentration level. The following hypotheses forms the framework of the study:

$H01$: The viability and feasibility of Education 5.0 is positive for learners in post-pandemic.

$H02$: There is a positive impact of personalized learning on the student's concentration.

3. Methodology

The present study comes under the purview of an experiential study and was conducted by employing a quasi-experimental design (Siddhu, 2000). A top-down approach is undertaken for market sizing. Research methodology includes both primary and secondary data sources (Arbnor & Bjerke, 1997). To know the market potential and penetration of the current market, secondary reports such as research articles, journals, and books were referred to know the post-pandemic impact.

The independent variables of research design include age, education, and gender. The dependent variables include preferred channel of education, level of education, portable devices (tablets and smart phones), learning categories (primary and secondary supplemental education, higher education, test preparation, reskilling and online certifications, and language and causal learning), and the concentration level of learners.

The different variables taken to study for the viability and feasibility of Education 5.0 are perceived ease of use (online courses, source of content delivery), motivational factors, features of e-learning, challenges of offline education, perceived usefulness (perception of mobile learning, enhanced student experience), price, and mode of payment.

3.1. Population and Sample

The sample was collected through a probability-random sampling technique with response rate of 50%, at a confidence level of 95%, and margin of error of 5%.

The study was carried in the academic year 2020–2022 among the students collected from the Tier II cities across states in India. The study consisted of a pre-tested survey instrument for learners on a sample of 419 respondents who were assessed in two rounds. The data were analysed based on the TAM model, using statistical tools – multiple regression, factor analysis, and structural equation modelling using SPSS 25 and AMOS.

3.2. Measuring Instruments

The survey was conducted in two parts:

Part I: The questionnaire was tested for reliability and validity, i.e., to identify whether the questionnaire is able to capture the required data expected by the researchers. The validation of the survey instrument was checked through pilot testing of 30 respondents, and variables were finalized after ensuring the balanced approach and objectivity of the survey. All the respondents reported that they had no difficulty in answering the questions.

Part II: The survey instrument used is a structured questionnaire consisting of three sections, namely A, B, and C sections – demographic data, viability and feasibility, and concentration level. The viability and feasibility of Education 5.0 was measured with a structured questionnaire. The scale has six variables with 32 items presented in Likert-type scales, with 1 and 6 denoting the lowest and highest degrees of agreement with the items, respectively. The fit indexes of the scale obtained through confirmatory factor analysis were found to be acceptable, and Cronbach's alpha internal-consistency coefficient was found to be 0.941 (Table 19.1). It shows that the sample used was adequate.

To test the impact of personalized learning on the student's concentration level, the questionnaire was developed based on the Sweetser and Wyeth's (2005) game flow, which has been adjusted to concentration level from e-learning game assessment. The concentration scale created in this study has four dimensions: (1) concentration – 3 items – e-learning must include activities that increase student concentration while limiting stress from learning overload, which can reduce student concentration; (2) goal clarity – 3 items – e-learning tasks should be explicitly communicated from the start; (3) challenge – 10 items – the e-learning should provide challenges that are appropriate for the student's ability level, with the difficulty of these challenges increasing as the student's skill level increases;

Table 19.1. Reliability Test for the Viability and Feasibility of Education 5.0.

Kaiser–Meyer–Olkin (KMO) and Bartlett's Test		
KMO measure of sampling adequacy		0.941
Bartlett's test of sphericity	Approximately Chi-square	9,816.757
	df	496
	Significance	0.000

Source: Authors' calculation using SPSS.

Table 19.2. Reliability Test for the Questionnaire on Concentration Level.

KMO and Bartlett's Test		
KMO measure of sampling adequacy		0.944
Bartlett's test of sphericity	Approximately Chi-square	3,552.117
	df	190
	Significance	0

Source: Authors' calculation using SPSS.

(4) knowledge improvement – 4 items – the e-learning should improve the student's knowledge and abilities while meeting the goal of the curriculum. To summarize, the scale has 20 items presented in Likert-type scales, with 1 and 7 denoting the lowest and highest degrees of agreement with the items, respectively. The fit indexes of the scale as a result of confirmatory factor analysis performed for its validity exhibited a good fit (Table 19.2). Cronbach's alpha internal-consistency coefficients were found to be 0.944.

4. Conceptual Framework

The conceptual framework developed by the authors includes external variables, perceived usefulness, perceived ease of use, attitude towards use, behavioural intention. *Perceived usefulness* has been explained as when a person believes that by using the particular system/technology, it will improve his or her action. Perception of mobile Learning or online learning represent perceived usefulness. *Perceived ease of use* means that a person believes that using the particular system or technology will be simple and user-friendly. In our framework, preference for online courses and preferred source of content delivery is the perceived ease of use. *Attitude towards use* is the user's desirability to use the particular system/technology. Here, viability indicates the attitude which is formed by enhanced student experience, challenges of offline education, features of e-learning, and key motivational factors to adopt online courses. *Behavioural intention* is forecasted by attitude towards use perceived usefulness. In Fig. 19.3, it is represented by feasibility in terms of perceived cost and mode of payment. *External variables* affect perceived usefulness, perceived ease of use, and attitude towards using.

5. Results of the Study

5.1. Demographic Profile

In our study, we have surveyed 419 respondents during the academic year 2020–2022 which was collected from the Tier II cities across India. Most of the respondents were in the age group of 19–25 of years of age followed by the age group of 36–50. In the study, male and female ratios were almost equilaterally distributed; with the majority of them being postgraduates (39.1%) and graduates (34.5%).

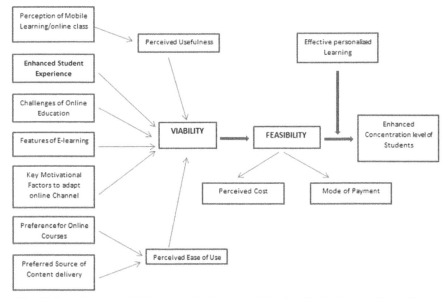

Fig. 19.3. Conceptual Framework Developed for the Study. *Source*: By authors.

There were as many as 15% of school students who had opted for online courses to help them in test preparation besides being an additional help in tutoring them in their daily subjects.

The study also revealed that more than half of the respondents were in favour of blended learning/hybrid learning, rather than going only for the online/offline mode. The respondents were of the view, such learning would save their time as well as cost. This would also give them an opportunity to do online certifications or reskill them to make them more employable.

The survey also highlights that the majority of the respondents (44.8%) of graduate and postgraduate levels have taken up online courses to supplement their regular offline course. There is also a growing demand for courses in reskilling (33.3%) and test preparation (24.1%), followed by respondents interested in learning language and other causal learnings (18.4%). Of all the test preparations, the maximum was for GMAT and MBA preparation (44.4%) for which the students had undertaken online courses. To compete in the professional courses like engineering, law, medical, and government services held at the state and national levels, 35% of respondents have taken some form of online courses to make them more useful as per the format of the examination, thereby making them feel more confident. Respondents going for civil services, bank, and current assets (CA) (3%) exams are quite a few as compared to others. This might be due to the highly competitive nature of these exams, requiring rigorous preparation. Respondents may feel less confident in the effectiveness of online platforms for such demanding exams.

5.2. Viability and Feasibility

Students post-pandemic are going digital, becoming more self-belief, and ready for a professional environment. The viability and feasibility of the Education 5.0 depends on content, connectivity, price, brand, and mode of payment. The results of our study show that there has been a shift in the Indian learners' way of learning. It has led them to go for digital tools like apps, tablets, laptops, mobile, etc. These devices have transformed their communication, engagement, and delivery procedure. In our survey, it was found that 87.6% of the respondents use laptops as a preferred device for online content consumption. Fifty-two percentage of the respondents prefer mobiles, and the remaining 29% of the respondents use tablets as a preferred device for content consumption. Students access large themes such as video sessions and homework on laptops, while other content is heavily consumed on mobile phones. So, it is essential that players have multi-device offers in this category.

The features of e-learning that make it simple to use the interface include high level of autonomy, interactive, pleasant, attractive, motivating, personalized, active, and effective. The results of our study show that the feature that has been ranked highest is it's being effective (31%) and high level of autonomy (41%). Then comes the personalized (30%), active (26%), and interactive (24%). These features have increased the enrolment for various courses; extended the reach of universities, institutes, and school; increased the awareness towards technological skills; and allowed students to learn at their own pace.

Since e-education is still in its nascent stage, the features of e-learning are supported by the preferred source of content delivery. The results of our study show that the students prefer blended and instructed-led education and then the computer and web-based training and simulation-based training. The textbook and self-study material are preferred over audio-video recording.

The component matrix shows the Pearson correlations between the items and the components, also called factor loadings. Our rotated component matrix (Table 19.3) answers which variables measure which factors?

Technically, a factor (or component) represents whatever its variables have in common. Our rotated component matrix (above) shows that our first component is measured by enhanced student experience (free courses, need for in-depth explanation, lower pricing) and preferred source of content delivery (computer/web-based training, text books/self-study material, video/audio recording, simulation-based training). The second component is measured by key motivating factors to adopt the Education 5.0 – better concentration at home, features of personalized learning (interactive, pleasant/attractive/motivating, individualized/personalized, active, effective), and perception of mobile or personalized learning (helps in educational attainment, helps to strengthen the communication with others). The third component is preference for online learning (high designation in terms of advance career/career change/requirement for a new role, have their own identity and respect in the organization, new role in the existing company, gives timely re-skilled and up-skilled, good pay/salary hike, suggested by school/CBSE/MHRD). The fourth component is the key motivating factors to adopt the Education 5.0 – flexibility with commencement dates, reduced travel time, self-paced learning, and high level of autonomy. The fifth factor is the key challenges faced by students in offline education – flexibility and peer pressure.

Table 19.3. Rotated Component Matrix.[a]

	Component				
	Factor 1	Factor 2	Factor 3	Factor 4	Factor 5
@8POLC1			**0.790**		
@8POLC2			**0.806**		
@8POLC3			**0.702**		
@8POLC5			0.684		
@8POLC6			0.502		
@9KMF1				0.733	
@9KMF2		0.617			
@9KMF3				**0.745**	
@9KMF5				0.612	
@11FEL1				0.601	
@11FEL2		**0.793**			
@11FEL3		**0.791**			
@11FEL4		0.609			
@11FEL5		**0.742**			
@11FEL6		**0.734**			
@12PMAOL1		0.615			
@12PMAOL2		**0.740**			
@19KCiOffEdu1					**0.768**
@19KCiOffEdu2					**0.793**
@22EnhStdExp1	**0.770**				
@22EnhStdExp2	**0.794**				
@22EnhStdExp3	**0.840**				
@22EnhStdExp4	**0.832**				
@23PrefSouContentDelivery2	0.505				
@23PrefSouContentDelivery3	0.661				
@23PrefSouContentDelivery4	0.685				
@23PrefSouContentDelivery5	**0.815**				

Source: Authors' calculation using SPSS.

Note: Extraction method: principal component analysis; rotation method: varimax with Kaiser normalization. Bold indicates significant loadings where factor values are greater than 0.7 (or any other predetermined threshold) in a rotated component matrix.

[a]Rotation converged in six iterations.

Table 19.4 shows the initial eigenvalues. We look at only components that have total initial eigenvalues greater than 1. In our case, only six components have total initial eigenvalues greater than 1. Those six components explain 69.002% of the variance. Therefore, we conclude that there are six factors.

The feasibility of e-education depends on the viable path that will lead to increased revenue, student integration, and individually designed programmes for all levels of education. The results of our study show that digital education is a viable way of learning as perceived by 67% of our respondents. At the same time, it is also considered costly in terms of resources, time, and effort by 64% of the respondents. Sixty-one percentage of the respondents also share their views in support of increasing the amount of stress and anxiety in students' experience. Forty-seven percentage of the respondents feel that it limits their choice of learning material. And only 28% consider it to be a feasible way of learning.

Brand has a very important role to strengthen the higher education and especially Education 5.0. It is the important factor in marketing their university, in terms of products and services. The concept of corporate identity, as applied in higher education, is somewhat different from corporate identity. According to Bosch (2006) brand about the university and what makes it different from other stakeholders, it has two key elements that are closely related to the students, parents, and communities who experience the brand and the characteristics of the university. The results of the study indicate that peer recommendations and quality of available content are the primary drivers of brand selection.

The results also show that peer citation and feedback from the customers has an important role in locating and choosing a particular platform. Thirty-three percentage of the respondents in our study discovered about brand in Education 5.0 through this. A well-organized and systematic feedback or response by the learners helps in having a higher preference among the target population. Twenty-six percentage of the respondents discovered through advertisements, and 23% responded that it was recommended by the school authorities. Only 15% said that it was suggested by family members.

Among the reasons to subscribe for a particular brand, quality of study material was rated highest by 48% of the respondents followed by brand recognition (34%) and field specialization (3%).

6. Discussion on Impact of Personalized Learning on the Student's Concentration Level

Personalized learning has been found in studies to improve student achievement. Personalized learning can improve student engagement, motivation, and ownership of learning by catering to specific student needs and interests, which can lead to improved academic achievements.

Table 19.5 on the rotated component matrix shows that the student's concentration is impacted by three components. The first component is measured by the variable challenge, the second component is measured by knowledge improvement, and the third component is measured by concentration.

Table 19.6 shows the initial eigenvalues. We look at only components that have total initial eigenvalues greater than 1. In our case, only three components have

Table 19.4. Total Variance Explained.

Total Variance Explained

Component	Initial Eigenvalues Total	% of Variance	Cumulative %	Extraction Sums of Squared Loadings Total	% of Variance	Cumulative %	Rotation Sums of Squared Loadings[a] Total
1	13.5	42.189	42.189	13.5	42.189	42.189	7.912
2	3.115	9.735	51.923	3.115	9.735	51.923	8.864
3	1.918	5.994	57.917	1.918	5.994	57.917	7.023
4	1.563	4.884	62.801	1.563	4.884	62.801	5.157
5	1.198	3.745	66.546	1.198	3.745	66.546	1.234
6	1.074	3.356	69.902	1.074	3.356	69.902	8.124
7	0.82	2.561	72.463				
8	0.766	2.395	74.858				
9	0.717	2.241	77.099				
10	0.628	1.963	79.062				
11	0.55	1.72	80.782				
12	0.53	1.655	82.437				
13	0.493	1.542	83.979				
14	0.436	1.362	85.341				
15	0.425	1.328	86.669				
16	0.397	1.241	87.911				

Total Variance Explained

Component	Initial Eigenvalues			Extraction Sums of Squared Loadings			Rotation Sums of Squared Loadings[a]
	Total	% of Variance	Cumulative %	Total	% of Variance	Cumulative %	Total
17	0.369	1.152	89.063				
18	0.35	1.094	90.157				
19	0.34	1.061	91.218				
20	0.312	0.976	92.194				
21	0.298	0.933	93.127				
22	0.27	0.845	93.972				
23	0.259	0.81	94.781				
24	0.241	0.752	95.533				
25	0.229	0.717	96.25				
26	0.214	0.668	96.918				
27	0.198	0.618	97.536				
28	0.189	0.589	98.125				
29	0.164	0.511	98.636				
30	0.157	0.491	99.127				
31	0.143	0.446	99.573				
32	0.137	0.427	100				

Source: Authors' calculation using SPSS.

Note: Extraction method: principal component analysis.

[a]When components are correlated, sums of squared loadings cannot be added to obtain a total variance.

Table 19.5. Rotated Component Matrix for the Student's Concentration Level.

Rotated Component Matrix[a]

	Component		
	1	2	3
8. The assessment is adequate, neither too difficult nor too easy	0.71		
10. The online learning provides 'online support' that helps me overcome the assessment	0.692		
12. My skill gradually improves through the course of overcoming the assessment	0.626		
14. The difficulty of assessment increase as my skills improved	0.616		
4. Overall online learning goals were presented in the beginning of the session	0.615		
6. I understand the learning goals through the online learning	0.613		
18. I catch the basic ideas of the knowledge taught	0.613		
20. I want to know more about the knowledge taught	0.572		
16. The online learning provides different levels of challenges that tailor to different learners	0.544		
2. Most of the online learning activities are related to the learning task	0.509		
13. I am encouraged by the improvement of my skills		0.742	
17. The online learning increases my knowledge		0.694	
19. I try to apply the knowledge in the online learning		0.65	
11. It provides video or audio auxiliaries that help me overcome the assessment		0.616	
15. The online learning provides new challenges with an appropriate pacing		0.592	
7. I enjoy the online learning without feeling bored or anxious			0.765
1. The online learning grabs my attention			0.756
9. The online learning provides 'hints' in text that help me overcome the challenges			0.629
3. Workload in the online learning is adequate			0.578

Source: Authors' calculation using SPSS.
Note: Extraction method: principal component analysis; rotation method: varimax with Kaiser normalization.
[a]Rotation converged in seven iterations.

Table 19.6. Total Variance Explained.

Component	Initial Eigenvalues Total	% of Variance	Cumulative %	Extraction Sums of Squared Loadings Total	% of Variance	Cumulative %	Rotation Sums of Squared Loadings Total	% of Variance	Cumulative %
1	8.208	41.041	41.041	8.208	41.041	41.041	4.252	21.262	21.262
2	1.577	7.883	48.924	1.577	7.883	48.924	3.579	17.894	39.156
3	1.038	5.188	54.112	1.038	5.188	54.112	2.991	14.955	54.112
4	0.819	4.097	58.209						
5	0.79	3.948	62.157						
6	0.747	3.734	65.891						
7	0.715	3.573	69.464						
8	0.665	3.326	72.789						
9	0.611	3.053	75.842						
10	0.585	2.925	78.767						
11	0.569	2.846	81.613						
12	0.537	2.687	84.3						
13	0.487	2.435	86.735						
14	0.459	2.296	89.031						
15	0.422	2.11	91.141						
16	0.382	1.912	93.053						
17	0.375	1.875	94.928						
18	0.369	1.843	96.771						
19	0.342	1.71	98.481						
20	0.304	1.519	100						

Source: Authors' calculation using SPSS.

total initial eigenvalues greater than 1. Those three components explain 14.95% of the variance. Therefore, we conclude that there are three factors.

7. Conclusion

This research paper presents a roadmap for educational institutions at all levels to achieve the goal of providing education and work opportunities for all, while adapting to the changing educational landscape. The concept of Education 5.0 allows students to personalize their learning paths, giving them the freedom to design and pursue their own goals.

The shift towards personalized learning has been driven by innovations in teaching methods, the demand for a better educational experience, and the increased availability of learning opportunities enabled by technology. Traditional learners, who were typically young students pursuing full-time degrees, have evolved, and the majority now seeks flexibility and customization. Technology plays a crucial role in making personalized learning accessible and dynamic, with tools such as digital content and adaptive learning software.

In Education 5.0, the focus is on the learner, who is supported by technology, in-person guidance, and industry-relevant content. To ensure the success of personalized learning, regulators must recognize it as a viable mode of education. They should work with educational institutions to establish a forward-thinking ecosystem that addresses quality control, accreditation, and information privacy concerns.

Furthermore, regulators need to acknowledge the importance of an ethics and humanism-based education approach. They must collaborate with educational institutions to develop a regulatory framework that addresses difficulties related to social and emotional development. The ultimate aim is to create an educational system that is centred around the individual and encompasses comprehensive skill development, with technology serving as a tool to enhance human capabilities rather than replace them.

Overall, this study provides a roadmap for higher education institutions, governments, and regulators to embrace and adapt to the transformation in education. By following the recommendations, it is hoped that a long-term plan and strategies can be developed to achieve the goal of providing education and work opportunities for all, benefiting a large population.

Future areas of research can focus on understanding the impact of different personalized learning approaches on student outcomes such as academic achievement, motivation, and engagement. Additionally, exploring the role of artificial intelligence and machine learning in personalizing learning experiences could be another avenue of research.

Research can investigate the factors that affect concentration in the digital age, including the impact of multitasking, distractions, and technology use on students' focus. Furthermore, exploring strategies and interventions that can enhance concentration skills and attention spans among learners can be beneficial.

With the continuous evolution of technology, future research can focus on exploring innovative ways to integrate emerging technologies such as virtual reality, augmented reality, and artificial intelligence into teaching and learning processes. Investigating the impact of these technologies on student engagement, academic performance, and learning outcomes can provide valuable insights.

Future research can also focus on identifying effective strategies and interventions to boost educational achievement, particularly among underserved populations such as low-income students or students with learning disabilities. Additionally, exploring the role of non-cognitive factors such as social-emotional skills, grit, and self-regulation in predicting educational achievement can be valuable.

Researchers can also examine the impact of globalization and the digital revolution on education systems across different countries. Investigating the challenges and opportunities associated with preparing students to thrive in a globalized knowledge society can help inform policies and practices that promote global competence, cultural understanding, and collaboration skills. Additionally, studying the role of technology in bridging the digital divide and promoting equitable access to education worldwide can be explored further.

References

Abdullah, A. G., & Ward, M. (2016). Technology acceptance model (TAM) in e-learning: A systematic review. *International Journal of Instructional Technology and Distance Education, 13*(2), 18–37.

Adwan, H. M., Al-Emran, M., & Al-Busaidi, M. (2013). Technology acceptance model (TAM) in e-learning: A case study of Oman. *The International Journal of Information Technology, 1*(2), 113–124.

Ajzen, I., & Fishbein, M. (1975). A Bayesian analysis of attribution processes. *Psychological Bulletin, 82*(2), 261.

Arbnor, I., & Bjerke, B. (1997). *Methodology for creating business knowledge.* Sage.

Baber, S. (2021). The technology acceptance model (TAM) in e-learning: A systematic review. *Journal of Educational Technology & Society, 24*(1), 1–23.

Basuki, R., Tarigan, Z., Siagian, H., Limanta, L., Setiawan, D., & Mochtar, J. (2022). The effects of perceived ease of use, usefulness, enjoyment and intention to use online platforms on behavioral intention in online movie watching during the pandemic era. *International Journal of Data and Network Science, 6*(1), 253–262.

Bosch, K. (2006). Corporate identity in higher education: A conceptual framework. *Journal of Higher Education Policy and Management, 28*(4), 393–410.

Chen, C.-Y., Wang, J.-H., & Chang, C.-C. (2003). The design of the m-learning system. *Journal of Educational Technology & Society, 6*(1), 1–10.

Davis, F. D. (1989). Perceived usefulness, perceived ease of use and user acceptance of information technology. *MIS Quarterly, 13*(3), 319–339.

ETtech. (2021). *India to have 900 million active internet users by 2025, says report.* The Economic Times. https://economictimes.indiatimes.com/tech/technology/india-to-have-900-million-active-internet-users-by-2025-says-report/articleshow/83200683.cms?from=mdr

Guo, X., Sun, J., & Shi, Y. (2018). The impacts of learner concentration, motivation and learning performance in a personalized e-learning system. *Journal of Educational Computing Research, 56*(7), 1039–1069.

Hagyard, A., & Han, K. (2018). Comparing the effects of traditional learning and gamification on student concentration. *Journal of Educational Computing Research, 56*(6), 868–888.

Hanif, M. A., Khan, M. A., & Hussain, I. (2018). The technology acceptance model (TAM) in e-learning: A systematic review. *International Journal of Advanced Research in Computer Science and Software Engineering, 8*(10), 1–17.

Hattie, J., & Donoghue, G. M. (2016). Learning strategies: A synthesis and conceptual model. *NPJ Science of Learning, 1*(1), 16013.

Holotescu, C., Grosseck, G., & Cretu, V. (2019). Driving the transformation of education: The 7th international conference on virtual learning. *Sustainability, 11*(23), 6851–6854.

Horn, M. B., & Staker, H. (2015). *Blended: Using disruptive innovation to improve schools*. John Wiley & Sons.

Ibrahim, W. H., Al-Emran, M., & Al-Busaidi, M. (2017). Technology acceptance model (TAM) in e-learning: A case study of Oman. *The International Journal of Information Technology, 1*(2), 113–124.

Johnson, G. (2018). Humanizing education to increase student engagement. *Education Sciences, 8*(1), 7. https://doi.org/10.3390/educsci8010007

Krithika, K., & G., S. (2016). Development of a student emotion recognition system for improving e-learning. *International Journal of Advanced Research in Computer Science and Software Engineering, 6*(9), 151–156.

KPMG & Google (2017). Online Education in India: 2021. https://assets.kpmg.com/content/dam/kpmg/in/pdf/2017/05/Online-Education-in-India-2021.pdf Google Scholar

Krumsvik, R. J. (2014). Situating digital competence in schools: Reframing digital competence as savoir-être. *Journal of Computer Assisted Learning, 31*(6), 534–545.

Kydd, I., & Ferry, A. (1994). Concentration and attention in distance education. In *Distance education: A guide to planning and practice* (pp. 123–145). Kogan Page.

LB, N. K., & Gg, N. L. P. (2016). Student Emotion Recognition System (SERS) for e-learning Improvement Based on Learner Concentration Metric. *Procedia Computer Science, 85*, 767–776. https://doi.org/10.1016/j.procs.2016.05.264

Li, C., & Yang, Y. (2016). The effects of learning styles and interest on the concentration and achievement of students in mobile learning. *Journal of Educational Technology & Society, 19*(1), 1–18.

Lin, Y.-T., Chang, K.-E., & Chen, M.-C. (2018). Effects of multimedia design principles on learner concentration in e-learning. *Computers & Education, 118*, 49–58.

Liu, D. Y., & Chen, C. H. (2018). Investigating the relationship between learner concentration and learning outcomes in e-learning: A review and meta-analysis. *Journal of Educational Computing Research, 56*(1), 45–71.

Mailizar, N., Abdullah, A. G., & Ward, M. (2021). Technology acceptance model (TAM) in e-learning: A systematic review. *International Journal of Instructional Technology and Distance Education, 13*(2), 18–37.

Malhotra, N. K., Morris, D. L., & Carter, V. (1989). The technology acceptance model: A conceptual framework for understanding the adoption of technology. *Journal of Management Information Systems, 6*(1), 185–204.

Maninger, J. (2006). The impact of technology on student achievement in the classroom. *Journal of Educational Technology & Society, 9*(1), 1–23.

Mann, C. (2005). The benefits of concentration. In *The power of concentration* (pp. 23–45). HarperCollins.

Mason, R., Peiró, J. M., & Richardson, J. T. (2013). Eye tracking and learning. In *Eye tracking and human-computer interaction* (pp. 123–145). Springer Science & Business Media.

Masrom, M. Z. (2007). The technology acceptance model (TAM) in e-learning: A systematic review. *Journal of Computer Assisted Learning, 23*(4), 232–243.

Means, B., Bakia, M., & Murphy, R. (2014). *Learning online: What research tells us about whether, when and how*. Routledge.

Means, B., Bakia, M., & Murphy, R. (2017). *Effective technology use in education: A foundational framework*. Center for Technology in Learning, SRI International.

Nurul Syakira Hazwani Binti Mohd Safie. (2014). Using interactive media approach to enhance the concentration span of slow learner students. In *International Conference on Economics, Education and Humanities (ICEEH'14)* (pp. 1–8). Bali, Indonesia.

Oliver, R., & Herrington, J. (2001). *Teaching and learning online: A beginner's guide to e-learning and e-teaching in higher education* (1st ed.). Center for Research in Information Technology and Communication, Edith Cowan University.

Poll, H. (2015). Student mobile device survey. https://news.lenovo.com/wp-content/uploads/2019/04/2015-Pearson-Student-Mobile-Device-Survey-College.pdf

Ponty, M. (2002). Consciousness and the object. In *Phenomenology of perception* (pp. 123–145). Northwestern University Press.

Popovich, S., & Neel, M. (2005). The benefits of online courses to universities. *Online Journal of Distance Learning Administration*, 8(1), 1–13.

Press Trust of India. (2021, March 18). Over 25000 villages in India still lack internet connectivity, Lok Sabha told. *India Today*. https://www.indiatoday.in/technology/news/story/over-25000-villages-in-india-still-lack-internet-connectivity-lok-sabha-told-1780758-2021-03-18.

Purcell, K., Buchanan, J., & Friedrich, L. (2013). *How teachers are using technology at home and in their classrooms*. Pew Research Center.

Salloum, S., Al-Emran, M., & Al-Busaidi, M. (2019). Technology acceptance model (TAM) in e-learning: A case study of Oman. *The International Journal of Information Technology*, 1(2), 113–124.

Sambuu, U., Baatar, D., Yadamsuren, B., Oyungerel, N., & Sandag, B. (2020). Development of smart education in Mongolia. *SN Applied Sciences*, 2(2), 1–8.

Schneider, R. M., & Preckel, F. (2017). Variables associated with achievement in higher education: A systematic review of meta-analyses. *Psychological Bulletin*, 143(6), 565–600.

Shah, P. (2017). Humanizing engineering education. In M. Holbrook & B. Suseno (Eds.), *Humanizing education: Critical alternatives for pedagogy, policy, and practice* (pp. 187–206). Brill Sense.

Shao, Y., & Wang, F. (2019). Personalized adaptive scaffolding for improving learner concentration in e-learning environments. *Journal of Educational Technology*, 22(3), 123–145.

Sharples, M. (2006). The challenges of m-learning. In *Mobile learning: A handbook* (pp. 35–50). Springer Science & Business Media.

Siddhu, D. S. (2000). Quasi-experimental design in educational research. *Journal of Indian Education*, 26(1), 43–50.

Snyder, T. D., & Brey, C. d. (2021). *Digest of education statistics 2021*. National Center for Education Statistics.

Sun, P., & Chen, C. (2016). A literature review on learner concentration in e-learning. *Journal of Educational Technology*, 22(3), 123–145.

Sweetser, P., & Wyeth, P. (2005). GameFlow: A model for evaluating player enjoyment in games. *ACM Computers in Entertainment*, 3(3), 1–24.

Tondeur, J., van Braak, J., Sang, G., Voogt, J., Fisser, P., & Ottenbreit-Leftwich, A. (2012). Preparing preservice teachers to integrate technology in education: A synthesis of qualitative evidence. *Computers & Education*, 59(1), 134–144.

Trucano, M. (2019). Can 'Education 5.0' usher a new era of self-paced, self-directed learning for students? World Education Blog, The World Bank.

Wagner, T. (2008). *The global achievement gap: Why even our best schools don't teach the new survival skills our children need – And what we can do about it*. Basic Books.

World Bank. (2019). Education systems in action: Transforming data into education policy implementation (SABER annual report 2019). [World Bank Documents]. https://documents1.worldbank.org/curated/en/675041599106965808/pdf/Education-Systems-in-Action-Transforming-Data-into-Education-Policy-Implementation-SABER-Annual-Report-2019.pdf

Yang, X., Zhao, X., Tian, X., & Xing, B. (2021). Effects of environment and posture on the concentration and achievement of students in mobile learning. *Interactive Learning Environments*, *29*(3), 400–413.

Yeh, Y.-C., Chen, Y.-W., & Nolan, J. (2019). Designing e-learning environments to enhance learner concentration: A systematic review and meta-analysis. *Educational Technology & Society*, *22*(4), 131–144.

Zhao, Y. (2009). *Catching up or leading the way: American education in the age of globalization*. ASCD.

Zhang, Y., & Liu, X. (2016). The technology acceptance model (TAM) in e-learning: A systematic review. *Journal of Educational Technology & Society*, *19*(1), 1–18.

Zhu, E., & Kaplan, M. (2018). Antiblackness and the eRacism initiative: Raising awareness and facilitating SBAR conversations. *Journal of the American College of Radiology*, *15*(2), 364–366.

Chapter 20

Assistive Technologies for Education: Fulfilling National Education Policy (NEP) Goals

Vijay T. Raisinghani

Welingkar Institute of Management Development and Research (WeSchool), Mumbai, Maharashtra, India

Abstract

The recent pandemic forced a rethink of education based on the classroom model. Digital modes of education became the only option available. Educators, students, parents, and all stakeholders aided and changed over to the digital mode rapidly, embedding innovative practices to facilitate student engagement. While the changeover was fast, and technology ensured that continuity in education was maintained, the students with disabilities faced a technology barrier. Disabilities could be visual, cognitive, learning, neurological, auditory, physical, or speech. Technological tools leveraged for online education did not meet the requirements of students with disabilities. The distance mode further accentuated the teachers' limitations about working with such students. India's National Education Policy (NEP) mandates barrier-free education. The Rights of Persons with Disabilities Act (2016) mandates free education for 6- to 14-year-olds with disabilities. The Sustainable Development Goals also focus on the education of children and young persons with disabilities. However, enabling technology itself could prove to be a barrier to education if it lacks adequate support. Assistive technologies integrated with online education tools would empower these students to maximize the benefits of technology online and in a classroom mode. In this chapter, we study the various assistive technologies, best practices followed in various countries, and provide recommendations for their integration with tools or technologies that should be leveraged for education. These recommendations would equip education technology organizations to adapt their tools to reduce accessibility friction for students and enable special educators and teachers in general to create a much-needed inclusive learning environment.

Keywords: Accessibility; online education; assistive technologies; barrier-free education; rights of persons with disabilities; UNCRPD; NEP

1. Introduction

The salient points mentioned in the preamble of the UN Convention on the Rights of Persons with Disabilities (UNCRPD) (UN-DESA, 2006; UN–Sustainable Development Goals, 2015) emphasize the dignity, equal, and inalienable rights of all humans. A crucial point mentioned is that

> disability is an evolving concept and that disability results from the interaction between persons with impairments and attitudinal and environmental barriers that hinders their full and effective participation in society on an equal basis with others.

The above point should challenge our perception of disability. The disability per se does not belong to the individual but is a result of attitudinal and environmental barriers. This is the social model of disability. The inherent impairment of the person and the restrictions forced by society create disabling environments. A perspective on the challenges in teaching disabled students in an online environment is presented in Aljedaani et al. (2023).

Article 24 of UN-DESA (2006) is about education. The article states that States Parties ensure inclusive education enables persons with disability to live a life of dignity, develop to their fullest potential their personality and skills, and engage with society. The States Parties should also ensure that persons with disabilities have access to and are not excluded from any level of education, with reasonable support for individual needs. Further, the State Parties should use appropriate languages and modes and means of communication suited to individual needs. The essence of the article is that education should be available and accessible to all without any discrimination. The environment and individuals supporting education must be sensitive to, and accommodative of, the needs of persons with disabilities.

Acts have been defined by various governments to address the requirements defined in UNCRPD. India enacted the Persons with Disabilities Act 1995, which was enhanced by the Government of India through the Rights of Persons with Disabilities Act, 2016 (IN-MoLJ, 2016). Also, the NEP emphasizes barrier-free education (NEP (India), 2020). The United States established the Individuals with Disabilities Education Act in 1975 (US-DoE, 1975). In the United Kingdom, the Special Educational Needs and Disability (SEND) Act of 2001 was enacted (UK-DoE, 2001). The European Commission introduced the European

Accessibility Act in 2015 (EU, 2015). The Australian government defined the Disability Standards for Education in 2005 to specify the requirements under the Disability Discrimination Act of 1992 (AU, 1992; AU Gov., 2005).

In Section 2, we provide an overview of the various acts listed above. In Section 3, we present an overview of various international guidelines and tools for accessibility. Sections 4–6 discuss the online learning tools, assistive technologies, and learning management systems (LMSs), and the barriers they pose to students with disabilities. In Section 7, we conclude this chapter with our recommendations for tool creators to ensure education without barriers.

2. Enabling Disability Education

Various governments worldwide have passed legislations to enable equal rights for persons with disabilities. The acts also provide guidelines on educational support for persons with disabilities.

2.1. India

The Indian Disability Act 2016 (IN-MoLJ, 2016) is a landmark legislation that aims to promote the rights of persons with disabilities in education. The act expands the definition of disabilities to include a wider range of conditions, mandates inclusive education in all educational institutions, and requires reasonable accommodation to be provided. It also stipulates a reservation of seats in all educational institutions and prohibits discrimination against persons with disabilities in any educational setting.

The act is aligned with India's NEP (NEP (India), 2020), which envisions a transformational shift in the education system, promoting holistic development, creativity, critical thinking, and inclusivity. The act complements the NEP's focus on early childhood care and education, vocational education and skill development, and multilingualism.

The successful implementation of the act requires raising awareness among stakeholders about disability rights and the importance of inclusive education. Regular training for educators and administrators can help overcome attitudinal barriers and ensure effective implementation. Adequate resources, qualified teachers, and continuous monitoring are also essential for ensuring access to quality education and equal opportunities for all learners.

To ensure a level field in higher educational institutions, the Universities Grants Commission (UGC) (IN-UGC, 1953) has defined the Accessibility Guidelines and Standards for Higher Education Institutions and Universities (IN-UGC-Accessibility, 2022). The UGC guidelines emphasize various aspects of access, including information and communication technologies and assistive technologies. These guidelines refer to the Indian standards for accessibility. The UGC guidelines also refer to the e-content accessibility guidelines defined by the Government of India (IN-MoE-E-content, 2021). Additionally, the Bureau of Indian Standards, the National Standards Body of India, has defined the standard *IS 17802* for accessibility for ICT products and services (IN-BIS-Accessibility, 2022).

Table 20.1. Accessibility Guidelines and Tools for Digital Content.

Content-Type	Standard	Validator
Microsoft word document	Office accessibility guidelines (Microsoft–Accessibility Guidelines and Requirements, 2022)	Word accessibility checker
Portable document format	PDF-universal accessibility (PDF-UA) (PDF/UA Foundation, 2021)	PDF accessibility checker
EPUB	EPUB accessibility guidelines	ACE (accessibility checker for EPUB) (Ace by DAISY, 2023)
Websites, videos, and apps	WCAGs or guidelines for Indian government websites (GIGW)	AXE (Axe Accessibility Testing Tools, 2023), WAVE (WebAIM, 2023), etc.
Audio	DAISY (2023)	Obi (2023)
Fonts for Indian languages	Unicode	–

Source: IN-UGC-Accessibility (2022).

A snapshot of the e-content accessibility standards and validating tools is shown in Table 20.1 (IN-UGC-Accessibility, 2022).

The UGC guidelines suggest various approaches for converting and/or providing e-content, and assessment systems, for students. For example, instructional material should be provided in EPUB, braille, large print, audio, easy-to-read, plain language, sign language, etc. Assistive technologies such as screen readers, refreshable braille displays, videos with sign language, hearing enhancement systems, closed captioning, sign language interpretation, etc. should be compatible with or integrated within the instructional material. The guidelines also state that higher education institutes should ensure training, awareness, availability of tools, etc. so that all stakeholders can participate in ensuring that persons with disabilities face no barriers to education.

2.2. United Kingdom

The Equality Act (UK-GOV, 2010) prohibits discrimination against disabled people in all areas of life, including education. It requires educational institutions to make reasonable adjustments to ensure that disabled students can participate fully in education. The Equality Act replaced the Disability Discrimination Act (UK-GOV, 1995). It prohibits discrimination against disabled people in employment, education, and other areas of life. The UK government's Department for Education and Department of Health and Social Care have provided guidelines for their SEND system for persons aged 0–25 (UK-GOV-DfE, 2014). The former has created multiple reports to help identify appropriate assistive technologies for use in education (UK-GOV-DfE, 2020).

2.3. United States

Listed below are the US acts relevant to accessibility.

Section 508 of the Rehabilitation Act: Section 508 sets accessibility standards for electronic and information technology, including online learning materials, to ensure they are accessible to individuals with disabilities (USA–The Rehabilitation Act of 1973, 1973). Americans with Disabilities Act (ADA) prohibits discrimination based on disability and applies to online educational services and materials provided by public entities (USA–American Disabilities Act–1990, As Amended, 2008). The Higher Education Opportunity Act (HEOA) requires institutions to ensure the accessibility of online education programmes and provides guidelines for accessible technology and course content (USA–HEOA–2008, 2008).

The US Department of Education provides accessibility guidelines and resources for educational institutions to ensure compliance with federal accessibility laws (USA–Accessibility Statement, 2013).

3. International Guidelines, Standards, and Tools

The Web Content Accessibility Guidelines (WCAGs) (Kirkpatrick et al., 2018) provide comprehensive standards and guidelines for making web content accessible to people with disabilities. These guidelines also benefit people without disabilities, as a key principle of accessibility is designing websites that are flexible to meet different user needs, preferences, and situations.

The WCAGs are organized around four principles: perceivable, operable, understandable, and robust (CUNY–Library Services, 2023). These principles are further broken down into guidelines and success criteria. The success criteria are written as statements that must be met to conform to the standard. Perceivable means making all the content accessible through multiple modalities. It involves providing text alternatives for non-text content and also a facility to transform text into other forms, creating adaptable content, i.e., presentation of the content should be customizable and independent of the sequence of information and making content distinguishable through proper hierarchy and contrast. The operable principle involves making the interface easily usable through different input modes such as keyboard and voice, providing enough time to read and act on content, giving warnings for flashing content, and options to pause or close distracting content. The third principle is 'Robust content and reliable interpretation' which ensures that content is compatible with different browsers and assistive technology, and giving a role or name to non-standard user interface components and ensuring markup can be easily interpreted can help with this. The 'Understandable information and interface' principle focuses on making content understandable and readable by the broadest audience through clear and simple language and providing definitions for complex words. It also involves making the content and components consistent and function as the user expects them to, keeping the user in control.

The WCAG success criteria are organized into three levels of conformance: Level A, Level AA, and Level AAA. Level A is a basic requirement for some users with disabilities to be able to access and use web content. Level AA indicates overall accessibility and removal of significant barriers to accessing content. The highest standard of accessibility in WCAGs is represented by Level AAA conformance, which holds organizations to the most rigorous accessibility requirements.

Quality Matters (QM) Higher Education Rubric (QM, 2023) is a widely used set of standards for online course quality that includes accessibility criteria to ensure that online courses are accessible to all learners.

3.1. Tools and Other Support for Accessibility

The Harvard Digital Accessibility Services website (Harvard University, 2023) discusses the use of automated tools to test for web accessibility. For example, tools are available to check whether web pages are adhering to the WCAGs. Some other free automated tools are WAVE (WebAIM, 2023) Siteimprove (2023), Axe (Deque-AXE, 2023), Accessibility Insights (Microsoft-Accessibility, 2023), Accessible Name and Description Inspector (ANDI, 2023), PDF Accessibility Checker (PDF/UA Foundation, 2021), Photosensitive Epilepsy Analysis Tool (PEAT) (University of Maryland, 2016), Contrast Checker (WebAIM, 2023), Colour Contrast Analyzer (The Paciello Group, 2023), and Contrast Ratio (Siegemedia, 2023). However, automated accessibility evaluation tools have their limitations (Manca et al., 2023).

Accessible Books Consortium (ABC, 2023) provides access to accessible books for persons with print disabilities. TCS Access Infinity (TATA Consultancy Services, 2023), created by TCS Research's Accessibility Center of Excellence (CoE), transforms reading for people with disabilities. It converts content into accessible formats and supports various devices. Launched officially in 2016 as the *Sugamya Pustakalaya* portal by the DAISY Forum of India (DFI) (Sugamya Pustakalaya, 2016) and the Government of India, it now offers content in 17 languages, with over 650,000+ titles, serving as a vital resource for all.

3.2. World Health Organization (WHO) – Priority Assistive Product List

The WHO has introduced the *Priority Assistive Products List (APL)* (WHO, 2016). The list includes 50 priority assistive products based on the widespread requirements of persons with disabilities.

Some of the products that would be helpful for digital education are noted from the list as follows: audio players with DAISY capability, Braille displays (notetakers), Braille writing equipment/braillers, closed captioning displays, communication software, deafblind communicators, gesture to voice technology, hearing aids, keyboard and mouse emulation software, magnifiers – digital and handheld, magnifiers – optical, personal digital assistant, recorders, screen readers, simplified mobile phones, spectacles, low vision, short distance, long distance, filters and protection, time management products, and video communication devices.

4. Barriers in Common Online Education Tools

In this section, we discuss the limitations of some common online tools that facilitate learning, Zoom, Google Meet, Microsoft Teams, etc., concerning accessibility.

- Keyboard Navigation Challenges:
    - All three platforms may have limitations in keyboard navigation, making it challenging for users who rely on keyboard input. Users with mobility impairments, including those who rely on alternative input devices or switch devices, may struggle with navigating using a keyboard.
- Screen Reader Compatibility:
    - While improvements have been made, users have reported issues with screen reader compatibility (Leporini et al., 2023), such as difficulty in navigating menus and identifying participants. Users with visual impairments who rely on screen readers may face significant challenges when the platform is not compatible, hindering their ability to access content and participate effectively.
- Captioning and Transcription Limitations:
    - Automatic captions and transcriptions may not always be accurate, affecting the experience for users who are deaf or hard of hearing. Users who are deaf or hard of hearing depend on accurate captions and transcriptions. Inaccurate or missing captions can greatly impede their comprehension and participation. For persons with speech disabilities, uttering clear sentences with adequate voice intensity may be difficult, and though voice user interfaces have machine learning systems, they are generally designed based on users with clear and intelligible speech (Pradhan et al., 2018). Pauses in between utterances, repeated words in utterances, and different pronunciations may confuse the speech-to-text converter on these online platforms. For input fields of online forms or chat, different sounds and repeat words in unclear speech could get included in the message. This becomes a barrier for persons having speech impairment.
- Complex Interfaces:
    - The interfaces of these platforms can be complex, with numerous buttons, menus, and options, potentially causing difficulties for users with cognitive or learning disabilities. Users with cognitive or learning disabilities may find it overwhelming to navigate complex interfaces, potentially affecting their ability to focus on content and engage effectively.
- Inconsistent Accessibility Across Devices:
    - The accessibility features may vary across different devices and browsers, leading to inconsistencies in the user experience. Users with disabilities who require specific devices or browsers for accessibility may face barriers if the platform's accessibility varies across devices, limiting their choice and flexibility.

- Meeting Host Responsibilities:
  o Effective use of accessibility features often depends on the knowledge and actions of the meeting host. If hosts are unaware or do not enable accessibility features, it can hinder the accessibility of meetings. This issue affects users with disabilities across the spectrum.
- Limited Customization:
  o These platforms may have limited customization options for users with specific accessibility needs, such as adjusting font sizes or colour schemes. Users with visual impairments may struggle if they cannot customize font sizes or colour schemes to suit their needs. This limitation affects users with low vision, colour blindness, or other visual impairments.
- Language Support:
  o While these platforms support multiple languages, the availability and accuracy of accessibility features, such as captions and transcripts, may vary for different languages. Users who speak languages that have limited accessibility support may face challenges in accessing content and engaging with others.
- Bandwidth and Connection Issues:
  o Some tools require higher bandwidth and better connectivity to function well. This could limit the access of users to high-quality video and audio content, affecting the overall learning experience for those who rely on real-time communication.
- Training and Awareness:
  o Many users and educators may not be fully aware of the accessibility features or how to use them effectively, highlighting the need for improved training and awareness. This primarily affects users with various disabilities, as they may not receive adequate guidance on utilizing accessibility features, making the learning experience less inclusive.
- Browser Compatibility:
  o Certain accessibility features may not work consistently across all web browsers, which can be a problem for users who prefer or are limited to using specific browsers. Users who rely on specific browsers for accessibility may face challenges if certain features do not work as expected on their preferred browsers.
- Third-Party Integrations:
  o Integration with third-party applications or plugins can introduce accessibility challenges for users if those integrations are not fully accessible.
- Real-Time Collaboration Barriers:
  o Real-time collaboration tools, such as virtual whiteboards and interactive elements, may present barriers to some users with disabilities. Any diagrams drawn with digital pens or pencils and text that is hand-written on digital whiteboards may not be converted to audio by a screen reader. Users with motor or speech disabilities may find it difficult to participate in collaborative activities. The future of online learning lies in immersive experiences. While research is ongoing, it is crucial to incorporate the right accessibility features as the technology is being developed (Robern et al., 2021).

- Limited Offline Access:
  o Offline access and downloadable content may not be fully accessible, impacting users who rely on offline materials. Users who rely on offline access to materials due to intermittent internet access or specific disabilities may struggle if offline resources are not fully accessible, affecting their ability to learn independently.

5. Barriers in Common Assistive Technologies

Many tools have been developed to support students with disabilities. Below we list some of the popular assistive technologies and discuss the barriers these tools help resolve but could still pose accessibility challenges for students with disabilities. Table 20.2 presents a summary of the tools and accessibility challenges.

Table 20.2. Accessibility Challenges in Assistive Technologies.

Assistive Technology	Tools Free/Commercial	Accessibility Challenges
Screen readers: screen readers convert text and graphical information into synthesized speech or braille output.	Free: non-visual desktop access (NVDA) (NV Access, 2023) Commercial: job access with speech (JAWS) (JAWS Screen Reader, 2023)	Complex web content and non-standard design can pose navigation difficulties for screen reader users. Some websites and applications are not designed with screen reader compatibility in mind, leading to navigation difficulties for users with visual impairments (WebAIM, 2019).
Voice recognition software: voice recognition software allows users to control computers and dictate text using voice commands.	Free: Microsoft. Use voice recognition in Windows 10 (2021) Commercial: Nuance Communications. Dragon naturally speaking (Nuance Communications, 2023)	Background noise can interfere with accuracy. It may be difficult to use in places that require silence or are too noisy. Users with speech impairments may have difficulty in using voice recognition effectively (Masina et al., 2020).
Braille displays: Braille displays provide tactile output of digital content for users with visual impairments.	Free: Android accessibility. TalkBack (Braille display). (Android Accessibility, 2023) Commercial: Freedom Scientific. Focus Blue Braille Displays (2023)	The cost of Braille displays can be a barrier for some users. Additionally, the limited availability of Braille-compatible content can make it difficult for users to access certain materials (Saigal, 2023).

(*Continued*)

Table 20.2. (*Continued*)

Assistive Technology	Tools Free/Commercial	Accessibility Challenges
Screen magnification software: screen magnification software enlarges on-screen text and graphics for users with low vision.	Free: Microsoft. Use a magnifier to make things on the screen easier to see (Microsoft Magnifier, 2023) Commercial: ZoomText. ZoomText magnifier/reader (ZoomText, 2023)	Excessive magnification can lead to a loss of context, making it challenging for users to navigate and understand the entire content of a page. This is also dependent on how the layout of the page is designed. Some magnifiers have started to support split screens where one side is magnified and the other is not to give context (Rempel, 2012).
Alternative input devices: devices like sip-and-puff switches or head-controlled mice enable individuals with mobility impairments to interact with computers.	Free: Microsoft. Type without using the keyboard (on-screen keyboard) (Microsoft OSK, 2023) Commercial: Tobii Dynavox. Eye gaze devices (Tobii Dynavox, 2023)	Users may face a steep learning curve when transitioning to alternative input methods, which can be challenging for some (Beukelman et al., 2023).
Augmentative and alternative communication (AAC) devices: AAC devices help individuals with communication disabilities express themselves through text or speech output.	Free: AssistiveWare. Proloquo2Go – symbol-based AAC (Proloquo2Go, 2023) Commercial: Tobii Dynavox. Communicator 5 (2023).	Setting up and customizing AAC devices can be time-consuming, and the vocabulary may not always meet the specific needs of users (Aydin & Diken, 2020).
Text-to-speech software: text-to-speech software reads digital text aloud for users with reading difficulties or learning disabilities.	Free: Natural Reader. Natural Reader Free (Natural Reader Software, 2023) Commercial: Kurzweil Education. Kurzweil 3000 (2023)	Some text-to-speech voices may sound unnatural or robotic, affecting comprehension and engagement for some users. Also, these software may not be equipped with supporting multiple languages.

Table 20.2. (*Continued*)

Screen contrast and colour adjustment tools: these tools allow users to adjust screen contrast, colours, and font settings for improved readability.	Free: Microsoft. Turn on high contrast mode (*Turn high contrast mode on or off*, 2021) Commercial: Microsoft. Accessibility in Microsoft Teams (*Change settings in Microsoft Teams*, 2023)	Not all websites and applications allow users to override their default colour and contrast settings, limiting customization options.
Closed captioning and subtitling: closed captioning and subtitling provide text-based representations of audio content for individuals who are deaf or hard of hearing	Free: YouTube Help. Add your subtitles and closed captions (YouTube closed captions, 2023) Commercial: 3Play Media. Captioning services (3Play Media closed captioning, 2023)	The accuracy of captions and subtitles may vary, affecting comprehension and accessibility for individuals who are deaf or hard of hearing. Often limited languages are supported in captioning, denying access to those who communicate in vernacular languages.
Assistive listening devices: these devices amplify sound for individuals with hearing impairments.	Free: Google Play. Sound amplifier (Google Accessibility, 2023) Commercial: Phonak (Phonak – Life is on, 2023)	Users need to carry and maintain specialized equipment, which can be inconvenient and may discourage some individuals from using these devices.

6. Barriers in Common LMSs

In this section, we list common problems in LMSs, we also list the common LMSs and the barriers they pose to students with disabilities.

6.1. Common Barriers in LMSs

Inaccessible Content Editor: Some LMSs may have content editors that are not fully compatible with screen readers, making it difficult for users with visual impairments to create or edit content (Nave, 2021).

Inaccessible Multimedia: Lack of captions, transcripts, or alternative formats for multimedia content, such as videos and audio files, can make the content inaccessible to users with hearing or visual impairments (W3C, 2022).

Complex Navigation: Complex navigation menus and structures can be challenging for users with cognitive disabilities or those who rely on screen readers to navigate through course materials (Burgstahler & Cory, 2010).

Inconsistent Design and Layout: Inconsistencies in design and layout can confuse users with disabilities who rely on consistent visual cues and organization to navigate an LMS (Slatin & Sharron, 2003).

Keyboard Navigation Issues: Keyboard navigation may be hindered by the lack of proper focus indicators or keyboard traps, making it difficult for users with mobility impairments to navigate effectively (W3C, 2022).

Inaccessible Assessments: Online quizzes, tests, and assessments that are not designed with accessibility in mind can disadvantage students with disabilities (Goegan et al., 2018).

Limited Compatibility With Assistive Technologies: Some LMSs may not work well with assistive technologies, such as screen readers or speech recognition software, preventing users from accessing content or participating fully (Brito & Dias, 2020).

Insufficient Training and Support: Lack of training and support for instructors and administrators on creating and maintaining accessible content can result in inaccessible course materials.

Inadequate Documentation: LMS documentation that lacks accessibility guidance may leave instructors and content creators unaware of best practices for creating accessible content.

Inaccessible Collaborative Tools: Collaborative tools within LMSs, such as discussion boards or virtual classrooms, may lack accessibility features, excluding users with disabilities from participation.

6.2. Common LMSs and Accessibility Barriers

1. *Moodle* (Moodle Accessibility, 2023):
   Inconsistent navigation and layout can confuse users with cognitive disabilities.

   - Inadequate keyboard navigation support, including keyboard traps.
   - Complex interface elements that may be challenging for screen reader users.

2. *Blackboard Learn* (Anthology Accessibility, 2023):
   Complex navigation and menus can be challenging for users with cognitive impairments.

   - Inconsistent layout and design may create accessibility barriers.
   - Limited compatibility with certain assistive technologies.

3. *Canvas By Instructure* (Canvas LMS, 2023):
   Complex navigation and inconsistent design elements.

   - Inadequate keyboard navigation support.
   - Challenges in creating accessible content, such as multimedia and assessments.

4. *D2L Brightspace* (D2L Brightspace, 2023):
   Inaccessible multimedia content, including videos without captions.

   - Partial support for keyboard navigation and screen readers.
   - Challenges in creating accessible assessments.

5. *Sakai* (Sakai Accessibility, 2023):
   Complex navigation and interface elements.
   - Limited compatibility with some assistive technologies.
   - Challenges in ensuring multimedia accessibility.

6. *Google Classroom* (Google Classroom, 2023):
   Limited support for screen readers and keyboard navigation.
   - Challenges in ensuring that content created within Google Apps is accessible.

7. *Microsoft Teams for Education* (MS Teams for Education, 2023):
   Challenges in navigating the interface with screen readers.
   - Limited support for keyboard navigation in some parts of the platform.

8. *Adobe Connect* (Adobe Connect, 2023):
   Inaccessible features in virtual classrooms.
   - Challenges in ensuring that content shared in Adobe Connect is accessible.

7. Conclusion

Enabling education for all is essential in today's world. All nations have well-defined laws to protect the rights of persons with disabilities. As nations like India move towards becoming a superpower, the need for universal design for education technologies is even more important. The learning tools should be interoperable with all types of assistive technologies. In addition, the content should afford features to enable assistive technologies to exploit them to the maximum. Accessibility is not only beneficial for a certain set of users but useful for all where one might face situational disabilities such as a fractured arm or a bandaged eye due to an operation, etc. Features such as voice navigation, gesture recognition, keyboard navigation, voice generation, affordable braille displays, multi-language support, low-bandwidth support, customization, immersion support, etc. are essential to enable barrier-free education for all. It is also essential that software and web developers are made aware of the need to integrate accessibility into the software design and development process (Shi et al., 2023; Tsaktsiras & Katsanos, 2023).

References

3Play Media closed captioning. (2023). https://www.3playmedia.com/services/captioning/
Accessible Books Consortium (ABC). (2023). https://www.accessiblebooksconsortium.org/
Ace by DAISY. (2023). https://daisy.org/activities/software/ace/
Adobe Connect. (2023, November 9). https://helpx.adobe.com/in/support/connect.html
Aljedaani, W., Aljedaani, M., Mkaouer, M. W., & Ludi, S. (2023). Teachers perspectives on transition to online teaching deaf and hard-of-hearing students during the COVID-19 pandemic: A case study. In *Proceedings of the 16th innovations in software engineering conference*. ACM.

ANDI. (2023). *Accessibility testing tool*. https://www.ssa.gov/accessibility/andi/help/install.html
Android Accessibility. (2023). *Connect to a Braille display*. https://support.google.com/accessibility/android/answer/3535226
Anthology Accessibility. (2023). https://www.anthology.com/trust-center/accessibility
AU. (1992). *Disability discrimination act*. Federal Register of Legislation, Australian Government. https://www.legislation.gov.au/Details/C2016C00763
AU Gov. (2005). *Disability standards for education*. The Federal Register for Legislation, Australian Government. https://www.legislation.gov.au/Details/F2005L00767
Axe Accessibility Testing Tools. (2023). https://www.deque.com/axe/
Aydin, O., & Diken, I. H. (2020). Studies comparing augmentative and alternative communication systems (AAC) applications for individuals with autism spectrum disorder: A systematic review and meta-analysis. *Education and Training in Autism and Developmental Disabilities*, 55(2), 119–141. https://www.jstor.org/stable/27077906
Beukelman, D. R., Fager, S. K., Sorenson, T., T, J., & Koester, H. (2023). Multi-modal access method (eye-tracking + switch-scanning) for individuals with severe motor impairment: A preliminary investigation. *Assistive Technology*, 35(4), 321–329. https://doi.org/10.1080/10400435.2022.2053895
Brito, E., & Dias, G. (2020). LMS accessibility for students with disabilities: The experts' opinions. In *15th Iberian conference on information systems and technologies (CISTI)* (pp. 1–5).
Burgstahler, S. E., & Cory, R. C. (Eds.). (2010). *Universal design in higher education: From principles to practice*. Harvard Education Press.
Canvas LMS. (2023). https://www.instructure.com/higher-education/products/canvas/canvas-lms
Change settings in Microsoft Teams. (2023, October 11). https://support.microsoft.com/en-au/office/change-settings-in-microsoft-teams-b506e8f1-1a96-4cf1-8c6b-b6ed4f424bc7#BKMK_HowDoIEnableHighContrastMode
Communicator 5. (2023). https://www.tobiidynavox.com/products/communicator-5
CUNY–Library Services. (2023). *Accessibility toolkit for open educational resources (OER): Accessibility principles*. https://guides.cuny.edu/accessibility/whyitmatters
D2L Brightspace. (2023). https://www.d2l.com/brightspace/
DAISY. (2023). https://daisy.org/
Deque-AXE. (2023). *Axe accessibility testing tools*. https://www.deque.com/axe/
EU. (2015). *European accessibility act*. European Commission-Employment, Social Affairs & Inclusion. https://ec.europa.eu/social/main.jsp?catId=1202
Focus Blue Braille Displays. (2023). https://www.freedomscientific.com/products/blindness/braille-display/
Goegan, L. D., Radil, A. I., & Daniels, L. M. (2018). Accessibility in questionnaire research: Integrating universal design to increase the participation of individuals with learning disabilities. *Learning Disabilities: A Contemporary Journal*, 16(2), 177–190.
Google Accessibility. (2023, September 5). *Sound amplifier*. https://play.google.com/store/apps/details?id=com.google.android.accessibility.soundamplifier
Google Classroom. (2023). https://edu.google.com/intl/ALL_in/workspace-for-education/classroom/
Harvard University. (2023). *Automated tools for testing accessibility*. https://accessibility.huit.harvard.edu/auto-tools-testing
IN-BIS-Accessibility.(2022).https://broadbandindiaforum.in/wp-content/uploads/2022/08/IS-17802_1_2021.pdf; https://www.services.bis.gov.in/php/BIS_2.0/bisconnect/get_is_list_by_category_id/24
IN-MoE-E-content. (2021). *Guidelines for the development of e-content for children with disabilities*. https://www.education.gov.in/sites/upload_files/mhrd/files/CWSN_E-Content_guidelines.pdf

IN-MoLJ. (2016, December 27). *The rights of persons with disabilities act*. Department of Empowerment of Persons with Disabilities, Government of India. https://disabilityaffairs.gov.in/upload/uploadfiles/files/RPWD%20ACT%202016.pdf

IN-UGC. (1953). https://www.ugc.ac.in

IN-UGC-Accessibility. (2022, July). *Accessibility guidelines*. University Grants Commission. https://www.ugc.gov.in/pdfnews/8572354_Final-Accessibility-Guidelines.pdf

JAWS Screen Reader. (2023). https://www.freedomscientific.com/products/software/jaws/

Kirkpatrick, A., Connor, J. O., Campbell, A., & Cooper, M. (2018, June 5). *Web content accessibility guidelines (WCAG) 2.1*. World Wide Web Consortium. https://www.w3.org/TR/WCAG21/

Kurzweil 3000. (2023). https://www.kurzweiledu.com/products/k3000.html

Leporini, B., Buzzi, M., & Hersh, M. (2023, March). Video conferencing tools: Comparative study of the experiences of screen reader users and the development of more inclusive design guidelines. *ACM Transactions on Accessible Computing, 16*(1), 1–36. https://dl.acm.org/doi/10.1145/3573012

Manca, M., Palumbo, V., Paternò, F., & Santoro, C. (2023). The transparency of automatic web accessibility evaluation tools: Design criteria, state of the art, and user perception. *ACM Transactions on Accessible Computing, 16*(1), 1–36. https://doi.org/10.1145/3556979

Masina, F. O., Pluchino, P., Dainese, G., Volpato, S., Nelini, C., Mapelli, D., Spagnolli, A., & Gamberini, L. (2020). Investigating the accessibility of voice assistants with impaired users: Mixed methods study. *Journal of Medicinal Internet Research, 22*(9), e18431. https://doi.org/10.2196/18431

Microsoft-Accessibility. (2023). *Accessibility insights*. https://accessibilityinsights.io/docs/web/overview/

Microsoft–Accessibility Guidelines and Requirements. (2022, June 25). https://learn.microsoft.com/en-us/style-guide/accessibility/accessibility-guidelines-requirements

Microsoft Magnifier. (2023, February 14). https://support.microsoft.com/en-us/windows/use-magnifier-to-make-things-on-the-screen-easier-to-see-414948ba-8b1c-d3bd-8615-0e5e32204198

Microsoft OSK. (2023, February 28). *Use the on-screen keyboard (OSK) to type*. https://support.microsoft.com/en-us/windows/use-the-on-screen-keyboard-osk-to-type-ecbb5e08-5b4e-d8c8-f794-81dbf896267a

Moodle Accessibility. (2023, May 24). https://docs.moodle.org/402/en/Accessibility

MS Teams for Education. (2023). https://www.microsoft.com/en-us/education/products/teams

National Education Policy (India). (2020). Ministry of Education, Government of India. https://www.education.gov.in/national-education-policy

Natural Reader Software. (2023). https://www.naturalreaders.com/software.html

Nave, L. (2021). Universal design for learning: UDL in online environments: The WHAT of learning. *Journal of Developmental Education, 44*(2), 30–32.

Nuance Communications. (2023). *Dragon naturally speaking*. https://www.nuance.com/dragon.html

NV Access. (2023). https://www.nvaccess.org/

Obi. (2023). https://daisy.org/activities/software/obi/

PDF/UA Foundation. (2021). *PDF accessibility checker*. https://pdfua.foundation/en/pdf-accessibility-checker-pac/

Phonak – Life is on. (2023). https://www.phonak.com/com/en/hearing-aids/accessories/roger-pen.htm

Pradhan, A., Mehta, K., & Findlater, L. (2018). "Accessibility came by accident": Use of voice-controlled intelligent personal assistants by people with disabilities. In *Proceedings of the 2018 CHI conference on human factors in computing systems* (pp. 1–13). Association for Computing Machinery. https://doi.org/10.1145/3173574.3174033

Proloquo2Go. (2023). https://www.assistiveware.com/products/proloquo2go

Quality Matters. (2023). *Higher education course design Rubric* (7th ed.). https://qualitymatters.org/qa-resources/rubric-standards/higher-ed-rubric

Rempel, J. (2012). *The bigger picture: A comparative review of magnifier for Windows 7 and Zoom for Mac OS*. American Foundation for the Blind. https://www.afb.org/aw/13/3/15829

Robern, G., Uribe-Quevedo, A., Sukhai, M., Coppin, P., Lee, T., & Ingino, R. (2021). Work-in-progress-exploring VR conference navigation employing audio cues. In *2021 7th International conference of the immersive learning research network (iLRN)* (pp. 1–3). https://doi.org/10.23919/iLRN52045.2021.9459330

Saigal, S. (2023). *Government needs to help with refreshable Braille displays. Hindustan Times.* https://www.thehindu.com/news/cities/mumbai/government-needs-to-help-with-refreshable-braille-display-says-expert/article66338659.ece

Sakai Accessibility. (2023). https://www.sakailms.org/accessibility

Shi, W., Moses, H., Yu, Q., Malachowsky, S., & Krutz, D. E. (2023). All: Supporting experiential accessibility education and inclusive software development. *ACM Transactions on Software Engineering Methodology, 33*(2), 1–30. https://doi.org/10.1145/3625292

Siegemedia. (2023). *Contrast ratio checker*. https://www.siegemedia.com/contrast-ratio

Siteimprove. (2023). *Siteimprove accessibility checker*. https://www.siteimprove.com/

Slatin, J. M., & Sharron, R. (2003). *Maximum accessibility: Making your web site more usable for everyone*. Addison-Wesley Professional.

Sugamya Pustakalaya. (2016). https://daisyindia.org/

TATA Consultancy Services. (2023). *TCS access infinity*. https://www.tcs.com/; https://www.tcs.com/who-we-are/newsroom/tcs-in-the-news/to-infinity-and-beyond

The Paciello Group. (2023). *Color contrast checker*. https://www.tpgi.com/color-contrast-checker/

Tobii Dynavox. (2023). *Eye gaze pathway*. https://www.tobiidynavox.com/pages/eye-gaze-pathway

Tsaktsiras, K., & Katsanos, C. (2023). ESALP 2.0: Educational system to support learning of web content accessibility guidelines by Greek web practitioners. In *Proceedings of the 2nd international conference of the ACM Greek SIGCHI chapter*. ACM.

Turn high contrast mode on or off. (2021, December 3). https://support.microsoft.com/en-us/windows/turn-high-contrast-mode-on-or-off-in-windows-909e9d89-a0f9-a3a9-b993-7a6dcee85025

UK-DoE. (2001). *Special educational needs and disability act*. The Official Home of UK Legislation. https://www.legislation.gov.uk/ukpga/2001/10/contents

UK-GOV. (1995). *Disability discrimination act*. UK Public General Acts. https://www.legislation.gov.uk/ukpga/1995/50/contents

UK-GOV. (2010). *Equality act*. UK Public General Acts. https://www.legislation.gov.uk/ukpga/2010/15/contents

UK-GOV-DfE. (2014). *SEND code of practice*. https://www.gov.uk/government/publications/send-code-of-practice-0-to-25

UK-GOV-DfE. (2020). *Research and analysis – Assistive technology (AT) stakeholder reports*. https://www.gov.uk/government/publications/assistive-technology-at-stakeholder-reports

UN-DESA. (2006, December 6). *Convention on the rights of persons with disabilities – Articles*. United Nations–Department of Economic and Social Affairs. https://www.un.org/development/desa/disabilities/convention-on-the-rights-of-persons-with-disabilities/convention-on-the-rights-of-persons-with-disabilities-2.html

University of Maryland. (2016, October 19). *Photosensitive epilepsy analysis tool (PEAT)*. Trace Research and Development Center. https://trace.umd.edu/peat/

UN–Sustainable Development Goals. (2015). United Nations–Department of Economic and Social Affairs. https://sdgs.un.org/goals

USA–Accessibility Statement. (2013, August 9). US Department of Education. https://www2.ed.gov/notices/accessibility/index.html

USA–American Disabilities Act–1990, As Amended. (2008). US Department of Justice Civil Rights Division. https://www.ada.gov/law-and-regs/ada/

USA–Higher Education Opportunity Act–2008. (2008, August 14). US Department of Education. https://www2.ed.gov/policy/highered/leg/hea08/index.html

USA–The Rehabilitation Act of 1973. (1973). US Equal Opportunity and Employment Commission. https://www.eeoc.gov/statutes/rehabilitation-act-1973

US-DoE. (1975, November 29). *Individuals with disabilities education act*. US Department of Education. https://sites.ed.gov/idea/about-idea/

Use voice recognition in Windows 10. (2021, November 1). https://support.microsoft.com/en-us/windows/use-voice-recognition-in-windows-83ff75bd-63eb-0b6c-18d4-6fae94050571

W3C. (2022, June 29). *W3C accessibility standards overview*. https://www.w3.org/WAI/standards-guidelines/

WebAIM. (2019, September 27). *WebAIM: Screen reader user survey #8 results*. https://webaim.org/projects/screenreadersurvey8/

WebAIM. (2023). *WAVE web accessibility evaluation tools*. https://wave.webaim.org/

WHO. (2016). *Priority assistive products list*. https://www.who.int/publications/i/item/priority-assistive-products-list

YouTube closed captions. (2023). https://support.google.com/youtube/answer/2734796?hl=en

ZoomText. (2023). https://www.freedomscientific.com/products/software/zoomtext/

Conclusion

Dieu Hack-Polay[a,b], Deborah Lock[c], Andrea Caputo[b,d], Madhavi Lokhande[e] and Uday Salunkhe[e]

[a]*Crandall University, Canada*
[b]*University of Lincoln, UK*
[c]*Birmingham City University, UK*
[d]*University of Trento, Italy*
[e]*WeSchool, India*

Although much is written about the role of the rapid adoption of learning technologies in response to the COVID pandemic, the evidence suggests that corresponding digital pedagogies remain embryonic as the models for various teaching and learning practices have yet to emerge and be absorbed into 'normal' academic practice. While Väätäjä and Ruokamo's (2021) dimensions for digital pedagogies identify the need for the development of philosophies which underpin 'classroom' practices, as well as academic competence to deliver engaging and meaningful student-centred learning, it is academics' ability to reflect and revitalize their practice through blending digital technologies into their teaching which is key to success (Sailin & Mahmor, 2018).

The discussions and examples within this book provide a clear indication of the challenges which many institutions across the world have faced as they either moved from traditional delivery mechanisms or tentative steps towards digital education, to full implementation within a very short scale, that is, crisis innovation and implementation. For all, the primary objective was to ensure the safety and well-being of staff and students alike while continuing to deliver meaningful education. As Chernova and J.-F. point out (see Chapter 2), these challenges encompassed topics such as information access, diverse communication infrastructures, collaboration, the use of digital platforms, variation in teaching rituals and communication protocols, unstructured digital proxemics, the absence of proven remote feedback loop models, and COVID-19 management protocols.

New debates have emerged as a result of technology enhanced learning which are proving particularly troublesome for the sector to address. For example, the absence of a shared understanding of 'student engagement' in the digital world and what constitutes engagement (Nkomo et al., 2021). The notion that an individual can be in a virtual classroom as a 'ghost' and not actively participate in any of the activities is no different to that of a student in a classroom not engaging, and yet it appears to be more visible in the online world due to the self-reporting nature of the classroom.

Likewise, there remains challenges around building inclusive learning communities among students who may have limited or no physical access to a campus and the usual trappings associated with 'going to university'. For academics, the art of creating fulfilling digital education communities is integral to fostering a sense of belonging both within the cohort and the institution in general. The risk of educational isolation has been brought into sharp focus as the forced study-from-home lockdown exposed the vulnerabilities of the most precarious, including students with disabilities (Louissi and Mielly, see Chapter 6). A key tenet of sustainable digital educational practices has got to be equality of learning opportunities in which no student is inadvertently disadvantaged.

Post-pandemic discussions and activities have moved on from crisis innovation to one where the sector is implementing changes because of the lessons learnt, ensuring sustainability by normalizing 'best' digital practices and divesting redundant approaches which add little or no value to the student learning journey.

References

Nkomo, L. M., Daniel, B. K., & Butson, R. J. (2021). Synthesis of student engagement with digital technologies: A systematic review of the literature. *International Journal of Educational Technology in Higher Education*, *18*, 1–26.

Sailin, S., & Mahmor, N. (2018). Improving student teachers' digital pedagogy through meaningful learning activities. *Malaysian Journal of Learning and Instruction*, *15*(2), 143–173.

Väätäjä, J. O., & Ruokamo, H. (2021). Conceptualizing dimensions and a model for digital pedagogy. *Journal of Pacific Rim Psychology*, *15*, 1834490921995395.

Printed and bound by CPI Group (UK) Ltd, Croydon, CR0 4YY
05/02/2025

14638643-0004